# PROJECT MANAGEMENT

Field    Laurie Keller

## SOUTH-WESTERN
CENGAGE Learning

Australia • Brazil • Japan • Korea • Mexico • Singapore • Spain • United Kingdom • United States

## SOUTH-WESTERN
CENGAGE Learning™

**Project Management**

Mike Field and Peter Cullen

Publishing Director: Linden Harris
Commissioning Editor: Tom Rennie
Senior Production Controller: Maeve Healy
Marketing Manager: Anne-Marie Scoones

For product information and technology assistance, contact **emea.info@cengage.com**.
For permission to use material from this text or product, and for permission queries, email **clsuk.permissions@cengage.com**.

British Library Cataloguing-in-Publication Data
A catalogue record for this book is available from the British Library.

ISBN: 978-1-86152-274-0

**Cengage Learning EMEA**
Cheriton House, North Way, Andover, Hampshire, SP10 5BE, United Kingdom

Cengage Learning products are represented in Canada by Nelson Education Ltd.

For your lifelong learning solutions, visit **www.cengage.co.uk**

Purchase your next print book, e-book or e-chapter at **www.CengageBrain.com**

Printed by RR Donnelley, China
16 17 18 19 20 – 13 12 11

# CONTENTS

# How to study this book

You may think that reading a book on project management is pretty much a waste of time. We agree. That is why we do not want you just to read this book - we want you to study it and try out some of the ideas on your projects.

The book is designed to provide you with interactive learning - which means that you have to work as you read. To help you to do this we have provided lots of questions for you to answer and activities for you to do.

The questions are known as self-assessment questions, or SAQs for short. You can assess whether you have really understood a topic by answering our questions on it and then seeing how your answer compares with ours. We give our answers to all the questions at the back of the book. (We don't pretend that all our questions have a single correct answer but you should be able to judge whether your answer is reasonable or not.)

The activities are rather more open-ended. From time to time we give you an activity which is something we think you can apply to a project of your own. This will generally make you think about whether a technique that we have described really could work in your project environment or not. You do not have to be a project manager to be able to do this. You may think that some techniques are inappropriate or too costly in terms of the effort that would need to be put in compared with the rewards that you would get. We want you to make up your own mind about that.

Do not feel that you have to study the book from cover to cover. The order that we follow is roughly the order in which problem areas arise in a project but projects are never quite so ordered as we would like and it isn't always possible to say that you have to do this first and that next until you have finished a project. It is same with the book. If you want to know about techniques that you could use and issues that you should think about when you are just coming to the end of a project then jump straight away to Chapter 7. The chapters do of course build on what you have studied in an earlier chapter so it helps if you have studied the earlier ones but even if you skip you should be able to make sense of what you read, especially if you are prepared to follow up any references back and use the index as a guide.

# 1 PROJECT INITIATION

## *AIMS AND OBJECTIVES*

Chapter 1 introduces projects: what they are and how they come about as a result of ideas, responses to problems and planning. Key players in the project game are introduced. The chapter then looks at how feasibility studies are carried out and how technical, social, political, environmental and financial feasibility is explored and assessed. Decision-making tools are discussed. Once a proposal for action has been accepted by management, a project results. This chapter looks at various ways of organizing the life-cycles of projects and what the project manager's job consists of. It ends with an extended case study of the London Ambulance Service's attempt to automate command and control.

Having studied this chapter you should be able to:

- define what a project is
- use a variety of knowledge-gathering and idea-generating techniques to develop objectives for action
- use Pareto analysis and cause-and-effect diagrams to explore problem areas
- generate simple matrix diagrams to relate objectives to strategies
- name and define the chief roles various people can assume in respect to proposals and projects
- relate all of these to the process of organizational planning
- explain different views of quality and show that a structured approach to planning improves quality
- describe the elements of a feasibility study
- state the general aims of a functional specification
- describe what a scenario is and generate some simple scenarios in response to a statement of a problem
- assess the maturity of a technology
- use tools for the development or assessment of a proposal
- understand the uses and limitations of payback, rate of return and discounted cash flow methods
- understand the importance of risk
- describe the basic project life-cycle, the phased development life-cycle and the prototyping life-cycle
- understand why projects with a software content are problematic and suggest ways in which phased development or prototype approaches can help
- list the main activities and tasks of a project manager.

# 1.1  *GENESIS*

This book is titled *Project Management*. To write about projects, we have to define what they are and describe how they arise. This chapter will concentrate on describing what a project is, how it can arise as a part of a planning process, as a response to a changing environment, a business opportunity, a problem or a newly identified quality requirement.

Projects often appear to be mysterious: it can be difficult to define exactly what a project is, and to the man or woman in the average organization they may appear to arise rather in the same way that mushrooms sprout – overnight. They are very diverse, and may range from one or two people making an effort over a few days or weeks to dozens or even hundreds of people working over a period of years.

## 1.1.1  What is a project?

Projects and project work are often contrasted with *process*: process describes the normal day-to-day activities of an organization, while the word *project* is often used to describe something outside normal day-to-day work. Of course, in some fields such as construction, research and software design, the normal day-to-day work is carrying out 'projects'. What then *is* a project?

Projects vary so much that they are difficult to define. What follows are some definitions offered by writers about projects.

> A *project* is a unique venture with a beginning and an end, conducted by people to meet established goals within parameters of cost, schedule and quality.
>
> Buchanan and Boddy (1992) p. 8

> A project is a set of people and other resources temporarily assembled to reach a specified objective, normally with a fixed budget and with a fixed time period. Projects are generally associated with products or procedures that are being done for the first time or with known procedures that are being altered.
>
> Graham (1985) pp. 1–2 (quoted in Buchanan and Boddy)

> [A project has] dedicated resources, a single point of responsibility, clear boundaries across which resources and deliverables move, limited duration, [it is a] one-off task and [has] objectives. It is a useful way of organizing work. Projects don't arise without deliberate intervention.
>
> Gray (1994)

> The simplest form of a project is a discrete undertaking with defined objectives often including time, cost and quality (performance) goals. All projects evolve through a similar 'life-cycle' sequence during which there should be recognised start and finish points. In addition the project objectives may be defined in a number of ways, e.g. financial, social and economic, the important point being that the goals are defined and the project is finite.
>
> APM (1993) p. 11

Key features of these quotations are that a project has the following characteristics:

- a project is a unique undertaking: each one will differ from every other in some respect
- projects have specific objectives (or goals) to achieve
- projects require resources
- projects have budgets
- projects have schedules
- projects require the effort of people
- measures of quality will apply.

The uniqueness of projects means that they take place in an atmosphere of risk and uncertainty. For our purposes, we will define a **project** as organized work towards a pre-defined goal or objective that requires resources and effort, a unique (and therefore risky) venture having a budget and schedule. A project's success can be measured in terms of how closely it comes to meeting the goal or objective (and this is an issue of quality) within the parameters of its budget and schedule. Once a project completes, it ceases; therefore project work is also characterized by impermanence.

---

### ACTIVITY 1.1

Think about how you might identify whether or not a project is successful. List those items that you would look at to determine a project's success.

### DISCUSSION

One way to identify whether a project is successful is to ask the following questions:

- Did the project achieve its time, cost and quality objectives?
- Does the project meet the customer's perceived requirements?
- Does the project's outcome make the client want to come back to do further business?
- Has the project been completed leaving the project organization fit and able to continue further work?

---

**Quality** in the context of projects will be discussed throughout this book.

Defining quality is not easy and there are a number of different perspectives from which quality can be viewed:

- *the product-based view:* quality is related to the content of the product (the quantity of ingredients or the attributes of the product)
- *the user-based view:* fitness for the user's purpose, meeting the user's requirements
- *the manufacturing-based view:* conformity to a specification; this may or may not be consistent with a user-based view
- *the value-based view:* providing what the user wants at an acceptable price, with conformity to a specification at an acceptable cost
- *the transcendent view:* quality cannot be precisely defined but equates to a notion of innate excellence (like a work of art).

The British Standards Institution's definition of quality is: 'The totality of features and characteristics of a product or service that bear on its ability to satisfy stated or implied needs' (BS 4778). In the context of a project, the product or service is 'the deliverables from the project'.

Standards exist for a wide variety of things, from the shapes of pipes to the classification of tea leaves. This book will generally refer to British (BS), European (EN) or international (ISO) standards where these exist. Some American standards, generally military standards (MIL-STD) and industry standards (e.g. IEEE) may be mentioned as well. International standards are increasingly widely accepted and used, particularly within Europe.

---

### ACTIVITY 1.2

From your personal experience choose a major item you have purchased and spend 10 minutes or so writing down an appreciation of its quality from the different points of view above. Our discussion will focus on the motor car, but you can choose whatever you like. The purpose of this activity is to help you to appreciate that there are several points of view.

### DISCUSSION

A product-based view of the motor car would focus on the standard of the materials used in the car.

A user-based view obviously depends on who the user is and what he or she wants out of the product. Your own preferences might range from the utilitarian to the exotic.

A manufacturing-based view would rate the quality against the given set of standards applicable to that particular model. On this basis it is possible for a cheap, low-specification car to be rated of high quality if it meets the standards set for it.

A value-based view would combine the user's requirements with a price or conformity to the specification at an acceptable cost.

A transcendent view of quality would yield something like a Rolls Royce, a top-of-the-line Mercedes Benz or one of the hand-built luxury sports cars.

Whatever you chose to evaluate, your list should contain examples of all the views of quality for that product, and you should have listed specific items or instances of how that quality is manifested in that view.

---

Generally, we will think of quality as *the totality of features and characteristics of a product or service that bear on its ability to satisfy stated or implied needs*. However, you should remember that not only are there different views, but different views may exist within the same organization.

## Examples of projects

Let's look at some illustrative examples of projects.

An aircraft manufacturer finds that the nose wheel on the prototype of a new aircraft collapses too easily and institutes a project to strengthen the nose wheel design. (Where designs are the result of a 'committee' or 'concurrent engineering' approach, as is often the case in the aircraft and automotive industries, what one group does with their part of a design may force another group to redesign. For example, when the wing strut in one aircraft design was strengthened, maintenance to part of the aircraft became impossible – the fitter couldn't reach existing wiring because the maintenance access shrank to make room for the stronger wing strut! A project had to be initiated to redesign the maintenance access.)

A construction firm may be asked to construct access roads and a group of small factory units on derelict land in order to generate business and jobs in a depressed area of the country. This may involve surveying, demolition of walls, clearing any rubble, removing trees and shrubs, levelling the site, laying out the access roads and constructing them, constructing foundations and erecting the buildings required by the plans.

A research and development department in a chemical firm may be asked to devote time to exploring the possibilities of developing new products using a new polymer.

A software development firm may be asked to make modifications to an existing database system in order to improve the ability of users to prepare reports directly using the data retrieved rather than having to transcribe it to a word-processing system. This may involve developing an understanding of the database and the word-processing systems, interviewing or observing users, developing specifications, writing and testing code, installing the new version of the software and providing training and documentation.

The marketing group of a company may be asked to prepare the launch of a new product. This may involve market research, planning and executing an advertising campaign, organizing promotional events and press releases and liaising with wholesalers and retail outlets.

A charity working in the Third World may determine in consultation with local people that a well needs to be dug. This may involve consulting people to determine a good site, consulting an expert hydrologist, organizing local labour and materials and carrying out the work. It may involve earlier effort to determine the best local materials available and the best ways of using them for this project. It may also involve training local people to maintain the well and working with local groups to ensure that the new resource is shared fairly.

A government body may have to respond to legislative changes. For example, the change in the UK from the old basis of local taxation, the rates (based on 'rateable value' which was in turn related to property value), to the community charge (the poll tax which was a charge on individuals) obliged local government bodies to make major changes to computer systems and undertake a major effort to identify whom to tax. Subsequently, the change from the poll to the council tax (which combines a highly modified element of the poll tax with an element of the tax based on property value) required further major system changes and another major effort to assess properties to assign them to tax bands. These formed, in a relatively short period, two separate major projects to institute the changes: one for the poll tax and then one for the council tax.

Sometimes the work needed to achieve a major organizational objective will be far greater than can easily be organized and carried out in a single project. This may mean that the organization will undertake a **programme** that consists of a number of interrelated projects. The Association of Project Managers defines a programme as:

> ... a specific undertaking to achieve a number of objectives. The most common examples of programmes are development programmes or large single purpose undertakings consisting of a series of inter-dependent projects. Examples include product and economic development programmes where the programme follows a concept/design/development life cycle before moving into implement-ation of multiple projects.
>
> APM (1993) p.10

**SAQ 1.1**

Based on the characteristics we have stated belong to projects and your own experience, draw up a table contrasting project management with managing operations.

# 1.1.2  Organizations and 'players in the game'

Projects take place within organizations whose structures, philosophies and cultures affect how work is planned and carried out. We shall briefly discuss organizations and how they go about planning. Projects also exist within a social environment consisting of people who are affected by and have an influence on the outcome of projects.

## Organizational structures

Business and other organizations in the West or based on Western models are normally structured as hierarchies using vertical lines of reporting. A person, usually called the managing director or chief executive officer, occupies the pinnacle of this hierarchy, takes advice from a board of directors on the strategic **objectives** of the business, and will seek the concurrence of the board for strategic, controversial or difficult decisions. Below the managing director the organization may divide into functional areas: marketing, product design and engineering, manufacturing, sales, personnel, finance. Some large organizations at this level may divide themselves by general groups of products. A large firm engaged in oil exploration might divide along lines of exploration, instrumentation, information systems and so on.

Often projects cross these functional or product group divisions: a project to develop a new product may, for example, involve the marketing, information systems, design and engineering and manufacturing divisions of a company. Yet the loyalties of people working in hierarchical organizations tend to follow lines of vertical reporting and conflicts may arise as a result of horizontal linkages required between different divisions, which may have different objectives and different cultures. A classic example is the complaint common in software development firms that the marketing people have promised something to customers which cannot be produced (either at all, or in time and to budget) by the people working in information systems.

Teams of people working on projects are often brought together from different areas for the duration of the project. This can be seen as beneficial, bringing to a group a diversification of knowledge, assumptions, ideas and skills. But the tension between vertical 'organizational chart' linkages and project-based linkages within an organization can have a detrimental effect on the outcome of the project unless care is taken to ensure otherwise. This will be discussed more extensively in Chapter 4.

## 'Players in the game'

A surprisingly large number of people in addition to the project manager and project team members can be involved in one way or another with projects. All of these people are important to some degree either because they are affected by the outcome of the project, or because they can influence its outcome, favourably or adversely. These various 'players' in the project 'game', who may only be involved peripherally, are still important. It is important to be aware of who they are and what role they play in the project environment. The terms we use here are drawn from Boddy and Buchanan (1992) and from Morris (1994).

## Sponsor

Almost all projects will have someone in the role of project (or earlier, proposal) **sponsor**. Morris's definition of this role is:

> The sponsor is the person providing the resources for the project: the person who should be responsible for ensuring that the project is successful at the business or institutional level.

> [The sponsor's] role, which is akin to the Chairman of the Board, is different from that of project *champion*.

> Morris, pp. 188 and 327

## Champion

The project or proposal **champion** may or may not be the same person as the sponsor. A champion is someone who acts as an advocate for a proposal or project; someone who has the ear of people who are in power and who promotes the cause of the proposal or project. Boddy and Buchanan (1992) use it in the sense of 'cajoling', 'providing support in times of difficulty', 'pushing changes through' (p.26).

## Client

A term often used in contracts to signify the person or organization contracting to obtain professional services is the **client**. This is the person or organization in the position of buying the services of a contracting organization or person. A client may be a sponsor or champion, or those roles may be taken by someone else (or several other people). We will use the term to mean the one who *pays for contractual services*, even in cases where the contract is an informal one, as it might be between, say, one department and another in the same organization.

## Customer

**Customer** is a term similar to *client*. Its most common meaning is one who buys, but it can mean also a person with whom one is concerned. In talking about quality, it is common to say that it is important to 'keep the customer satisfied' and it is in this sense that we will use this term.

## Owner

Although it does appear in Boddy and Buchanan (1992), we will not use the term **owner** much. The term owner can be taken to mean something similar to client or customer, though in a legal sense is much more narrowly defined, as you will see in Chapter 2, where we note problems that may arise with the legal concept of property (that is, ownership). Boddy and Buchanan use the term *owner* more in the sense of one with an attitude of strong attachment to the aims of a project.

## Stakeholder

The politics of organizations are such that many people who may not be directly involved with a project nevertheless have an interest in its completion and success. Any such person, whether directly involved or not, can be called a **stakeholder**, someone for whom the success of the project is important in any terms – the project manager, project team members, the sponsor, the champion, the client – for reasons of anticipated increased profitability, job security, financial reward, personal satisfaction, improved working conditions. Much more will be said about stakeholders and how to identify them in Chapter 4.

# 1.1.3 The project environment: strategic planning

Projects have to be planned. Indeed, an organization must plan to have projects. By **planning** we mean the process of formulating an organized method of achieving something which is to be done (such as a project) or of proceeding. Projects do not take place in isolation: they have an environment which gives birth to them and with which they interact for the rest of their lives.

## The environment of the organization

An early step in planning is the gathering of information about the environment in which an organization operates – the market, the economy, the technology and the legislative and regulatory climate. Knowing the market implies understanding the *present* market an organization and its products have, and *forecasting* markets for new or revised products and services.

## The mission

A common starting point is for the group to prepare a **mission statement** for itself. The mission statement should be a brief description of what the group (which could be the entire organization or some part of it) believes it has been organized to do. Ideally, a single sentence should encapsulate what the group believes it exists to do. Certainly it should be no more than a short paragraph in length. Longer statements tend to become confused and confusing, too long to read and too long to remember. It should be succinct enough to be recalled readily, and compared to the activities the group is actually doing or is contemplating doing. For example, one possible mission statement for the Open University is: 'to provide high-quality university-level and post-graduate education at reasonable cost to students who may not have previous qualifications and who are studying at a distance.'

There is some feeling that mission statements are 'old hat' and of little value. This may be because many published mission statements in the past have sounded too much like public relations exercises with no substance behind them, or were long and complicated. However, properly written in the right spirit they have genuine value, focusing attention on what an organization thinks it is or ought to be doing. The good mission statement creates boundaries within which objectives can be set. For example, if it were suggested that the Open University might undertake the manufacture of computers for students and others in order to increase its income, it should be immediately obvious that this activity would fall well outside the boundaries set by its mission statement. This should signal that the proposed objective is beyond the organization's likely available expertise, experience and infrastructure. To attempt to meet such an objective would require major organizational change.

A mission statement is effective when it encapsulates the core *values* of an organization concisely and clearly, allowing immediate comparison with any suggestions for activities. But more than a mission statement is required in order to identify what the *objectives* of the organization are.

## Change from above

**Strategic planning** sets the direction and route for an organization at a macro level. Within business organizations it is the normal function of a board of directors to formulate the strategic plans. They will do this at least to maintain the organization's place in the market and to meet the requirements of their customers, and will also consider strategic plans in the search for new growth and new business. In other types of organization, for example campaigning or charitable organizations or government, a comparable responsible body will exist: in the case of charities and campaigning organizations these are normally boards of trustees. These bodies formulate strategic plans for their organization in response to changes in their environments or changes in legislation. The result of this activity is, in the end, *projects* because projects are one of the major ways in which an organization can effect change. The role of the project is to move from a starting place to the end point defined in strategic plans as a goal for the organization.

## Change from below and from outside

Change can also be prompted from within the organization. A bright idea from a member of staff that appears to offer the organization something valuable (more diversity, new income, improved ability to survive, a need amongst customers or users hitherto unperceived, improved quality of product or service) can develop into a project to realize that idea.

---

### EXAMPLE 1.1

A worker at a catering firm noticed that there was no place to obtain lunch on the large industrial estate where the firm was located. He realized that many workers on the estate were having either to bring packed lunches or to travel some distance to eat. He suggested to his management that the catering firm could open a small restaurant with a take-away food bar in a little used area of their premises and thereby increase their business. The resulting restaurant drew on existing space, expertise and staff, brought in new income, and was particularly useful because all of the trade was in cash, which improved cash flow. This in turn helped improve the firm's ability to survive.

---

Planning activities for some types of organization will involve a simultaneous flow of ideas from the top down and from the bottom up to generate ideas which can become organizational objectives for change.

Change often comes from outside the organization: responses to changes in legislation might be required, work to meet a new standard needed, or a potential customer approaches a firm with an idea that will require change.

Notice that in the example above the worker was employed by a *catering* firm. What is the significance of this in the context of the preceding discussion?

# Strategic planning

The ways in which strategic planning takes place in an organization are as varied as the organizations themselves. Planning may be conducted autocratically, by orders from the board of directors; it may be conducted consensually by wide consultation and discussion throughout an organization; it may be proactive or reactive; it may be a mixture of these things – real life, including that encompassed by planning in organizations, is less well defined, less clear cut and much messier than descriptions of it would lead one to believe.

In what follows we suggest some ways of planning and some tools for doing so. Our descriptions are not exhaustive. They suggest ways of proceeding which are not the only ways and which will not fit easily into all organizational cultures. We hope that what we suggest provides an orderly way to progress from an organization's present situation towards a future that is more the result of planning than of whim or chance. What we suggest is also a process that can be carried out in top-down fashion, starting with the highest levels of an organization and advancing downwards through divisions, groups and even to the team level.

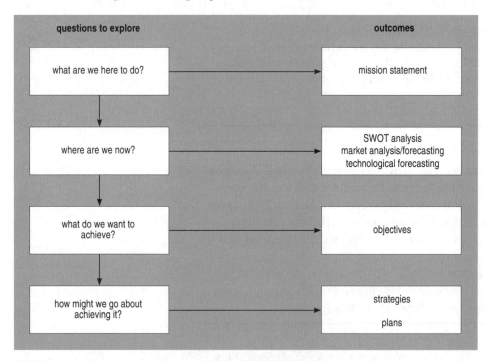

**FIGURE 1.1** Strategic planning questions and their outcomes

The decision making involved in strategic planning is not trivial: there are a number of tools available to help the organization to come to an informed decision about change. Once the questions shown in Figure 1.1 have been explored and their outcomes drawn up at the level of the whole organization, they are passed downward: a strategic plan at organizational level becomes an objective at the divisional level. The division then asks the questions in the figure again, develops the outcomes, and passes the results downwards. This way of planning can also work where there is no 'downwards' – for example in a co-operative where groups within the organization may use these tools and then negotiate with other peer groups.

## Strengths, weaknesses, opportunities, threats

One of the commonest analytical tools is **SWOT analysis** (SWOT is an acronym for Strengths, Weaknesses, Opportunities, Threats). This form of analysis provides a structure for studying both the internal and the external environments of an organization. The organization's strengths, weaknesses, opportunities and threats will be documented, investigated, and discussed. The strengths and weaknesses generally arise in an organization's internal environment (present products or projects, customers, staff, morale, information flows) and the opportunities and threats arise in the organization's external environment (competition, economic climate, potential market, legislation). These external factors are social, technological, economic, ecological and political (sometimes known as the STEEP factors).

Consider a SWOT analysis that might be done by a company that makes computer peripherals for industrial use, as in Example 1.2 overleaf.

Such an analysis can be made, not only for the whole organization, but for any part of an organization. A group concerned with a single product can, for example, carry out a SWOT analysis on that product and the way it is produced and marketed.

---

### ACTIVITY 1.3

Do a brief SWOT analysis for the group or department where you work, or for a group, such as a club or affinity group, to which you belong. Try to list at least three things in each category.

---

NO, NO SWOT STANDS FOR STRENGTH WEAKNESS OPPORTUNITY AND......

---

## EXAMPLE 1.2

### Strengths

1   The company has an established customer base and a growing reputation.

2   The business is now economically viable and profitable.

3   We now have an established group of salespeople, committed to our products, experienced with the products and with selling them.

4   Our new CD-ROM, soon to be released on the market, is in an exciting area.

### Weaknesses

1   Income is still too low to enable research and development into new areas related to our business.

2   The products to date have been marketed solely for industrial needs and we have not explored other potential markets.

3   Some products have low sales.

4   The process of developing new products or improving existing products is lengthy, and we do not respond to customer requests quickly enough at present.

5   Some products are now dated.

6   Our unrelated product lines hinder sales.

7   It is difficult to recruit industrial design personnel with appropriate skills and knowledge of our specialized needs.

### Opportunities

1   Significant numbers of our products have a commercial market as well as an industrial market.

2   There are new areas related to our present product lines, ripe for exploration and development.

3   There is customer interest in products related to our present lines but which we do not currently produce.

### Threats

1   Competitors might copy and modify our designs to produce an improved or cheaper product.

2   We may face legal action due to leaks of toxic materials.

---

Having studied such analyses a board of directors or trustees may use them to decide how to emphasize or build on an organization's strengths, address its weaknesses, take advantage of its opportunities and avoid or reduce its threats. A project or projects may then arise as a result. Although the need for the organization to undertake a project will normally be formulated by senior management or a customer, the project itself is, as yet, unborn. All there may be is an uneasy thought by someone 'up there' that all is not well or that something is needed.

# 1.1.4   Two investigative tools

Some objectives will necessarily be concerned with improving an existing situation, procedure, process or product in order to address a weakness; in other words, they will be concerned with reducing or eliminating *problems*. In order to do so effectively, the problem has to be investigated thoroughly to determine whether or not the problem is serious and whether it is worth tackling. There are two commonly used tools for this purpose, **Pareto analysis** and **cause and effect diagrams**.

## *Pareto analysis*

An Italian economist, Vilfredo Pareto, is credited with the development of this technique, which relies on an almost universal truism concerning the relationship between *value* and *quantity*. There are countless everyday examples: in a warehouse 20% of items will usually represent 80% of total stock value, 80% of quality problems will be accounted for by 20% of the possible causes of failure, etc. The ratio of 20 : 80 occurs so often that many people think of this ratio as 'Pareto's law'.

For example, in a computer system there will be frequent but minor failures in disk accesses: these failures are normally corrected simply by re-trying the access. Far more rarely, a disk's read head will touch the delicate magnetic surface, but then the disk is effectively destroyed and access is impossible under any circumstances. The former occurs frequently but with little impact, the latter rarely but with great impact. Pareto analysis consists of drawing columns that represent the magnitude of a problem, or of each aspect of a large problem. These columns are then arranged in order of magnitude, starting with the largest. (The column height represents the value of correcting the problem, so columns of the same size may refer to small but frequently occurring difficulties *or* to major difficulties that occur less often.)

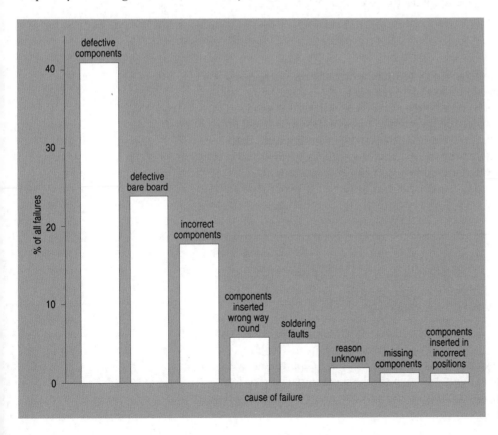

**FIGURE 1.2**
Pareto analysis of printed circuit board failures

Figure 1.2 shows a Pareto analysis of printed circuit board failures. If a project to improve the quality of these circuit boards were to be set up, it should concentrate on addressing those failures caused by defective components, defective bare boards and the use of incorrect components. Addressing all of the remaining causes of circuit board failures could cost a great deal of effort and money, but would gain little in terms of value in preventing circuit board failure.

### SAQ 1.3

Assume that following an examination of the production records for widgets you find the following: of a weekly production of 100 000 widgets worth £10 each, quality control staff remove 5 due to unacceptable burring remaining on the metal, 200 because they are unbalanced (out of round), and 50 to be re-polished as the polishing isn't good enough. Customers in the same week returned a shipment of 500 because they arrived scratched and gouged and so were unusable, and a shipment of 350 because the size despatched was not the size ordered. (Both returned shipments incurred additional shipping charges, but for this question you should focus only on the values of the shipments.) Either draw columns or use the figures given here to undertake a Pareto analysis.

(a)  Place these categories of faulty widgets in order from most to least value.

(b)  Where does the analysis suggest you could achieve the greatest improvement in quality?

Having identified which problems might merit further investigation, the next stage will be to study the symptoms of the problems, develop theories of the causes of those symptoms and then carry out further analysis and experimentation to establish true causes. A technique which is likely to be useful here is cause and effect diagramming.

### *Cause and effect diagrams*

Cause and effect diagrams are often known as **Ishikawa** or **fishbone diagrams**. Their construction begins with the definition of an occurrence (an effect) which is then reduced to those factors which contribute to it (causes). These are then examined in order to determine which are the prime causes of the effect, for it is the *prime causes* that must be tackled. An example is shown in Figure 1.3. Note that major causes are connected directly to the main arrow, sub-causes (such as incorrect storage in the figure) are connected to these lines, and sub-sub causes (such as dampness in storage) are connected to these. This establishes a chain of major and minor causes.

### ACTIVITY 1.4

While you haven't enough information to draw a cause and effect diagram for the widget problem, you should see that there may be a common factor in the two largest problem areas. What do you think it is?

### DISCUSSION

Both would appear to involve to some extent the shipping department. Were you to investigate further, you might find that carelessness in packing orders was responsible for both problems. In turn, the apparent carelessness could be

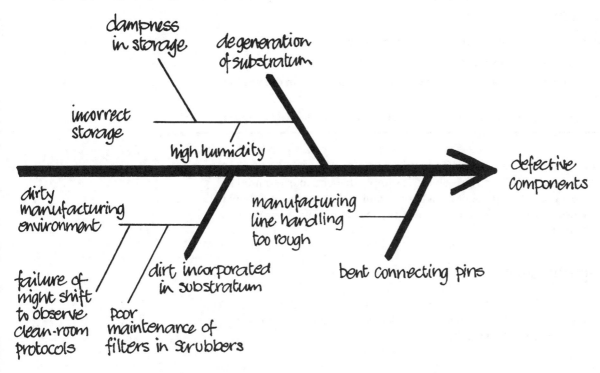

**FIGURE 1.3**  A cause and effect diagram for determining the causes of defective components

caused by a number of factors: poor lighting, packing materials not right for the product, poor layout of the packing area, lack of training of packers, low morale in the shipping department are all possibilities. Only a thorough investigation will determine the source of the problems.

Having determined the source of a problem and the value that would accrue to the organization if it could be eliminated or at least greatly reduced, the resulting objective should become clear, and possibly so should some strategies to achieve the objective.

# 1.1.5  Organizational objectives

Objectives are those things the organization wants to achieve, the 'whats' of the organization. A typical top-level objective in a profit-oriented organization might be: *to increase profit.* In a producer co-operative a top-level objective might be: *to improve the standard of living amongst our members and their families.* In a campaigning organization with a 'green' outlook a high-level objective might be: *to encourage the public to reduce their dependence on the private motor car.*

---

ACTIVITY 1.5

Think of a group of which you are a member; it could be any group such as a group where you work, your family or a club. Write down three to five high-level objectives such a group, in your opinion, would have.

---

DISCUSSION

In thinking of a family group three high-level objectives might be:

- to provide financial security for each family member
- to provide an environment of peace and safety, away from the world at large
- to provide a sound educational and social upbringing for any children.

---

Notice that all the items mentioned so far contain verbs such as *to improve, to encourage, to provide*. This is because objectives imply that action is required in order to achieve a **goal**. A goal might be 'a happy family life', but the members will need to take action to provide the financial security, peaceful, safe environment, and the sound upbringing.

## Identifying objectives

As we have mentioned earlier, it is usually the function of the board of directors or a similar body to determine what the high-level objectives should be. There are a number of techniques for achieving this.

### Brainstorming

A common technique is *brainstorming*. The technique has three phases. In the first phase, participants, ideally a close-knit group of five or six people working in a private area and without interruptions or interference, call out ideas for objectives. A 'compère', who encourages participation and discourages criticism at this stage, writes the ideas on a black- or whiteboard, on a flip-chart, on notes stuck to a bulletin board, or any combination of these, where every participant can see them all. When the pace of the interaction amongst the participants begins to falter or when the participants agree to stop presenting ideas, the group can move to the second phase, where they discuss the products of the first phase and can reject (possibly with reference to the mission statement) or keep individual ideas. Those which are kept can then be criticized constructively and roughly ranked in order of importance, interest or a perception of their feasibility. A suitable form of criticism is to ask whether an idea can be developed in some way to make it more usable. The process may be repeated, which may involve rejecting some of the ideas kept in the first round of this phase. In the final phase the participants seek consensus on a form of ranking and use this to develop a ranked set of objectives.

### Nominal group technique

Another technique for obtaining objectives is *nominal group technique*, developed by Delbecq and Van de Ven at the University of Wisconsin. This involves the silent and individual generation of ideas in writing in a group setting over a defined period of time (typically an hour or so), the recording of those ideas as simple phrases on a board or flip-chart, discussion to clarify the ideas, and a voting on the priority of ideas to achieve a rank ordering or rating. Thus it is similar to, but not so free-wheeling as, brainstorming.

### Affinity diagrams

Both brainstorming and the nominal group technique result in a ranked list of objectives. The group can then classify their organizational objectives using *affinity diagrams* – drawing connecting lines between different objectives that in some way are related. A thick line can be used to indicate a strong affinity, and a thin line a weaker affinity. This helps to group related objectives together. Once these affinities have been identified, objectives can be classified under descriptive headings. An example of headings under which objectives were classified by an organization devoted to promoting quality assurance and management techniques is:

- to increase the effectiveness of the service provided
- to increase customer satisfaction
- to increase profitability
- to increase job satisfaction
- to build a strong European organization.

We are less interested in how these objectives are identified and codified within an organization than in how these objectives, which describe *what* the organization wants to do, are developed into proposals (and ultimately into project plans) which enable the organization to achieve its objectives. From a quality point of view we are also concerned with how the organization and the people working within it can ensure their activities, including project activities, all work towards achieving their objectives.

## Towards project proposals

Objectives are *what* the organization wants to achieve. The effort required to do so occurs within some period of planning: this year, over the next five years, over the next decade.

Turning objectives, the *whats* of an organization, into plans, which are the highest-level *hows*, is the next task. We all frequently have objectives we want to achieve. Say, for example, that we want to eat. We might plan how to achieve this objective by preparing a meal at home or going to a restaurant. Even this simple example shows us something important: *there is almost always more than one way to achieve an objective.* When there is more than one way to achieve an objective and more than one person or group involved, some degree of disagreement or conflict may arise. Someone who likes home-cooked food may well want to prepare a meal at home, but another person who is tired of eating the same sorts of food so frequently may want to visit a restaurant that serves exotic cuisine. Even one person can feel ambivalent about how an objective is to be accomplished: a tired mother may welcome a trip to a restaurant as a break from cooking, but may also dread having to deal with her small children in a public setting. These disagreements, conflicts and ambivalences can adversely affect the outcome of any decision. In organizations, they can cause a programme or project to stray from the spirit of the objectives it was designed to achieve and thereby can seriously compromise the quality of the result.

The use of organized brainstorming and group planning, particularly if widely practised in an organization at all levels, will generally have two beneficial effects: people will feel that their attempts to contribute are welcomed and treated seriously; a good chance therefore exists that they will feel a measure of support for the outcome. People will be clearer about what the desired outcome is and how individuals and groups should work towards achieving it. Both these factors are unquantifiable, but contribute to the achievement of quality.

### *Matrix diagrams*

The brainstorming technique together with an organizing principle can be used to achieve the next level of planning within an organization. This may still be a rather high and strategic level of planning, but the techniques described here can be repeated at lower levels where more detailed work is done to develop programme and, finally, project plans.

Identified objectives form the 'what' column in a *matrix diagram*, as in Figure 1.4. Scale ratings are given to indicate the importance of each objective based on an analysis of organizational requirements. The group (which may not be the same group that has identified the objectives) then brainstorms as described above, but the goal of this brainstorming session is to identify key strategies ('hows') to meet the already identified objectives. Strategies are then linked to objectives by placing them in the other dimension of the matrix diagram and indicating whether links are non-existent, weak, medium or strong.

| | | strategies | | | | | |
|---|---|---|---|---|---|---|---|
| **Objectives** | importance rating | identify and quantify costs | identify customer needs | undertake marketing research | study and improve quality assurance techniques used | identify and eliminate areas of wasted effort | reduce paperwork |
| reduce operating costs | | strong | | | weak | medium | medium |
| provide better customer service | | | strong | | weak | | medium |
| increase marketability of systems | | medium | strong | strong | medium | | |
| increase employee satisfaction | | weak | | | medium | strong | strong |

weak link | medium link | strong link

**FIGURE 1.4**
A simple matrix diagram relating ranked objectives to strategies for achieving them

## ACTIVITY 1.6

Produce a short matrix diagram for the following objectives: develop study skills, study project management, pass a professional examination. List your key strategies and indicate broadly their links to these three objectives.

## DISCUSSION

Your key strategies might be: attend a course on study skills, read this book, take notes, revise notes, take a course in how to relax. The relationships might be: taking a course on study skills has a strong link to developing study skills, and medium links to the other two objectives; reading this book has a medium link to the objective 'study project management' (you need to do more than simply read the book to study it effectively!); taking notes has a strong link to 'study project management', a medium link to passing the exam and a medium link to developing study skills (practising techniques like note-taking helps to improve skills); studying the notes has a strong link to passing the examination.

You might have said something different.

Reiterating this process can be used to identify lower-level objectives and lower-level strategies and finally tactics. Taking Figure 1.4 as a brief example, in the next iteration the *strategy* of identifying and quantifying costs can become an *objective*, and a group can brainstorm or otherwise identify strategies for doing so: for example, looking at past invoices for certain items, identifying cheaper sources, identifying handling costs for those items, and so on. You might ask customers to participate in this process, perhaps through market research or by direct participation in identifying and ranking objectives.

At the strategic level a project manager may have no input at all. However, as the key strategies are identified and increasingly refined through iteration, strategies can turn into programmes of change, and the tactics of realizing those strategies can become projects. A project, to give it yet another definition, becomes a way of employing a strategy or strategies to achieve an objective or objectives. This process – identifying objectives, refining and classifying them, rating them according to an agreed scale of importance, brainstorming key strategies and establishing the links between objectives and strategies – can also be used at the project level.

One clear advantage of carrying out planning in this top-down fashion is that it helps to keep people's minds focused on the key mission and objectives of the organization as they resolve strategies into finer and finer detail. Suggestions for changes from lower down in the organizational hierarchy can be evaluated by a similar method: how well does this suggestion fit with the organization's mission and objectives? This reduces the chances of creating projects that will not have, or may eventually lose, the support of higher management, or projects that diverge significantly from the main 'business' of the organization. Having a project mission statement and objectives that are clearly stated and understood by all the participants and management can be a major factor in the success of the project.

## EXAMPLE 1.3

A successful project to develop a system to check whether telephone bills had been paid and, if not, to remind customers by telephone is described in Norris *et al.* (1993). The authors note that having a strongly stated project objective prevented effort on this project from going astray. At one point the project team was tempted to apply a great deal of expensive and difficult technology to the problem. By going back to the project's objective – to maximize the number of outstanding bills that get paid each month – the project team realized that the project was not about developing and implementing exciting new technology but about reminding people to pay bills. As a result, the final design was quite different from the initial thoughts of the project team. They avoided focusing on an isolated technical solution that was itself problematic and concentrated instead on the problem of reminding users who hadn't yet paid to do so. Norris *et al.* (p. 29) ask why the project went so well and answer their own question: 'The main thing was kept the main thing. The project team never lost sight of their objective. They could easily have been seduced by "clever" solutions – the use of [automatic] message senders, smart software to detect answer-phones, etc. They continually asked the question, "will this clear more unpaid accounts?"'

## From objectives towards actions

We have not yet indicated where in this cycle objectives become actions and organizational plans turn into *proposals* for action. Drawing such a line is very difficult. However, as the process of identifying objectives and then determining the strategy or strategies to achieve those objectives continues, two things occur. One is that the rankings of objectives, combined with a notion of the strength of links between objectives and strategies, will gradually emerge as a set of priorities: of objectives and of strategies deemed most effective to realize those objectives. As yet, no attempt has been made to determine the benefits of achieving a particular objective, nor whether a strategy is feasible and what it is likely to cost to effect that strategy. This is a necessary step before a project can be organized and authorized. It is a rare organization that can afford to try all identified strategies to meet all of its objectives. That is why it is important to be able to rank objectives in importance and to identify those strategies which will be most effective at achieving the most important objectives.

The second is that the proposals for action become increasingly detailed, and this enables a more accurate judgement to be made of their desirability, likely costs and likely benefits. Different proposals compete against each other for organizational attention, and it becomes clearer as these become more detailed which are likely to be more 'do-able' and of greater benefit.

The process of determining benefit increasingly is one of determining the *value* a proposal has for the organization. This also provides a measure by which one proposal can be compared to another in a case where choices must be made. However, *value* in this sense is not simply a matter of 'cost to build' or 'cost to buy'. It is a complex process, called the **value process**, of assessing each aspect of a proposal over its lifetime. At this early stage in planning, before any investment is made, the process is called **value planning**. Later you will meet with some methods for assessing the financial costs and benefits of proposals. These form a part of value planning provided such aspects as an assessment of running costs (energy, maintenance, repair and replacement) and, ultimately, decommissioning costs are included.

## Requirements

One of the best ways to ensure the quality of any project, or any deliverable or product, is to get the requirements for it right. If the requirements are not clearly and completely set out, any project or design based on them cannot succeed. And getting the requirements right at an early stage will prevent escalation of costs due to rework, client dissatisfaction and excessive changes during project execution and maintenance of the product afterwards.

Getting the requirements right involves the successful identification of:

- what constitutes acceptable and appropriate requirements
- what constitutes an acceptable demonstration of each element of those requirements
- the resolution of technical, financial or organizational conflicts of interest that may appear in the requirements
- the agreement on and documentation of the requirements and demonstrations in the proposal.

## EXAMPLE 1.4

A large computer system often requires a data communications network. The network consists of a number of separate components. It is exceedingly complex and the suitability of particular components cannot be judged solely on simple criteria such as their cost. Instead, they have to be judged on a number of complex and interlinked criteria: compatibility with all the other components used on several levels ranging from the mechanical and electrical to the use of different protocols; capacity, dependability, ease of installation, and size; the financial soundness and reputation of the manufacturer (can the manufacturer deliver the products wanted on time, and will the manufacturer still be in business when it becomes necessary to expand the network and more components are needed?), maintainability (ease and cost), ability to allow interconnection to other networks, running and purchase costs and so on. All of these will have some bearing on whether component A is more suitable than components B, C or D, which may appear to do the same function and be cheaper to purchase. *Making the correct choice is an important quality issue.*

A **requirement** is a statement of what is expected of a product or project. Drawing up the statement of requirements is one of the earliest steps in planning. A requirement is different from a **specification** in that the requirement is the starting point of a development and is an expression of those aspects which will define the thing to be done and the product to be developed. A specification is a statement of the characteristics of a project or product, such as its size or performance standards. A requirement might be 'to be able to travel independently of the public transport system'. This could be met in a number of ways: by motor car, motor cycle or bicycle or by travelling on foot. A specification resulting from such a requirement would vary depending upon the stage of definition, but could be stated as: 'a super-mini car' or 'an 1100cc petrol-engined motor car capable of carrying four passengers' or even one that specified in detail length, width, height, colour, etc.

It is only after much further work in feasibility studies and design, and often after prototypes have been built and tried, that a firm technical specification can be made.

A requirement must be *appropriate and well defined*. It is important to determine whether the proposed requirement is *appropriate* to real needs and expectations and to the value that the potential client will put on it. Then the client has to *agree* that the requirement is appropriate and meets his or her needs.

Even when a requirement is appropriate and well defined and everyone agrees on its meaning, if the parties have not agreed on how to demonstrate that a requirement has been met, the way is left open for that agreement to break down over time. Setting out how it will be possible to demonstrate that a requirement has been met is therefore very important. Desired characteristics are often set out in simple terms such as 'easy to use', 'safe', 'reliable' – but how will anyone know when 'safe' or 'reliable' have been achieved? It is best to avoid abstract terms. One way is to state the required quality, say 'easy to use', and then list what factors contribute to this quality. For example, 'easy to use' can include:

- appropriate documentation written in an easy-to-understand style
- clues on the thing itself which indicate how it should be used (for example an item's shape could mean it will only fit with another item in one obvious way)

- displays on the item directing clearly how it is to be used
- parts ergonomically designed for typical users, remembering that many people are not 'typical' (they may, for example, be colour-blind or left-handed or of above average height or users of a wheelchair).

This isn't an exhaustive list of ways in which the quality 'easy to use' can be refined, but you should see how important it is to define a quality in a concrete way. It will be necessary to look at these specifics at a later stage and turn them into demonstrations. For example, the first item on our list above is 'appropriate documentation'. Later on, we might want to specify that the demonstration of this is 'the existence of a user's manual which is complete, contains several useful and accurate worked examples and accurate and uncluttered illustrations'. Demonstrations must also be measurable.

## ACTIVITY 1.7

Assume you are drawing up the requirements for a door. First list two or three qualities that a door should exhibit, then refine these by listing two contributing factors for each quality.

## DISCUSSION

Three qualities that we could think of were: easy to use, draught-proof, attractive appearance. (You may have a different list.) The contributing factors we identified are shown in Table 1.1 (in some cases we've listed more than two).

**TABLE 1.1** Qualities and contributing factors

| Quality | Contributing factors |
|---|---|
| easy to use | handle opens easily |
| | door swings or slides out of the way with minimal effort |
| | door is wide enough to permit easy passage |
| draught-proof | frame overlaps with door edges and fits well |
| | seals used to improve draught-proofing |
| attractive appearance | smooth surface |
| | pleasing proportions |
| | attractive hardware used |

We haven't said anything about demonstrations here, but it would be possible at this early stage to set some additional qualities and contributing factors, such as extending the quality 'easy to use' by specifying that 'the door must be usable by wheelchair users, people with Zimmer frames or pushchairs or with their arms full'. This would have a bearing on the door being wide enough, needing only minimal effort to open and close it, and the handle being easy to reach.

Requirements will affect the cost of any item and any project, and yet cost is only one criterion and may not be the most important. Other aspects may be vital to the success of the proposal.

**EXAMPLE 1.5**

The design team for an early space satellite did not communicate to the purchasing manager the fact that all electronic parts needed to be 'high reliability' – able to perform after having been subjected to the pressures and vibrations of a launch, under conditions of near vacuum and alternating very low and very high temperatures. The purchasing manager proceeded to acquire electronic parts on the basis of price alone. High-reliability electronics are, of course, far more expensive than their ordinary counterparts. One of the key electronic components of the satellite failed to survive the launch because it was of the ordinary type.

## Next step: feasibility

Once you have identified and ranked objectives and strategies at the organizational level and analysed major problems and their causes, made decisions about which to pursue further, and set out your requirements and specifications, the next step is to identify those potential strategies which should be surveyed to see how feasible (how profitably 'do-able') they are. This stage is referred to as a **feasibility study**. Feasibility studies may be undertaken for one or more potential strategies and the results of these studies may be used to decide which proposals to pursue. More will be said in the next section on aspects of assessing feasibility.

# 1.1.6　Summary

This section has set the scene for projects by describing organizations and the 'players' – sponsor, champion, client, customer, owner and stakeholders. It shows how organizations can go about identifying their mission and objectives, how those objectives and the strategies to achieve them can be explored and refined in a structured way, how problems can be analysed and then, broadly, how the feasibility of various possible actions can be determined. It is then up to management to decide which actions to pursue.

Having studied this section you should be able to:

- define in your own words what a project is
- name and define the chief roles various people can assume in respect to proposals and projects
- explain the purpose of a mission statement
- define and carry out a simple SWOT analysis
- explain how to carry out a Pareto analysis of a problem
- explain the role of cause-and-effect diagrams
- generate simple matrix diagrams to relate objectives to strategies
- relate all of these to the process of organizational planning
- explain how quality is improved when a structured approach to planning is used, ensuring that mission, objectives and strategies are clearly identified
- set acceptable requirements for proposed projects.

# 1.2 *FEASIBILITY*

Undertaking a full assessment of whether a proposal is feasible or not is a substantial project in its own right. Sometimes the potential project manager may be involved and sometimes not. However, it is important for any project manager to understand the processes by which proposals are evaluated and assessed.

At this point, let's assume that we have a project proposal, or quite probably several proposals, to consider. We need to decide next whether any of them are worth pursuing further. We need to assess their feasibility.

In what follows, we don't expect you to learn all the details or memorize all the terms, particularly those associated with cost–benefit analyses and accounting. However, you will find it beneficial as a practising project manager to be able to read proposals with a critical eye. How complete is the functional specification? How sound is the method used to calculate profitability? How good is the assessment of the technical and technological factors? Have social, political and ecological factors been considered adequately?

As you study this section, bear in mind that your aim should be to develop your critical faculties for when you assess proposals.

## 1.2.1 The feasibility study

A team should be designated to undertake a feasibility study for any proposal that appears to be worth accepting. This study should attempt to generate **scenarios** which are potentially acceptable solutions. The resulting scenarios – different versions of what might be done – and all objectives that are to be addressed by the study should be used to prepare a **functional specification** that spells out a proposal's scope, objectives, financial and time constraints, and addresses the questions of technical and economic feasibility. A functional specification says *what has to be done* and *what constraints apply to doing it*. It ensures that there is *at least one satisfactory way* of doing it but it does not specify how the objective is to be achieved. That step occurs as part of the project planning, if the proposal is accepted and authorized by management.

Assessing the feasibility of a proposed scenario requires an understanding of the social, technological, ecological, economic and political (STEEP) factors involved. Note that the financial and technical aspects – the 'hard', quantifiable aspects – are only part of the problem to be analysed. The other factors are 'soft'. Soft systems analysis (SSA) is an approach that deals with information beyond the 'hard' information of quantities and facts (see, for example, Checkland (1981) and Checkland and Scholes (1990)). SSA can be used early in a study to identify the interactions that need to be considered in any assessment. It is particularly useful for identifying those aspects of any problem or proposal that fall outside normal operations research and 'engineering' concerns with function, construction and operation. A particular technique employed by SSA that is useful in feasibility studies is *rich picture analysis*. This is an analyst's holistic (describing the situation as a whole) representation of a situation: it identifies problem areas, structures, processes and political, psychological and social factors. Financial, technical or regulatory constraints can be captured in the picture. Figure 1.5 is a rich picture of the project to construct the bridge over the Humber.

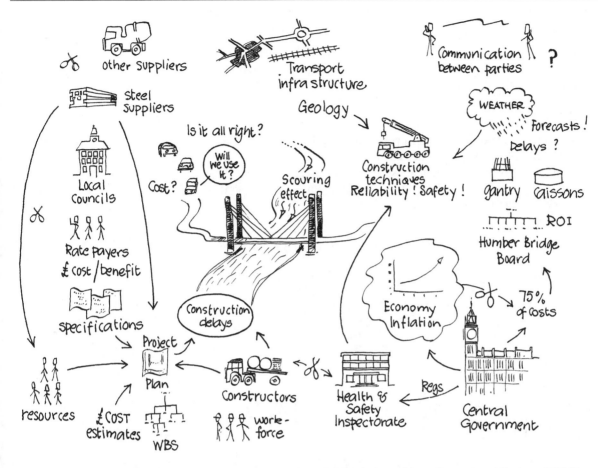

**FIGURE 1.5** Rich picture of the construction of the Humber Bridge (adapted from Stewart and Fortune (1994))

Note that the rich picture also calls attention to areas which require further analysis of the technical feasibility of a project. Figure 1.5 notes in particular: geology, gantry, caissons, scouring effects and the transport infrastructure. The appearance of these suggests that before the project begins they all merit further investigation: the geology by a consulting geologist, perhaps, the proposed designs for the gantry and caissons by an experienced consulting civil engineer, and so on. Other items draw attention to the social and political aspects of the project (e.g. local councils, potential users). Yet others highlight aspects of the project that must enter into planning (e.g. suppliers, resources) or execution (safety, reliability).

## ACTIVITY 1.8

Sketch a quick rich picture of a 'project' for you to study with the UK's Open University. Include all the elements you think affect you and your project, or that your project has an effect on.

## DISCUSSION

Your picture will, of course, be unique to you. But you probably have included your job, your boss(es), partner and other family members if you have them, and your costs of studying, as we have in our picture (Figure 1.6). Perhaps you've pictured how it affects your living arrangements, what strains and stresses (or benefits!) it gives to your social life, etc.

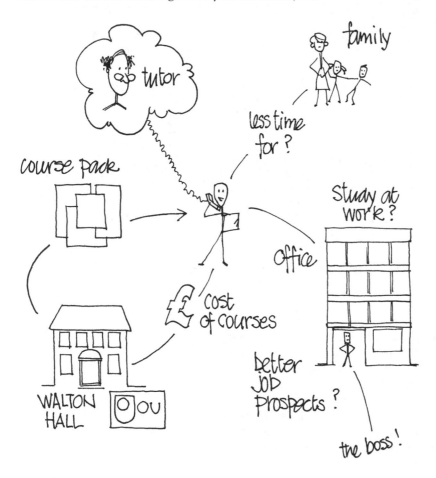

**FIGURE 1.6** A 'rich picture' of studying with The Open University

# Generating acceptable scenarios

A scenario is a brief description of a system, process or set of procedures that should meet the identified objectives. As noted above, for every objective there are a number of possible strategies – the objective of eating can be satisfied by: assembling raw food in a salad, assembling and preparing ingredients for a cooked meal at home, going to a friend's for a meal, going to a café or restaurant, or getting a meal to take away. Each of these would be a possible scenario for satisfying a need to eat. Developing scenarios is an activity in which brainstorming again can play a role. Many ideas can be generated, but then must be looked at critically and modified, selected or rejected.

---

### ACTIVITY 1.9

Make a brief list of possible scenarios to meet the need to move people and their baggage around a large site like a major airport or resort complex. 'Brainstorm' on your own if you like, or ask friends or colleagues to join in.

### DISCUSSION

Some possible scenarios are:

- provide wide pavements, stairs, road crossings, etc., with free or hired baggage carts allowing the movement of people on foot, pushing carts containing their baggage

- provide moving belts (travelators), escalators and elevators and free or hired baggage carts for movement on foot as above

- provide individual electric carts in which one to four people can load their baggage and drive themselves or be driven by a hired driver around the site

- provide petrol- or diesel-driven buses with baggage racks to move groups of people and their baggage around the site

- provide a fixed-roadbed or rail system of automatically controlled cars or wagons in which groups of people and their baggage can be moved around the site (e.g. a monorail, a form of small train or tram, or similar).

The scenarios above describe current ways of transporting people and baggage at major airports. Brainstorming may generate some more 'far-fetched' ideas:

- provide booths to teleport people and baggage from one place to another by converting them into pure energy which can be beamed at the speed of light

- provide anti-gravity discs of, say, 1.5 metres diameter upon which one to three people and their baggage can stand; the discs then move under automatic control.

You may have thought of other possible scenarios.

---

We have included far-fetched ideas in our discussion of this activity to show briefly how an idea which may appear so far-fetched as to be silly can be modified to use an existing or emerging technology. Look at the second of our far-fetched ideas. Anti-gravity is, at best, a very long way from achieving reality. However, it is possible to use the technology of superconductors to lift a weight and then to move it using linear electric motors; this is an *emerging technology* currently being explored for its application to public transport. While it may still seem far-fetched, such a technology may in future be used to lift a disc on which people and their baggage stand and to move the disc and its burden under automatic control around a site such as an airport.

### SAQ 1.4

What is the role of a scenario and how is a scenario developed?

## 1.2.2   Technical feasibility

We've generated some scenarios for moving people and luggage around a site like a major airport or resort complex. How do we assess the technical feasibility of these scenarios? We do not intend to answer such a broad question but note that from the point of view of minimizing risk we need to be sure that the chosen technology is sound.

We can determine whether a technology is *mature*. For example, the technologies of laying pavements, building stairways and so on are very mature, though new materials will from time to time appear on the market and influence the technology. An example is the use of extremely hard-wearing rubber tiles in places such as railway stations, airports and the like to provide a more pleasant and safer surface to walk on, reduce noise levels and yet be nearly as durable as harder surfaces.

Some technologies are only relatively mature and are still undergoing active development. The use of fixed-rail or fixed-bed cars, trains and trams is an example: there has been continuous change in such a technology to increase safety, improve the comfort of the ride, increase speed, and reduce running and maintenance costs and side-effects such as noise. The Paris Metro originally used iron-wheeled vehicles on fixed iron rails but has moved to rubber-tyred vehicles running on concrete 'tracks'; both Gatwick and Stansted Airports have automatic, driverless rail vehicles to move people.

Other technologies, such as superconductors and linear motors, are only just emerging: a few scale-model prototypes have been built to develop an understanding of the characteristics of the technology and to help make it usable at full scale and at an affordable cost.

Not only do we need to assess whether a technology is mature, sound and applicable – we also need to assess a variety of technical aspects of any proposal. These vary enormously and often require experienced or expert people to evaluate them properly. Even the building of a house by an experienced building contractor requires this sort of assessment. For example, the soil on the building site will affect how the foundations have to be constructed. A house built on clay has different requirements from one built on sandy soil; one built on a hillside with the potential for slippage is different yet again from one built where the earth is stable. (A soil engineer may be called to take samples and prepare a report before building commences.) Marketing projects have to take into account the fact that 'markets' vary due to climatic, cultural and economic differences: you can't market air-conditioners very successfully in a cold climate, nor to people who can't afford them. A software developer may need expert advice from the hardware manufacturer before undertaking a project using that manufacturer's platform. A project to dig a well in the Third World will need an assessment from a hydrologist about the depth, suitability and extent of the local aquifers and water table.

You should bear in mind that cost is by no means the only factor determining whether a project is worth while, though its ease of measurement may tend to give it prominence. Several techniques exist for dealing with anything where cost is of less importance than other aspects of a project or product.

## Features analysis

**Features analysis** is a method of gathering and organizing information about different products which can be used for the same purpose and comparing them in terms other than those of cost. **Features** are those elements of a piece of equipment, a system, or some other major constituent of the project which are regarded as important in the context of the project's requirements.

Assume that your company plans to publish a series of 'how to' books on a highly technical subject. You are asked to interview a number of 'typical' buyers and users of this type of book to find out what the requirements are. You find that most of your subjects mention: durability, portability, ability to keep the pages clean, ability to prop the open book up and have it stay open at the correct page. What then, are the features?

If you look at the requirement for durability, then a feature might be the materials used for covers and pages, and the type of binding used. The binding is also a feature that will dictate whether an open book can be easily propped up and will stay open at the right page. Portability will probably be determined more by dimensions and weight. (You may have to find out more about this requirement: do people want to be able to carry the book under an arm, in a briefcase, in a pocket?) Being able to keep the pages clean will depend upon the paper used, which will also have a bearing on the weight of the finished product.

Note that a feature, such as the type of paper used, can have a bearing on two or more other features (such as weight and ability to keep clean). One sample of paper may contribute more to one feature (saving weight) and less to the other (ability to keep clean), while another sample may be easier to keep clean but weigh more.

A features analysis of the proposed system components will focus attention on the features of any requirement that are likely to prove important to the achievement of something that works and that satisfies needs. The importance of these features needs to be determined so that competing proposals or products can be judged accordingly. (One inevitable feature is of course cost, but it may not be the most important feature.)

Undertaking a features analysis entails identifying those features in the requirements likely to be vital, or very important, to the final outcome of the proposal. When important features have been identified they can be given a weighting, an assignment of a value indicating the *relative importance* of one feature to all the others.

Each feature so identified becomes a category with several constituent elements. If we take robustness of a system for an example, we can analyse ways in which a system can be robust: it continues to operate in spite of power failures, the communications channels will not fail, the central computer has to be designed so that a failure in the hardware will not cause the system to cease to operate, and so on. These elements are painstakingly listed. Each will have a point value attached to it such that the total number of points for the elements listed under one feature will be 1.00. Each feature will be assigned a weight factor which indicates its relative importance to other features looked at in the analysis. An example using the factor *passenger/luggage capacity* in choosing a new motor car is shown in Table 1.2. The weight factor here (0.25) indicates that passenger/luggage capacity will make up one quarter of the value we give to the overall analysis of the new car.

**TABLE 1.2**  Part of a features analysis for choosing a new motor car

|  | Weight factor | Point value |
| --- | --- | --- |
| passenger/luggage capacity | 0.25 | |
| front seat head room | | 0.13 |
| front seat leg room | | 0.17 |
| back seat head room | | 0.10 |
| back seat leg room | | 0.10 |
| total seating capacity | | 0.16 |
| internal luggage capacity | | 0.14 |
| luggage capacity on roof rack | | 0.08 |
| ability to rearrange seating | | 0.06 |
| glove box capacity | | 0.03 |
| other small item storage | | 0.03 |
| **total** | | **1.00** |

In this case we have chosen as an important feature of a new motor car the passenger and luggage carrying capacity. We can go further and identify other features for choosing a motor car, as shown in Table 1.3. Each such feature will then have the elements that constitute that feature also listed and given point values, and the total value of the features for an item will be 1.00.

Following the descriptions of features, weight factors and the elements that make up the features and their point values, each candidate product must be rated. Using the feature described in Table 1.2, motor car A might have sufficient front seat head room for people 1.8 metres (6 foot) tall while motor car B may easily accommodate people of 1.95 metres (6 foot 4 inches). If a taxi firm employs several drivers who are over 1.8 metres tall, they will have a preference – because of this element of the passenger and luggage feature – for motor car B, though other elements and features must enter into the final choice. In carrying out the features analysis, you would have to decide whether to give motor car B the full point value for front seat head room of 0.13 and how much point value (perhaps only 0.09) to give motor car A. When all the elements of a feature have been rated for all the candidate products, these are summed up. Let's say that motor car A has a point count of 0.58 for feature passenger and luggage capacity and motor car B has a point count of 0.71.

All the features identified are assessed and point values summed up. Then the point value for each feature is multiplied by the weight factor for that feature. Thus motor car A in our example will have a weight-adjusted rating for passenger and luggage capacity of 0.145, derived by multiplying motor car A's point count of 0.58 by the weighting assigned to passenger and luggage capacity (0.25) to give 0.145; similarly B's point count of 0.71 times 0.25 gives a weight-adjusted rating of 0.1775.

The weight-adjusted scores for all features being considered are then summed for each candidate to obtain a **figure of merit** (FOM), and the candidate with the highest FOM *should* normally be the product chosen. (A figure of merit assigns a numeric value to a cost or benefit based on an arbitrarily decided and often weighted scale: for example you might rate a computer according to the desirability of its speed, memory capacity and reliability.)

The problems with features analysis are fairly obvious:

- there may be many constituent elements for each feature
- features must be weighted in terms of their relative importance
- qualitative ranking systems (e.g. those using categories like poor, average, good and excellent) are more difficult to analyse though they may be easier to use when rating elements
- complete consensus about the weightings of features and rankings will rarely occur.

Thus the result of a features analysis is to some extent arbitrary. Nevertheless, a features analysis can be a highly valuable exercise since it will help an organization to identify, rate and rank those features of a system which they find important more objectively.

**TABLE 1.3**

Features and weight factors for choosing a new car

|  | Weight factor |
| --- | --- |
| driver comfort | 0.25 |
| passenger/luggage capacity | 0.25 |
| safety | 0.25 |
| handling | 0.10 |
| reliability | 0.10 |
| passenger comfort | 0.05 |
| **total** | **1.00** |

## ACTIVITY 1.10

Imagine you are planning to buy some luggage to use in your new job, which will involve a great deal of long-distance international travel over the next two or three years. You may need to be away from your home for up to six weeks at a time. You will need to be able to carry sufficient clothes for up to six weeks for a variety of climates, as you may spend a couple of weeks in Moscow in winter, followed by a couple of weeks in equatorial Africa. You should also expect to carry small amounts of paperwork and perhaps some samples.

List what you feel will be important features to judge in comparing different makes of luggage. Assign weighting factors to these.

## DISCUSSION

Possible features of importance are: durability, empty weight, capacity, ease of carrying, security of locks, internal compartmentalization, degree of water-proofness, ease of recognition at the luggage conveyor at the airport, appearance. You may have suggested others, depending upon what you consider to be important to *you*. Likewise, any weighting you assign to these features will also vary, though the specification that you will do a great deal of travel for the next two to three years probably means that durability will have a relatively high rating.

## ACTIVITY 1.11

Now take the feature *ease of carrying* and list some elements that you feel make up this feature.

## DISCUSSION

Some that occurred to us are: comfort of handle, balance of case, presence of shoulder strap (on smaller cases), presence of wheels on larger cases, ease of using the wheels (e.g. does the case fall over when pulled along), strap or handle for pulling of sufficient length and strength to allow one to walk upright while pulling case along. You may have thought of others.

## SAQ 1.5

(a) List the main steps of a features analysis.

(b) What is the value of doing a features analysis?

# Ecological and social factors

Increasingly, ecological factors must be considered when assessing the feasibility of any plan. Ecological considerations may be prompted by a feeling that an organization's existing and potential customers would prefer to buy products which are less harmful to the environment than alternatives, or by concern amongst shareholders or employees, or may be mandated by health and safety legislation. It is beyond the scope of this book to discuss in detail the assessment of ecological factors, but Example 1.6 gives an idea of the types of things looked at in such an environmental impact assessment. When assessing the environmental impact of any project it is important to consider it 'from the cradle to the grave'. In a manufacturing project this means taking into account not only the impact of the product itself and any pollution created in the manufacturing process but also the raw materials and energy used for its manufacture and the method of its eventual disposal.

It is also increasingly common to assess social factors in determining feasibility; this is particularly true in projects undertaken in the under-developed world. These may range from social factors within a single group or office (for example where a new technology is likely to be introduced) to broader social concerns about the effects of a project, process or product on employment, the health of workers and the general public, and safety issues. An example of an attempt to incorporate these concerns into the development of software is the ETHICS method (Mumford, 1983). ETHICS (Effective Technical and Human Implementation of Computer Systems) looks at using participative methods to explore organizational issues such as goals, values and sources of job satisfaction in designing computer systems, and incorporating these issues with technical solutions into a design.

## EXAMPLE 1.6

In the UK 2 million tonnes of glass are used each year to make bottles. The raw materials – sand, limestone and soda ash – are quite plentiful but their extraction causes a considerable amount of damage to the environment. The best sand for glass manufacture in Britain comes from Norfolk and Surrey and the limestone comes from the Peak District National Park. These materials then have to be transported to the major glass manufacturing plants, which are located in the north of England. Every tonne of glass that is recycled saves the energy equivalent of about 140 litres of oil and 1.2 tonnes of the raw materials that would have gone into an equivalent amount of new glass.

Most glass which is not recycled will eventually be disposed of into landfill sites. In many parts of the country there is shortage of disposal sites and consequently the cost of disposal is rising. Even where there are existing holes in the ground from previous mineral extraction neighbouring communities often campaign against their use as waste tips, fearing smells and health hazards. Broken glass which has been thrown away thoughtlessly is a hazard to both people and wildlife. Recycling glass saves the extraction of raw materials and some of the energy, and alleviates the problem of waste disposal.

The re-use of glass bottles is, however, even more environmentally beneficial. Whereas recycling old glass ('cullet') saves less than 10% of the energy consumed, re-using bottles saves most of the energy consumed in their manufacture; some energy is still required to clean the bottles before re-use. Currently in the UK re-use is limited mainly to milk and beer bottles but could easily be extended to other types. The average milk bottle is used 24 times. So, to minimize the environmental impact of glass bottles, re-use is preferable to recycling but recycling is preferable to disposal as waste.

## Other technical factors

An article in the *Independent* newspaper ('City puts transport future on the line', 23 February 1994) highlights some of the other technical factors that may apply to a project. The article looks at the new tram system in Sheffield launched the previous day and compares it to the then year-old tram system in Manchester. Tram systems are seen as an important way of addressing problems of traffic congestion and public transport needs in large cities. Sheffield chose to route its trams through areas in need of redevelopment, such as the derelict industrial area in the Don Valley, on streets where disruption to car traffic would be minimal. However, blocked access to shops and local traffic delays during construction alienated many local people along the route. This raises questions as to whether the new trams in Sheffield will attract sufficient passengers (20 million passengers are needed in the first year to break even). Manchester converted existing track owned by British Rail for its use, which minimized disruption to road traffic during the construction phase. By concentrating on popular commuter routes, Manchester's trams attracted nearly 20% more passengers than they expected.

Technical factors other than the maturity of a technology may be:

- the utility of the technology (for example in the selection of computer systems)
- the usability of systems
- the degree of disruption during the construction or installation phase
- use of and improvement to existing infrastructure or the development of new infrastructure
- notions of general social utility (Sheffield's choice in their tram routes)
- marketability (Manchester's choice in their tram routes).

Assessing whether a particular technology is suitable for a particular situation will depend on the situation and the objectives of the organization. Returning to our activity of developing scenarios about moving people and baggage, an airport authority with a large and busy existing airport will want a technical solution which will not be too disruptive to install and will work immediately, perhaps instituting a system of buses. An airport authority building a new airport can more safely choose a technical solution which might cause too much disruption if attempted in an existing facility, such as a fixed roadbed system like a monorail. An organization exploring novel applications for superconductors and linear motors may want to develop the technology of moving discs.

In addition to purely technological factors, technical constraints may apply to any plans. If you plan to start a restaurant business, opening hours allowed by a local authority will be a constraint to consider, as perhaps will the availability of car parking facilities or public transport.

---

### ACTIVITY 1.12

Make a very brief technical, social and ecological assessment in terms of *questions* to be asked – take no more than three to five minutes – of a plan to collect and recycle steel and tin-plate cans in a medium-sized town. (Note that we are not looking for the technical *answers* here, just the questions that might be asked.)

### DISCUSSION

Our list of questions for this assessment follows.

*Technological factors*

- How mature is the process of recycling steel and tin-plate?

*Social factors*

- Could local people be persuaded to recycle their tins?
- Are there reasonable places to put recycling collection points; or would it be better to have collections from homes?

- Is this likely to affect employment in the area?
- Would local people object to the siting of a recycling plant here (smells, noise, generation of more road traffic)?
- How much disruption would there be in building the plant?

*Ecological factors*

- How much energy is consumed by the processes, compared to energy consumed in extracting raw materials for making steel and tin-plate? Where does the energy originate? How 'clean' or 'dirty' is the process of energy generation used in the locality?
- What are the waste products (including air, water and soil pollutants) generated by the recycling process, and how can these be minimized and handled safely?
- Can permission for the plant be obtained from the local authority?
- Is the road infrastructure able to support another industrial site in the area?

You may have other questions in your list.

# 1.2.3  Financial feasibility

Before investment of resources in selecting and carrying out a potential project can proceed, two sets of questions need to be considered:

1   Will the investment of resources in a particular project be worthwhile? How worth while will it be?

2   Where there are several alternative opportunities for investing resources, which one gives the best rewards?

## Cost–benefit analysis

The technique that should almost certainly be used during any feasibility study is the **cost–benefit analysis**. This means:

- identifying, specifying and evaluating the costs, including purchase, construction, maintenance, repair, running costs such as energy consumption, and decommissioning, of the proposal for its projected lifetime
- identifying, specifying and evaluating the benefits of the proposal over its projected lifetime.

No matter what the size and nature of a proposal, the methods of evaluation are always the same: the specification of costs and benefits is the first stage. The types of cost and types of benefit involved in a particular project obviously depend upon the nature of the proposal and can vary as much as the proposals themselves.

For every item of proposal cost and every item of proposal benefit, you need to specify:

- its value in money terms or its value in terms of desirability (using some numeric scale)
- whether it is capital or revenue in nature (see below)
- its likely timing (when it occurs)
- whether it occurs once or recurs

- whether recurring items will remain constant or vary as time goes by (e.g. because of inflationary factors)
- where recurring items are expected to vary, for what reasons and by how much.

Fortunately, many of the types of costs and benefits are common to many projects. In some cases it is of value to be able to look at each phase of a project in terms of that phase's costs and benefits and to assess these in isolation from the rest of the project – a technique called **value engineering**.

Some costs and benefits will not be easily translatable into financial terms. These are called **intangible** costs and benefits. As we have already seen, some intangible costs and benefits can be rated by developing a figure of merit. Other intangible costs and benefits may not be expressible in any numeric way – an example might be improved employee morale. The term *cost–benefit analysis* is often applied in a broad way to allow management to judge non-monetary and non-quantifiable costs and benefits as well as financial costs and benefits. A cost–benefit analysis may look not only at the financial feasibility of a potential project but also at intangible costs and benefits.

Another piece of information needed in carrying out a cost–benefit analysis is whether an item of financial cost or benefit is of a capital or of a revenue nature. (You should learn the difference between **capital** and **revenue** and what **financing costs**, **overheads**, **depreciation** and **inflation** are. You do not need to memorize how to calculate these, but should be able to do so using standard tables and descriptions of the formulae used. You should be able to state which methods are likely to yield sound results.)

We have provided a checklist of costs and savings in Appendix 1, *Evaluating Proposals Financially*. Use this checklist as an *aide-mémoire* to ensure that nothing is overlooked.

### Capital costs

**Capital costs** are incurred in the acquisition or enhancement of **assets**. Assets are usually **tangible** things such as land, buildings, plant, machinery, fixtures, fittings, stocks of materials and cash *owned* by the organization. Capital costs include:

- the basic purchase price of an asset
- any additional costs which are incurred in installing and commissioning an asset and putting it into working order.

Capital expenditure usually occurs at the outset of work but there are exceptions. Any subsequent costs which are in respect of the acquisition or enhancement of assets should be treated as capital and regarded as part of the total investment.

### Revenue costs

Any cost incurred in a project other than for the acquisition or enhancement of assets is called **revenue cost**. Revenue costs (sometimes referred to as **running costs**) are those costs incurred on a continuing basis as part of day-to-day operations. These need to include projected maintenance and repair costs, the cost of replacing worn-out components and the like. Examples are given in Table 1.4 on page 40 which shows a sample **cash flow** statement.

One type of revenue cost sometimes attributed to a project, even if that project doesn't use internal resources, is overhead allocation. The term **overheads** refers to the day-to-day revenue expenses (the running costs) which appear as charges against income which apply to the organization generally and are not directly attributable to any specific area within the organization (which is why they are sometimes called *indirect costs*). Examples are:

- administrative costs such as rent and rates, staff salaries, mains and other services, insurances, stationery etc.

- general management salaries and costs

- depreciation on administrative offices, machinery and furniture.

If a proposal results directly in an increase in any of the overhead costs the amount of the increase represents a revenue cost directly attributable to the proposal and the increase must be allowed for when calculating a project's financial viability. Examples are additional rates or taxes, additional insurance costs and salaries of additional staff. Depreciation is another revenue cost.

*If you are interested in learning how depreciation costs are calculated see Appendix 2, Depreciation Costs.*

## Financing costs

Every project has to be financed. Money has to be found to pay for the initial investment in the project and perhaps also to finance subsequent revenue costs if the benefits in the initial years are inadequate to cover these. As with other resources, the use of financial resources itself costs money: financing costs. These are usually the interest that has to be paid on the outstanding balance of funds invested in a project until such time as the project benefits have paid those balances off. (This is exactly like paying interest charges on a reducing bank loan.) To determine whether the proposal is economically viable, the percentage rate of a project's financing costs is compared against the calculation of project profitability. It is therefore vital in proposal evaluation to know what your financing costs will be, otherwise there is no way of deciding whether a project will be worthwhile as an investment.

Unfortunately, the determination of the financing cost rate is not altogether straightforward. It depends upon where the funds come from. In business, there are only three possible sources of funds for investment in a project:

1   finance already available in the business

2   finance borrowed from someone else (e.g. a bank)

3   additional capital invested by shareholders.

Where the organization is not a business, other sources of finance may be available and have minimal or no associated costs:

- grants from governments or foundations (these are sometimes available to businesses as well)

- subsidies from governments (sometimes available to businesses)

- donations from other organizations or individuals

- tax income (in the case of government organizations).

Of course, a mixture of these sources may be possible. Grants and subsidies reduce the capital costs in a project, and are best treated as reducing the costs of the project in respect of which they are granted (a process called *netting off*).

Funds already in a business will not be simply lying around – they will be used to finance assets and generate profits, and so these funds will already be earning money themselves. If, therefore, a proposal calls upon these funds to finance a project, there will be a lost opportunity cost. It is important that the expected **rate of return** from the proposal is at least equal to, and preferably higher than, the rate of return currently earned by the funds in their present use.

The financing cost of funds borrowed from someone else is quite simply the rate of interest they charge for the loan.

Obtaining additional capital from shareholders is normally only used to finance substantial long-term projects. The financing cost will be the rate of dividend that will have to be offered to subscribers to tempt them into contributing the funds.

To be really prudent and to ensure that a cost–benefit analysis cannot be criticized for underestimating the financing costs, the best course is to use as the financing cost rate the highest of:

1    the rate of interest that would be charged on borrowed funds
2    the rate that could be earned on funds if invested to the best advantage elsewhere
3    the current return on investment (ROI) of the business.

If a proposal's evaluation shows a potential rate of return in excess of the selected financing cost rate, its viability cannot be questioned on financial grounds, and it becomes management's responsibility to try to find the funds from the cheapest source available.

## Effects of time on values

For reasons that will become clear later, project benefits obtained early in the life of a project are worth more in real terms than the same benefits received in the more distant future. Similarly, costs incurred early in a project have a greater impact than if those costs are deferred to a later time. The **payback period** and average annual rate of return methods of evaluation ignore this fact because they are based on the unrealistic assumption that every pound (Euro or other unit of currency) of cost and benefit is the same no matter when it is received or spent and no matter what rate of interest could be earned or charged on it as time goes by. Only the **discounted cash flow** methods of evaluation take the effects of time and interest rates on money values into account.

This is not the only consideration. Recurring costs and benefits can vary year by year for a number of reasons. If such variations can be predicted with a reasonable degree of certainty they must be accounted for in the proposal evaluation. An obvious example is where the implementation of a proposal results in fewer people being needed in a department. The initial saving in payroll costs is easily evaluated and is a revenue benefit. But the saving will become worth more and more in currency unit terms each year because the payroll cost per capita increases every year irrespective of inflationary factors as a result of progressive wage and salary structures and pay bargaining. (If the reduction in people is part of a larger trend of rising unemployment, however, taxes and levies may also rise to fund increased levels of unemployment benefit, retraining programmes and other such social effects. This is much more difficult to calculate, but should remain a factor to be considered.) Another example is the escalation of fuel costs. An initial saving in fuel consumption becomes worth more each year in money terms (provided, of course, that the lower consumption rate is maintained *and* that the real cost of fuel continues to rise).

Finally, many organizations adopt the policy of allowing for inflation in proposal evaluations. Having established the basic values of recurring costs and benefits, a blanket percentage increase is then applied to all values, year by year, on a compound basis (the increases of one year being included in the calculations of the following year). Inflation may not affect all types of benefits and costs equally (for example, fuel costs may rise faster than the rate of general inflation). It is also difficult to predict with any acceptable degree of certainty the trend in inflation rates more than a single year ahead.

# Cash flow statements

Once all the data in respect of every cash outflow and inflow have been assembled, a **cash flow statement** for the project can be prepared. Let's take an example.

## *FatPac Haulage*

Ten years ago your organization acquired an ailing warehouse and road transport company (FatPac Haulage) whose assets consisted of some insubstantial buildings used as garages and a storage depot, together with five trucks which at that time were relatively new and in good condition. The business has grown rapidly. The premises are now inadequate, expensive to heat and maintain and expensive to insure as there is only a primitive sprinkler system installed. The five trucks are now uneconomic to run. Diesel and repair bills have become prohibitive, breakdowns and lost operating hours are excessive. With more truck capacity, better reliability and faster service FatPac could easily obtain more business. A project is under consideration to replace the trucks and to rebuild the depot with better equipment, full insulation, an effective sprinkler system and in-company truck maintenance.

Table 1.4 shows a sample cash flow statement that might be prepared to show the expected cash flows arising from the project.

**TABLE 1.4** A sample cash flow for a project for the FatPac Haulage Company

| | Year 0 | Year 1 | Year 2 | Year 3 | Year 4 | Year 5 | Year 6 | Year 7 |
|---|---|---|---|---|---|---|---|---|
| **Capital inflows** | £k | £k | £k | £k | £k | £k | £k | £k |
| Grants | 50 | | | | | | | |
| Profits on trade-in | 5 | | | | | | | |
| **Revenue inflows** | | | | | | | | |
| Outside repair and maintenance savings, heating savings, fuel savings | | 60 | 73 | 86 | 100 | 113 | 113 | 113 |
| Increased profits | | 45 | 55 | 65 | 75 | 85 | 85 | 85 |
| Insurance savings | | 5 | 5 | 5 | 5 | 5 | 5 | 5 |
| **Total inflows** | **55** | **110** | **133** | **156** | **180** | **203** | **203** | **203** |
| **Capital outflows** | £k | £k | £k | £k | £k | £k | £k | £k |
| New trucks | 170 | | | | | | | |
| Buildings | 150 | | | | | | | |
| Fixtures and fittings | 50 | | | | | | | |
| Site clearance etc. | 20 | | | | | | | |
| Machinery | 20 | | | | | | | |
| Installation costs | 15 | | | | | | | |
| **Revenue outflows** | £k | £k | £k | £k | £k | £k | £k | £k |
| Materials, garage power | | 7 | 9 | 10 | 12 | 13 | 13 | 13 |
| Payroll costs | | 15 | 16 | 17 | 17 | 18 | 19 | 20 |
| Increased rates | | 3 | 3 | 3 | 3 | 3 | 3 | 3 |
| **Total outflows** | **425** | **25** | **28** | **30** | **32** | **34** | **35** | **36** |
| **Net cash flow*** | **(370)** | **85** | **105** | **126** | **148** | **169** | **168** | **167** |

*( ) = a negative net cash flow, or, if you prefer, a cash outflow. Note that the savings projected as revenue inflows from outside repair and mainenance, heating and fuel are obtained by determining the running costs for the present equipment and buildings, the running costs for the proposed buildings and equipment, and taking the difference.

## Choosing the correct number of years

To decide what is the most appropriate number of years over which a proposal should be evaluated is difficult. Too short a period (say three years in the example of FatPac Haulage) would ignore the very real possibility of longer term project benefits. Many projects, especially those of a substantial nature, often prove unprofitable in early years but, once consolidated, produce rapidly increasing and very substantial benefits in the medium and longer term which more than justify their early shortfalls in cash flow. In the case of a tree farm or an advanced and speculative research and development project, however, a perfectly suitable period may be quite long: 20 years or more.

Conversely, to try to evaluate a project over too long a period means that one may be trying to justify an investment from benefits that are so far in the future that they may never happen. The longer the timescale, the greater is the possibility of a wrong decision being taken to pursue a proposal because:

- there is an increasing possibility of business problems
- there is a greater likelihood that assets in use will become less reliable and economic to run and could require replacement
- market factors could change significantly
- risk and uncertainty upset forecasts.

## Establishing a method for calculating value

In this section we look at three methods for evaluating project proposals financially:

- the payback method
- the net present value method
- the internal rate of return method.

Note that we will show our calculations in full so that you can follow what we are doing. This degree of arithmetical accuracy can mislead people into believing that there really will be, say, £21 736.37 profit at the end of the third year, when in fact figures like these are forecasts based on 'best informed guess' estimates, which can often be quite rough. Hence it is more sensible to show projected profits and losses in round figures. In our example, it would be accurate enough to say that we estimate about £22 000 profit at the end of the third year.

### *The payback period method*

This is the simplest of all the methods. It is also the one which produces the *least* meaningful results and yet it is by far the most commonly used! All this method does is calculate how long it takes to recover the initial project investment out of the subsequent net cash flows, i.e. how long it takes for a project to recoup the initial capital outlay.

We refer you to Appendix 1 where you will find two other methods also discussed.

As a simple example, an organization invests £20 000 in a proposal for which the estimate states that the positive net cash flow *each year* (i.e. the excess of cash inflows over cash outflows) will be £5000. So the organization can expect to recover its initial investment in

$$\frac{£20\ 000}{£5\ 000} = 4 \text{ years}$$

Even if the net cash flow varies year by year, it is just as simple to calculate the payback period. Look at this next example which we will call *Proposal A*:

| Initial investment (£100 000) | Expected pattern of net cash flows (all positive): |
|---|---|
| Year 1 | £45 000 |
| Year 2 | £35 000 |
| Year 3 | £20 000 |
| Year 4 | £20 000 |
| Year 5 | £15 000 |

It obviously takes exactly three years to recover the initial investment.

There are three important points to be borne in mind when using this method of proposal evaluation:

1    The cash flows should be calculated after tax. The reason is that this method is based on the recovery of the project investment out of *net* project income and it is only what is left out of one's income after the tax authorities have taken their share that is available for use.

2    Exclude depreciation charges from revenue costs. Again, this is because this method is looking for the complete reimbursement of the total project investment (including capital expenditure on fixed assets). If depreciation costs are included with your proposal's cash outflows, these would be recovered twice over. (See the appendix entitled *Depreciation Costs* for a discussion of methods of depreciation.)

3    Until the payback point is reached, there is an outstanding (but decreasing) balance of funds being used to finance the investment and therefore incurring financing costs (either real or notional depending where the funds come from). If it is possible to calculate what these financing costs are, they should be included as revenue costs (cash outflows) in the cash flow statement.

The chief advantage in using the payback period method is that it is easy to understand and to calculate.

There are also serious limitations:

•    It completely ignores positive net cash flows received after the payback point. (In some proposals these later cash flows are the most significant – for example, investors in the Channel Tunnel project know that it will be many years before cash flows from passenger revenue will start to produce a return on their investment.)

•    The method looks *entirely* at cash flow and completely ignores profitability or return on investment.

•    The method assumes that all money is of equal value no matter when it is spent or received (though if financing costs are incorporated in a cash flow statement this partly relieves this criticism).

•    If a short payback period is required this method will miss many worthwhile longer-term proposals.

Many organizations use the payback period method by itself and look for payback periods of two, or at the outside three, years. As a result many worthwhile (but longer-term) proposals which would give a high rate of return on investment never get accepted. If you must use this method, then use one of the 'rate of return' methods *as well* to get a second point of view.

### SAQ 1.6

Assume you want to invest £20 000 and there are two proposals you can choose. Proposal A requires an investment of £20 000 and should have a positive net cash flow of £3200 annually for the first seven years. Proposal B also requires an investment of £20 000 and estimates net cash flows of: Year 1, –£2000; Year 2, £2675; Year 3, £3200; Year 4, £4550; Year 5, £6550; Year 6, £7000; Year 7, £8000. How do the projects compare using the payback method?

The advantage of this method is that it is very quick to calculate. Perhaps it is also an advantage that it is very common. It is best to use this method, if at all, in conjunction with a second method – one of the **rate of return** methods – to reach a better overall decision when comparing proposals.

*Discounted cash flow methods*

The payback methods provide limited and sometimes inadequate measures of proposal viability. Though simple to use, they have significant limitations.

The average annual rate of return methods are described in Appendix 1.

We now move to discounted cash flow techniques and two important methods:

(a)    the net present value (NPV) method

(b)    the internal rate of return (IRR) method.

However, before looking at them in detail, it is necessary to remember that the more familiar reverse process to discounting is *compounding*.

# Compounding

If you deposit a certain amount of money in a place where it will attract interest, such as a savings account, the total amount of money, if left there, will build up by a constant factor every year. To take a simple example, consider what happens if you invest £1 in a savings account offering 10% p.a. interest. The amount after year 1 is £1 + (10/100 × £1) = £1.10. This is equivalent to multiplying the original £1 by a factor of 1.1. Repeated every year, provided there are no withdrawals and assuming constant interest rates, the money builds up as follows:

| | |
|---|---|
| Year 0 | £1.00 |
| Year 1 | £1.10 |
| Year 2 | £1.21 |
| Year 3 | £1.33 |

In a similar way, a company starts with a sum of money, say £100 000, which it will invest in plant, the hiring of a work force, etc. The sale of its goods and services will (one hopes) more than repay the initial investment costs. In other words the cash flows from these sales should be equal to or exceed the interest that would have been earned had the company simply put its money on deposit. If the company has an *internal rate of return* (rate of compounding) of 10%, the value of this project will look like this:

| | |
|---|---|
| Year 0 | £100 000 |
| Year 1 | £110 000 |
| Year 2 | £121 000 |
| Year 3 | £133 000 |

If a finance house provided a £100 000 loan with an interest rate of 10% to finance the proposal, the proposal would just about be viable, but there will be no net profit to hand over to shareholders. If the project were to be terminated after one year, the amount of money owed to the finance house would exactly match the value of the project at that time; after two years, the company would owe £12 100 and so on.

# Discounting

The principle of discounting reverses the reasoning behind compounding. Go back to the savings account example and assume an interest rate of 10%. We could say that if we were to be promised £1.33 in three years' time, this would be equivalent to being paid £1 now, for, with that £1, we could obtain £1.33 in three years' time through suitable investment. Using the 10% discount rate, values of £1.10 in a year's time, £1.21 in two years' time and £1.33 in three years' time have a *present value* of £1.

Similarly, the present value of £1 in one year's time would be £1/1.10 = £0.9091, or just under 91 pence. The *present* values of *future* money for different rates of interest can be set out in a discount table, and Table 1.5 does this for a future, mythical £1.

Looking at the discount table and the first entry in the 10% column in particular, you can see straight away that £1 received in a year's time has, as calculated previously, a present value of £0.9091. The present value reduces as the future period is increased; thus the present value of £1 to be received in five years' time is only £0.6209. For present values of future receipts other than £1, simply multiply by the required factor, e.g. the present value of £5000 in five years' time at 10% interest rate is £(0.6209 × 5000) = £3104.50.

The idea of present value can be applied to both inflows and outflows. As an example of outflow, assume that in five years' time you have to meet a bill of £1. You can meet it by investing £0.62 now (at 10% interest). The outflow of £1 in five years' time can be equated to an outflow of £0.62 now, or that the present value is −£0.62 (the minus indicates the direction of cash flow). As an example of an inflow, suppose that you were to receive £1 in five years' time. You would be justified in regarding the present value of this amount as +£0.62, since you could match this future receipt by investing £0.62 now.

A manufacturing company can regard its future inflows and outflows from a project in the same way. If its IRR (internal rate of return) is 10%, then an anticipated fuel bill of £5000 in year 5 of the project, for instance, should be discounted and called a cash flow with a PV (present value) of −£(0.6209 × 5000) = −£3104.50, because, in order to meet this outflow, £3104.50 can be invested now in the company's production resources to meet this bill. Similarly, an income of £5000 through the sale of finished goods in five years' time can be equated to an investment of £3104.50 now. Such a future receipt will have a PV of +£3104.50.

Of course, the argument applied to a single future payment or receipt also applies to the stream of revenues and costs encountered by the firm in the course of a project. The net discounted sum of such streams is called the *net present value* (NPV). (There are tables showing cumulative discounting factors for costs/revenues expected to have the same values for the life of a project.)

Earlier we considered a proposal with an IRR of 10%, the company in question obtaining loans from the money market at 10% interest rate. As pointed out, such a proposal will not make a profit, i.e. its NPV will be zero. If the performance of the firm could be enhanced, then a positive NPV would appear, which represents the PV of money available as dividends for shareholders, or which can be retained for use in other proposals. For investment purposes, then, the *decision rule* is that only proposals which show a positive NPV should be accepted.

**Table 1.5**  Discount table (opposite)

| n | 1% | 2% | 3% | 4% | 5% | 6% | 7% | 8% | 9% | 10% | 11% | 12% | 13% | 14% | 15% | 16% |
|---|----|----|----|----|----|----|----|----|----|-----|-----|-----|-----|-----|-----|-----|
| 1 | 0.9901 | 0.9804 | 0.9709 | 0.9615 | 0.9524 | 0.9434 | 0.9346 | 0.9259 | 0.9174 | 0.9091 | 0.9009 | 0.8929 | 0.8850 | 0.8772 | 0.8696 | 0.8621 |
| 2 | 0.9803 | 0.9612 | 0.9426 | 0.9246 | 0.9070 | 0.8900 | 0.8734 | 0.8573 | 0.8417 | 0.8264 | 0.8116 | 0.7972 | 0.7831 | 0.7695 | 0.7561 | 0.7432 |
| 3 | 0.9706 | 0.9423 | 0.9151 | 0.8890 | 0.8638 | 0.8396 | 0.8163 | 0.7938 | 0.7722 | 0.7513 | 0.7312 | 0.7118 | 0.6931 | 0.6750 | 0.6575 | 0.6407 |
| 4 | 0.9610 | 0.9238 | 0.8885 | 0.8548 | 0.8227 | 0.7921 | 0.7629 | 0.7350 | 0.7084 | 0.6830 | 0.6587 | 0.6355 | 0.6133 | 0.5921 | 0.5718 | 0.5523 |
| 5 | 0.9515 | 0.9057 | 0.8626 | 0.8219 | 0.7835 | 0.7473 | 0.7130 | 0.6806 | 0.6499 | 0.6209 | 0.5935 | 0.5674 | 0.5428 | 0.5194 | 0.4972 | 0.4761 |
| 6 | 0.9420 | 0.8880 | 0.8375 | 0.7903 | 0.7462 | 0.7050 | 0.6663 | 0.6302 | 0.5963 | 0.5645 | 0.5346 | 0.5066 | 0.4803 | 0.4556 | 0.4323 | 0.4104 |
| 7 | 0.9327 | 0.8706 | 0.8131 | 0.7599 | 0.7107 | 0.6651 | 0.6227 | 0.5835 | 0.5470 | 0.5132 | 0.4817 | 0.4523 | 0.4251 | 0.3996 | 0.3759 | 0.3538 |
| 8 | 0.9235 | 0.8535 | 0.7894 | 0.7307 | 0.6768 | 0.6274 | 0.5820 | 0.5403 | 0.5019 | 0.4665 | 0.4339 | 0.4039 | 0.3762 | 0.3506 | 0.3269 | 0.3050 |
| 9 | 0.9143 | 0.8368 | 0.7664 | 0.7026 | 0.6446 | 0.5919 | 0.5439 | 0.5002 | 0.4604 | 0.4241 | 0.3909 | 0.3606 | 0.3329 | 0.3075 | 0.2843 | 0.2630 |
| 10 | 0.9053 | 0.8203 | 0.7441 | 0.6756 | 0.6139 | 0.5584 | 0.5083 | 0.4632 | 0.4224 | 0.3855 | 0.3522 | 0.3220 | 0.2946 | 0.2697 | 0.2472 | 0.2267 |
| 11 | 0.8693 | 0.8043 | 0.7224 | 0.6496 | 0.5847 | 0.5268 | 0.4751 | 0.4289 | 0.3875 | 0.3505 | 0.3173 | 0.2875 | 0.2607 | 0.2366 | 0.2149 | 0.1954 |
| 12 | 0.8874 | 0.7885 | 0.7014 | 0.6246 | 0.5568 | 0.4970 | 0.4440 | 0.3971 | 0.3555 | 0.3186 | 0.2858 | 0.2567 | 0.2307 | 0.2076 | 0.1869 | 0.1685 |
| 13 | 0.8787 | 0.7730 | 0.6810 | 0.6006 | 0.5303 | 0.4688 | 0.4150 | 0.3677 | 0.3262 | 0.2897 | 0.2575 | 0.2292 | 0.2042 | 0.1821 | 0.1625 | 0.1452 |
| 14 | 0.8700 | 0.7579 | 0.6611 | 0.5775 | 0.5051 | 0.4423 | 0.3878 | 0.3405 | 0.2992 | 0.2633 | 0.2320 | 0.2046 | 0.1807 | 0.1597 | 0.1413 | 0.1252 |
| 15 | 0.8613 | 0.7430 | 0.6419 | 0.5553 | 0.4810 | 0.4173 | 0.3624 | 0.3152 | 0.2745 | 0.2394 | 0.2090 | 0.1827 | 0.1599 | 0.1401 | 0.1229 | 0.1079 |

| n | 17% | 18% | 19% | 20% | 21% | 22% | 23% | 24% | 25% | 26% | 27% | 28% | 29% | 30% | 31% | 32% |
|---|-----|-----|-----|-----|-----|-----|-----|-----|-----|-----|-----|-----|-----|-----|-----|-----|
| 1 | 0.8547 | 0.8475 | 0.8403 | 0.8333 | 0.8264 | 0.8197 | 0.8130 | 0.8065 | 0.8000 | 0.7937 | 0.7874 | 0.7813 | 0.7752 | 0.7692 | 0.7634 | 0.7576 |
| 2 | 0.7305 | 0.7182 | 0.7062 | 0.6944 | 0.6830 | 0.6719 | 0.6610 | 0.6504 | 0.6400 | 0.6299 | 0.6200 | 0.6104 | 0.6009 | 0.5917 | 0.5827 | 0.5739 |
| 3 | 0.6244 | 0.6086 | 0.5934 | 0.5787 | 0.5645 | 0.5507 | 0.5374 | 0.5245 | 0.5120 | 0.4999 | 0.4882 | 0.4768 | 0.4658 | 0.4552 | 0.4448 | 0.4348 |
| 4 | 0.5337 | 0.5158 | 0.4987 | 0.4823 | 0.4665 | 0.4514 | 0.4369 | 0.4230 | 0.4096 | 0.3968 | 0.3844 | 0.3725 | 0.3611 | 0.3501 | 0.3396 | 0.3294 |
| 5 | 0.4561 | 0.4371 | 0.4190 | 0.4019 | 0.3855 | 0.3700 | 0.3552 | 0.3411 | 0.3277 | 0.3149 | 0.3027 | 0.2910 | 0.2799 | 0.2693 | 0.2592 | 0.2495 |
| 6 | 0.3898 | 0.3704 | 0.3521 | 0.3349 | 0.3186 | 0.3033 | 0.2888 | 0.2751 | 0.2621 | 0.2499 | 0.2383 | 0.2274 | 0.2170 | 0.2072 | 0.1979 | 0.1890 |
| 7 | 0.3332 | 0.3139 | 0.2959 | 0.2791 | 0.2633 | 0.2486 | 0.2348 | 0.2218 | 0.2097 | 0.1983 | 0.1877 | 0.1776 | 0.1682 | 0.1594 | 0.1510 | 0.1432 |
| 8 | 0.2848 | 0.2660 | 0.2487 | 0.2326 | 0.2176 | 0.2038 | 0.1909 | 0.1789 | 0.1678 | 0.1574 | 0.1478 | 0.1388 | 0.1304 | 0.1226 | 0.1153 | 0.1085 |
| 9 | 0.2434 | 0.2255 | 0.2090 | 0.1938 | 0.1799 | 0.1670 | 0.1552 | 0.1443 | 0.1342 | 0.1249 | 0.1164 | 0.1084 | 0.1011 | 0.0943 | 0.0880 | 0.0822 |
| 10 | 0.2080 | 0.1911 | 0.1756 | 0.1615 | 0.1486 | 0.1369 | 0.1262 | 0.1164 | 0.1074 | 0.0992 | 0.0916 | 0.0847 | 0.0784 | 0.0725 | 0.0672 | 0.0623 |
| 11 | 0.1778 | 0.1619 | 0.1476 | 0.1346 | 0.1228 | 0.1122 | 0.1026 | 0.0938 | 0.0859 | 0.0787 | 0.0721 | 0.0662 | 0.0607 | 0.0558 | 0.0513 | 0.0472 |
| 12 | 0.1520 | 0.1372 | 0.1240 | 0.1122 | 0.1015 | 0.0920 | 0.0834 | 0.0757 | 0.0687 | 0.0625 | 0.0568 | 0.0517 | 0.0471 | 0.0429 | 0.0392 | 0.0357 |
| 13 | 0.1299 | 0.1163 | 0.1042 | 0.0935 | 0.0839 | 0.0754 | 0.0678 | 0.0610 | 0.0550 | 0.0496 | 0.0447 | 0.0404 | 0.0365 | 0.0330 | 0.0299 | 0.0271 |
| 14 | 0.1110 | 0.0985 | 0.0876 | 0.0779 | 0.0693 | 0.0618 | 0.0551 | 0.0492 | 0.0440 | 0.0393 | 0.0352 | 0.0316 | 0.0283 | 0.0254 | 0.0228 | 0.0205 |
| 15 | 0.0949 | 0.0835 | 0.0736 | 0.0649 | 0.0573 | 0.0507 | 0.0448 | 0.0397 | 0.0352 | 0.0312 | 0.0277 | 0.0247 | 0.0219 | 0.0195 | 0.0174 | 0.0155 |

$n$ = Number of years

## SAQ 1.7

Assume that you have £250 in your possession.

(a) If you do not invest this money but leave it tucked away in a drawer for five years, and inflation runs at 3% a year, what will your £250 be worth in present terms at the end of that period?

(b) If you invest this money in a savings scheme that guarantees an after-tax annual return of 3% and you leave all interest earned in the account for the full period, what will your account contain at the end of that period?

(c) Imagine that you have invested your money in this scheme, but you want to determine what your money will be worth at the end of the five-year period in present terms (taking inflation into account). How much will your savings scheme yield you in present day terms at the end of five years?

### Net present value (NPV) method

We will now show you how this method works by applying it to the proposal described earlier (staying with the 10% discount rate). The net cash flows (NCFs) for that proposal were as follows:

| Year | Net cash flow (£) | |
| --- | --- | --- |
| 0 | (100 000) | Negative |
| 1 | 45 000 | Positive |
| 2 | 35 000 | Positive |
| 3 | 20 000 | Positive |
| 4 | 20 000 | Positive |
| 5 | 15 000 | Positive |

From our reference table, we must now find the discounting factors relative to 10% per year (compounded) for the years 1 through 5. We will not apply a discount factor to cash flows in year 0; year 0 is regarded as being the outset of the proposal and for all practical purposes to be the present-day value of that cash flow.

The discounting factors we need are those in the reference table in the column headed 10%. These discount factors are now applied to the yearly net cash flows of the proposal to establish the total net present value (NPV) of those cash flows.

| Year | Net cash flow (£) | Discount factors | NPV (£) |
| --- | --- | --- | --- |
| 0 | (100 000) | 1.0000 | (100 000) |
| 1 | 45 000 | 0.9091 | 40 909 |
| 2 | 35 000 | 0.8264 | 28 924 |
| 3 | 20 000 | 0.7513 | 15 026 |
| 4 | 20 000 | 0.6830 | 13 660 |
| 5 | 15 000 | 0.6209 | 9 313 |
| Total net present value of proposal net cash flows | | | 7 832 |

This result means that after allowing for financing costs at 10% per year compounded, this proposal will more than pay for the initial investment. It is financially viable. If two or more alternative proposals were being evaluated, the one which had the highest total NPV would probably be selected. If, at the end of calculations, a proposal shows a *negative* total NPV, it means that the rate of return generated by that proposal is less than the rate required, and so that proposal would not be implemented unless there were some overriding non-financial reason for doing so.

The only difficult part of the NPV calculation is establishing the financing cost rate (or the required rate of return) for the proposal. Companies often are not sure exactly what will be the financing cost of the funds needed for the investment, especially when a mix of sources of funds is involved. To overcome this difficulty, you should find the IRR implied by the cash flow – this calculates what rate of return a proposal will generate and management can then decide whether this rate is adequate for their purposes.

## SAQ 1.8

Assume that by investing £20 000 cash in the stock market you could be certain of a 12% rate of return. Now calculate the NPV of Proposal B in SAQ 1.6, using 12% as the discount rate.

The main problem with NPV evaluations is the difficulty of comparing small projects with large projects. A small project might have only a modest NPV compared with a much bigger project, but require a much smaller initial investment. To make a ranking possible for projects of different sizes the NPV method may be extended to give a figure called the internal rate of return.

### Internal rate of return (IRR) method

This is really the NPV method in reverse. Exactly the same data and the reference table of discount factors are needed, but it is not necessary to *predetermine* the required rate of return from the proposal. The IRR method calculates the rate of return to be obtained from the proposal, based on the assumption that the discounted values of future net cash flows will exactly pay for the initial investment. For our sample proposal, therefore, start with the following table:

| Year | Net cash flow (£) | Discount factors | NPV (£) |
|---|---|---|---|
| 0 | (100 000) | 1.0000 | (100 000) |
| 1 | 45 000 | ? | ? |
| 2 | 35 000 | ? | ? |
| 3 | 20 000 | ? | ? |
| 4 | 20 000 | ? | ? |
| 5 | 15 000 | ? | ? |
| NPV of proposal net cash flows | | | = £ zero |

In other words, what discount rate will give discount factors which reduce the values of the positive net cash flows in years 1 through 5 to exactly £100 000 in total?

The answer is found by trial and error using progressively higher discount rates until the NPV is reduced to zero, or nearly zero. In the example above, the IRR works out to 14%, as shown below.

| Year | Net cash flow (£) | Discount factors | NPV (£) |
|------|-------------------|------------------|---------|
| 0 | (100 000) | 1.0000 | (100 000) |
| 1 | 45 000 | 0.8772 | 39 474 |
| 2 | 35 000 | 0.7695 | 26 933 |
| 3 | 20 000 | 0.6750 | 13 500 |
| 4 | 20 000 | 0.5921 | 11 842 |
| 5 | 15 000 | 0.5194 | 7 791 |
| NPV of proposal net cash flows | | | (460) |

This means that our sample proposal is worth implementing if management will accept a rate of return of less than 14% per annum (which they might well do if, for example, it were possible to finance the proposal from funds costing, say, 12% per annum).

The IRR method is not infallible, and it is not always possible to judge the relative viability of proposals by ranking their IRRs. It is much better to rank proposals by their NPVs under a given rate of interest, if this is possible.

### SAQ 1.9

What is the IRR of Proposal B to the nearest percentage point?

### SAQ 1.10

To see the effect of project size on the value of IRR and NPV consider:

(a) What is the value of IRR of a project twice the size of Proposal B in every respect (i.e. all cash flows are doubled).

(b) What is the effect on NPV of doubling the size of a project?

# 1.2.4   Risk and uncertainty

**Risk** and **uncertainty** are present in most projects. Risk represents the *chance* of adverse consequences or loss occurring. Generally, risks can be identified and once identified the probability of the risk occurring needs to be assessed. However, there may also be doubt about the *validity* of qualitative or quantitative data: this is called uncertainty. We can also use the term uncertainty to mean a state where too little is known about something, and the very lack of knowledge represents a danger that can only be addressed by gathering more information. Example 1.7 illustrates the distinction between risk and uncertainty.

---

### EXAMPLE 1.7

Your company is asked to store some substance you know nothing about. What risks are associated with this request? They are difficult to determine until you find out whether, for example, the substance is explosive, flammable, corrosive, poisonous, and so on. If you find that the substance is explosive, you now know that there is a risk of explosion in storing the substance. Further investigations of the uncertainty surrounding the substance might reveal to you that it is only explosive if heated above a certain temperature. You now know not only the risk, but can make a probabilistic assessment of whether temperatures in your storage area are likely to be within the safe limits during the time you need to store the substance. (The knowledge also allows you to plan actions that might reduce the risk of explosion further, for example by installing air conditioning or refrigeration. More will be said about this aspect of risk in Chapter 2.)

Any person preparing a proposal must take risks and uncertainties into account. To do either requires first that areas of uncertainty and risk are identified. At the stage of making proposals, perceived risks must be brought clearly to the attention of those in authority to make decisions in the matter – the problem is 'escalated' to more senior managers. The problem may then be delegated to someone with the express purpose of investigating further. Crockford (1980) listed the following categories of risks:

- fire and natural disaster
- accident
- political and social risk (war, civil disturbance, theft and vandalism)
- technical risk
- marketing risk
- labour risk (stoppages and strikes, turnover of personnel)
- liability risks (product liability, safety).

Some people would expand this list to include environmental problems (problems short of natural disaster but nevertheless serious), and would include under social risks demonstrations against a project and adverse social effects (for example from having to relocate large numbers of people to make way for the project).

## High-risk proposals

It is likely that the potential for variation of costs should be considered a risk if novel elements predominate in a project. Proposals involving research, development or immature technologies tend to be of higher risk than projects in more mature areas such as civil engineering. However, Chicken (1994) notes that major civil engineering projects which are novel, such as the Sydney Opera House, the Thames Flood Barrier and the Channel Tunnel, suffer from variation in costs, often by factors of from 10 to 200 times original estimates (p. 6). Information systems developments are particularly prone to this problem, as the designers must often design *today* for *tomorrow's* technology, while their experience gained in *yesterday's* project becomes rapidly obsolescent.

Three dimensions of risk exist:

- size
- technological maturity (the incorporation of novel methods, techniques, materials etc.)
- structural complexity.

The larger a proposed project is the greater the risk. Increase in size usually means an increase in complexity, including the complexity of administration, management, communication amongst the participants and so on. Technological risks lie in the extent to which the technology and the methods proposed to be used are new and untried, innovative or unfamiliar. Structural complexity refers both to the arrangement of the component parts of the proposed project and to the structure of teams, management and relationships between groups.

Risk assessment will be considered in detail in Chapter 2.

## 1.2.5  Summary

A practising project manager – indeed, anyone who works regularly in a project environment – can benefit from being able to apply his or her critical faculties to proposals. People can also find themselves in the position of participating in drawing up a feasibility study for a proposal. The feasibility study develops a scenario and a functional specification (what the new or revised system should *do*); it should identify whether the scenario is technically feasible, its likelihood of success in ecological, social and political terms and whether it is financially feasible. Financial feasibility is assessed in a cost–benefit analysis that thoroughly identifies and assesses tangible and intangible costs and benefits. A cash flow statement for the proposal is produced, then analysed by one or more of a number of methods ranging from the simple payback period to the internal rate of return. You have been given some practice in each of these methods in this section. The risks inherent in a proposal also affect its feasibility. More will be said about risks – identifying, assessing and managing them – in Chapter 2. At such an early stage as the feasibility study, risks are brought to the attention of more senior managers and may be delegated to someone to explore further. Proposals resulting in projects that are large, or with many novel elements or depending upon an immature technology, or structurally complex to manage, are identified as very risky ventures.

Having studied this section, you should be able to:

- describe the elements of a feasibility study

- state the general aims of a functional specification

- describe what a scenario is and generate some simple scenarios in response to a statement of a problem

- assess the maturity of a technology, given that you know something about the area (for example, people working in civil engineering would not be expected to assess the maturity of software development methods, and people working in software engineering would not be expected to assess the maturity of some area of materials science)

- sketch a rich picture to represent the 'soft' (social, political, ecological) elements of a proposal

- frame some questions to be investigated in an ecological assessment of a proposal

- carry out a features analysis and explain how a figure of merit can be derived

- identify and distinguish between capital and revenue costs, and tangible and intangible costs and benefits

- understand what is meant by finance costs, internal costs and overheads or indirect costs

- describe the effect of time on values

- draw up a simple cash flow statement and justify your choice of the period used
- make a simple evaluation based on payback period, but know the limitations of this method
- calculate net present value and internal rate of return from given cash flows
- list categories of risk
- list the three dimensions of risk in proposals.

# 1.3 *MAKING DECISIONS*

Given a set of proposals for which the feasibility has been assessed, management must now decide which proposals to pursue. What decision-makers are looking for is the *best* option available.

Decisions are too often made on the basis of personal inclination and interest, for 'political' reasons – enhancing the power or prestige of an individual or a group within the organizational hierarchy – or for better reasons but in the absence of full information about the possible risks and outcomes of the decision. We have laid more stress on investigating how and why decisions are made and whether structured and scientifically based methods of decision making are possible, since making a bad decision will be costly. Below we describe some factors to be considered and some methods to aid decision making.

## 1.3.1 Coherence

A decision-maker needs to ask whether a proposal for a project has *coherence*. Coherence is the degree of relationship of the different parts of a proposal to each other and to the objectives and needs of the organization. The following Activity will develop an analogy (adapted from Lindley, 1985) to help you understand what is meant by coherence: remember that it is only an analogy!

---

### ACTIVITY 1.13

Think of a large building consisting of a number of floors and different wings, such as a hospital. Now concentrate entirely on the dimensions and ignore such considerations as building materials, the uses of different parts of the building or the people who will inhabit the building. Think about the sizes of rooms, corridors, stairs, windows and doors and furniture.

### DISCUSSION

Without you having to think consciously about it, your thoughts about this building will use certain 'rules' to determine (roughly) the consistency of the dimensions and relationships of the different parts of the building. For example, a window or door can't be bigger than the wall it is set in, and the window and door frames must not be smaller, or significantly larger, than the windows and doors. A room can't be wider than the building is. A stairway has to be as high as the distance between floors. Two wings cannot occupy any common ground. An upstairs room has to be placed at least a little higher than the ceiling of the room below it. These relationships show the coherence of the design.

---

Proposals should exhibit this internal coherence, and should cohere to the previously identified objectives of the organization. Just as an architect designing a building will use a standard to measure the dimensions – a millimetre, centimetre or metre – structured aids to making decisions can be applied to evaluating and comparing proposals and deciding upon a course of action.

The principle of coherence aids comparison as well. Compare like with like. If two competing proposals use different methods of calculating profitability, you will find it very difficult to make an informed decision about which is better.

# 1.3.2 Aids to decision making

*Decision trees*

One particular decision-making technique is to use a **decision tree**. A decision tree is a way of representing graphically the decision processes and their various possible outcomes. They are particularly useful when you have to make a decision about a choice of route when there are uncertainties about the results of adopting that route.

Let's take a simple example. Suppose that you are developing a software product and you want to decide whether to buy in a package to form a part of that product or to develop that package yourself. You believe that the chances of good sales will be improved if you develop your own package although developing your own package will cost more. This situation can be represented in the decision tree of Figure 1.7.

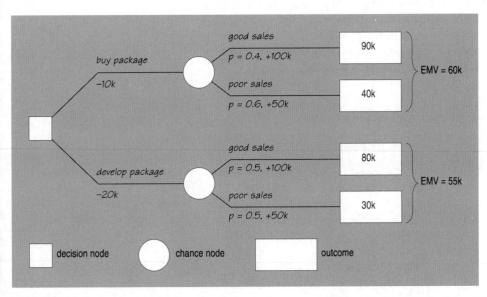

**FIGURE 1.7** A simple decision tree (monetary values are expressed in thousands of pounds)

In this decision tree, options or *decision nodes* are represented by squares, and *chance nodes* by circles. The main decision is at the left, whether to buy or develop a package. The costs of the options at that point (£10 000 to buy, £20 000 to develop) are shown against the branches. Each of these branches has a chance node shown, with the probabilities of reaching particular outcomes given (e.g. 40% probability of achieving good sales of £100 000). The final rectangle (the leaf at the end of each branch) gives the total value of reaching that particular outcome, including any costs and benefits attached to branches en route. For example the top leaf on the right of the tree is worth £90 000, as a result of profits of £100 000 less the cost of buying the package initially, £10 000.

It is now possible to arrive at the *estimated monetary value* (EMV) of the two options, using the formula:

$$\text{EMV} = \sum_{i=1}^{n} P_i V_i$$

where $V_i$ is the value of outcome $i$, $P_i$ is the probability that the outcome will occur, and $n$ is the number of possible outcomes. (Note: for the non-mathematical, $\sum$ means 'sum', the $i = 1$ subscript says: 'start from the first item' and the $n$ superscript means 'continue until all are calculated and summed'.)

This formula applied to the option to 'buy the package' gives:

$$\text{EMV} = 0.4 \times 90 + 0.6 \times 40 = 60k$$

The probabilities assigned at the chance nodes are subjective probabilities, perhaps arrived at by using one or more forecasting techniques, and the values of outcomes may be estimated using one or other of the financial appraisal techniques referred to earlier.

### SAQ 1.11

(a) Construct a decision tree to choose between three possible products that might be developed. The costs of developing each product are shown in the first column of Table 1.6. Estimates have been made of the probability of getting high or low growth for each of the products. The value of the product is in each case higher if high growth can be obtained. The values of the products in each case are as estimated in column 5.

(b) Calculate the EMV of each option.

**TABLE 1.6**  The probabilities and values of the different options

| Product | Cost £k | Growth | Probability | Value £k |
|---------|---------|--------|-------------|----------|
| A | 18 | High | 0.6 | 33 |
|   |    | Low | 0.4 | 19 |
| B | 20 | High | 0.5 | 30 |
|   |    | Low | 0.5 | 18 |
| C | 15 | High | 0.7 | 25 |
|   |    | Low | 0.3 | 15 |

The users of the decision trees shown so far have only had one decision to make. This has been the decision shown at the left hand side of the tree. However, a decision tree can be more elaborate and include further decision nodes, representing further decisions that you will have to make along the route to the outcome. Such a tree is shown in Figure 1.8, where the primary decision is to choose between the development of two products, A and B. We have already seen Product A in Figure 1.7. If you choose Product A you still have to decide whether or not to buy a package as discussed earlier.

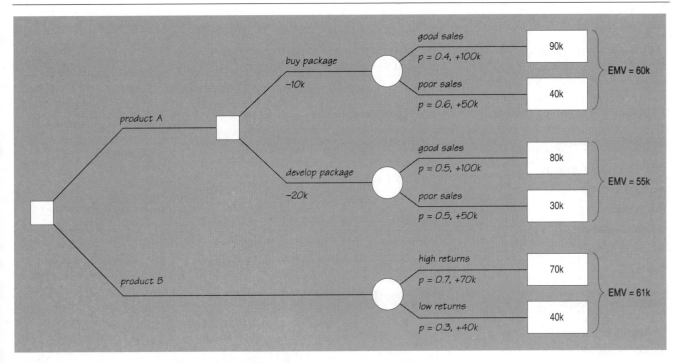

**FIGURE 1.8** A tree with more than one decision node

The way to tackle such trees is to look at the subsidiary decision first. In fact we have already done this for Product A, and found that the EMV of buying a package was higher than the EMV of developing one, so we conclude that at that decision point we will take the higher value branch. The tree can then be simplified by cutting out the irrelevant branch and removing that decision node. Since the EMV of Product A, as found in Figure 1.7, is at best £60 000, the decision tree of Figure 1.8 now indicates Product B as the higher valued choice. (As with all such decisions you must remember the likely accuracy of the estimates, and there may be other, non-monetary, reasons for choosing Product A.)

In a tree that had a number of subsidiary decisions you would need to eliminate each one in turn until the tree was reduced to the principal decision, all the other decisions having been taken in the way that gives the optimal value.

### Proposal ranking formulae

The technique of *proposal ranking formulae* is unsophisticated and suitable only when fairly low expenditure is being considered. The viability of different proposals is compared by ranking them in order according to payback time or rate of return.

### Proposal selection index

Proposals can be ranked according to a *proposal selection index* of the form:

$$I = P_T \times P_C \times NPV$$

where $P_T$ is a measure of each proposal's anticipated technical success, $P_C$ is a similar measure of anticipated commercial success, and NPV is the anticipated net present value of each proposal.

*Checklists*

Checklists of the type shown in Table 1.7 can be used to assess various aspects of a number of proposals – in this case R & D proposals – and then used to make comparisons between the different options.

**TABLE 1.7**  A project comparison checklist (after de la Mare, 1982)

| Economic merits | 1 | 2 | 3 | 4 | 5 |
|---|---|---|---|---|---|
| estimated sales revenue | | | | | |
| production costs | | | | | |
| R & D costs | | | | | |
| capital investment | | | | | |
| return on capital | | | | | |
| risk level | | | | | |

KEY:
1 = Unacceptable
2 = Unfavourable
3 = Adequate
4 = Favourable
5 = Most favourable

| R & D implications | 1 | 2 | 3 | 4 | 5 |
|---|---|---|---|---|---|
| probability of success | | | | | |
| degree of novelty | | | | | |
| company's existing know-how | | | | | |
| time to develop product | | | | | |
| manpower requirements | | | | | |
| patent status | | | | | |

| Production implications | 1 | 2 | 3 | 4 | 5 |
|---|---|---|---|---|---|
| process familiarity | | | | | |
| process flexibility | | | | | |
| compatibility with existing operations | | | | | |
| equipment availability | | | | | |
| raw materials availability | | | | | |
| production hazards | | | | | |
| freight or transport problems | | | | | |

| Marketing implications | 1 | 2 | 3 | 4 | 5 |
|---|---|---|---|---|---|
| market size | | | | | |
| market variability | | | | | |
| number of customers | | | | | |
| number of competitors | | | | | |
| growth rate | | | | | |
| compatibility with existing products | | | | | |
| promotional requirements | | | | | |
| product adaptability | | | | | |
| competitors' ability to imitate | | | | | |

*Measured checklists*

This method is almost identical to the previous one but instead of various aspects being rated on a scale that stretches from 'unacceptable' to 'most favourable' they are scored numerically. An example of a measured checklist, again for an R & D project, is shown in Table 1.8.

## Limitations of techniques

One of the main problems associated with these and similar techniques is that they all require estimates to be made of the cash flows that will be realized throughout the economic life of a project. To put this another way, they assume, for a capital investment project say, that it is practicable to meet the information needs shown in Figure 1.9. This may patently not be the case when a proposal has not even reached the drawing board stage. The costs of gathering such information are usually too substantial to be incurred lightly. Sometimes the only alternative is to accept the risks that are inherent in making decisions based on hunches and incomplete information and to try to keep some of the rejected options open until the front runner has been evaluated more fully.

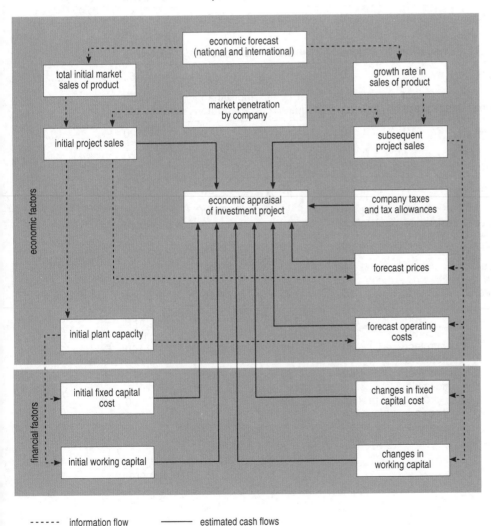

**FIGURE 1.9**   The information needs of a prospective capital project (de la Mare, 1982)

**TABLE 1.8** A measured checklist (after de la Mare, 1982)

Score

| | | | | | | | | |
|---|---|---|---|---|---|---|---|---|
| 1 Peak sales revenue | Value (millions) | 0.5 | 1 | 2 | 5 | 10 | | |
| | Score | 10 | 40 | 80 | 130 | 190 | → | ........... |
| 2 Production costs (as % of 1 above) | % | 20 | 30 | 40 | 50 | 60 | | |
| | Score | 60 | 40 | 20 | 10 | 0 | → | ........... |
| 3 Capital investment (as % of 1 above) | % | 0 | 50 | 75 | 100 | 150 | | |
| | Score | 50 | 40 | 30 | 20 | 10 | → | ........... |
| 4 R & D costs | Value | 10 000 | 50 000 | 100 000 | 300 000 | 500 000 | | |
| | Score | 150 | 100 | 60 | 30 | 0 | → | ........... |
| 5 Extent of competition | Degree | none | slight | moderate | appreciable | extensive | | |
| | Score | 100 | 70 | 50 | 20 | 0 | → | ........... |
| 6 Synergy with existing products | Degree | negative | none | little | appreciable | extensive | | |
| | Score | −20 | 0 | 5 | 10 | 50 | → | ........... |
| 7 Production know-how | Degree | most inadequate | needs training | adequate | more than adequate | most appropriate | | |
| | Score | −10 | 0 | 5 | 10 | 20 | → | ........... |
| 8 Probability of technical success | % | 20 | 40 | 60 | 80 | 100 | | |
| | Score | 0 | 30 | 40 | 50 | 60 | → | ........... |
| 9 Market acceptance of product | Degree | much resistance | some resistance | neutral | willing acceptance | ready acceptance | | |
| | Score | −50 | 0 | 10 | 20 | 50 | → | ........... |

| 10 Project/product life | Product life (years) | 2 | 5 | 10 | 15 | 20 or more | |
|---|---|---|---|---|---|---|---|
| From R & D time to build sales to 50% peak | 0.5 | 100 | 120 | 140 | 160 | 180 | → |
| | 1 | 80 | 100 | 120 | 140 | 160 | → |
| | 2 | project unfeasible | 80 | 100 | 120 | 140 | → |
| | 3 | project unfeasible | 60 | 80 | 100 | 120 | → |
| | 5 | project unfeasible | project unfeasible | 60 | 80 | 100 | → |

→ ..........

Standard ratings:
more than 600 excellent
500–600 good
400–499 fair
less than 400 poor

Total score =

Array

## 1.3.3 Summary

The genesis of a project from organizational plans through proposals to decisions is often a protracted process which in itself calls for the use of special management skills and techniques. Certain questions need to be asked. Phrased in everyday jargon-free language, these are shown in Figure 1.10. The decision-maker in the diagram is the person or people responsible for authorizing a proposal.

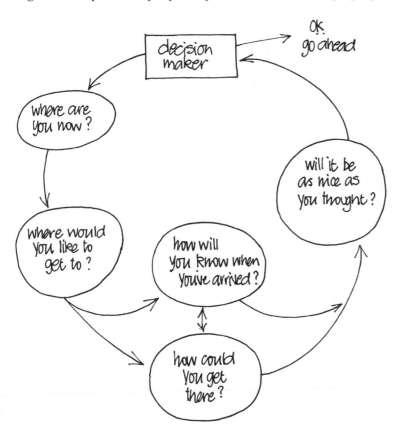

**FIGURE 1.10** Decision-maker's questions

If we define a project as the means whereby an existing state of affairs is transformed into a desired state of affairs, then before the project begins we have to be able to specify both the existing and the desired states. The difference between the two defines what needs to be done. Even in cases where the existing and desired states of affairs are the same, the organization must be aware that the desired state can deteriorate in the future into something undesirable. In such a case the organization needs to do something to prevent the future adverse state of affairs from arising. Of course the gap between an existing and desired state of affairs is not necessarily sufficient stimulus to cause an organization to embark upon a project: the organization will pay attention to those problems and opportunities which the value system of that organization suggests are important.

When proposals reach a stage where a decision is required it is important to base the decision as firmly as possible – to avoid political expediency and the personal inclinations of the decision-maker. A proposal needs to demonstrate an internal consistency: the parts need to fit together in a way which suggests that no part is grossly 'out of scale' with the other parts. Decision trees can assist in guiding decisions, as can proposal ranking formulae (when expenditure is estimated to be low), selection indexes, checklists and measured checklists. However, all these techniques require estimates of cash flows to be made for the economic life of a project: something that may not be feasible at the time the decision whether to proceed is required. Sometimes it is necessary to accept that a decision can be based on incomplete information. If that is the case, then it is important to keep other options open.

Having studied this section you should be able to:

- decide generally whether a proposal exhibits coherence
- explain why it is necessary to calculate profitability in the same way for proposals which are being compared in order to choose amongst them
- calculate expected monetary value (EMV) for possible outcomes in a decision tree
- explain how proposal ranking formulae work
- use a checklist or measured checklist
- state the main limitation of these techniques
- list some of the questions a decision-maker needs to ask before making a decision.

# 1.4   PROJECTS: THE LIFE-CYCLE

Once a feasibility study has been undertaken, presented to management and then identified as an area in which a programme of change or one or more projects should be authorized, we enter the realm of the project itself.

## 1.4.1   Project life-cycles

Earlier we said that a project is: '… a unique venture with a beginning and an end' (Buchanan and Boddy, 1992, p. 8). But it must have a middle, too. We say that a project has a *life-cycle*, based on an analogy with living things which are born, live for a period of time doing things like consuming food and water, breathing, moving, etc., and then finally end (die). There is much discussion about whether there is only one 'true' model of a project life-cycle or many, and whether any of these are reasonably accurate descriptions of what happens in real life. Some writers include the feasibility study as part of the project life-cycle; others believe that the project proper only begins once the feasibility study is completed and the proposal accepted, or only when cost headings for the project are defined. We will use proposal acceptance, since management normally give approval *after* they have been presented with the feasibility study and decided to go ahead with further work. If you find it helpful, you can think of the work needed to carry out a feasibility study as being a mini-project in its own right.

Even with the best of plans and most stringent of controls, real life is always more chaotic than the models we apply to it; the same is true of projects. Nevertheless, in the case of projects, models are useful to help us recognize different ways of moving from the project's beginning to its end, and the broad phases where the activities that take place change from one type to another.

There is no single life-cycle that applies to all projects and we discuss below three different life-cycles which might be a model for a given situation, depending on the approach to be taken. These three life-cycles are:

- a basic project life-cycle, adapted from a five-phase model described by Weiss and Wysocki (1994)

- a phased development life-cycle (a sequence of mini-projects) from Jordan and Machesky (1990)

- a prototyping life-cycle.

### The basic project life-cycle

We have adopted a somewhat different terminology here from that which has been commonly used in the past, in an attempt to describe a basic life-cycle which will fit many projects. The terms used for the five phases (many writers use only four phases) are taken from Weiss and Wysocki (1994).

The basic project life-cycle is shown in Figure 1.11 as a series of arrows proceeding from definition to closure.

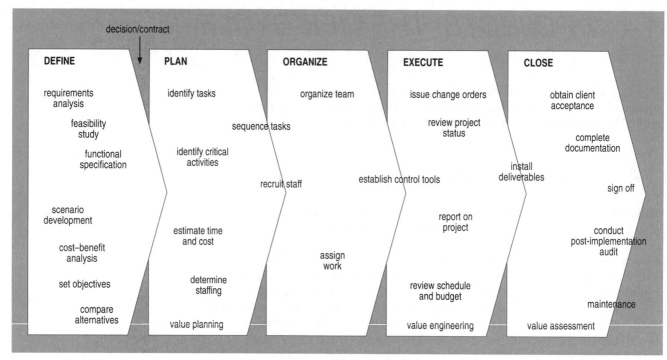

**FIGURE 1.11** The basic project life-cycle

The overlapping areas between the major phases of work in Figure 1.11 are intended to show that the change from one phase to the next is not abrupt: in many projects activities that seem to be part of the planning phase can overlap with activities from the organizing phase, and so on.

Proposals are formulated, estimated and tested for feasibility, and sufficient plans are made to enable a 'go/no-go' decision to be made, often in the form of a contract. The decision forms the end of the stage often called the **definition phase**. Many writers refer to this as the **feasibility phase**.

Once a decision to go ahead has been made, a project enters a **planning phase**. Some plans and general costs, of course, will probably have emerged from the definition phase, but more refinement will need to be done in this phase as earlier plans and cost estimates will have been developed to enable a decision to be made about whether to pursue the proposal further, not to plan its execution in detail. The major tasks that must be carried out in the planning phase include:

● task identification and sequencing

● identification of activities critical to success

● estimating and budgeting

● staffing.

By the end of the planning phase, work can begin on the **organization phase**. Some or all of this phase may overlap with the planning stage. The aim during the organization phase is to put in place the teams, the controls, tools, and communications that will be required for the next phase.

The next phase is the **execution** or **implementation phase**. The important activities in this phase are:

● communicating with management, client, users and others

● reviewing progress

● monitoring costs

● controlling quality

● issuing orders for change

● managing changes.

This phase comes to a close as the agreed deliverables are installed.

The final stage of the project is the **closure phase**. The results of the project can then be put into operation.

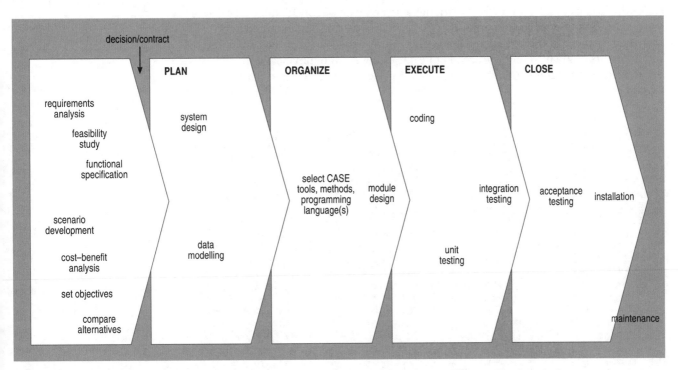

**FIGURE 1.12** The basic software project life-cycle (note: CASE = Computer-Aided Software Engineering)

*Concurrency*

When there is significant overlap in time between activities in different phases, for example when planning activities continue at the same time as organization is under way and execution may even have begun, we say that these activities exhibit **concurrency**. Since changes are an inevitable fact of project life, there will also be times when activities such as estimating or even recruiting or assigning work have to be done again in response to such changes. Many people who regularly work with software development projects know that, while they follow the basic pattern of planning, organizing, executing and closing, many of their own activities and terminology are peculiar to software development. Figure 1.12 shows these activities as an amplification of the basic project life-cycle. In software development, *maintenance* is sometimes considered a part of a software development project. Whether this is the case depends upon whether the client accepts delivery of a flawed piece of software (as that client may, in order to get a system into operation in spite of problems). If that is the case, there may be an intensive period of error detection and correction that continues even after acceptance testing and installation. Otherwise, the task of maintaining software may fall to a different team or group of people and be treated more as a normal system of production, in that minor errors will be logged and the client helped to work around them. An accumulation of errors will then be dealt with as a minor or major redesign of the software in a new project.

## The phased development life-cycle

Phased development is a strategy in which the activities of requirements determination, the evaluation of alternatives, design specification and the implementation of the design are repeated in several iterations. Thus it forms a series of closely linked 'mini-projects' (though each may be of considerable size), at the end of each of which some portion of the overall project is implemented and reviewed by the users. The feedback from the review is used to help determine the requirements of the next mini-project. Figure 1.13 shows diagrammatically the life-cycle of a project carried out as four mini-projects, each forming a phase of the overall project.

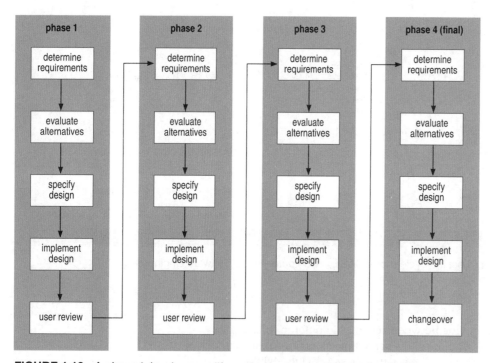

**FIGURE 1.13**   A phased development life-cycle (Jordan and Machesky, 1990)

An example will illustrate this. A large insurance company decided to automate the handling of insurance claims. After initial discussions, they decided to undertake the automation in phases.

There were a number of reasons for this.

- Previous attempts to automate major functions had resulted in serious problems arising, which had proved costly to fix.

- The resources available to undertake the work were few, so there was no possibility of making a concentrated effort to achieve complete automation in the course of a single project.

- The disruption to the normal flow of work in the claims adjustment department would be minimized.

- Training could occur in phases: people would learn to use the system bit by bit, in a natural way.

- Feedback at the end of each phase from the users would inform the development and implementation of the next phase.

It was decided that the phases would mirror the way a claim entered the claims adjustment department and moved through it to adjudication and issuing of payment.

The first phase of the project concentrated on the claims form submitted by the claimant. This phase of the project resulted in the creation of a 'form' on a computer terminal screen which could be filled in by an operator talking to the claimant over the telephone. At first, the operators simply took handwritten forms and entered them on the screen form, but quite quickly this changed to the operators using lightweight telephone headsets and entering the information directly on screen. The claim form was then simply printed by the central computer and posted to the claimant for checking and signature.

The second phase made some minor improvements in the 'form' on the screen and the resulting print-out. Furthermore, the central computer, as well as printing the form out for checking and signature, passed the form, once approved by the claimant, electronically to the claims adjuster, who no longer worked with a paper copy. The claims adjuster reviewed the electronic form and entered information electronically from quotations from prospective repairers. Any arithmetic needed was performed automatically and then the form was printed out.

The third phase again made minor improvements to the 'forms' and automated the approval by the adjuster and the quality control review by a manager, and simply printed a cheque to the claimants for all approved claims and a printed report of all rejected claims to be used to prepare letters to those claimants.

The final phase used word-processing software to assist the preparation of letters to claimants whose claims either were rejected or required further information: the operator could select pre-written phrases for inclusion in the letter but could also add custom-written paragraphs. The letters were automatically printed together with envelopes.

A phased development project life-cycle is suitable for projects with a high degree of technological risk attached to them, or as illustrated above, projects where the resources are not available to do everything in one concerted effort. They have the benefit of minimizing disruption and of having several stages at which the feedback from users can result in beneficial changes to the end product.

## Prototyping project life-cycle

*Prototyping* is a form of phased development. In prototyping a model, or prototype, of the proposed system is built quickly and shown to the users in order to obtain rapid feedback. The model may or may not become part of the final system offered to the users. Prototyping reserves the right to 'throw away' a less successful model, build on a more successful model and fine-tune a very successful model. The model may begin as something quite crude (for example, it may ignore function in order to obtain information on, say, ergonomic aspects of the model) and gradually be refined, or it may be rebuilt at each iteration, or after several iterations a 'formal' project may be constituted to turn the approved model into a working artefact or system.

The advantages of a prototyping project life-cycle are similar to those of a phased development project life-cycle. They have a disadvantage, however, in that it is far more difficult to estimate costs and schedules (due to the experimental nature of the early prototypes) and more difficult to control.

## Using a life-cycle model

Real life is messy and projects, however well organized and run, are likely to run into problems. You may think that there is little value in adopting a life-cycle model for a project. In fact, such models are useful in planning, then in guiding the stages of a project and in helping a project manager to manage it, provided that the manager remains aware that the model is only that, a *model*, and not an exact description of how a project will proceed from start to finish. More important than the life-cycle are the *milestones* and *deliverables* agreed as part of the project plan. These will be described in Chapters 2 and 3.

# 1.4.2   Software: why is it such a problem?

Software development projects are particularly vulnerable to problems.

> In practice, most software developments bear only a passing resemblance to the published 'life cycles' and the so-called quality control procedures are sometimes more concerned with damage limitation than guaranteeing quality in the end product.
>
> Norris *et al.* (1993), p. 15

Software is an intangible product, realized in the form of texts of various sorts: design documents, program code, user and operator manuals, forms, and ultimately only in the observable actions of a computer system. Such systems may be highly complex, multi-functional, and linked to a wide variety of other such systems of software, computer hardware and networks.

Intangibility and the notorious complexity of software make it prone to error. The change from a comma to a full stop in a program in one particular programming language where the difference is key to how the program behaves (in this case changing the item from 1,10 – a number of iterations a program loop is to do – to 1.10 – a variable data value) meant a space probe entirely missed its target (Norris *et al.* p. 10). The error was undetected because both the forms 1,10 and 1.10 were legitimate expressions and both appear visually very similar. However, each causes radically different actions in the resulting program. If that particular part of the program is not thoroughly tested – something that can be impossible due to the amount of time it takes to test all possibilities in a complex program, or impossible to do because the circumstances in which that part of the program should be activated are not possible to simulate for testing – the error won't appear until it is too late.

## Software immeasurability

Not only is software intangible, it is exceedingly difficult to measure. Even experts cannot agree on *what* to measure, let alone *how* to do so. The following example is drawn from Norris *et al.* The program below is a simple program in the popular C language designed to translate degrees Fahrenheit from 0° to 300°, in 20° steps, to degrees Celsius.

```
#define        LOWER        0
#define        UPPER        300
#define        STEP         20

main ()
     {
              int fahr;
              for (fahr=LOWER; fahr<=UPPER; fahr=fahr+STEP)
              printf ("%4d %6.1f\n", fahr, (5.0/9.0*(fahr−32))

     }
```

---

### ACTIVITY 1.14

How many statements does the program contain? (If you don't know much about software and programming, skip this activity, but read the discussion.)

### DISCUSSION

A group of 44 experts were asked at a meeting discussing software measurement to do this exercise. Results are shown in Table 1.9.

**TABLE 1.9**  Results of an experiment on the difficulty of measuring software

| Number of statements | Number of experts stating this was the correct number |
|---|:---:|
| one statement | 1 |
| two statements | 6 |
| three statements | 5 |
| four statements | 1 |
| five statements | 4 |
| six statements | 11 |
| seven statements | 4 |
| eight statements | 1 |
| nine statements | 11 |

If expert practitioners interested in software measurement can't agree on the number of statements in such a short program in a commonly used programming language, it is not surprising that software is therefore very difficult to quantify and measure. Yet some software estimation methods (introduced in Chapter 2) rely on such measures as 'the number of program code statements' likely to be produced.

## Software complexity

Software is enormously complex. Programs can be written to make decisions based on data values and the data values can change depending upon conditions, either in the data itself or in the outside world. Many decisions offer only two possibilities, of the form: IF A IS TRUE DO X OTHERWISE DO Y. If I feel like being active, I go for a walk, otherwise I watch television. Grouping and ordering such either/or decisions can produce quite complex actions. However, in order to test a program thoroughly for correctness, *every possible combination of either/or decision must be tested*, and for many programs this is an impossibility. Assume that a program of nine interlinked either/or decisions exists. Testing one decision requires two tests. Testing two, where the second depends on the first, requires five to six tests (depending on the linkage between the first and second). By the time all possible combinations for nine such are considered, even if each test takes a tiny fraction of a second, a full test of all possible combinations and paths through the program will require *millennia*. Instead of full tests, programmers rely on their understanding of a program to help them design and perform tests that can be done within the time available and will show up errors – but testing to prove correctness of a program is almost always impossible except for the most trivial examples. This means that undiscovered errors can persist in the software and can even lie dormant for years before manifesting themselves.

Then, to compound matters, software interacts with other software on the same machine, and with the hardware that supports it, often in very complex ways. Such complexity often results in the frustration of encountering a seemingly intractable problem even on so simple a machine as a personal computer used by itself only for word processing.

## EXAMPLE 1.8

I recently attached a printer to a personal computer for a friend, who only wanted it to do word processing. At first, nothing worked. The problem proved to be the connecting cable, which was mis-wired. After correcting this problem, he could only print the first page of any document. Eventually he found that he could print every page of the document, but only one at a time, and that the printer demanded that each sheet of paper be hand-fed to it, rather than taking paper from the automatic feeder. The only-one-page-printed-at-a-time problem turned out to lie in the word-processing software; he had a version that was known to be defective. A new version was obtained which allowed all pages of a document to be printed with a single print command, but it still remained apparently impossible to make the printer use the automatic feed. This was finally solved by changing no less than nine different parameters: one in the DOS operating system, two in two different parts of the word-processing software, and six others, one in each document he had been unable to print properly before!

How much worse it is when a complex applications program may run under a so-called environment (such as Windows or CICS), which in turn runs on some operating system, which in turn runs on hardware that varies somewhat from one manufacturer or one model to another, where different parts of the hardware system may come from different manufacturers and may be connected to a local area network, which may be connected to a wide area network, and so on!

## Software quality

We have as yet no widely agreed measures of the 'goodness' of software produced as the result of a project; neither can we measure its quality accurately or positively. Quality measures for software are largely confined to the relative *absence* of faults. There has been some research effort to quantify and locate the likely source of faults. In one study the percentage of faults by area is shown in Table 1.10.

Requirements definition occurs at the very beginning of a software project. As with any engineering project, the software engineer or analyst visits the client and users and interviews and observes them in order to determine what they require. The problem with this phase is the fact that the eventual product, the software, is intangible and invisible. There isn't much that can be shown to prospective clients and users. And unless the users themselves are experts, they may not be fully aware of the capabilities and limitations of software, nor may they be fully aware of its complexities or the problems of integrating new software with existing systems. In any case they may have difficulty in expressing their requirements; or the analyst or systems engineer, who is rarely an expert in the client's line of business or the users' tasks, may have difficulty in understanding fully the requirements they do express.

There are no simple answers for the problems of obtaining a sound requirements definition document. The analyst or software engineer prepares this and then 'walks through' it with the client and perhaps with some end-users, but as there is nothing to 'try out' it is difficult to determine from such a walk-through whether all requirements are covered, and whether those that have been are covered satisfactorily. One possible solution is the prototype approach mentioned earlier; an early prototype, perhaps crudely giving the function and feel of the eventual

**TABLE 1.10** Areas giving rise to faults in software

| Phase giving rise to fault | Percentage of total faults |
| --- | --- |
| requirements definition | 38 |
| maintenance (operation) | 32 |
| design | 23 |
| installation | 7 |

(adapted from Norris *et al.* 1993)

product, can be tried out to see what its deficiencies, limitations and errors are, and the requirements definition can then be refined.

Software design is plagued by the problem of change: since there is nothing tangible, it is easy to think that nothing has been built, and therefore anything can be changed, and the change is simple. However, the complexity of software, which emerges quickly in the design phase, is such that even relatively simple-sounding changes can have knock-on effects that are very difficult to determine until testing. Again, prototyping or phased development are approaches which can help in this respect. However, the problems of controlling this type of development and the increase in the time needed to complete a product can make these approaches unsatisfactory.

Installation, interestingly, gives rise to the fewest significant errors. This is perhaps the one task that is relatively straightforward in a software project, although the project team may not think so when they are scrambling to get everything up and working!

Maintenance generates another large proportion of errors. This again is related to the complexity of the software. A 'fix' applied in one area may generate problems in other areas and have cascading knock-on effects.

As well as the problems mentioned so far, you should note that software development involves a series of 'translations'. The requirements document has to be 'translated' into designs, and later the designs have to be translated into a programming language, which in turn gets translated into machine language. At each step, it is possible to make errors: to miss part of what needs to be translated, to insert something that wasn't there before, to mistranslate. And at each stage, it is also all too easy to make apparently simple errors, like the substitution of the full stop for the comma mentioned earlier, that have enormous effects.

Having read all the reasons why software is so problematic, you may be forgiven if you wonder how any usable software ever gets written. If you have much experience with *any* software at all, even a simple word-processing or spreadsheet package, you will have found things that don't work as you think they should, or don't work as they are described. Nevertheless, even somewhat flawed software can be an enormous boon in carrying out daily tasks such as letter and report writing and financial record-keeping and planning. If your word processor only prints one page at a command instead of a whole document, it may be annoying but it isn't threatening. The real problem arises with the software that we increasingly depend upon to fly aircraft, monitor radar at busy airports, manage power stations (including nuclear power stations) and even to manage systems within our motor cars. If such software fails, the consequences may be much more serious than simply having to enter a new print command for each page of a document. This is why software engineering, program proving and the development of safety-critical software are such active areas of research.

# 1.4.3  Success factors

What is the definition of project success? According to Norris *et al.* (p. 1) it is that:

- the product is delivered
- it meets customers' perceived requirements
- the supplier is able to continue future production (how many suppliers complete a project 'successfully' but are unable to continue in business?)
- the customer is willing to use the supplier again.

How can we know if a project is likely to be successful? A number of researchers have established a set of factors which, taken together, indicate that a project has a high likelihood of success.

### Project objectives

The project's objectives are clearly defined in the project plans (and *kept to* in carrying out the project work).

### Project personnel

The project manager is competent; project team members are competent. (Boehm (1981) found that the capabilities of personnel were more than twice as important as any other factor in software projects; this would be less so in 'hard' fields, those with tangible outputs.)

### Support from above

The project is supported by top management. This is best obtained by making sure that the project is important to the achievement of the organization's mission and its major objectives.

### Resources

Resources of money, time, material and people are sufficient to do the job.

### Communication and control

Communication channels between project manager and senior management, the project manager and team leaders and team members, the project group and the client, are in place and are adequate. There are channels for feedback on reports, deliverables and quality.

Control mechanisms in are place and used. Milestones are checked against the schedule. Deliverables are tangible (even if these are in the form of reports) and are reviewed for quality.

Contractors are responsive to their clients.

# 1.4.4   Why manage projects?

Each of the paragraphs below will discuss a point briefly and signpost forward to where these topics will be amplified in subsequent chapters.

It is necessary to develop a specification of what is to be done. (It is important to be aware of the iterative nature of this activity: pilot studies, feasibility studies, the project itself, specifying changes that will inevitably occur while a project is under way, all result in the need to modify the specification of what is to be done.) In this chapter we have discussed ways of identifying what is to be done and, at the highest level, how that should be done. In Chapters 2 and 3 we look at the detailed planning of the project itself.

Proposals need to be 'scoped' (for effort, elapsed time, cost and likely effects) at an early stage. We discussed this briefly at the start of Section 1.2.1. Projects that result from successful proposals also need to have effort, time, cost and effects planned, and dependencies between tasks and between resources and tasks identified (Chapters 2 and 3).

Once a project is planned and perhaps put out to tender, it is necessary for the relevant parties to agree what is to be done, by when and at what cost – the contract. It may be an informal contract between different departments of the same organization or a formal, legal instrument drawn up between two or more organizations (Chapter 2).

Effort has to be co-ordinated and communication has to take place amongst all the 'players'. It is necessary to organize and manage the team – direct it and co-ordinate its efforts. It is also necessary to liaise with clients, senior management, potential users and others (Chapter 4).

Once a project is under way, it becomes necessary to control the process of getting from plan to reality. This will be described in detail in Chapters 5 and 6. Most projects require some degree of change in what they are undertaking even as they progress, so it is also necessary to 'correct the course' of the project in a controlled way. This will also be described in Chapters 5 and 6. A project also needs to close down in a planned way – closure. This will be described in Chapter 7.

A disciplined approach is very important to achieving a project's goals. There are a number of project management methodologies in existence – disciplined methods of proceeding. The collection of techniques and methods mentioned in this book also constitute a methodology, albeit an informal one.

# 1.4.5   What does a project manager do?

What follows is a broad description of the major areas a project manager concerns him- or herself with, and the knowledge, skills and tools a project manager will need. This will be elaborated in each of the subsequent chapters. As above, each area will be discussed briefly, with forward signposting.

Project management is quite different from line (so-called 'system') management. As noted earlier, projects are designed to change something: the manager must be able to cope with the risk inherent in managing such changes. People working on the project may come from other areas; indeed, they may be contractors or subcontractors or employees of member firms in a consortium.

*Estimating and planning*

The project manager, or someone under his or her direction, has to collect information about what exactly needs to be done and how it is to be organized; how much it will cost and how long it will take; and then look at the interdependencies of various tasks, skills and other resources. The results are a project plan and a project budget (Chapters 2 and 3).

*Assembling a team*

A project team can make or break a project. Often the project manager has little say in who works on the project: the team will be assembled from people with the right skills (if they are available) who are not assigned to work of a higher priority than the project. Even if the project manager has a free choice, the pool of people from whom he or she can select is limited. A project manager's skill lies in assembling people and *making* them into a team – motivating them, managing conflict amongst them and ensuring good communication (Chapter 4).

A project manager's skill lies in making people into a team

### Reporting and liaising

The project manager is the spokesperson for the project. It is his or her job to liaise with senior management, clients, regulatory bodies and everyone contributing to the project (Chapters 4 and 5).

### Putting tools in place

A number of tools exist to help manage and control projects, and to undertake estimating and reporting. Specific tools also exist for specific types of projects: in the case of software projects tools range from appropriate hardware and operating system software, through language compilers and test harnesses to computer-aided software engineering (CASE) tools. The manager has to see that the appropriate tools for the job are available or obtained (Chapters 5 and 6).

### Managing and co-ordinating work

Once the project work begins, the project manager's job is to manage the work that is done and to co-ordinate the efforts of different team members and different bodies within the organization in order to achieve the project's objectives (Chapters 5 and 6).

### Managing change

Few, if any, projects end exactly as they were initially planned. Problems arise that require changes to plans: these may be short-term (for example delaying a particular task because a necessary material or resource is not available at the right time) or long-term. The users or clients may change their requirements as they learn more about the product they will be receiving at the end of the project. The regulatory, legislative or financial climate in which the project operates may change during the execution of the project. Unless someone – normally the project manager – institutes a formal way of noting, estimating and carrying out approved changes (change control) the project can deteriorate into chaos (Chapter 6).

## 1.4.6 Summary

Projects rarely proceed smoothly through a series of well-ordered and well-organized phases to a perfect conclusion. Nevertheless, there is value in having a model for project life-cycles. Projects can follow a basic project life-cycle, use a phased development cycle, or involve prototypes which may then be developed (or simply serve as a model for the final product).

All projects take place in an atmosphere of at least some risk. The occurrence of adverse circumstances may mean that extra time, cost or some reworking of the project plans are required in order to complete.

Even in the best organized and run projects the distinction between phases is not always clear-cut: design may overlap to some extent with development, development with implementation, and implementation with operation. The project organization has to be prepared for setbacks and has to plan so that those setbacks remain minor and do not become so major as to jeopardize the success of the project. (In Chapter 2 we will discuss risk analysis and management, and how contingency planning can help ensure that the project succeeds.)

Projects with a significant software content are particularly problematic. Software is invisible, difficult or impossible to measure (there is wide disagreement about what measures can or should be applied and how they can be used), very complex, and subject to human error as the outputs of one project phase are translated for the next phase. This is most serious where the software is critical to human safety.

One thing that every project manager or person responsible for a project can do is to see whether any of the success factors are present for that project: the more factors present the greater the likelihood of success. The management of a project is very important and includes a number of tasks that are the responsibility of the project manager: estimating and planning, assembling a team, getting the tools into place, managing and co-ordinating work, managing change and reporting and liaising.

Having studied this section you should be able to:

- describe the basic project life-cycle and list some of the tasks that belong to each phase
- describe the phased development life-cycle and state how it differs from the basic project life-cycle
- draw up a brief plan for a phased development project based on a simple scenario of the project requirements
- describe the prototyping project life-cycle
- state four major reasons why projects with a software content are problematic and suggest ways in which phased development or prototype approaches can help
- list five areas in which to look for the presence of success factors in any project and state what these factors are
- list the main activities of a project manager.

# 1.5   CASE STUDY: THE LONDON AMBULANCE SERVICE

The automation of the despatch of ambulances in London, which was implemented on 26 October 1992, was subject to very severe problems on the 26 and 27 October, and to failure on 4 November 1992.

This case study, based on the Report of the Inquiry into the London Ambulance Service of February 1993, will look at what the project's objectives were, how these were realized and why they resulted in such severe problems.

As you work through this case study you should note any aspects of failure that you consider failure of *project management*. In an Activity at the end of the section we will ask you to list these points and in the discussion following we will indicate where in this book we will address those issues.

## 1.5.1   Background

The London Ambulance Service (LAS) was founded in 1930. By 1965, when the Greater London Council (GLC) replaced the previous London County Council (LCC), the LAS was enlarged to take in all or part of eight other ambulance services. In 1974 responsibility for all British ambulance services was transferred to the National Health Service. This meant that ambulance services had to be managed, but at 'arm's length', by a regional health authority – in the case of LAS this was the South West Thames Regional Health Authority – but had service agreements with the four regional health authorities whose territories it covered. (The LAS was, however, a quasi-independent body with its own board.) The LAS covers a geographical area of just over 600 square miles with a resident population of about 6.8 million people (though the daytime population, boosted by workers and visitors, especially in central London, is much higher). This makes it the largest ambulance service in the world. The LAS transports over 5000 patients and receives between 2000 and 2500 calls daily. Of these, between 1300 and 1600 are emergency 999 calls.

The LAS is divided broadly between accident and emergency (A & E) and patient transport service (PTS). Of ambulance journeys, about half a million per year are accident and emergency patients, and 1.3 million are patient transport service. As of January 1993 there were 2700 full-time equivalent staff positions (two half-time positions will constitute one full-time equivalent position), of which just over 50% were operational A & E staff, 21% were operational PTS staff, and 200 (roughly 7%) were control assistants responsible for taking calls for ambulance service. The service had 305 A & E ambulances, 445 PTS ambulances, plus other emergency, rapid response, driver training and motorcycle response units, and one helicopter.

---

### ACTIVITY 1.15

To help appreciate the LAS's operating environment, draw a rich picture of it based on this description.

## DISCUSSION

Your picture should include the NHS as the responsible body, the regional health authorities (with one, South West Thames, as the 'managing' body), the LAS board as the more direct 'managing' body, the large population and area, the two different types of ambulances, the staff in their different categories, etc. (You should omit the GLC and LCC, which have historic associations only.) Our own rich picture is shown in Figure 1.14.

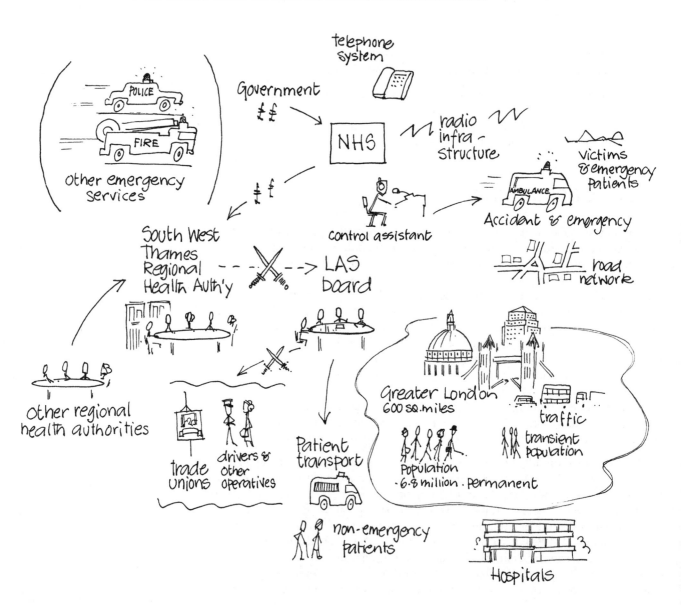

**FIGURE 1.14** A rich picture of the London Ambulance Service

The LAS first considered introducing a computerized command and control system in the early 1980s. This was intended to address shortcomings in both the manual system of call taking and the identification and mobilization of resources.

The manual system operates (at the time of writing) as follows:

1    A 999 or urgent call is received in Central Ambulance Control.

2    A control assistant (CA) writes down the call details on a pre-printed form. The incident location is identified from a map book, which provides the map reference co-ordinates.

3    On completion, the form is placed on a conveyor belt system with other forms from other CAs and is transported to a central collection point.

4    Another Central Ambulance Control staff member collects the forms from the central collection point, reviews the information on each form and decides which resource allocator should deal with it (based on the three London divisions: north east, north west and south). At this point potential duplicated calls are also identified.

5    The resource allocator examines the forms for his or her sector.

6    Using status and location information for each vehicle, obtained from the radio operator who notes this on forms maintained in the 'activation box' for each vehicle, the resource allocator decides which ambulance should be mobilized. This is then also recorded on the form which is then passed to a despatcher.

7    The despatcher telephones the relevant ambulance station (if that is where the ambulance is) or passes mobilization instructions to the radio operator if the ambulance is already mobile.

This process should take no more than three minutes. However, there are deficiencies in the totally manual system including:

- Callers can give incomplete or inaccurate details requiring an exploration of a number of alternatives through the map books to identify the precise location of an incident.

- Moving pieces of paper around the control room is inefficient.

- Knowing where an ambulance is relies on the allocators' intuition and reports relayed through the radio operator: this is a laborious process.

- Communicating with ambulances by voice radio is time-consuming and can, at peak times, lead to queues of mobilization messages building up.

- Identifying duplicated calls requires error-prone human judgement and memory.

- Callers may call back; dealing with these call-backs is labour intensive and the control assistant may have to leave his or her post to talk to the resource allocators.

- Identifying those incidents requiring a rapid response unit or the helicopter relies totally on human judgement.

---

ACTIVITY 1.15

Modify your rich picture to include the points made above. List separately those features which you think could be addressed by a computer-based despatch system.

DISCUSSION

Your rich picture should now include callers, maps, paper flow, communications.

A computer-based despatch system could provide features to address these problems, such as:

- a computer-based gazetteer (a map with an index) with public telephone box identification

- elimination of paper movement around the control room

- timely automated ambulance availability and location

- computer-based intelligence to help identify duplicate calls and major incidents requiring special responses

- direct mobilization of an ambulance on completion of an emergency call.

---

The LAS had already made an unsuccessful attempt to computerize its command and control system in the late eighties. This was abandoned in 1990 when testing revealed that the system would not cope with the demands likely to be placed upon it. After abandoning this attempt, the LAS began working on a requirements specification for a 'state of the art' command and control system.

## 1.5.2 Requirements analysis and tendering for the contract

A team to look at the requirements for the new system was assembled in the Autumn of 1990. It consisted of the Director of Support Services (chairing the team), the systems manager, a contract analyst who had worked with the LAS on the previous, unsuccessful system, and the control room services manager. Other individuals representing training, communications and other areas were also involved but there was little involvement from ambulance crews. The aim of the team was to create, as far as possible, a totally automated system: the bulk of calls would be handled automatically from location identification through ambulance allocation to mobilization, and only the most complex cases would require a human allocator.

The team recognized that they were treading fresh ground. At that time no other emergency service had attempted to go so far, though several other UK emergency services had computer-based call taking. Some also had vehicle location mapping and were considering automating the choice of vehicle for voice radio mobilization or mobilization through mobile data terminals in each vehicle.

The team contacted other ambulance services (West Midlands, Oxford and Surrey) to see whether their existing command and control systems might be made to meet the LAS 'vision'. All of these were rejected. Surrey's system was only partly what was wanted and the team felt it would be prohibitively costly to extend it; West Midlands' was closest to the needs and size of London, but there was no spare IT (information technology) capacity in West Midlands to develop or support a system for London; Oxford's was originally provided by McDonnell Douglas for fire brigade use and at the time McDonnell Douglas seemed unwilling to amend their system to meet the LAS's requirements.

The contract analyst, working with the systems manager, then progressed work on the systems requirements specification, and this was completed in February 1991, with a companion paper describing revised operational methods that would be required by the new system. The proposed system consisted of three main elements:

- computer-aided despatch
- computer map display
- automatic vehicle location system (AVLS).

These elements needed to interface with existing mobile data terminals which had already been installed in LAS vehicles as a part of the rejected earlier system. Integrated communications would be through the radio interface system provided for the earlier system by one of the contractors (SOLO Electronic Systems Ltd). The firm would be given a new contract for this.

A team consisting of the contract analyst, the systems manager and a supplies manager from the regional health authority's regional procurement department undertook procurement for the system. The invitation to tender was advertised and 35 companies expressed interest in all or part of the system. Meetings were held with prospective suppliers, many of whom raised concerns over the proposed timetable: full implementation in less than a year. The team also had a proposed budget of £1.5 million.

The very tight timetable seems to have come from a report commissioned from management consultants in the autumn of 1990 about action to be taken on the previous, rejected system. The report recommended abandoning the old project and starting work on the specification and acquisition or development of a new system. A packaged solution, the report stated, would cost about £1.5 million and require 19 months from specification to implementation. The report went on to warn that such estimates should be significantly increased if a packaged solution was not possible. However the estimates for both the cost and the timescale of a packaged solution seem to have been accepted as adequate for new development.

---

### ACTIVITY 1.16

Whether or not you are familiar with the problems of information technology systems development, you should be able at this point to spot one or two serious potential problems. What are they?

### DISCUSSION

The unusual transference of an estimate for a packaged solution to a 'bespoke' (tailor-made) solution is one serious shortcoming, especially as the earlier management report advised that a significant increase in this estimate was required if a packaged solution was not available.

It was also becoming clear at this stage that the LAS was looking for a solution with many novel aspects to it – a sure sign that the risk would be high.

---

Seventeen prospective suppliers provided full proposals for all or parts of the system. The team developed a checklist of the main LAS requirements, including time and cost, and used a points scoring system to rate potential suppliers.

Only one of the proposals met all the LAS requirements, including timetable and price. This was from a consortium of Apricot Computers, Systems Options (a small software development firm) and Datatrak (for the automatic vehicle location system), bidding at just under £1 million.

Procurement guidelines for the regional health authority stated that the lowest tender should be accepted unless there are 'good and sufficient reasons to the contrary', but otherwise provided little qualitative guidance to procurement teams. Although a number of other permutations of bidders might have produced a system meeting the requirement within the tight timescale, they were not considered because of their failure to compete on cost.

### ACTIVITY 1.17

List two or three possible ways of assessing the bid that you think could have been included in the procurement guidelines.

### DISCUSSION

The team should have ascertained exactly what kinds of procurement were covered by the guidelines (it is entirely possible that they did not cover such novel projects as this). Perhaps guidelines of this kind in any organization could suggest having a second and critical look at tenders that are significantly lower than all others before accepting them. There is also the possibility of taking references for the tendering companies from previous clients, and asking to see details of the estimates that went into making up the tender. You may have listed others.

No questions were asked as to why the software development bid from Systems Options, at £35 000, was so much lower than any other bidder's, but with hindsight it was taken to mean that Systems Options had seriously underestimated the complexity of the task. The selection process was audited, and the audit endorsed the procurement team's decision.

Though the original proposal had come from Apricot Computers, who were expected to be the lead contractors in the consortium, Software Options became the leaders in fact, though they were not keen to do so.

## 1.5.3   Development of the system

The LAS decided to adopt the PRINCE project management methodology, but team members received only cursory training and failed to follow the method fully. They expected the lead contractor to be responsible for project management, but this was not covered explicitly in the contract. Project management was undertaken by the Director of Support Services, who had no real experience of controlling major software development and who needed to continue his normal duties, and by the contract analyst. Systems Options, despite being the lead contractor, appeared to exercise no responsibility beyond providing planning schedules to early project group meetings. There were regular project management meetings throughout the project.

Systems Options were regularly late in delivering software. This was partly blamed on a two-month delay in starting the programming while the system design specification was written, and partly on delays in the delivery of the radio interface system specification and protocols by SOLO. Indeed, the separate contract with SOLO for the radio interface system was only signed in mid-September of 1991, just four months before the system was due to be implemented, and some three months after the original systems design contract was awarded to Software Options.

In October, 1991 a new systems manager was recruited by the LAS, and though he was not directly involved in the project he carried out a review of progress in November. The report recommended that the January implementation date be kept in order to maintain pressure on the suppliers, and it stressed the need for quality but did not contain any real conclusions. By mid-December it was clear that the deadline of 8 January for full implementation wouldn't be met. The project group then took a decision to implement a partial solution during January. The call-taking routines were implemented and the reports printed out for manual allocation and voice despatch. The computer-based gazetteer was also brought into operation, enabling control assistants to identify the locations of incidents more easily. This partial implementation was broadly successful though some problems – screens 'locking up', failure of the file server (the unit providing access to data files) and the loss of an incident due to a printer being switched off at the wrong moment – were experienced and caused staff to lose confidence in the system. Many problems were due to the hasty expedient of using printers, which were not a part of the original specification.

Work on all aspects of the system continued, and various elements of the system were tested. The next step was to report the locations of vehicles automatically in order to supplement the information available to the allocators. The trials identified many problems with this aspect of the system:

- frequent incomplete status reporting by ambulance crews
- inaccurate Datatrak location fixes caused by faulty equipment, transmission black-spots or software error
- the inability of the system to cope with established working practices such as taking a vehicle other than the one allocated by the system
- overload of communications channels particularly during shift changes
- continued occasional problems with the central ambulance control hardware
- bugs in the resource proposal software that caused it sometimes to fail to identify the nearest available ambulance
- continued difficulties with mobile data terminals through failures to transmit or receive signals or the occasional lock-up of mobile data terminals.

---

## ACTIVITY 1.18

Recall that ambulance crews had no input to the planning process for this system. Identify in the list of problems above those which appear to be related to the behaviour of ambulance crews. Can you suggest any remedies that could have ameliorated any of these problems?

## DISCUSSION

One problem is obvious: the incomplete status reporting. Another problem is the conflict with established working practices. The incompatibility with established working practices should have been addressed by consulting the ambulance crews at the proposal stage. At least the problem would then have been identified early on. A possible problem is the overload of communications channels during shift changes, which might be exacerbated by many private 'see you after work' messages being transmitted. Problems of incompatible working practices and overloading of communications channels could have been addressed by training, though it is possible that ambulance crews will have felt disgruntled at their exclusion from the proposal stage, when their inputs as to 'real' (as opposed to 'rule book') working practices could have been very valuable.

---

The system was implemented piecemeal across different LAS divisions over the first nine months of 1992 and during that period was never in a stable state, with changes and enhancements constantly being made to the computer-aided despatch software and the radio interface system. In March 1992 the LAS systems manager carried out a further review of project progress, which reported almost daily failures of the radio interface system. The report from that review noted that volume testing of the whole communications infrastructure still had to be carried out. Recommendations were made to prepare a fully documented implementation strategy which should then be signed off by all parties, to bring the change log (the software company's record of the changes they made to the software) under the formal control of the systems team and not allow piecemeal changes outside this formal system, and to review the training of staff.

### SAQ 1.12

What aspect of project management is referred to by the phrase 'to bring the change log under the formal control of the systems team'?

Automated ambulance selection was implemented on 26 October 1992 – the first time that the full system was in operation. The decision was taken to 'go live' and use the system as it had been envisaged: with no paper records or activation boxes. In addition it was decided to:

- reconfigure the control room
- install more computer-aided despatch terminals and radio interface system screens
- separate the ambulance allocators from radio operators and those expected to deal with exceptional cases
- cover the whole of London rather than operate in three separate divisions
- use only the ambulance allocations proposed by the new system
- allow some of the call-takers to allocate ambulances if the nearest ambulance was less than 11 minutes away
- use separate allocators for 999 calls, doctors' urgent calls and patient transport calls.

ACTIVITY 1.19

Can you see any problems likely to arise from the decisions listed above?

DISCUSSION

There are many. Perhaps the most significant is the decision to 'go live' without leaving the old system at least physically intact so that it would be possible to fall back to it in the event of serious problems with the new system. Since the piecemeal implementation of the new system had revealed a significant number of problems, one might have expected that the live new system would also exhibit problems and errors, some of which (especially if combined) could be serious enough to warrant going back to old methods for a time while fault diagnosis and repairs were enacted. The change to the configuration of the control room means that it would have a layout unfamiliar to the people working in it at a crucial time – when they are also trying to cope with new working practices. The decision to cover the whole of London was also a risky one: it meant that should problems arise, call-taking and despatch in the problem area could not be switched to another location. The decision to use only the ambulance allocations from the new system was also risky given some of the problems detailed earlier (poor status information and mistaken location information).

# 1.5.4  Failure

On 26 and then 27 of October 1992 response times for ambulances became at times unacceptable, but generally the system functioned as it was designed to do. However, there were flaws in the new system that would lead to its total failure. In order to be effective the system needed near-perfect information all of the time, otherwise it could not be expected to allocate the most appropriate ambulance to an incident. While imperfections in the information available to the system were not individually very serious, cumulatively they could lead to system failure. The changes made to the operating procedures and layout of the central ambulance control room made it extremely difficult for staff to intervene and correct problems. As a result, the quality and accuracy of the information available to the system rapidly deteriorated: the locations of fewer and fewer vehicles were known. Sometimes several ambulances were sent to the same incident, and sometimes the nearest ambulance was not sent. People who had called for an ambulance grew increasingly alarmed at the delays and called back, indirectly causing severe lengthening of response times to incidents. Higher numbers of 'waiting attention' and exception messages caused the system to slow down. Unrectified exception messages generated further exception messages. Ambulance crews grew frustrated with problems and increasingly didn't press the status buttons in the correct sequence. The higher level of radio traffic increased the number of failed mobilizations and created voice communication delays.

Following the problems that arose on the 26 and 27 of October, central ambulance control returned to partially manual methods of operation. The system then operated reasonably successfully up to the early hours of 4 November, when at 2 a.m. it slowed significantly and then locked up altogether. Attempts to switch off and restart workstations failed to overcome the problem. Because of this calls could not even be printed and mobilizations from incident summaries could not take place. Central ambulance control management and staff reverted fully to a manual, paper-based system with voice or telephone mobilization.

Software Options were called in to investigate the failure. In particular, the LAS wanted to know why fall-back to the standby system had not worked. The inquiry team concluded that the system failure was caused by a minor programming error. A piece of code caused a small amount of the memory within the file server to be used up every time a vehicle mobilization occurred. This small amount of memory was then not released, as it should have been. Over three weeks this gradually used up all the available memory in the system and caused it to fail. The failure of the fall-back procedures was found to be a consequence of the temporary addition of the printers, which had not been part of the original specification but simply a stop-gap means of getting some parts of the system going as near to the scheduled date as possible. The fall-back system was designed to operate as part of the completely paperless system, but there is no record of this having been tested, and failure of the printer-based system had not been tested at all.

The report of the inquiry team states in its conclusions:

> What is clear from the ... investigations is that neither the Computer Aided Despatch (CAD) system itself, nor its users, were ready for full implementation on 26 October 1992. The CAD software was not complete, not properly tuned, and not fully tested. The resilience of the hardware under a full load had not been tested. The fall back option to the second file server had certainly not been tested. There were outstanding problems with data transmission to and from the mobile data terminals. There was some scepticism over the accuracy record of the Automatic Vehicle Location System (AVLS). Staff, both within Central Ambulance Control (CAC) and ambulance crews, had no confidence in the system and were not all fully trained. The physical changes to the layout of the control room on 26 October 1992 meant that CAC staff were working in unfamiliar positions, without paper backup, and were less able to work with colleagues with whom they had jointly solved problems before. There had been no attempt to foresee fully the effect of inaccurate or incomplete data available to the system.... These imperfections led to an increase in the number of exception messages that would have to be dealt with and which in turn would lead to more call backs and enquiries. In particular the decision on that day to use only the computer generated resource [ambulance] allocations (which were proven to be less than 100% reliable) was a high risk move.

(p. 56)

## 1.5.5  Summary

The inquiry team identified a number of problems and risks with the LAS's attempt at full automation. We summarize them here.

The LAS can benefit from the introduction of a computer-aided despatch system, but the system implemented in 1992 was too ambitious and was developed and implemented against an impossible timetable.

The development of a strategy for the future of computer-aided despatch with the LAS must involve full consultation between management, staff, trade union representatives and information technology advisers, and perhaps should be extended to include experts in computer-aided despatch from other emergency services.

The particular geographical, social and political environment in which the LAS operates and the cultural climate of the service itself require a more measured and participative approach from management and staff.

Advice from many sources outside the LAS, and concern voiced by potential suppliers on the high risk of the system and the timetable, were ignored or not accepted.

The procurement guidelines were followed fully but were inadequate in that they emphasized open tendering and obtaining the best price and ignored qualitative aspects.

Independent references for the lead contractor were not taken up.

Since the software contractor was a small company with no previous experience of similar emergency systems, the risk of failure was high.

The LAS adopted but failed to follow the PRINCE project management method.

Project management throughout development and implementation was inadequate, being a part-time responsibility of someone with no experience in this area of project work, and it was often unclear who was responsible.

Each stage of development and implementation should have had an analysis of qualitative and quantitative costs and benefits (referred to in the report as 'value engineering').

Management, the project team and the lead supplier failed to identify or to recognize the significance of many problems.

The majority of its users distrusted the system because of problems identified with early 'releases' of the system, to the point where staff expected the system to fail rather than willed it to succeed.

Changes to working practices required by the implementation of the system were not discussed with those likely to be affected. Training was incomplete and inconsistent.

The system relied on near perfect information at all times and the project team failed to appreciate the impact of a high level of imperfect information on the system.

The system was not fully tested to a satisfactory level of quality and resilience before it was implemented.

The system relied on a communications infrastructure that was overloaded already and unable to cope easily with the additional demands placed upon it in an already difficult large urban environment.

The LAS Board and the regional health authority management, while they realized that there were problems, accepted assurances that problems were being rectified and implementation would occur. At no time was a full independent review commissioned on the true state of the project.

It is easier to say, with hindsight, what happened with this project and why, than to have said, at any time between the setting of the system requirement specification and the failure of the system on 4 November 1992, what was going wrong. As you progress through the chapters of this book you should refer back to the London Ambulance Service system and ask yourself: was the method or technique I've just studied applied? If not, how might its application have improved the situation?

## ACTIVITY 1.20

As indicated at the beginning of this section you should have been looking at this case study with a critical eye to see what went wrong from a *project management* point of view. Review the points that you have noted and make a list of them.

## DISCUSSION

A check through the summary of the inquiry teams findings yields a whole range of problems which could be attributed to poor project management. Nearly all the points made in the summary relate to the management of the project rather than to technical problems. The following are some of the points that you may have noted. In brackets we have added the chapters of this book which are the most relevant to each issue.

*General*  The project management was part-time and responsibilities were unclear. Problems that arose were not properly analysed (Chapters 4, 5 and 6).

*Estimating*  The work was seriously underestimated. There seem to have been no checks on the validity of low-priced estimates (Chapter 2).

*Planning*  An impossible timetable was set (Chapter 3).

*Contracting*  No check was made of the suitability of contractors (Chapter 2).

*Risks*  Risk assessment and management were either non-existent or wildly optimistic (Chapters 2 and 5).

*Quality assurance*  Quality was not as relevant as price. Testing was inadequate (Chapters 2, 3 and 5).

*Value engineering*  This was not applied (Chapter 5).

*Communications/team building*  There was a lack of participation and communication with the stakeholders in the project. Training was inadequate (Chapter 4).

*Auditing*  This was not undertaken (Chapter 6).

*Project management methodology*  The PRINCE methodology was adopted but not followed .

# 2 RISK, ESTIMATES AND CONTRACTS

## *INTRODUCTION*

We've discussed how projects arise in Chapter 1. In this chapter we assume that management has decided to support further work on a proposal, at least so far as providing resource for more detailed estimating and planning. (A certain amount of rough planning and estimating has probably taken place earlier, and as a project progresses, more and more detailed planning and estimating takes place; some degree of planning and estimating may continue almost to the end of a project.)

## Aims and objectives

Having studied this chapter you should be able to:

- determine what tasks need to be done and how they should be organized to aid proper project and budget control procedures
- identify and evaluate risks and draw up risk-management plans
- determine the costs of either managing or incurring risks
- draw up an estimate and assist in drawing up a budget
- find the costs of a task or element of work as part of drawing up an estimate
- appreciate the process of tendering, evaluating a bid and contracting
- understand the possible problems that can be introduced by the contract and plan to deal with these in a positive way.

# 2.1 *ORGANIZING PROJECTS*

This section describes how projects can be organized and looks at the production of work, product and cost breakdown structures as initial planning activities.

We begin by looking at the initial steps in actual project work: determining exactly what must be done and how much it will *really* cost to do it. You should not assume that these activities are done *once* at the beginning of a project, documented and then 'carved in tablets of stone'. Projects *do* require that an initial plan and estimate be prepared. But they also require that all *changes* be incorporated into plans and estimated, as you will learn in Chapter 5. And as the project progresses from its early stages towards completion, it may be necessary more than once to re-plan and re-estimate the project or parts of it on the basis of newly acquired information, changing client requirements or a changing project environment.

Planning will be discussed in much greater detail in Chapter 3. While you need to study first this chapter and then Chapter 3, you should always bear in mind that the processes and tasks described in both units are related to each other and are often carried out in parallel with each other. In real life a project manager might find him- or herself moving between doing a work breakdown structure, some scheduling, a product breakdown structure, team building (discussed in Chapter 4) and other tasks.

## 2.1.1 How projects can be organized

There are many ways to organize projects.

- They can be done entirely within an organization: one group can be deputed to carry out the project on behalf of the whole organization, a division or a department – **in-house projects**.

- Parts of the project work can be put to **tender** for bidding. Other organizations interested in taking on the work will prepare an **estimate** and use it to develop a **bid** which they will submit (they are referred to as **bidders**), with the successful bidder making a **contract** with the **client** organization. In other words, the successful bidder becomes a **contractor**.

- All the project work can be put to tender and contracted for. The contractor can do all of the project work, or can divide it and let parts be done by **subcontractors**.

- Part or all of a project can be tendered for by **consortia** of organizations (this is particularly likely in cases such as the Channel Tunnel which require such large amounts of cash and other resources that a single contractor cannot finance them by itself, or like the London Ambulance Service (LAS) case study you met in Chapter 1 which require the bringing together of a number of specialisms).

We need to make a distinction between contracting and subcontracting on the one hand and putting together a consortium of companies that will bid for a contract on the other. The biggest difference is in the process of putting together a bid or a tender – the intending contractor may put subsets of work out for formal tender by potential subcontractors before, during or after making its own bid to the client, or even after the bid has been accepted and a contract drawn up. A consortium initially comes together in a more informal way, as interested organizations seek each other out and determine a strategy for bidding. A consortium will also choose an 'umbrella' name for itself and develop a more formal organization. The Channel Tunnel is an example of a project that involved a consortium *and* used 'traditional' contractual arrangements. A prime consideration in either case is *where the responsibility lies* – with the lead contractor or in shared responsibility.

Where parts or all of a project are to be put to tender, the organization wishing to do the project will need to specify in some detail the work to be done. Specifying the work in some detail will give the organization and the project manager some idea of how the work can be split up into packages which can be put to tender for contracts and will be used by a bidder to make an estimate and put in a bid. It would be unusual for the organization wishing to sponsor the project to undertake a detailed estimate, although it may wish to make a rough estimate in order to judge the merits of various bids (an exception is the construction industry where it is the norm to prepare detailed estimates using 'blue-book' methods – described in Section 2.3.2).

We will discuss the practice of contracting in Section 2.5. In the meantime, we will describe the estimating process as though it were for an in-house project. You should bear in mind as you read that it is a potential contractor who would do the detailed estimating for a package of work in order to draw up and submit a bid. The potential contractor may also undertake further definition of the work to be done (down to the detailed level) either in order to plan and estimate it or to pass on a subset of the work for tendering by a potential subcontractor.

## ACTIVITY 2.1

Recall the case study of the London Ambulance Service described in Chapter 1 Section 1.5. Draw a rough diagram showing how the project was organized in terms of client and contracting consortium. What failure of project organization do you feel strongly contributed to the eventual failure of the project?

## DISCUSSION

The fact that no lead firm within the consortium was ever identified and legally contracted to be responsible for project management is likely to be a major factor. Systems Options were assumed to be the lead contractor but never really took on the role. (See Figure 2.1 overleaf.)

# Large projects: how to break them up and why

Some objectives are simply too uncertain of success for one project to be defined to meet that objective. Typically, these would be longer-term objectives that depend on, for example, the development or even discovery of new technologies or materials. In this case the long-term, uncertain objective needs to be realized in a **programme** of work that seeks to progress towards it by means of projects phased to develop the technology over a long time. To develop something totally new or significantly different from all that has preceded it, one or more projects are specified at the beginning to explore the feasibility of a technology. Subsequent projects follow in order to develop the technology to the state where a prototype of the main objective is possible. If the prototype (there may be several) is successful, then a design and finally a product may emerge. Each stage of such a programme will constitute a separate project. In the beginning, only the initial exploratory projects will be closely specified, since further development will depend on the outcome of the exploration of technical possibilities. This incremental way of proceeding is useful when technical risk and uncertainty are very high: it limits expenditure to that which is financially prudent at the time, establishing a basis of technological or marketing exploration for future action and deferring further specific planning until the degree of uncertainty is reduced considerably.

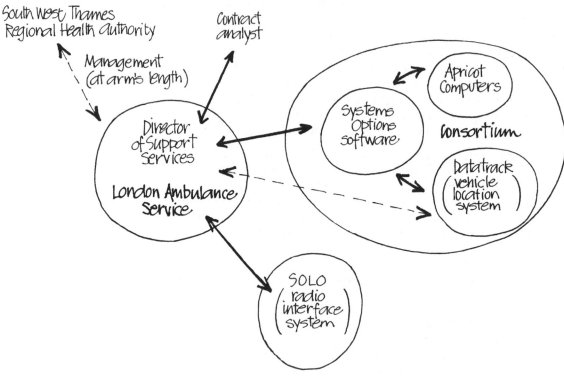

**FIGURE 2.1**   The contractual structures of the LAS project

## EXAMPLE 2.1

A good example of a programme of work is the development of fixed-wing vertical take-off and landing jet aircraft. The result was the successful Harrier 'jump jet', but the programme began about two decades earlier, with a project exploring the control of vertical take-off and landing in a test-harness referred to lovingly as the 'Flying Bedstead'. Later projects that grew out of the Flying Bedstead explored what was required to allow a fixed-wing aircraft hovering, lifting or descending vertically to change to travelling forward horizontally. Over the years the technology, techniques and design were refined until it was possible to build and test a prototype aircraft, and finally to announce the design, take orders and build the Harrier. Each phase of this programme of development contained one or more projects which had proper schedules and budgets, while the overall programme tended to 'develop' as the projects successfully produced answers to key questions in the effort to find out whether such an aircraft was feasible, and if it was, what design parameters were necessary for it to work satisfactorily.

Suppose that one of the early exploratory projects in developing the Harrier had shown that the overall objective – a fixed-wing vertical take-off and landing jet aircraft – was unfeasible for some reason, such as the likely cost of the final product far exceeding what the market could afford to pay. When this becomes known, management can cease continuing this development and use the financial and other resources freed thereby to do other things of importance to the organization.

There are other reasons for breaking up a large project or objective into a programme of smaller ones. One reason might be that an appraisal of the financial situation in an organization will show that even if the whole of a large project cannot be achieved at once, benefit can be gained by taking a phased approach to the work. A smaller project, which can quickly achieve part of the objective may be worth doing now, while further work is delayed until the financial situation improves. It is also possible that an organization will wish to gain experience with a particular part before proceeding with the rest, or feel it desirable to minimize the inevitable disruption to working that the change inherent in a project always brings with it.

## ACTIVITY 2.2

You work for UNICEF, which has an objective to develop a cheap, palatable children's drink with a high vitamin and mineral content for use as a dietary supplement in areas where the diet most children receive is deemed inadequate. A lot is currently known about vitamins and minerals at a biochemical level, but production tends to be expensive. Would you proceed with a closely specified project, or a series of phased projects? Justify your choice.

## DISCUSSION

While there is no one correct answer to this question, the best solution may be to use a phased programme of development. It will be necessary first to explore the technology of vitamin and mineral supplement manufacture in order to identify ways of reducing production costs very considerably. It will be necessary to explore what constitutes palatability amongst children in many different cultures, and what problems of packaging, transport and storage exist in different climates and places. Once these have been identified, it should be possible to institute a project to set up a production facility and begin production. You may have had a different answer, but if you said a single project would be an appropriate strategy in this situation, we would suggest that the degree of uncertainty is too high to specify the route to the objective clearly enough.

Once the bounds of a project are decided, once its objectives become clear and resources are available, work can begin to escalate. This may mean appointing a project manager if one is not already in post, settling the estimates, contracting work as deemed necessary or suitable (Chapter 2), planning (Chapter 3) and assembling a team (Chapter 4). We shall now describe what an estimate is and what needs to happen to set estimating, planning and contracting in motion.

## What is an estimate?

An estimate for a project is a document that ends with a sum – almost always expressed in monetary units such as pounds, dollars, yen, Deutschmarks, guilders or francs – of costs for materials, labour, acquiring capital assets, overheads, etc. If the estimate is part of a bid or tender it will also include an element of profit, though this may not be labelled as such. An estimate is not used solely for the purposes of predicting how much a project will cost; it has a central role to play in **budgeting** and controlling costs. Since not all costs will be known at the outset of a project, the process of estimating requires methods of determining likely costs where some uncertainty exists. The estimator needs to look more closely at the risks involved in the project and what can be done about them as they often have cost implications. The estimator also needs to determine what tasks are to be done and the space, raw materials, supplies, equipment and manufactured components and subassemblies required. He or she then needs to know how long tasks are likely to take and in what order they can be done to optimize the resource needs of the project, to achieve a balance between the amount of resource required and the effective use of it. Since we cannot discuss everything mentioned here within this chapter, the problems of developing a project schedule (when tasks will be done, what their order should be, and when resources are required and in what amounts) will be covered in Chapter 3. Once all this is known, an estimate for the project can be developed.

# 2.1.2   Preparatory work

You cannot estimate accurately how much a project, or part of a project, will cost to implement until you know what it involves.

In Chapter 1 we discussed using an iterative cycle to find objectives and then identify strategies to meet those objectives. The strategies were the *hows* at each level in this process. At the lowest levels, these *hows* translate into items of work to be done by an individual, a team or a subcontractor. It is sometimes difficult to know where to stop this cycle.

How do we know when to stop? How do we identify everything that needs to be done, omitting nothing, and yet not go too far? We've chosen Example 2.2 deliberately because it brings up some points to remember.

- What appears to be a description of work to be carried out at one level can be broken down into finer detail, forming a hierarchy of descriptions of what is to be done ranging from the very general to the highly detailed.

- At some levels, work on a project of any significant amount can be assigned to another organization, group or individual (the contractor, on to the subcontractor and finally to the individual worker).

- The most likely point at which to contract work to a contractor, subcontractor, team of people or individual worker, depending upon the level of description, is the point where the work to be done can be described so that it forms clearly delineated subcategories.

- There are as many ways of dividing up the work and determining who is to do it and how as there are projects.

## EXAMPLE 2.2

If a high-level goal is 'a new organizational headquarters' then a *how* at that
level is: 'acquire a site and build a new building'. But there is more to it than
that. If 'acquire a site' becomes a goal at the next level down we then have to
consider how to bring this about: locate a site, determine whether planning
permission would be forthcoming and negotiate for its purchase with its
present owner. Putting a building up on the site would involve commissioning
an architect, getting a building loan, contracting for the work to be done with a
building contractor, monitoring the construction, paying for the building and
moving into it. Each of these *hows* can be broken down further. A building
contractor is likely to subcontract work to specialists: the plumbing to a firm of
plumbing contractors, the electrical supply to a firm of electrical contractors,
and so on. If the builder plans to undertake all the less specialized work, then
there may be concreting to be done, bricklaying, rough and finish carpentry,
glazing, tiling, flooring and so on. Bricklaying requires someone to work out
how many bricks are needed and how long it will take bricklayers to lay those
bricks in a particular configuration dictated by the design of the building. We
could take this further and describe the delivery of the bricks, their movements
on the building site before laying, the mixing of mortar and the detailed
actions of bricklaying (pick up a brick in one hand, use the trowel to form a
'sausage' of mortar, lift the mortar using the trowel and 'butter' it onto the
brick…).

### Produce the work breakdown structure

What we have just described is a **work** (sometimes called an **activity**) **breakdown
structure** (WBS). The WBS is basic to the management of the project. Estimates and
risk assessments are based on the WBS. Cost control and progress monitoring
(described in Chapter 5) will usually be organized to reflect the project's split into
packages of work. As the WBS provides the basic framework for the organization
and control of work, it is worth spending some time to achieve as good a structure
for the work breakdown as possible. More will be said in Section 2.1.3 about how to
produce one.

### Draw up a statement of work

In order to make an estimate of costs, resources and times required to complete a
package of work, it is first necessary to use the WBS to prepare a **statement of
work** (SOW) for each package, specifying the work to be done by an individual or
small team. This will be described further in Section 2.1.4.

### Produce the product breakdown structure

As well as incurring the costs of work to be done, many projects involve the
acquisition of complex assets such as a mainframe computer system or hardware
and machinery, and these too will need to be estimated. In some cases these
computer systems or systems of machinery are of the 'turnkey' variety: one supplier
supplies the entire package at a single quoted price. Even if your project happens to
be the creation of such a turnkey system, your organization needs to be able to
estimate how much it will cost, what components *you* need to acquire to build the

system, and so on. Many organizations prefer to assemble a customized package of components, perhaps drawing different components from different vendors and manufacturers. In these cases, it will be necessary to produce a **product breakdown structure**: the hierarchically arranged list of components that allows the project manager eventually to estimate the cost of the 'product'. An example appears in Section 2.1.5.

*Produce the cost breakdown structure*

The **cost breakdown structure** draws on the work and product breakdown structures to produce a breakdown of project costs. This breakdown in turn will be the main source for preparing the formal document setting out the estimate for the project. An example of a cost breakdown structure appears in Section 2.1.6.

### SAQ 2.1

List the four documents that constitute the preliminary work for estimating and planning.

## 2.1.3   Work breakdown structure

To carry out a work breakdown, the work on a project is, as we have stated, specified in ever finer detail until, at the lowest level of this decomposition, a **task list** emerges, equivalent to the statement of work that describes in detail the work one individual or a very small team (two or three people) will carry out. This is a *top-down approach* to the enumeration of tasks. When the structure of the resulting list is well organized, it has the added advantage that it allows the work to be divided into work packages among different teams, contractors or departments. Rook (1991) defines the work breakdown structure as:

> … a product-oriented task hierarchy of all the work to be performed to accomplish the project contractual objectives. The products may be software, hardware, documents, tests, reports, support services, or other quantified elements of the objectives…. Use of the term 'product-oriented' does *not* mean … that the WBS should follow a structural decomposition of the functions of the delivered product [unless this is] appropriate.

(Chapter 27, p. 20)

There are some guidelines to bear in mind when preparing a work breakdown.

- The split of work into major 'packages' should be logical and compatible with splits to be used for cost control and reporting.
- It should be possible to test whether a 'package' of work is complete.
- At the very lowest level, the work elements should be well-defined tasks for an individual to perform within a reasonable period of time.

In practice it may be impossible to meet these guidelines perfectly, so the project manager will have to weigh up the possibilities and decide which split seems to fit the guidelines best.

Any changes to the higher levels in a WBS need to be agreed and then protected from further alterations early in the project planning stage. This allows the individual workers, teams or departments (or the contractors or subcontractors) to use them when preparing the input to the estimates and schedules for the project plans. It may not be possible to complete the lower levels until later in the project when more detailed information is available.

Assume we are planning to dig a well and install a wind-powered pump in a remote village in an undeveloped area of Africa. We have already done a hydrological survey and located the site. Figure 2.2 shows the division of the project into major categories, each with an identifying number.

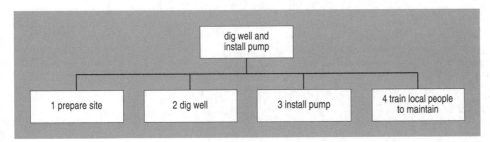

**FIGURE 2.2**
Beginning a work breakdown structure: the top-level divisions

Further breakdown might proceed as shown in Figure 2.3, where first of the top-level divisions has been subdivided to form a package of work. The numbering within each of these packages as 1.1, 1.2, 1.3, etc. identifies them as subdivisions of the first top-level element. In a large project these subdivisions may themselves constitute packages.

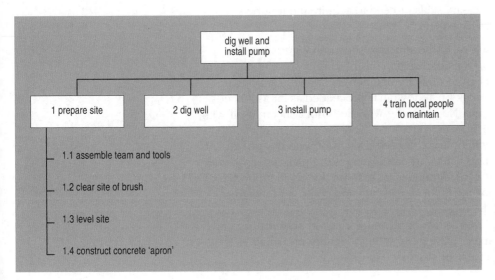

**FIGURE 2.3**
The work breakdown structure: expansion of the site preparation work into packages

In the example we have chosen, we will assume we are using local labour rather than experienced contractors who know exactly how to construct a concrete 'apron' for the well, so we must carry the breakdown a bit further, as shown in Figure 2.4 to include some training. In other contexts, we would probably assume that a local building contractor had experience with concrete mixing and pouring and with form-making, and that we needn't specify the work in such detail that it amounted to 'how to' instructions.

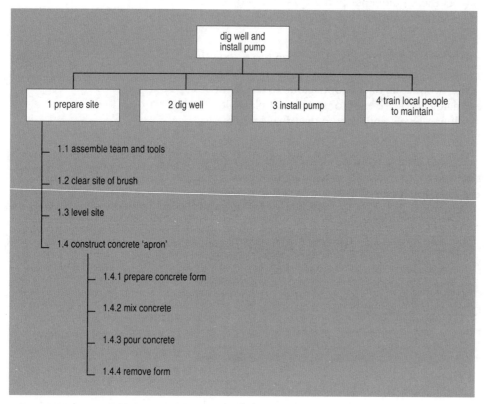

**FIGURE 2.4**  Expansion of a package into tasks

Our example shows that developing a WBS depends upon a certain amount of knowledge acquired beforehand: of the skills, tools and materials involved and whether the workers have the necessary skills or need to acquire them or be supervised by someone who does have them.

You will notice that, at the lowest level of the structure shown in Figure 2.4 (for example 'prepare concrete form') each task list item has become a specific statement of the task to be done, and that it can be done by one person or a very small team. This indicates that the process of work breakdown has proceeded as far as it needs to down this 'branch' of the structure. Note that the WBS does not concern itself with the order in which tasks are done, how they are done, how long they might take, who might do them or how many people are needed. Details of who will do the work and any scheduling constraints can be inserted later, as the planning proceeds. The WBS is simply a structured way of identifying tasks to be done and grouping those so that the divisions are convenient for monitoring and control. In digging a well, it is likely that the hole will be dug before the concrete 'apron' is constructed, but the WBS doesn't tell us that. (That aspect of planning is called **scheduling** and will be discussed in detail in Chapter 3. Using the WBS to identify measurable milestones and quality criteria will also be discussed in Chapter 3.)

*Numbering systems*

The structure of the work breakdown exercise can be preserved in a numbering system which can provide a convenient way of classifying and organizing documents developed from the WBS. We have used one common system which is to number each of the top-level components as 1, 2, 3 and so on. All items appearing in the next level below are numbered 1.1, 1.2, 1.3 and so on. Items at the third level are numbered 1.3.1, 1.3.2, 1.3.3 and so on.

A variant is to number the top level 100, 200, 300 and so on, the next level under 100 as 110, 120, 130, etc. and the next level under 110 as 111, 112, 113. The important point is to number so that you can reconstruct the hierarchy from the numbering system, and also insert new components in their proper places as they are thought of. Such a hierarchical scheme allows you to develop an index of tasks labelled with numbers which can be used as cross-references. This will be useful in relating documents to each other, in controlling paperwork and in costing and scheduling activities.

Although the levels in a WBS are most commonly referred to by a number, sometimes meaningful names are attached to them. For example, the lowest level at which responsibility for cost control is delegated is sometimes called the **cost account level**, and the level immediately below it is called the **work package level**.

The hierarchy we have described in Figures 2.2, 2.3 and 2.4 begins the work breakdown by making the top-level major division a functional one. Such an approach is useful where different trades will be brought in as contractors (such as a general builder to carry out civil work, an electrical contractor to carry out electrical work, and so on). Each contractor can be given a list of his or her tasks. But this is not the only possible breakdown. In the case of the well, it is as valid to divide work into preliminary tasks (what must be done *before* well-digging is started), concrete-based tasks (making the concrete lining rings, the apron forms, etc.) and installation tasks (testing the pump and the quality of the water and training those who will maintain the equipment). Another possibility is to divide work according to which organization will carry it out: construction crew, the charity's own personnel, the hydrological engineer's personnel and any equipment supplier's personnel.

---

### ACTIVITY 2.3

Produce a WBS of no more than three levels for setting up a fully-furnished new office in office-space rented by your firm in another town. Assume that you will need to change such items as the lighting, wiring and partition walls to suit your needs, but plumbing and heating are satisfactory as they are.

### DISCUSSION

Our answer to this activity appears in Figure 2.5. Your answer may differ. No WBS is the only possible one. The important point is to establish from the top downwards a hierarchy of work and tasks in an organized fashion.

---

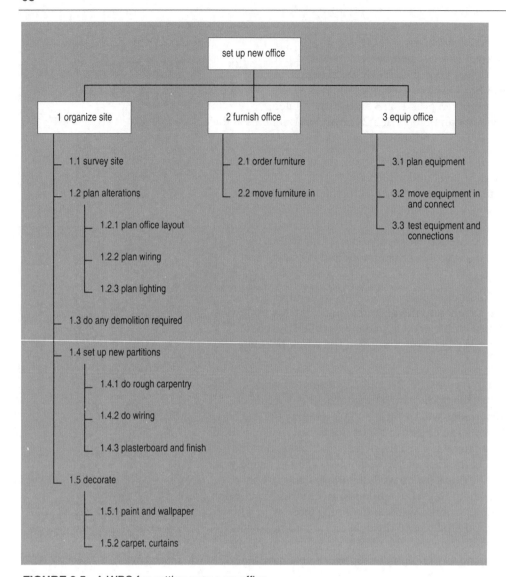

**FIGURE 2.5**  A WBS for setting up a new office

A WBS can develop in a number of possible ways. (You will see an example of this in Chapter 3.) You may decide to divide the work according to specialisms such as civil, electrical, mechanical, or according to broad phases such as clearing, digging and excavation, stabilization and equipment installation, or in some other way. Although no one way is invariably 'right', this does not mean that you can treat the WBS as a dynamic document. Once you have decided on your high-level breakdown and proceeded beyond that, it becomes very difficult to make substantial changes. It may be wise to sketch some alternative WBSs down a few levels, then determine what appears to be the best breakdown for this project before committing yourself to doing any detailed work.

SAQ 2.2

What is the main purpose of a WBS?

# 2.1.4 Work packages and statements of work

Work packages (WPs) are defined in BS 6046 Part 1 (1984) as:

> … related products and functions brought together … [to form] parcels of work which can be individually planned, resourced and costed. These normally represent the smallest entities to carry costs at the total project level, although further breakdowns may be possible depending upon each participating organization's own cost collection and control systems. WP costs (estimates and actuals) can then be used, firstly to produce a project budget and secondly to monitor performance against this. They are not restricted by calendar date boundaries or by project phases. Such attempts at restriction may result in unnecessary re-planning. Nor is it necessary to restrict a WP to a single area of responsibility.
>
> (p. 26)

The WP document specifies the work to be done for each package described in the work breakdown structure. *Such a document should specify exactly what is to be delivered when the package has been completed* (**deliverables**). Deliverables will include not just identifiable hardware to be delivered, but also less tangible elements such as tests to be performed, software to be written, or training to be given. In other words the document specifies *all* the items to be delivered. A **work package definition** such as the one shown in Figure 2.6 overleaf defines a work package, as determined from the WBS, in terms of what is to be done, who is responsible, start and completion dates, deliverables and milestones for the package. When it is completed to a sufficient level of detail it can be signed by the person who will be responsible for ensuring that the work it describes is executed.

The work packages will be broken down further, often by the person responsible for the package, to produce *statements of work* (SOWs) for each work element. This can be done either at the planning stage or as the need arises during project execution. These lower-level SOWs can be given to individual members of a project team to perform. A SOW is similar to the work package definition document shown in Figure 2.6. In addition to the work to be done, it lists the inputs expected from elsewhere, the deliverables to be produced, the time allowed, the expected start and finish dates and the relationship to other tasks. There are areas on the form for signatures of the person to whom the work is assigned and the person who issued the statement.

The work package definitions for the project as a whole and for subcontracted packages will be central to the contracts drawn up between a client and a contractor and between the main contractor and the subcontractors, so it is important to be able to specify work to be done as unambiguously as possible. These documents should be as 'watertight' as any legal document. This will create a point from which change can be effectively managed. This precision is recommended even for projects carried out within the scope of a single organization so that the 'client' and the 'contractor', and the leader or manager and worker know exactly what has been agreed.

How to determine task start and finish dates and dependencies is discussed in Chapter 3. Assigning people to a job is discussed in Chapter 4.

---

**WORLDWIDE NETWORKS LONDON**                    ISSUE 1

**MAJOR CHANGE PROJECT MANAGEMENT**              DATE: DEC 1992

**NATIONAL CODE CHANGE WORK PACKAGE AGREEMENT**

| WP TITLE: EXCHANGE SYSTEMS TXE4 | WP NO: |
|---|---|

WP DESCRIPTION:

To manage and co-ordinate the rollout of a package of activities in accordance with NCC NCR's thus ensuring TXE data requirements are implemented for NCC within time, cost and quality parameters.

| WP MANAGER: Dave Colloff | TEL: 071 587 7481 | FAX: 071 820 1839 |
|---|---|---|

| START DATE: 1 January 1993 | COMPLETION DATE: 16 May 1995 |
|---|---|

DELIVERABLES:

Space capacity in network, dial code table file, OPX file implementation, cyclic store changes, MCU data changes.

MILESTONES:

| | |
|---|---|
| Dial Codes Loaded | February 1994 |
| Dual Access Available | April 1994 |
| Parallel Running | August 1994 |
| Phone Day | 16 April 1995 |

WORK PACKAGE ACCEPTANCE

As nominated Work Package Manager your signature is requested to indicate that you formally accept responsibility for completing this Work Package, within time, cost and quality parameters.

If for any reason there is a requirement to change the scope of the work package, the change will be agreed with you before the package is reissued and forwarded for signature.

Activity sheets will be issued in association with this work package and will require individual acceptance and completion sign-off.

I accept the above work package.

NAME: _____          SIGNATURE: _____
                Work Package Manager          DATE: _____

**FIGURE 2.6**   A work package definition document

Statements of work should also specify the standard(s) to which work is to be performed, if any are applicable. While it is difficult to suggest a standard for something such as a purchase order, if the purchasing agent were not very experienced, the statement of work might specify that the purchase order needs to be checked for completeness against the product breakdown structure by a more senior purchasing agent.

Activities described in Chapter 3, for example working out the optimum level of resources and inputs to minimize cost without jeopardizing a schedule ('resource smoothing'), will affect estimates. An estimate can't be considered firm until the project manager is sure that extra resources or time won't be required. Estimating is an iterative process of gathering more and more cost information and *simultaneously* developing plans so that the final result is a project plan *and* as accurate a costing as possible. (Since you will not study details of planning until Chapter 3, any activities in this chapter will be in determining rough or 'first-cut' estimates.)

WP definitions and statements of work are important tools for ensuring the quality of the project, since it is the accumulation of deliverables specified in these documents that will be judged by the client. Thus quality measures can be specified and the deliverable checked against them *for every item of work* in the project.

It is commonly agreed that the best way to specify what work is to be done is to specify what shall be delivered. This may be fairly straightforward for a tangible item such as a building or a piece of equipment, but it is not so easy for less tangible items such as any tests to be performed. Considerable effort may have to be devoted to specifying precisely what is to be delivered. This is in the interests of both the client and the contractor. At the lowest level it is a form of contract between an individual project team member and the team's manager.

---

## EXAMPLE 2.3  Loosely specified work

A contractor was given a requirement to: 'allocate personnel on a regular basis to provide input data and participate in formal hazard and operability studies'. This requirement was rejected by the contractor as a part of the statement of work because he was unable to quantify the amount of effort that would be involved, and this meant that he would be unable to make the estimates.

---

## ACTIVITY 2.4

How could the requirement in Example 2.3 be re-specified so that it was more easily quantifiable?

## DISCUSSION

One way would be to state how many people of what job or skill categories should be assigned to this duty. Additionally, you could try to determine how many studies are likely to be needed and how long each might take. Lastly, it might be possible to estimate the amount of input data (even knowing the *kind* of data needed could be helpful here). You may have thought of other ways.

---

A SOW form normally contains a section called *inputs*. In preparing estimates you need to know what supplies, materials, purchased components and manufactured parts will be required. It can be helpful to use the WBS to prepare cross-referred lists of such inputs: you can prepare for each task a list of such likely inputs. When the inputs are well specified they can be added to the SOW form and used to draw up the cost breakdown structure described in Section 2.1.6. The cost breakdown structure in turn can be used to draw up purchasing instructions or requisition forms when the time comes. (A preliminary list can provide a basis for contacting potential suppliers to get technical, price and delivery information.)

**SAQ 2.3**

What are the main purposes of the work package definition and the statement of work?

# 2.1.5  The product breakdown structure

The product breakdown structure is a tool for dealing with complexes of machinery, equipment and software which consist of components that need to be estimated separately. The breakdown structure provides a way of identifying the components. If components can be purchased from different vendors or manufacturers, the product breakdown structure can also be used to identify 'best buys'. The product breakdown structure can also be used as an alternative to the work breakdown structure. (The project management methodology PRINCE uses the product breakdown structure in this way.)

A computer system provides a good example of a complex product that can be purchased as a turnkey system or broken down into its components and separately estimated. A computer system consists of the following major components:

> a central processing unit
>
> a number of peripheral data storage devices
>
> a number of peripheral input and output devices
>
> the interconnections for these parts
>
> basic software.

It may also include a data communications network; for the purposes of this example we will assume it does.

Each of these major components, except the first, can be broken down into another level of components. For example, the peripheral data storage devices (for a mainframe or large server-based system) can be broken down into:

> magnetic tape drives
>
> magnetic disk drives
>
> a mass storage subsystem.

A further step would be to specify which model(s) were required. For example, disk drive models (even if from the same manufacturer) have different characteristics: they may be fixed or movable head, the disk packs may be removable or permanently mounted, and data capacities and access speeds may differ. Once the models have been determined and someone has estimated the storage capacities (e.g. capacity for data always required on line and capacity for data held on media that can be removed from the system) of each type required for this hypothetical computer system, numbers can be applied to these components. (Normally you can only buy a tape drive, not the subcomponents of a tape drive.) At this point it may be possible to say that 16 Model X tape drives are needed.

To carry the breakdown further, we may need to look at the basic software. This breaks down into:

> operating system
>
> application support systems software which in turn consists of
>> database support
>>
>> telecommunication support
>>
>> system management support software
>>
>> compilers
>>
>> interface support software, etc.
>
> applications software consisting of
>> database query language
>>
>> electronic mail
>>
>> file transfer applications, etc.

The communications network can consist of:

> cable and conduits
>
> communications controllers
>
> network support software
>
> data terminals.

The examples of communications controllers and network support software show that, as with the work breakdown structure, there is often more than one way in which to carry out the breakdown. If some of the network support software is contained within the communications controllers, then that network support software could be considered a subcomponent of the category 'communications controller'. However, it is also possible to consider the component 'network support software' as entirely separate from the communications controllers, as we have done in the list above.

As with the work breakdown structure, the product breakdown structure can be described as a hierarchy of components and subcomponents, down to the level of what is purchasable. The structure can be organized using a numbering system which can in turn be used to establish cross-references to manufacturers' literature, specifications and price sheets.

## ACTIVITY 2.5

You are in charge of planning and setting up an office in another town. Your manager thinks of an office as a king of product; all she wants to see is the finished product waiting for people to move in. Assume the office will house up to eight people who will be primarily desk workers using the telephone and facsimile (fax) to communicate with customers and personal computers networked to the head office to communicate with that office. Sketch a product breakdown structure of this office, with up to three levels in it. Take no more than two minutes for this.

## DISCUSSION

Our answer appears in Figure 2.7. Yours may be somewhat different in shape but should contain the main products.

Note that the breakdown's hierarchical nature can be reconstructed from the numbering system used. Elements in the product breakdown structure can be cross-referred to such things as manufacturers' catalogues and price lists (in this example it could be to a floor plan).

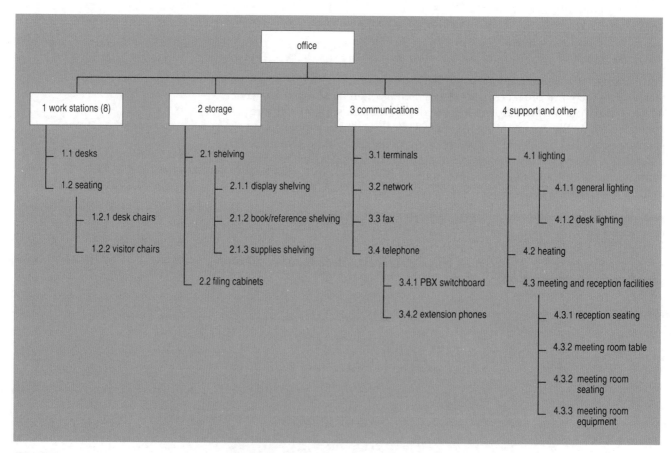

**FIGURE 2.7**  A product breakdown structure for an office

## SAQ 2.4

What is the main purpose of a product breakdown structure?

# 2.1.6  Cost breakdown structure

The cost breakdown structure, showing details of all the cost categories for a project, can only be completed when the work breakdown structure and product breakdown structure (if any) plus the input parts of statements of work are as complete as possible (though the process of assembling information can begin as soon as some of the WBS is known). The cost breakdown structure is a tool for identifying in one document *all* cost categories and for arranging them to suit the purposes of the project. Thus the costs of labour and the inputs required for that labour will be cross-referred to the WBS and its related statements of work, while capital cost categories will, in part, be related to any product breakdown structure, together with the inclusion of other capital and revenue costs *not* directly associated with either the labour or with any product. For example, renting office space would appear on the feasibility document but would not normally appear as part of a product breakdown structure, and it would appear on a WBS or a statement of work in the form of, say, 'acquire office space' or 'negotiate lease agreement'.

The cost breakdown structure will include information garnered from:

the WBS, work package definitions and statements of work

product breakdown structures

capital and revenue costs identified in the cost–benefit analyses and feasibility study documents.

Other cost items may also be present that were not thought of when the feasibility study and cost–benefit analysis were done; these need to be included in the cost breakdown structure. The organization of the hierarchy for cost breakdown may also differ significantly from both the WBS and any product breakdown structure; it will more closely resemble the categories used by an organization's accountants. Likely categories are: labour costs (direct and indirect), capital acquisition costs (which will include products identified and costed using the product breakdown structures), expenses, overheads and other categories.

---

### ACTIVITY 2.6

Use the WBS for setting up an office that appears in Figure 2.5 (page 98) and prepare a cost breakdown structure, assuming that *every item* for an office has to be acquired.

### DISCUSSION

Our answer appears in Figure 2.8 overleaf. Again, your answer may differ either in some details or in the organization of the structure.

---

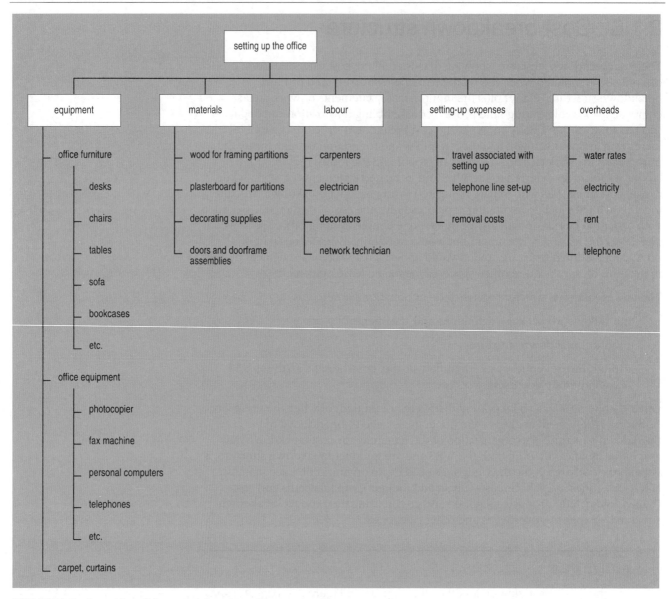

**FIGURE 2.8** A cost breakdown structure for setting up an office

## 2.1.7 Controlling documents

As we have seen, the number of documents associated with even this early stage of a project proliferates rapidly. The project manager and many others will need to be able to refer to the documents frequently as more information is known and as the project develops and changes. At this stage, however, in order to prepare a high-quality estimate the estimator (and the planner, as you will see in Chapter 3) needs to be able to link items on one document to items on other documents. Hence cross-references of items on the product breakdown structure, the work breakdown structure and the cost breakdown structure will prove very useful when cost items are grouped and categorized and the sums are done for each category. Note how the numbering systems we have advocated help establish simple links from one kind of document to another.

While the amount of documentation, cross-referring and indexing that is required in undertaking this 'ground work' for estimating may seem excessive at so early a stage in the project's life, it has important implications for achieving *quality*. The documents produced are early deliverables for the project, and reviewing their contents will help to establish a firm basis for estimating, planning and eventually for financial, scheduling and quality assurance controls and change controls for the remainder of the project work.

### SAQ 2.5

What is the main function of the cost breakdown structure?

## 2.1.8  Summary

There are many ways to organize projects: wholly in-house, partly in-house and partly contracted out, entirely contracted out. Parts can be subcontracted or a contract can be given to a consortium of organizations where financial or other resource constraints can only be met by a group of organizations. Where the objective is uncertain of achievement, a project may involve only initial explorations of the technology or other factors, with subsequent projects to develop from these initial findings.

The estimate is the document showing the costs of carrying out a project; it plays a central role in budgeting and cost control. To prepare an estimate it is necessary to prepare a work breakdown structure (WBS), a product breakdown structure, statements of work and deliverables and a cost breakdown structure. The WBS is a hierarchical, top-down view of the work to be carried out. A work package definition describes work to be done by a group or team of people as defined in the WBS, and a statement of work describes work that can be done by one person. Both are important in achieving quality. A product breakdown structure is a tool for dealing with complex, multi-component machinery or equipment. A cost breakdown structure can be assembled once other information from the WBS, statements of work and product breakdown structure are available. It assigns the costs to the categories used by an organization's accountants bringing together for example all the labour content of an estimate. A cross-reference helps to control documentation. If these documents are lacking, the project will be very difficult to keep under control.

Having studied this section you should be able to:

- describe in your own words how projects can be organized

- give reasons why it may be better to break a large project down into smaller projects

- state two ways in which large projects can be broken down into smaller projects and state a benefit for each

- give a brief definition of an estimate

- produce a work breakdown structure for a simple project

- produce a product breakdown structure for a simple 'product'

- produce a cost breakdown structure for a simple project

- explain why cross-referring these documents is important

- explain why document control is required.

# 2.2  *RISK*

This section is about the analysis and management of risks associated with a project.

It has sometimes been claimed that all project management is risk management. The aim of the project manager is to combat the variety of different hazards to which a project may be exposed.

Essentially there are two parts to this work:

- risk identification and analysis
- risk management

Risk identification and analysis means assessing the probability of risks occurring and their impact on the project. Risk management is what the project manager does to counteract or prepare for the risks.

" I DON'T SEE WHAT
COULD POSSIBLY
GO WRONG....."

## 2.2.1  Risk identification and analysis

We noted in Chapter 1 that risk is an inherent – and inevitable – characteristic of projects (though the degree of risk may vary widely) and we gave a definition: risk represents the *chance* of adverse consequences or loss occurring. That is a very general definition. How does one recognize a risk when planning and estimating a project? We want to be able to do more than identify general risks such as fire or flood! We want to know *what is risky about this particular project*, and at a later stage, *what is risky about this particular activity*. What we are seeking is a particular characteristic, circumstance or feature of this project that could potentially have an adverse effect on important deliverables or, worse, on the whole project. What risks are there, and what is the likelihood that they will come to pass? We say that a project is *sensitive* to a risk when, if the risk occurs, it can jeopardize a key aspect.

---

### EXAMPLE 2.4

A key employee with wide access to restricted and privileged information about a project to develop a new product becomes disgruntled, leaves her employer and takes the knowledge she has acquired to a new employer – the firm's main rival. This has now jeopardized the project to develop the new product, since it becomes highly likely that the rival firm will develop a competing product very quickly. The project was *sensitive* to the risk of specialist knowledge becoming available to a rival firm.

---

Only when we have identified risks and have an idea of their likelihood can we plan what to do about them, and gauge their impact on project estimates, budgets and schedules.

Risks related to deficient deliverables can lead to:

- unmet marketing claims, complaints, loss of image or reputation, loss of market
- legal claims
- liability
- waste of human and financial resources
- compromises to health and safety
- problems with availability and delivery
- loss of customer confidence.

## Risk assessment

We discussed risk at the strategic level in Chapter 1. At this stage the project manager has to make a careful identification and analysis of specific risks in order to make 'tactical' plans that affect the shape of detailed project plans and estimates. The process of **risk assessment** is more than simply identifying specific risks. It means obtaining a clear definition of risks, including how important the risk is to the project – what the severity of its occurrence would be, its sensitivity – and the likelihood of that risk occurring. Risk assessment:

- identifies risks
- analyses these in terms of their impact on performance, cost, schedule and quality
- estimates the probability of the risk occurring during the execution of the project – the project's *exposure*

- prioritizes the risks according to exposure, effect and problems associated with compounding risks
- enables management to monitor risk factors and take action during the execution of the project.

Figure 2.9 shows how assessments of risk fit into the tactical planning of a project.

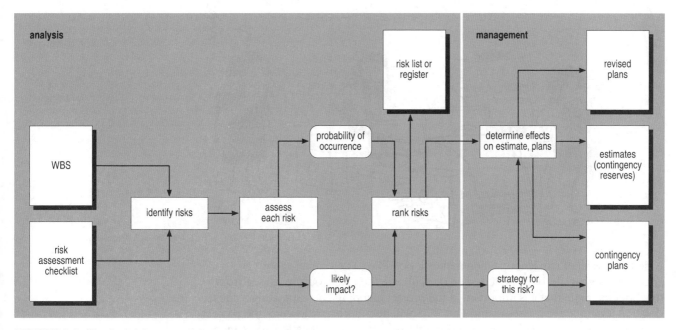

**FIGURE 2.9**  Tactical risk assessment and management

The technique illustrated in Figure 2.9 starts with an examination of the WBS using a checklist to help identify the risks. (Brainstorming is another means of identifying risks that might not appear on a checklist.) The next step is to assess each risk for its probability and likely impact on the project. The outcome will be a list or register of the risks ranked according to their significance. You can then decide how to manage the risks.

There are important psychological 'truisms' to bear in mind here. The scope of risk identified in an assessment will be in keeping with the scope and level of project definition used to identify risks. If a project manager asks, 'What can go wrong with this project?' thinking will be in terms of *the entire project*. Using our well-digging example, what could go wrong might be: no funding materializes, no tools are available, the people supposed to do the work don't do it, or the well, once dug, collapses. Small details that could jeopardize the whole project might be missed.

If the WBS forms the basis for risk assessment the questions asked would be of the form: 'What can go wrong with obtaining the tools for digging the well?' The planner is more likely to think in terms of: tools not being delivered to the site due to transport problems, not enough tools to go around, wrong tools delivered, the workers not knowing how to use the tools.

Once these potential risks are identified in detail, the project planner can decide what to do. If transport is key, someone can check that the roads are open or work out alternative routes; a vehicle in a reasonable state of repair, with a driver, can be made available at the time the tools need to be delivered; someone reliable can be asked to check that the tools to be sent are the right tools *before* they are loaded on the vehicle.

A detailed level of risk identification makes it possible to determine more specifically what can be done to lessen or eliminate the risk. You should see from this brief example that it is important at the project planning and estimating stage to develop a *detailed* risk assessment. The WBS will help: its breakdown of the project into work packages and elements is a good starting point for a detailed assessment of risks.

Another psychological 'truism' is that two minds are better than one (and three better than two, up to a number beyond which the debate would get too confused and too expensive). No one person can think of all the things that can possibly go wrong with more than the simplest project.

There are many kinds of risk. Many projects today are so complex that they will involve several kinds of risk. Different kinds of risk may require different kinds of risk assessment.

### Technical risk factors

Technical risk factors of a project often cover a very wide range. According to Chicken's (1994) survey of risk assessment practice, there is no universally accepted way of assessing risks and methods are often matters of opinion and experience. A system such as a project or a complex product may consist of a network of interacting components which may have non-linear and multidirectional or even unpredictable interactions. There are proposed techniques for analysing such multivariable systems, but the most common technique employed is to consult technical experts. Table 2.1 shows some methods employed for assessing technical risk.

We shall not discuss in any detail either statistical methods or computerized simulations. All these require knowledge and skill of a highly specialized nature which we do not have the space here to attempt to impart. However, if you are interested in learning about these further you could consult Chicken (1994) and Lindley (1985).

**TABLE 2.1** Some methods for assessing technical risks

| Method | Strengths | Weaknesses |
|---|---|---|
| Expert evidence, giving guidance to project personnel about risk | Simple to organize if an expert is available; usually the non-expert can understand the presentation of the evidence and accompanying guidance | What project team hears limited to one or two experts' opinions unless wider canvass is made; does not include systematic comparative analysis and may not improve decision-maker's understanding of significance of risk. |
| Systems analysis | Useful for identifying interacting factors involved and establishing their relative significance | Does not produce a quantitative comparison of the significance of various factors |
| Statistical methods, e.g. Bayesian inference or multivariate analysis | May give a good indication of possible outcomes in cases where data are inadequate; quantitative methods (multivariate analysis expresses the relationship between factors in mathematical terms) | Experts required to prepare data and use these methods; findings difficult to present to non-specialists; confidence in them low if analysis based on inadequate data |
| Computerized simulations, possibly based on an expert system | Good when all options and uncertainties have to be explored in detail and interaction between the various factors is well known | Confidence in this method yet to be established; only as good as the input data, simulation and the expert who provided the knowledge for the expert system; could give misleading results for novel proposals; reliable relevant quantitative data must be available |
| Soft systems analysis | Aids understanding of factors and relationships among factors | Does not normally quantify significance of relationships and interactions |
| Past experience (regression analysis) | Tries to predict future quantitative significance of factors from analysis of past experience | Only of value to the degree to which the project relates to past projects. |

Adapted from Chicken, 1994, pp. 79–81

Most risks can be assessed by identifying what kinds of risks may occur, rating their probability of occurring and their impact if they do, and then assessing the result of this data-gathering exercise. Used by experts in risk assessment, this technique is probably also the most accessible one for the project manager who is not an expert. We discuss the risk checklists that result from such an exercise below.

Stakeholders can give valuable assistance in carrying out a risk assessment. This can be a group effort organized by the project manager and including anyone having a significant stake in the outcome of the project. Other people who may have little or no stake in the project can usefully participate if they have experience of similar projects, are experts in particular technical or other subject areas, or are familiar with the risk assessment process. Working in a group this way, everyone will build an understanding of what risks exist.

We discussed in Chapter 1 how brainstorming and nominal group technique are used to determine organizational objectives and strategies and develop these into proposals. The same or similar techniques can be used to identify risks, and later to identify strategies for dealing with them. These are particularly useful in very novel projects or where pre-existing aids to risk identification and analysis don't exist. One possibility is to undertake a 'negative' brainstorming session: ask the question, 'How could we sabotage this aspect of the project?'

*Risk factor lists*

A number of aids to risk assessment exist in the form of risk factor lists. Some of these are part of proprietary systems of project management. Some have been drawn up by organizations as they have gained experience of projects. Some are simply the result of an experienced project manager keeping a log for each project of what went wrong, why it went wrong, and what was done about it. Such lists are rarely exhaustive and can often usefully be extended by the project manager or others.

We recommend that, if such lists do not exist in your organization or the process of developing them is not formalized, you start a risk log for your next project. You should begin by listing all identified risks, any plans for dealing with them should they occur, and then carefully logging those that do occur and what is done in each case.

---

## ACTIVITY 2.7

Think about the relationship a project might have with a primary supplier. Assume that the project stretches over several months or even over a year or more. Take no more than one or two minutes to write down as many risk factors associated with the supplier as you can think of.

## DISCUSSION

This is our list (yours may differ).

- The supplier could go out of business during the period of the project.

- The supplier could fail to deliver key components on time.

- If the supplier is not the manufacturer, the manufacturer could go out of business or cease making the required components.

- Whoever manufactures the components could make significant design changes that would affect their usability in this project.

- The project may not specify the right components.

This should give you some idea of the nature of a risk assessment list and how it can be developed if one does not already exist, or expanded to fit the present project if one does.

---

Most risk assessment lists take a common form: they identify risk factors and ask the project manager to score the risk on a scale such as low, medium or high likelihood of occurrence and perhaps also to assess the risk as having a low, medium or high impact on the project or its key deliverables. Such a list is shown in Figure 2.10.

To make such ratings the project manager has to have a specification of what is involved in the project: the tasks to do and the deliverables to be made. It is worth beginning the risk assessment process with a fairly firm work breakdown structure and even the work package definitions or statements of work in hand.

Figure 2.11 is a variant of the previous checklist. The assessor ticks the box that most closely describes the project being assessed, but in this case the box is labelled 'low', 'medium' or 'high' and overall project risk is not a matter of summing up weightings. The emphasis in this type of checklist is more on identifying high-risk factors than on arriving at an overall project risk figure.

| Risk Description | Probability (1=low, 5=high) | Impact (1=low, 5 =high) |
|---|---|---|
| Problems due to system interface with other systems? | | |
| System more complex than planned? | | |
| System less reliable than required? | | |
| System larger than estimated? | | |
| System requirements subject to change? | | |
| Likelihood of major changes after project start? | | |
| Likelihood of minor changes after project start? | | |
| Mechanisms for introducing change inadequate? | | |
| Difficulties in defining parameters? | | |
| Data definition tool not available on time? | | |
| Data definition and dictionary tools unavailable? | | |
| Hardware platform subject to change? | | |

**FIGURE 2.10**  A risk assessment checklist with probability and impact weighting columns

| Risk Factor | Risk Description | Score |
|---|---|---|
| Complexity: interface to other systems | The system must interface with:<br>0<br>1 to 5<br>>5 other systems | ☐ low<br>☐ medium<br>☐ high |
| System type | The system is:<br>batch processing<br>real-time (not safety-critical) or interactive<br>real-time, safety-critical or distributed | ☐ low<br>☐ medium<br>☐ high |
| System size | The system will consist of approx.<br>1 to 10 modules<br>11 to 25 modules<br>>25 modules | ☐ low<br>☐ medium<br>☐ high |
| System requirements | The system requirements are:<br>agreed and signed off<br>minor changes remain to be made<br>major changes are possible | ☐ low<br>☐ medium<br>☐ high |
| System data | The data and relationship of items as defined is:<br>simple<br>moderately complex<br>very complex | ☐ low<br>☐ medium<br>☐ high |

**FIGURE 2.11**  A risk assessment checklist (risk-factor style)

There are other kinds of risk assessment list which can be used to assess whether a project is a risky venture. Figure 2.12 shows a form of questionnaire that can be used to diagnose potential areas of risk.

In Figure 2.12 the risk assessor ticks which statement in each category most closely describes the project being assessed. The numbers in square brackets on the right are the risk weighting indicator associated with that statement: 1 indicates low risk and 6 indicates very high risk. The risk scores can be added together to produce an overall risk figure, which will help the project manager to know whether he or she is dealing with a low-, medium- or high-risk project. Note that there is no guidance given as to what to do about any of the risks (we shall discuss this in Section 2.2.2).

**A. Project structural risks**

For each question, tick the answer that most closely applies to the project you are assessing.
The risk score for each answer is contained in square brackets on the right. Add all risk scores for each category and refer to Section 3.3 ('Risk Assessment') in the Standards and Procedures Manual for guidance in interpreting the results.

1. Is this project:
- a modification to an existing system/existing equipment? [1]
- a replacement for an existing system/existing equipment? [2]
- a new system/new equipment? [3]
- a pilot study or pilot project? [5]

2. Who identified most of the requirements?
- the client [1]
- the project team expected to undertake the project [2]
- another group within this company [3]
- other, specify_____ [4]
- requirements not fully identified [5]

3. Is completion of this project defined as these items to be reviewed and signed off separately?
- standard deliverables for project of this type [1]
- non-standard but agreed deliverables [2]
- non-standard deliverables [4]
- deliverables not identified [6]

4. Are project planning, tracking and reporting methods and techniques committed for this project?
- yes, tried and tested [1]
- yes, but new to this team [2]
- no [5]

5. Has the client been briefed on change control and status reporting methods and:
- agreed? [1]
- disagreed? [4]
- not been briefed? [5]

**FIGURE 2.12** A risk assessment checklist (questionnaire style)

There is little point in assessing the risks of a project if the only purpose such an assessment serves is to disturb the peaceful sleep of the project manager! A thorough risk assessment must lead to something being done about the risks or planned for the eventuality that they might occur.

# 2.2.2 Risk management

Having analysed the situation the next step is to decide what to do about the risks. This is called **risk management**: the 'identification of countermeasures necessary to meet the requirements identified in risk analysis' (PRINCE, 1993, p. 5).

Risks identified in the risk analysis should be tackled in the following order:

- high-impact, high-probability risks
- high-impact, lower-probability risks
- lower-impact, high-probability risks.

Low-impact, low-probability risks are probably not worth expending much effort on (but see the discussion of *risk acceptance* below). The manager can then look at these high-impact or high-probability risks one by one to determine whether there are ways either to reduce the impact if the risk occurs or to reduce the probability of the risk occurring, or both.

For each risk to be managed, the project manager needs to identify what cost-effective countermeasures can be applied. These may need to be specified in great detail, depending upon the complexity of the countermeasures. Possible countermeasures are:

- avoiding the risk
- reducing the risk (likelihood or impact)
- transferring the risk to others (insurance)
- contingency plans (to be implemented should the risk occur)
- accepting the risk (just monitor the situation).

Let's review strategies for risk and give some examples.

## Avoiding the risk

Avoiding the risk means removing the risk totally from the work to be done. Avoiding a risk may mean not doing the project, if the risk occurs in one of the key elements of the project. It may be possible to redefine the project to *exclude* the risk area.

---

### EXAMPLE 2.5  Avoiding risks on a major construction project

It is proposed to provide fixed links from mainland Denmark to Denmark's large islands of Fünen and Lolland. From Fünen another link is planned across the Store Bælt (Great Belt) strait to the main Danish island of Sjælland (also known as Zealand, which contains Copenhagen) and finally to southern Sweden in place of existing ferry links (Pearce, 1995). There already exists a fixed link between Lolland and mainland Germany. These links will provide Sweden and Copenhagen with their only fixed links to the mainland of western Europe. Intergovernmental agreements were signed in 1991 and the first 17 km link, between Fünen and Sjælland, opened in 1997, was the largest construction project in Europe. The proposed 16 km combined tunnel and bridge between Sjælland and Malmö, Sweden, in particular creates a risk of restricting the vital periodic flow of salty, oxygen-rich waters from the North

Sea through the narrow Store Bælt and Øresund straits into the brackish and relatively stagnant Baltic and 'strangling' it. The Swedish Government is concerned at the risk and insisted in late 1993 on a complete redesign of the proposal for the Øresund link to avoid the risk of further restricting the flow between the Baltic to the North Seas. A further redesign has subsequently been ordered by the Swedish Water Rights Court to limit damage that might be caused by proposed compensatory dredging and reduce the risk of adversely affecting the flow to below one per cent. The resulting changes to the designs have increased the estimate for the link by more than $100 million, but the problems have yet (in 1995) to be resolved to the satisfaction of the expert oceanographic panel advising the Swedish Water Rights Court. Opponents of the bridge option who say it is too damaging in any form favour a tunnel.

## Reducing the risk

Reducing the risk means reducing either the likelihood or the impact of the threat (or both).

**Risk reduction** is an important strategy; it can be an expensive one or it can be a very cheap one, but in most cases it is likely to be cost-effective when compared to the cost of incurring the unreduced risk. Common risks which can be reduced are shown in Table 2.2.

This is not an exhaustive list; there are dozens of other possible risks which can be reduced.

**TABLE 2.2** Common risks: reducing their probability and impact

| Risk | How probability can be reduced | How impact can be reduced |
|---|---|---|
| Lack of experienced staff | Recruit experienced people, train staff, use outside consultants or subcontractors who are experienced | Have experienced staff informally supervise the work of less experienced staff; increase project time to accommodate a 'learning curve' |
| Lack of technical infrastructure in the form of tools or access to tools | Purchase or hire appropriate tools | Increase project time |
| Project manager has no prior experience of working with a contractor or vendor | Develop and maintain a good relationship; establish formal communication mechanisms | Increase project time to deal with problems of complex communications and co-ordination |
| Multiple vendors or contractors involved | Name one vendor or contractor as the prime contractor | Increase project contingency times |
| Vendor's or contractor's reputation shaky | Choose another contractor with a sounder reputation | Involve management, particularly to discuss concerns regarding vendor's or contractor's ability to provide work |
| Potential users lack commitment to outcome of project | Review with them all expected benefits; show how this fits with their strategic plans or working practices | Introduce the products of the project in a phased fashion to spread the impact over a longer period (may involve increasing project time) |
| People potentially affected by project outcome fear changes, resulting in their non-co-operation | Use consensus-building techniques to obtain their input where possible when defining requirements. | Review with them all expected benefits; show how this fits with their plans or practices |

You have been appointed project manager on a project where several of the people assigned to your project are unfamiliar with the methodology you have been mandated to use. Suggest one way of reducing the risk inherent in having inexperienced staff working on the project.

## DISCUSSION

*Training* is a simple answer to this problem. However, training can range from simple familiarization to intensive learning and practice. The training needs to be appropriate to the project's requirements and to the person being trained and the role that person will occupy, and it needs to be timely. Too early, and the learning will be extinguished from lack of rehearsal and practice. Too late, and there won't be time for newly trained people to make, correct and learn from their inevitable early mistakes.

Another possibility is to assign someone knowledgeable in the methodology to oversee and informally guide more inexperienced staff.

# Transferring the risk to others (insurance)

Insurance is a means of transferring the financial impact of having a risk occur. Insurance against fire or theft simply provides financial compensation for losses actually incurred. Compensation as the result of an insurance claim may not be adequate to keep a project on track, because the financial compensation may only be enough to compensate the organization for time and resources lost, not for repairing the damage so that the project can continue.

Subcontracting the risk to a specialist subcontractor can reduce the risk considerably by combining two risk management strategies: risk reduction and **risk transfer**. The risk reduction element arises if the subcontractor has specialist skills in this area of work and so is less likely to fail to meet standards. The risk transfer element arises if the subcontractor undertakes to complete the work to the standard required at the time required at a fixed price. If the subcontractor is reliable and backed by sufficient resources to cope with the identified risks (which should of course be discussed with the subcontractor) then the risk will be effectively transferred. However, transferring the risk doesn't always help in the long run, as Example 2.6 shows.

Note that, while a contractor or client may wish to transfer risk to a subcontractor, it is not always clear in such a situation *who* will be held responsible should a risk actually occur and result in problems. The client or contractor needs to give a detailed specification to the subcontractor which *includes* known risk factors and the parties need to understand clearly who has identified the risks, what those are, who will be responsible for risk management and who (if worst comes to worst) will have to shoulder the financial and legal responsibilities, and this should be backed up by the wording in the contract and other documents. The most that the client can gain from risk transfer is some financial protection in the event that the project fails. Risk transfer does not guarantee that a project will be completed successfully, and the financial protection may not be sufficient to prevent the bankruptcy of the client if the project was key to his or her business. The project manager can't simply dispose of his or her responsibilities by subcontracting and insuring.

---

**EXAMPLE 2.6**

In the London Ambulance Service (LAS) case study, the subcontractor's lack of experience in developing command and control systems was a large factor in the project's failure. If the subcontractor had been a specialist in the area of command and control systems this risk would have been very greatly reduced or could even have been avoided. In both cases the risk would have been transferred from the LAS to the subcontractor.

While the risk may have been transferred to the subcontractor, who – upon failing to perform – lost a great deal of money (and some subcontractors in this situation are bankrupted), the failure of a key subcontractor to deal adequately with a risk was itself a prime cause of failure in the LAS project.

---

# Contingency plans

Contingency planning involves 'identifying the range of alternative options for providing acceptable recovery strategies in the event of a loss' (PRINCE, 1993, p.13). **Contingency plans** can involve the allocation of a fund of money to cover minor cost-overruns or elaborate plans for alternatives or the restoration of lost resources, work or services. For each alternative option identified, its benefits and disadvantages must also be identified so that the optimum solution can be presented to management for a decision. General contingency strategies are:

- do nothing (choosing this option should be a positive choice, not a default because no one has taken the time to identify other possibilities!)

- alternative procedures, previously identified and described in detail (for example, a retreat to an earlier stage in the project so that work can recommence), or alternative ways to proceed from the point at which the hazard occurs

- reciprocal arrangements with other organizations, the client, contractor or subcontractor to provide specific resources and facilities in the event of a hazard arising.

---

ACTIVITY 2.9

Imagine that it is important for you to be able to open your firm's new office in time to coincide with a visit by the chief executive officer. He will want to see the office 'working'.

Use the WBS you produced in Activity 2.6 to help you identify potential risks. List three risks that you have identified as a result and suggest one action to reduce or otherwise deal with each risk.

DISCUSSION

Our answer is contained in Table 2.3.

**TABLE 2.3** Three risks to the office project and potential actions to take

| Risk | Potential action |
|---|---|
| Building work or decorating incomplete | Specify completion date well in advance of actual opening date to builders and decorators. |
| A supplier lets you down and either furniture or equipment is delivered late | Identify in advance alternative supplier for furniture, equipment, or both. |
| Some items of equipment incompatible with remainder | Ask supplier to let you view equipment or furniture well before delivery, to check consignment is correct in every detail. |
| | Set delivery date for furniture and equipment some time before office opening date, so there will be sufficient time to take corrective action. (You could do both in order to be doubly safe.) |

This activity was designed to give you a brief flavour of the kind of thinking necessary to develop contingency plans. You may have suggested other solutions.

Depending upon the risk, contingency plans can be quite detailed. If the risk probability is high and the impact could be severe, it may even be wise to distribute copies of the detailed plan to all likely participants and even to hold rehearsals on what to do should the risk actually occur. *Rehearsal* has the advantage of helping to highlight any problems that may exist in a contingency plan, enabling the project manager to alter the plan accordingly.

## Accepting the risk

The final strategy for managing a risk is the possibility of **risk acceptance**: the project manager decides nothing can or needs to be done at present, but notes that the situation needs review from time to time during the course of the project. It will be too costly to develop a contingency plan against everything that could go wrong. During the course of the project's execution it will be necessary to review the list of risks and risk factors to determine:

- whether any risk has become or is likely to become critical at any time soon

- whether any new risks have arisen which require assessment and possible planning or even immediate action.

In any case, each risk and any management and contingency plans should be reviewed on a periodic basis to ensure that, should the worst happen, the project manager will have given some thought about what to do.

### SAQ 2.6

Overleaf is a short table of some risks related to suppliers, together with strategies identified for dealing with the risks. Complete the table by identifying which type of strategy is used in each case. (The first one is completed for you.)

**TABLE 2.4** Risk, strategy and type

| Risk | Strategy | Type |
|---|---|---|
| Supplier goes bankrupt | Identify and approach alternative supplier | Contingency plan |
| Supplier does not deliver on time | Insert penalty clause in contract with supplier | |
| | Add extra time to project plan after date told to supplier | |
| Specification of components must be met as they interface with items from other suppliers | Stipulate exactly what specification must be met in contract with supplier | |
| Key expert in supplier's organization may leave | Watch this situation | |

## Risk monitoring

In Chapter 5 we will discuss this topic more fully. Here we will simply note that the purpose of risk assessment is to allow the project manager to identify and plan for risk. The manager manages risk by monitoring the situation and controlling it when it occurs. Monitoring risks can be tied to the tracking of milestones (milestones are discussed in Chapter 3), setting aside time periodically to examine the situation for the most likely and most damaging risks, reassessing risks as the project progresses, and, of course, taking corrective action.

# 2.2.3 Summary

This section has been concerned with those project elements which involve risk.

Risk analysis consists of two elements: risk identification and risk assessment. Identification means listing the risks to which the project might be exposed. Assessment means assessing how probable is the risk and how great an impact it would have if it occurs.

Risk management means deciding what to do about the risks. The management techniques include risk avoidance, risk reduction (probability and impact), risk transfer (insurance), contingency planning and risk acceptance.

Having studied this section you should now be able to:

- give a general list of the kinds of risks related to deficient deliverables
- describe the process of risk assessment and, using the WBS, carry out a simple risk assessment, listing risks and appropriate strategies for them in an area with which you are familiar
- describe risk management techniques and suggest appropriate strategies for defined risks in an area with which you are familiar
- describe risk reduction and suggest risk reduction strategies for defined risks in an area with which you are familiar
- explain what is meant by risk avoidance and give a simple example
- explain how risk transfer can be used to compensate for a hazard
- explain where contingency planning fits into risk management.

# 2.3  *ESTIMATING A PROJECT*

This section looks at the processes of gathering, organizing, and evaluating data which then are used to develop an estimate for a project.

Estimating may be done by different people for different purposes. It may be done by engineers in the sponsoring organization for in-house projects; by a potential contractor for tendering; by a subcontractor for subcontracting. Later, you will draw general conclusions about how this factor affects the degree of accuracy possible and required. For example, a potential subcontractor may draw up an estimate in order to bid for work on part of a larger project. This introduces as potential cost items factors of complexity (such as interfacing with the main contractor and with other subcontractors) but also simplifies estimating in that a detailed statement of work and deliverables should be available, though perhaps at a less detailed level than one would ideally want, to aid the estimating process.

There are distinct tasks to be undertaken in the process of estimating:

- Organize.
- Draw up a task list (WBS or other).
- List materials, supplies, component parts, etc.
- Draw up a product breakdown structure if needed.
- Draw up a cost breakdown structure and cross-references.
- Gather data not already held in the product and cost breakdown structures, materials lists, etc.
- Prepare costings associated with the risks identified and listed for the project.
- Classify items and consolidate them under distinct headings.
- Ensure the quality of your estimates. *Always* apply checks at each step.
- Prepare and present the estimate to management or the client.

## 2.3.1  Organizing for estimating

There are two schools of thought on who should undertake the estimating process:

- A *professional estimator*, not involved in the project itself, undertakes the estimating. Proponents argue that this eliminates the bias that can occur when the estimator is emotionally involved in getting the project accepted. It is also the only way an individual is likely to gain significant estimating experience. Opponents argue that the estimator's lack of personal involvement will always lead to a safe and unchallenging estimate.

- The *people who will carry out the work* undertake the estimating, with effort co-ordinated by the project manager. Proponents argue that responsibility for an estimate they have created means that project personnel will use the resulting budget and schedule more effectively than they would if it were imposed from outside. Opponents argue that project staff are insufficiently skilled in estimating and this adds an unnecessary element of risk to the estimate.

These approaches could be used together, with each providing a quality check on the estimates produced by the other, though this would increase the cost of making estimates. Whoever undertakes the estimating, it is extremely important that this complex activity be organized: that it be planned and carried out as though it were itself a project.

## Planning for the quality of estimates

A question you should always ask yourself is: 'What do I hope to achieve with my estimate?' This may seem a silly question, to which the obvious answer is: to obtain a reasonably accurate idea of the costs, resources and timescale necessary to do the project. (The estimation phase of the project is inseparable from the planning phase.) The following points are important though frequently neglected because they are unacknowledged.

*What are the requirements for this project?* If the requirements for the project are wrong, the results of the estimate cannot be right. This is the same as getting the requirements phase of any project right. One question to ask is: 'Have the client's and the contractor's own aims been considered?' These may have important implications for the success of the project. Were the requirements identified for this project complete and correct? Have the aims of the client and the contractor (especially those which are implicit rather than explicit) been taken into account? If the answer to any part of these questions is 'no' then action to rectify the situation needs to be taken immediately prior to preparing any estimates.

One thing any estimator should hope to achieve with any estimate is to *communicate with the contractor's management and with the client* about the costs and risks of the project.

*A high-quality estimate must identify factors which need to be controlled*, measures by which these factors can be gauged and the means for monitoring them as the project proceeds.

A sound estimate allows the client, the project team and the contractor's own management to make decisions about their project and about alternatives within the scope of the project.

Try to set measurable objectives for each estimating exercise, just as though you were planning a project. The more specific the objective, the easier it is to see that it has been achieved. The objectives of the planning step of an estimating 'project' might be:

- assign responsibilities
- train the staff
- schedule the estimating project
- determine reliability and validation measures.

You will know that the objective to *train the staff* has been met when the staff have completed the necessary training courses.

*If one does not already exist, establish a formal estimating process*. A formal process recognizes, organizes and perhaps automates the distinct steps in the estimating process we shall describe below; it helps to produce and measure quality. If one exists already see that it accomplishes the objectives set. Be sure to keep a record of previous experience: post-project reviews (which we cover in Chapter 6) should feed into this process.

*Teach people how to use the process*. Many people who are likely to carry out estimation do not have any training in how to do it. The mere existence of a formal process is insufficient if people do not understand its terminology or how it is to be used.

*Provide reviews and evaluation*. This is to ensure that the process is carried out correctly. By doing so, it is possible to identify and remedy errors of omission and execution. A good test of an estimate is whether an independent assessor can replicate its outcome.

*Measure whether the objectives set for the estimating process have been met*. There is no point in establishing measurable objectives if they are not measured. Any failure to meet such objectives is a signal that something is wrong. If measurement shows that the objectives are not being met, look at the reasons for this failure. The reason may lie with the people responsible or it may lie with the process. If the latter is the case, the process should be modified so that the amended process *does* meet the objectives.

**EXAMPLE 2.7**

A software development firm sought to improve its estimates by adapting the technique of peer review to the estimating process. The objective was to improve the accuracy of estimates by bringing the experience of several reviewers together and by giving the estimator an incentive to draw up estimates which could be defended from criticism. The measure of success was to be the accuracy of the estimates. To obtain results quickly, peer reviews were at first introduced only for projects or subprojects of short duration.

A half-yearly review of this plan showed that accuracy had not improved. Investigation showed that managers had put pressure on their subordinates to side-step the review process because of the time it required to review and correct an estimate compared with the time required to execute these short projects.

**ACTIVITY 2.10**

To what would you attribute the failure described in Example 2.7? Suggest another measure or procedure to improve this situation.

**DISCUSSION**

The failure could be attributed to the unco-operativeness of the managers or to the measurement process. Managers were under pressure to produce within tight constraints. Perhaps the process for measuring achievement of this objective created a further burden which proved too much for the managers and was counterproductive to the achievement of a worthwhile objective.

The firm amended the peer review procedure to take in only larger projects, where managers felt happier about the value of the review relative to overall project costs. Small project estimates were instead reviewed by one other person in order to reduce the time spent carrying out such a review. Later investigations showed that the accuracy of the estimates for both types of project increased significantly.

**SAQ 2.7**

List the objectives of making an estimate.

# 2.3.2   Data gathering

The work breakdown structure (WBS) lists tasks. Product breakdown structures list components to be acquired or produced. (The work itemized in a WBS will produce products which may also appear in a PBS: the estimates need to be checked for any double counting that could arise.) The cost breakdown structure includes other costs and the cross-reference documents show their relationships. Each aspect of the project must be reduced, as it has been for the WBS and other planning tools, to something *easily comprehensible* and therefore *easily measurable*.

Looking at similar aspects in past project cost histories can be helpful. Items in these histories are valuable guides to the same or similar items in the estimate to be made. This can aid the drawing up of checklists.

In identifying items to be costed, it is important to realize that the finer the level of detail the more effective will be cost control, but the more costly that control will be in relation to its potential value.

---

### ACTIVITY 2.11

Take the common item *stationery* to be used in a project. What are the ways in which this term can be further broken down? Why might you decide to do so? Why might you not?

### DISCUSSION

Unless stationery use has been a problem in the past, it might be better *not* to break such an item down at all. You could, of course, break it down into many constituent elements: headed notepaper, plain notepaper, pencils, ball-point pens, felt-tipped pens, feint-ruled A4 pads of paper, and so on. Consider the work (and its attendant costs) involved in costing and then in monitoring the use of stationery items at such a level.

---

The data gathering step should include both cost and schedule consideration based on the project's definition. For example, it may be necessary for the project work to expand the use of space and facilities temporarily (say with the use of a temporary building to house the project's staff). The costs of this *and* the timescale are both important, for instance one temporary office rented at a cost of so much per month for the period of so many months. (The timescale of projects will be discussed in detail in Chapter 3.)

## Approaches to estimating costs and time

There are several approaches to estimating costs and time. They are *not* mutually exclusive. One or more may be used to gather data for a single estimate. The approaches are:

- reliance on the judgement of the person doing the estimate

- breaking an item down into smaller component parts and estimating each component

- relying on data from one or more similar projects done in the past

- using standard data for a task or component.

The *judgement* of the estimator is one of the commoner methods of obtaining values for cost and, especially, for estimating durations of tasks. This method relies heavily on the experience of the estimator and should be rigorously subjected to tests of reasonableness and consistency: is the estimate reasonable and is it internally consistent? For example, the London Ambulance Service estimate might have usefully been questioned as to its reasonableness, given that several bidders expressed grave reservations about the target cost of the project and that the winning bid was considerably less than that. The estimator should be able to justify the use of judgement and the basis for considering the judgement a reasonable one in each case. The larger the piece of work being estimated the less reliable will that judgement be.

The second approach listed above, which we can call the *component method*, uses the work breakdown structure to break the project down into its component parts, estimate the components individually and then sum the figures. This reduces the scale of the application of judgement to more manageable proportions. Tasks may be broken into finer detail if necessary, as in Example 2.8.

---

### EXAMPLE 2.8

A systems analyst working on developing a requirements specification will need to conduct interviews with personnel in the client organization. The analyst should be able to determine how many people will need to be interviewed. Some will need to be interviewed twice. Each interview will take about 45 minutes. The analyst also needs to spend half an hour preparing for each interview; a quarter of an hour after each interview is needed to organize notes and list points to be raised in subsequent interviews. Then there is travel time and telephone time. All of these would be estimated separately using one of the other methods, such as judgement, and then summed to estimate total analyst-hours (which is *not* the same as elapsed time, of course).

---

Although this breaking down sounds tedious it is invaluable in helping people estimate if they have not done this before. It can help people develop the experience needed to use the judgement method above. It can also provide a very useful discipline in organizations which have a poor history of estimating accurately.

The *similar project* approach compares the project or task to be estimated with the *actual* costs and times of a similar previous task or project. The actual costs and times of the previous task or project become the basis for estimated figures for the new task or project. This requires a knowledge of what has happened, particularly to costs, since the earlier project was completed. It also relies on a judgement of the differences between the task or project now being estimated compared with the base task or project for which the actual data are available. There may be differences in type, scope, complexity and size.

**Standardized estimating** (also called 'blue-book' estimating) is the ideal method but it can only be used when a sufficient body of detailed data has been accumulated for statistically valid standards to be set. It is in common use in the construction industry, where a quantity surveyor estimates quantities required according to a known formula derived from a statistical standard. Its advantage is that the quality of an estimate so derived can be measured by its adherence to standards.

One problem inherent in using any of these approaches is the variation possible in some key factor such as the expertise of the people who will be performing the project work.

---

**EXAMPLE 2.9**

A comparative study in the US of computer programmers showed that there was an eleven-fold difference between the slowest and fastest workers. There was a comparable difference between those least and best able to produce correct code, but any correlation between speed and correctness was unclear. Some writers have called these findings into question because the study was conducted using programmers who were not using structured methods. However, even these sceptical writers believe that there is a considerable difference in ability and speed amongst programming staff.

---

Data about tasks or items of different types in the same project may be gathered by combining different methods. For example, data about costs of facilities (such as premises, communications and infrastructure) are best based on the **historical method**, whereas data about new development and design tasks can best be gathered using breakdown into components and/or comparison with a previous similar task or project. It is not necessary to choose a single method to gather data on all aspects of one project, so long as the method used in each case is *defensible, consistent* and *appropriate* to the item to be estimated.

### SAQ 2.8

(a) What is the 'similar project' approach to estimating?

(b) Explain how the component method is carried out.

(c) What precondition is necessary for the standardized method?

# 2.3.3  Consolidating and evaluating data

If the data gathering task has been widely distributed among a number of people, the data will need to be consolidated and evaluated. Consolidation involves grouping like items together (for example, several groups may have estimated clerical times and rates for different tasks and these may need to be grouped or made consistent). Any accidentally duplicated items need to be identified and subsequently eliminated.

Each participant in the data gathering should, of course, have applied tests for appropriate data and method, correct application of method and consistency and reasonableness of the data. *These tests should be applied again at this stage and with rigour*, before individual data are subsumed into the budget and schedule and their origins are lost. It is while you still know that 'Elizabeth was responsible for this' that you can return to Elizabeth with questions. By the time a senior manager or the client questions why such-and-such an item in the proposed budget seems so high or a task seems to take an inordinate amount of time it is probably too late to verify the component figures that made up the questioned sum, and it may be too late to prepare an adequate justification.

In making an estimate, several different project areas will probably have returned data for what can broadly be termed *salaries and wages*. These figures may also be further subdivided. The project manager will estimate only for her own organization's personnel and for any labour which she needs to hire directly. She might estimate: her own time on the project at a known rate, a portion of the production engineer's time at a known rate, some time from some of the employees on the shop floor to shift materials to a new location, and perhaps the time of some casual labour hired to demolish a wall. So she might see several figures:

- the tasks she needs to do, her estimated time and her rate

- the production engineer's tasks, time and his rate

- the shop floor employees' tasks, estimated times and median wage rate

- the estimated time to demolish the wall and an estimated or quoted rate for casual labour.

In accordance with standard accounting practices, she would probably consolidate these under headings: *salaries, wages* and *casual labour*. In addition, she might determine that, in order to meet her schedules, some workers might have to work overtime, for example, to shift materials when this will not hamper normal production. So she might have an additional category: *overtime*. All these categories in turn might be consolidated under a single budgetary heading called *salaries and wages*, and this would appear on a single line of her project budget, even though the various categories of labour would be paid for out of detailed categories.

The degree to which categories are broken down and reconsolidated is governed to a large extent by an organization's accounting policies. Table 2.5 shows a typical accounting hierarchy for a commercial firm. The hierarchical arrangement is first by area within the company (RD stands for the research and development department), the next two digits indicate whether the category is income, project costs (indicated by the digits 33 in our example), production or any of the other major activities. Two digits then indicate major category (such as salaries, wages and fees, the 11 in the example in Table 2.5). This is further divided into scientific/engineering salaries, technicians' salaries, consultants' fees, using the next two digits. The final four digits (left blank in this table) are devoted to a code which indicates a particular project or process. AS45 might be a code to indicate avionics software project number 45. This would be appended to each code to indicate which project is responsible for this item.

**TABLE 2.5**  A firm's accounting categories (partial list)

| Budget code | Item |
|---|---|
| *RD 33* | *Research and Development Department: project costs* |
| **11** | **salaries, wages and fees** |
| 1120 _ _ _ _ | scientific/engineering salaries |
| 1130 _ _ _ _ | technician salaries |
| 1140 _ _ _ _ | secretarial/clerical wages |
| 1160 _ _ _ _ | consultant fees |
| **12** | **people-related non-salary costs** |
| **25** | **testing** |
| 2510 _ _ _ _ | test bed equipment |
| **67** | **miscellaneous** |
| 6743 _ _ _ _ | telephone |
| 6755 _ _ _ _ | office supplies |
| 6756 _ _ _ _ | computing supplies (disks, etc.) |
| 6764 _ _ _ _ | other supplies |
| **69** | **maintenance** |
| 6910 _ _ _ _ | computing equipment |

A problem likely to appear at this stage is that the data gathered are incomplete. The data can usefully be cross-checked with items in similar projects or by using self-checking forms.

# 2.3.4  Completing the estimate

To convert an estimate of the effort required into cash requires a figure for the cost of staff time. The estimator must choose a **rate** to be applied to the time estimated for a task. The rate chosen can vary: some organizations use a median rate for the job title, though there may be a 'junior' rate for a less experienced person and a 'senior' rate for a more experienced person, depending upon which is most likely to do the work. (Median rates can be used to make a basic estimate and the senior rate used to make a 'worst case' estimate.) If someone is already assigned to the task, that person's true rate can be used, but at the stage of estimating a project it would be unusual for the names and rates of specific people who will work on the project to be available. An estimator must take these factors into account, present alternatives and re-estimate as firm choices are made. Some estimators always use a median figure and refine this in subsequent re-estimations. Some estimators prefer to use a junior, median and senior rate to derive low, median and high estimates for each task, then to refine this when the required skill level becomes clearer or the individual assigned this task becomes known.

---

**EXAMPLE 2.10**

We know that interviews will require a total of 37 analyst-hours. We can apply a rate or rates to this to obtain an estimate. In the particular organization we work for, a low, median and high estimate is made for all such tasks. The junior rate for analysts is £10 per hour, the median is £15 per hour and the senior is £25 per hour. Thus our three estimates are: low £370, median £555 and senior £925. The estimator can present an estimate showing the cheapest *and* most expensive options (best- and worst-case), or the cheapest and most likely options (best- and most-likely-case), or use the most likely costs on the assumption that in fact the project will balance in the long run. In the last case, the estimator is likely to make the worst-case estimate known so that there will be no unpleasant surprises.

---

Once a team is selected, *actual* rates can be used to refine the estimates. In Example 2.10, the inexperienced junior analyst will cost £370, but it may be determined that the interviews will be difficult, and the organization will be faced with paying more either because a more senior person is required or because it is deemed necessary to allow the junior person to carry out the interviews under the supervision of a senior analyst. In most cases an inexperienced person will require longer to carry out a task than an experienced one, and many estimators use this fact to optimize budgets, schedules and human resources.

If the junior analyst requires not 37 but 100 hours to carry out the work, it would cost £1000. The senior person would cost much more but will require only the estimated 37 hours at a cost of £925. If time is of the essence, it may be best to pay a higher rate to an experienced person in order to have the work done quickly. If time is less important but the inexperienced person needs on-the-job experience, then it may be best to take more time.

## Cost escalation

The estimator must bear in mind the likelihood of **cost escalation** – the change in final costs relative to estimated costs that occurs with the passage of time as a result of inflation and problems that may arise related to elapsed time. Harrison (1992) reports that cost escalation on smaller projects of 10 to 20% is relatively common. Escalation on large projects, especially those with a high development component or which are very novel, seems boundless: the design of the Concorde aircraft suffered a cost escalation above estimate of 545% and the Channel Tunnel, originally forecast in 1987 to cost £4.7 billion, was estimated to have cost over £10 billion by October 1993. (This included some £8 billion owed to a consortium of 220 banks, which means that every 1% rise in interest rates increases its financing costs by some £50 million a year.)

The estimator should include allowance for cost escalation in the initial cost estimate. Because they are cumulative, the effects of periods of high inflation can be particularly insidious, especially if accompanied by delays in the project, as shown in Figure 2.13. A contractor firm can protect itself to a large extent by including a price adjustment formula escalation clause linked to an appropriate price index in the contract. (A model clause is shown in Appendix 3.)

## Contingency allowances and reserves

In addition to protecting the project estimate against inflation, the contractor will still need to include **contingency allowances** in an estimate, as not all factors which affect the costs of the work will be reflected in the price index cited in the contract. Local conditions, for example, may not show up at all in a national index used as the basis for a price adjustment formula in a contract. The client has less protection against inflation than the contractor with an escalation clause and must forecast it and take it into account when making major project decisions. One means of doing this is to make a time-phased estimate, use forecasts of inflation and prepare a separate inflation estimate. Figure 2.13 shows estimated costs in a project lasting five years. The lowest line is an estimate based on costs *at the time the estimate was made* (called the **base date**) and the other lines show the potential cost effects of 5%, 10% and 15% per annum inflation. Note that the 15% p.a. inflation rate leads to a 47% escalation in the total cost at the end of the fifth year, but its effects become obvious only at the end of the third year.

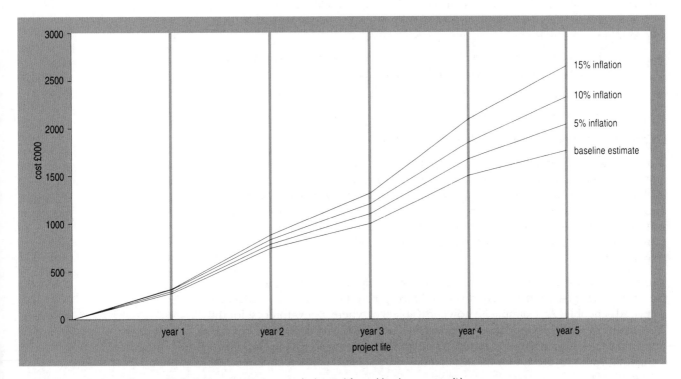

**FIGURE 2.13**   The effects of inflation on project costs (adapted from Harrison, *op. cit.*)

Once the base date estimate is established, indices of inflation forward from this date permit an estimate to be corrected for inflation during the life of the project. This means that actual costs, as they are gathered, must be 'deflated' (if they have been increased by inflation) by a formula that allows them to be compared meaningfully with their baseline estimates.

In addition, the estimator must consider adding **contingency reserves** or **management reserves** to an estimate. This is for two reasons:

- to cover minor changes and omissions, normal variations about the averages used in preparing the estimate, minor compensations and other small uncertainties
- to provide some insurance against risk.

134

---

## EXAMPLE 2.11

As you saw above, the need to carry out interviews by an analyst can be estimated using, for example, a median rate. A contingency allowance can be added to this in case the early interviews uncover problems that will require additional interviews lasting several hours to resolve. If the most-likely rate cost (in this case the median rate) for the estimated interviews is £555, a contingency allowance of, say, 10% can be added to this to cover the likelihood that more time may be needed. Thus we would say that the interviews would cost £610.50 (£555 + £55.50); this gives us a base estimate and a contingency allowance. If no additional problems were in fact uncovered then this contingency allowance would not be used.

---

How much contingency an estimator should add depends on the uncertainty of the estimate. Traditionally, 10% of the estimated project cost is added on for a contingency reserve but the figure chosen should reflect the degree of risk of over expenditure. Another formula for contingency reserves is to:

- add on 5% of funds committed but not expended (for example where firm orders for materials have been placed but not yet paid for)

- plus 9% of funds planned but not yet committed

- plus 1% of total project costs (committed and planned).

Again, the actual percentages should reflect the degree of risk.

No contingency reserve is necessary for funds already expended (you already know how much you've paid). The amount of contingency reserve needed may change with time (as it certainly does with the formula listed above). An innovative or novel project needs a much greater contingency reserve than a project whose parameters are well understood. Expenditure of contingency reserves should be very carefully controlled in order not to lose sight of the problem which occasioned the expenditure.

Changes need to be estimated, taking account of any ripple effect they may have. The revised estimates must be approved and incorporated into a revised budget and a revised schedule. An example is shown in Table 2.6, where a new forecast for the next month is produced, updating an older forecast, which may have been made some time ago. This updating is based in part on the reported actual expenditure compared with the forecast for the last month – but may also take account of other information available to the project manager.

### SAQ 2.9

(a) How can an estimator deal with a situation where it is impossible to use an actual rate of pay because the team member has not been chosen yet?

(b) Describe two ways of determining how much contingency reserve to add to an estimate.

(c) What is the purpose of a base date estimate and how does it work?

**TABLE 2.6** A rolling month re-estimation

| Budget code | Item | Actuals | Last forecast | Actuals – last forecast | Previous forecast | Next month |
|---|---|---|---|---|---|---|
| *RD 33* | *project costs* | | | | | |
| **11** | **salaries/wages** | **8.3** | **7.9** | **0.4** | **8.2** | **8.3** |
| 1120 | scien./eng. | 4.0 | 4.0 | 0.0 | 4.2 | 4.2 |
| 1130 | tech. | 3.0 | 3.0 | 0.0 | 3.2 | 3.1 |
| 1140 | sec/clerical | 0.8 | 0.9 | −0.1 | 0.8 | 1.0 |
| 1160 | consultants | 0.5 | 0.0 | 0.5 | 0.0 | 0.0 |
| **25** | **testing** | **5.0** | **5.2** | **−0.2** | **5.2** | **5.0** |
| 2510 | test bed equip. | 2.5 | 2.5 | 0.0 | 2.5 | 2.5 |
| 2550 | test consumables | 2.5 | 2.7 | −0.2 | 2.7 | 2.5 |
| **67** | **miscellaneous** | **1.5** | **1.5** | **0.0** | **1.5** | **1.5** |

## 2.3.5 Classification, final consolidation and presentation of estimates

These last steps take the results of the previous steps and turn them into a budget and schedule ready to be presented, approved or reworked, and used. The staff who have gathered data and made estimates have identified tasks and resources they *believe* are needed for a project. Now those items which will actually meet the project's needs must be selected.

Items should now be classified. A classification for budgetary purposes will be quite different from classifications used in constructing a schedule, because classifications for budgetary purposes are often dictated by an organization's accounting practices. It may be necessary to classify the data in two different ways: one suited to the project and the other suited to the organization's annual budget.

Preparation involves quality checks. Are the classifications valid? Has the risk associated with each item been identified and sensitivities noted? Project overviews and justification material should be included here, as should clarification of any items excluded from the project. The result should be a first draft budget and schedule. When the drafts are satisfactory, the budget and schedule can be approved by internal management and packaged for presentation.

The circumstances in which the project work will be carried out will influence the estimate. For example, the contractor will want to add a profit margin; yet the desire for a good margin will be tempered, if the purpose of the estimate is to bid for work, by the need to be the most attractive estimate (usually, but not always, the cheapest).

*The presentation step is very important*, especially when presenting to potential clients. The project must be marketed through its justification and budget proposal – why it should be done and how much it should cost – with the schedule playing a secondary role at this stage. Concern is likely to be centred on the question of when it will be completed, rather than on any scheduling detail. *It should also be made very clear what has been excluded from the scope of the project.* This will help reduce any possible misunderstandings between client and contractor later. For this reason it is important that the presenter be fully versed in what is contained in and excluded from the proposed budget and schedule, so that he or she can justify and defend them.

### SAQ 2.10

List the steps necessary to implement an estimate.

## Quality of estimates and project outcomes

The estimate is key to cost control. The quality of an estimate therefore is proven by the project manager's ability to keep costs under control (and the quality of project management depends in part on good cost control). Table 2.7 illustrates the quality interrelationships in four aspects of a project: estimates, project management, cost control and the quality of data obtained for purposes of future estimating.

**TABLE 2.7**  Expectations of quality from available data

| Quality of estimates | Quality of project management | Expectation of good cost control | Value of data for future cost estimating |
|---|---|---|---|
| Good | Good | High | Good |
| Good | Poor | Fair | Fair |
| Poor | Good | Low | Low |
| Poor | Poor | Very poor | Doubtful |

(taken from Wellman, 1992, p. 28)

However, it wouldn't do to wait until the project is well underway before deciding that an estimate is of poor quality. Quality should be assured at the outset by checking and cross-checking for the thoroughness of the requirements, completeness and accuracy of the data, soundness of the assumptions or historical data used (especially in models like COCOMO and function point, discussed in Section 2.3.6). If possible, you should have independent estimates made and compare them.

## 2.3.6  Software

In Chapter 1 we showed you an example of a small piece of code and noted that a panel of experts varied widely on how many statements that small bit of program contained. This highlights one serious problem with software development: measurement is difficult and there is little agreement even amongst experts on what to measure.

Software development is always 'research and development' in the sense that

- every piece of software is a unique endeavour
- there is no standard measure by which software quantity can be judged
- there is no standard measure by which software quality can be judged
- there exists enormous variation amongst individuals who design, write and test software as to how much they can produce in a given time and to what quality
- such measures as exist are subject to wide variation even amongst experts.

Even changing existing software can be problematic: the simplest changes in the operational demands made on a piece of software can be very difficult to design and incorporate, and more major changes can result in the entire system having to be redesigned and replaced. While this is not a course in software design, all those concerned with software projects should:

- look to establish a long life-cycle, with a long product life to profit from the initial investment
- look at ways to integrate, now or later, the software with other systems.

A 'long life-cycle' here refers not to an extended development period, but to the life of the product from the inception of the design to the time it is replaced. Too often in the past writers have restricted the software life-cycle to its development cycle and ended the cycle either with implementation or 'maintenance'. This tends to focus developers' attention on getting their software implemented and 'finishing' it. They then tend to stop worrying about it, as the maintenance phase becomes 'someone else's problem'. According to DeMarco (1982) this has a detrimental effect on software quality because it affects attitudes about what the objective is: quick work or defect-free, well-designed software. Integration also remains a problem, generally because it is not planned for from the outset. Thus a database application written two or three years ago may produce data in a format that is not acceptable to a report generator designed the year before that, and neither will interface with a graphics package bought this year in order to make data more presentable. Such problems generate frustration in the user population and may cause people to waste time developing individual 'work arounds' to problems that should have been anticipated.

There are three basic choices in obtaining software as a component of a project or as a project in itself.

The organization can *buy a package* if one exists on the market. This is a very common solution to obtaining software for well-known areas of office automation (e.g. word processing, spreadsheets) and has the advantages that the vendor often provides documentation, training, help lines and service.

The organization can *undertake a bespoke development* – core software is acquired and supplemented with new software, or a package is purchased and then modified to meet the organization's particular requirements. This has some of the advantages of purchasing a package, and the additional advantage of being more tailored to an organization's particular operational and business requirements. Problems can arise, however, with interfaces to other software and it may be difficult to determine who is responsible when there are problems.

The third alternative is for the organization to *undertake a custom development*, based on a new specification. This requires considerable time and expense and does not have the support of a vendor; nor does it have the advantage of having a user group to put pressure on the supplier. However, the software will be custom-made for use in the organization and therefore will more closely mirror the organization's business and operations and its philosophy.

## Modularity in software

According to Wellman in his 1992 book on software estimating:

> ... modularity must be seen as essential, at the design stage, so that parts of the system can at a later time be taken out and replaced with little or no disruption to the system as a whole or to other software to which it is interfaced.
>
> (p. 129)

The development and operation of software systems can be viewed as having five quantifiable aspects:

- scope
- size
- complexity
- cost
- elapsed time.

The first two of these can be derived from the specification. The complexity of the project can be identified by examining its technical feasibility and identifying a low-risk approach to development and implementation. Wellman notes that complexity exists in two different dimensions, that of the construction of the software and that of its functionality. It is necessary to know the measures of scope, size and complexity before costs and elapsed time can be derived to form an estimate.

## Stepwise estimation

The process of *stepwise estimation* is derived from the technique of stepwise refinement in developing a specification and is similar in concept to the work breakdown structure. What is to be estimated is decomposed into finer and finer detail until the decomposition reaches a state in which the quantity can be estimated because the scope of each piece has been reduced to something easily comprehensible and therefore more easily measurable.

If a project group is experienced with a particular application, or with the tools and techniques of development of the particular type of software to be produced and the stepwise decomposition (and preferably of both), estimates can be drawn up based on experience within the project group. This is a particularly effective method where the experience of the team members reduces the risk of problems occurring during the design, development and implementation phases of the software project. It is an unsuitable method where there is little experience of the application or type of software, or of the tools and techniques. This is amply illustrated in the London Ambulance System case study, where the software suppliers had no previous experience of developing command and control systems and therefore no experience on which to base estimates of risk and hence estimates of timescale and cost.

The decomposition of the software 'problem' proceeds with the express goal of arriving at items which, within themselves, are well understood and therefore measurable and of low risk. However, it should be noted that risk arises when even the best-understood pieces of software must interface with each other, because interfaces increase the complexity of the problem several-fold. In novel software development projects the risks inherent in interfaces between software components, or between software, hardware and human components are especially large and difficult or impossible to judge (other than to recognize that the problem exists and will be difficult!).

## Prototyping and evolutionary methods

**Prototyping** consists of implementing in some form some key features of the envisioned system in a *simulated operational environment* which can be used as a model to:

- evaluate complex or difficult algorithms
- validate design techniques and tools
- design test facilities
- assess the model in use to obtain feedback for input to the design (for example of the interface in an operational environment) or the estimating process or both
- assess aspects of system integration
- provide experience for team members
- persuade suppliers and users to accept the solution.

Prototypes can also help in the reduction of risk by allowing team members to gain experience and by giving feedback that identifies particularly risky parts of the design or problems of integration and operation. One problem, however, is that they often show the 'glittering prize' at the end of the project when most of the painstaking, detailed work still remains to be done.

Piloting is slightly different. A **pilot** implements a version of the software which provides the basic features required in the finished product in a *real operational environment*. (A prototype can become a pilot, so the distinction can be blurred.)

The pilot may be used as the first phase in **evolutionary development**. Evolutionary development may be the best way of proceeding with software development in a high-risk situation. Evolution seeks to provide a significant benefit early in the development, even if the original objective can't be achieved. Gilb (1988) says of evolutionary development that it is:

> ... evolutionary because it is based on the principle of a single step forward – feedback – adapt and proceed – feedback – adapt and proceed – feedback – and so on. ... By conscious and full exploitation of evolutionary ideas we can not only exercise far better control over risk elements, but we can gain many other important benefits.
>
> (p. 18)

Rather than develop a complete estimate before doing a system definition and starting development, both the prototyping and evolutionary approaches allow a limited amount of work to take place in order to make an early decision on the viability of the approach being used. A 'macro' estimate then emerges early as a result of such an assessment of feasibility. Following the 'macro' estimate, detailed requirements specifications and system design take place, and the detailed estimates and project plans are then based on the system design. Each stage is subjected to a quality review, as shown in Figure 2.14 overleaf.

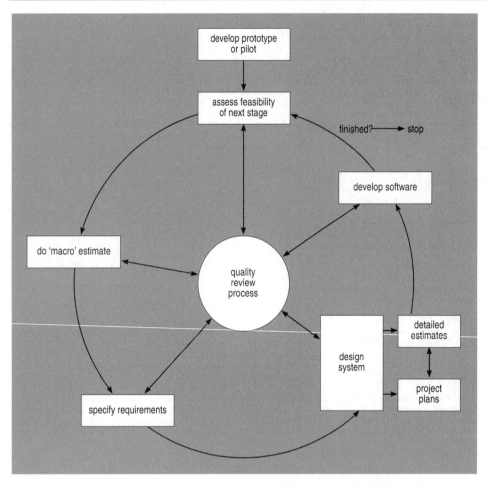

**FIGURE 2.14** Estimating software projects using prototype and evolutionary development models

The estimate and the plan for developing the software need to be updated when the software has been designed. After the software has been developed it is necessary to evaluate what has been done and to decide whether to continue to another stage or not.

## Statistical methods of estimating software

Sampling techniques and modular software development methods form the heart of statistical methods of software project estimation. In order to obtain samples, something has to be designed and written which is representative of the entire project or of a class of objects such as programs or databases which form a part of the project. Stepwise refinement can be used to identify the lowest level modules in the hierarchy; samples of characteristic modules at this low level are then designed and written, and the actual experience of design and writing then yields values used to estimate the entire project. According to Bennatan (1990) the following basic steps are required in order to use this method:

1    Identify all software components requiring new development (i.e. do not concern yourself at this stage with purchased, subcontracted or re-used software components).

2    Identify the modules that will implement the component.

3    Divide the modules so identified into categories according to:

complexity (or degree of difficulty)

function (communications, database, human–computer interface, etc.)

type (operating system, library utility, service task, etc.).

4    From each category select one module that is deemed to be representative of the others in that category.

5    Design, write and test the selected modules.

6    Based on information derived from step 5, estimate the resources required for the remaining modules in each category.

7    Combine the estimates for each category together with estimated costs for other system components such as purchased or subcontracted software to obtain a full estimate of all the software.

---

### ACTIVITY 2.12

Do you see any problems with applying statistical methods to software development? Note them down before reading the discussion below.

### DISCUSSION

One problem is that this method is not compatible with top-down software development, where the first modules designed, written and tested are the highest-level modules in the hierarchy. These modules would not be typical of the lower-level modules, which will of necessity carry more of the processing detail within them, and the top-down testing, integration and implementation method is not suitable here either. This method of estimating cannot be used in an organization which uses top-down software development, and invites all the problems of bottom-up software development (for example problems of software module integration).

It requires extensive experience of software development to be able to categorize modules as recommended in step 3. Step 2 requires initial design to take place, and this then becomes a critical activity. If this design needs to be changed, two problems occur. One is that changes in macro-level design may eliminate or fundamentally change low-level modules which then, if they have been written, must be rewritten or even discarded and replaced. The second is that the estimate based on one form of the high-level design is largely invalid for a different design.

As a method, it ignores an area of software development which is known to be high-risk: the interfacing and integration of modules and the achievement of the synergy necessary for a quality software system. This is a particularly difficult and troublesome aspect of software development when it is carried out from the bottom up (i.e. low-level modules written and tested first, then integrated).

---

A different form of statistical estimating effort for software depends upon the previous collection of records and experience of software development in the same or a very similar set of projects and the same or a similar organization. Some organizations do record how long it took to develop software modules and systems, and how much it cost. As the 'database' of information becomes larger, it becomes increasingly valuable as an estimating tool. In this type of statistical method, steps 1, 2 and 3 above are carried out, but then the resulting modules are compared with modules of a similar nature previously written *for other projects*. Actual times and costs of previous work then become the basis for creating an estimate for a new project. In turn, the data from the new project can be added to the database and used to modify future estimates.

An advantage of this form of statistical method is that it can be applied regardless of the development method used, so long as the method used in both the database projects and the new project are the same or very similar. It encompasses as well the same risk factors as the previous projects encountered.

## COCOMO (COnstructive COst MOdel)

The COCOMO model for software estimating was developed by Barry Boehm at TRW. It has subsequently been refined and many similar models have been developed. We do not intend you to learn the details of the COCOMO method, nor do we present the 'pure' COCOMO method here, but use the name COCOMO to cover a number of related and similar methods. If you are interested in knowing more, see Boehm (1981) and Bennatan (1990).

The method recognizes four modes (not discussed here) and allows three levels of estimation: basic (a non-specific gross estimation), intermediate (cost driver attributes are introduced into the estimate) and detailed (development-phase-sensitive effort multipliers are introduced as the project proceeds).

COCOMO starts by making an estimate of the number of lines of program code to be developed (but remember that there is no agreement even amongst experts as to what constitutes a *line* of code) and applies algorithms that take into account:

- the levels of ability of personnel assigned to the project
- the level of software complexity
- project size
- how reliable the software has to be
- what the development environment is like.

Reliability in software is expensive and may be unnecessary if a failure causes slight inconvenience. It becomes more and more necessary as the project software edges towards the safety-critical range. Safety-critical means human lives are at risk if the software fails to function according to its design parameters for even a short time. Reliability is also of importance in areas where ecological damage or severe financial loss may result from system failure.

It is relatively easy to create a scale for rating the levels of ability of personnel assigned to a project. For example, each software engineer working on the project can be given an expected performance value of between 1 and 4, 1 for a beginner and 4 for a very experienced engineer. The sum of these expected performance values for all engineers on the project is divided by the number of engineers. This is then an estimate of the average ability level of the whole team, presented together with cost multipliers for projects of different sizes (because project size is approximately inversely proportional to the importance of the ability of personnel). The cost multipliers indicate how much to increase estimates. There are also multipliers for reliability and development environment level.

# The function point model of estimating

The **function point model** uses the number and complexity of the functions to be delivered (e.g. functions for input, output, interface, etc.) to estimate the development effort (Jordan and Machesky, 1990). There are five steps.

1 Categorize the functions according to type and complexity and estimate the number of functions in each category.

2 Multiply the number of functions in each category by a complexity weight based on one of five difficulty levels to calculate the number of *function points* in each category. Table 2.8 illustrates this, although for simplicity we have used three difficulty levels.

**TABLE 2.8**  Complexity weights for functions in software

| Function | Simple | Average | Highly complex |
|----------|--------|---------|----------------|
| Input | 2 | 4 | 6 |
| Inquiry | 2 | 4 | 6 |
| Output | 3 | 5 | 7 |
| Interface | 4 | 7 | 10 |
| Master file | 5 | 10 | 15 |

(adapted from Jordan and Machesky, 1990, p. 149)

3 Total the number of function points for all categories.

4 Assign values to factors that influence the project and total them. (Factors are those that can contribute to the difficulty of the overall project, e.g. development environment.)

5 Compute the months of effort required by using an algorithm that relates effort-months to function points and influencing factors.

Each organization needs to develop its own specific function point model based on its own history to make this an accurate estimating tool. Example 2.12 overleaf demonstrates a typical calculation.

The function point method has the advantage that it is intuitively sensible because it is easy to see that developing three master files is more effort than developing one, and a complex master file is more effort than a simple one. Of course, the method is no more accurate than the data that go into it. It is possible to use it to make a rough estimate, as we have in Example 2.12. Combine it with a careful investigation of the required functions and the result will be more accurate – provided always that the model fits the circumstances of the project being estimated. A good function point model can only result when an organization undertakes a careful study of its own past projects – indeed, the model was developed not as an estimating tool but as a measure of productivity on past projects. Some computer packages are available to do function point estimating.

## EXAMPLE 2.12 Function point estimation

Assume that you have a project in which two input functions are simple, one is average and one highly complex, one function is a master file and is highly complex, four are inquiries which are all simple, and one is an interface which is average.

Table 2.9 shows how these are handled to produce the function points, multiplying the number by the complexity weight for each difficulty level.

**TABLE 2.9**  Determining function points

| Function | Difficulty level | Number | Complexity weight | Function points |
|---|---|---|---|---|
| Inputs | simple | 2 | 2 | 4 |
| Inputs | average | 1 | 4 | 4 |
| Inputs | highly complex | 1 | 6 | 6 |
| Master file | highly complex | 1 | 15 | 15 |
| Inquiry | simple | 4 | 2 | 8 |
| Interface | average | 1 | 7 | 7 |
| **Total unadjusted function points** | | | | **44** |

The next step is to evaluate the project influencing factors. Jordan and Machesky suggest using 0 for little or no difficulty, 3 for average and 5 for great difficulty.

If our project requires computer communications (worth, say, 5) but uses little distributed processing (worth 1), is online (worth 3), has large data volumes and high performance objectives (5), we can set these out and sum them as in Table 2.10.

**TABLE 2.10**  Evaluation of influencing factors

| Factor | Difficulty |
|---|---|
| Communications | 5 |
| Distributed processing | 1 |
| Online processing | 3 |
| Large data volumes and high performance objectives | 5 |
| **Total project influencing factor (PIF) value** | **14** |

The last step is to calculate the effort-months. The 0.36 is a constant (calculated by comparing actual to estimated times and determining the factor needed to adjust the estimates so that they equal the actuals) derived from using the function points and influencing factors to study productivity in past projects in one organization.

$$EM = 0.36 \times FP \times PIF$$

$$= 0.36 \times 44 \times 14$$

$$= 221.76 \text{ or } 222 \text{ effort-months.}$$

## 2.3.7 Summary

Budget (and plan) approval will signal the end of the major estimate preparation process. The approval authorizes expenditure and effort in order to achieve the objectives of the project; it sets constraints for that expenditure; it signals the apparent end to bargaining and negotiation about the project. Yet very few projects emerge from the weeks and months of effort and expense exactly as they were approved.

Estimation may require several iterations. As more is known about tasks, materials and human resources the estimate must be refined. Perhaps choices must be made in order to optimize the project plan or adjust plans in the light of newly revealed facts. *Any* changes made during the execution of the project will have some effect on the project's budget and schedule.

Software remains a problem, often poorly understood at the outset of a project and poorly estimated. A number of development models and estimating approaches are available to help: stepwise refinement in developing the software design and stepwise estimation; prototyping and evolutionary approaches to software development; 'macro' and detailed estimating statistical approaches to software estimation; and the COCOMO and function point models. (There are others, not mentioned in this chapter.)

Don't forget that the collection, analysis and documentation of all this information is an overhead, which adds to your project costs!

Having studied this section you should be able to:

- state the objectives (other than arriving at a sum for the project) for undertaking an estimate
- describe the two schools of thought on who ought to undertake the estimating process
- describe the important steps in preparing to undertake an estimate
- list the main categories to be estimated for most projects
- name those factors likely to affect the quantities of resource, time, cost or risk and state how they are likely to affect these
- describe four ways to obtain estimating data and explain why these are not mutually exclusive
- describe the steps of consolidation and evaluation of the data
- explain the purposes of contingency allowances and reserves
- explain the importance of presentation.

In addition, you should be able to explain why software estimating is more problematical than other forms of estimating and:

- describe stepwise estimation
- describe prototype and evolutionary methods of development and estimation
- describe statistical methods, state what their weaknesses are and describe a way of improving the statistical base of estimates for software
- describe in general terms the COCOMO model
- describe in general terms how the function point model works.

# 2.4 TENDERING AND CONTRACTING

This section discusses the processes of tendering and contracting. You are not expected to be become a legal expert, but should become familiar with the terminology and concepts involved.

Why study tendering and contracting? It is rare for a project manager to be more than peripherally involved in drawing up or signing a contract. Neither is the project manager normally responsible for contract management. However, the quality of the contract, its terms and conditions and the relationships it establishes between the two parties have a considerable effect on the project manager's work. For that reason every project manager should understand what is involved in tendering for, drawing up, signing and administering a contract.

## 2.4.1 The legal background

Every legal system makes assumptions about contracts, how they are made and implicit (as opposed to explicit) conditions that will apply between the contracting parties. As these can cause trouble for the parties to a contract and trouble costs time, money and upset, it is worth becoming acquainted with some of the principles governing contract law. (Here we will limit our discussion to English contract law) You should approach studying this section with the objective of familiarizing yourself with the terminology of contracts, the process of contracting, and the difficulties you may encounter if you have to deal with a poorly drafted contract.

The project manager may, if appointed early enough, be asked to provide information that will end up as a part of the contract. For example, an organization's legal representative may want to know about technical standards (such as ISO 9000) to which work is to be done or standards to which products of the project or components for the project must adhere. If the project manager is lucky enough to be involved at this stage, then he or she should ensure that the contract specifies not only such standards, but such things as liaison arrangements between the client and contractor, how the work will be managed and who will be responsible for what aspects of the work. (We give some questions to ask in Section 2.4.3.)

### Terms

Any part of a project which an organization decides to contract to another organization should be regarded as a subproject, normally defined by a work package definition document. More detailed plans will then be produced as part of a proposal by any organization seeking to undertake the work. The proposal is termed the tender (the price stated in the tender is generally known as the bid). A period of negotiation may take place between one or more **tenderers** and the original organization (known as the client or employer). The signed agreement between tenderer and client is known as a contract, an agreement for the tendering organization (now referred to as the contractor or **supplier**) to provide work, services or goods for a price, to be paid to the contractor or supplier by the client. Client and contractor or supplier are known as **parties to the contract**.

Figure 2.15 indicates the relationship of clients and contractors and shows the stages at which various activities are done and documents are drawn up.

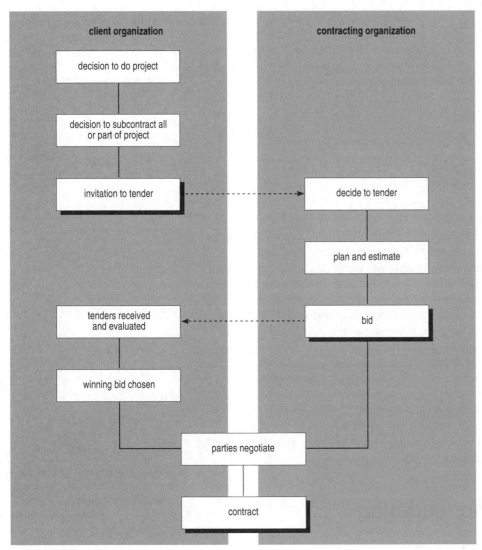

**FIGURE 2.15** Steps in reaching a contract

## Commitments

The contract commits the contractor to complete *all* the work specified to the *standard* specified and agreed between the parties and set out in the contract.

Project objectives may not change substantially in the course of a project's execution, but what needs to be done in order to achieve those objectives almost certainly will change in response to risk factors, changes in project environment and changes in detailed design. Neither party to a contract is free to alter plans unless this eventuality is explicitly provided for in the contract. Not only should there be explicit provision for alterations to the plans, but the mechanisms whereby requests for change are introduced, negotiated and incorporated into the plans should also be explicit. A contract is enforceable by law, so it is in the interests of both parties to build into it this sort of flexibility. Yet it is important not to leave so great a latitude for changes that there is no way of maintaining control.

If a client introduces substantial changes and is simply presented with a 'late' project and a much-increased bill at the end it could result in a legal dispute, since the client wasn't informed of the effects on cost and time of the changes. Likewise if a contractor introduces changes, however necessary to the completion of the work, without informing the client of them, the client is likely to take delivery of a product that is not, to the minds of its management, what was specified, and this can also result in a dispute. Changes are possible, but are legal only if the contract contains explicit clauses allowing them. Changes can be well managed only if the contract describes the mechanism by which these can be requested by either party and then agreed by both.

## Subcontracting

A contractor or, if the process has not advanced to the stage of a contract, a tenderer may in turn wish to let parts of the subproject to still other organizations. The same process applies – asking for proposals, evaluating them and either setting up binding contracts (usually if the first party already has a contract signed with the client) or less formal agreements (if the first party is bidding for the work but has not yet signed a contract, or if the first party is trying to assemble a consortium to undertake the project work). In attempting to assemble a consortium to bid for work the parties may have only the most informal of agreements but are likely to have explored the work and how it would be divided amongst them in some detail. All parties in a potential consortium are likely to have collaborated on drawing up the proposal; they may even have chosen a consortium name and settled the relationships amongst themselves: for example, which firm is to be the lead contractor and is to supply overall project management. A tenderer who wants to subcontract work to other suppliers is unlikely to have a formal contractual arrangement with those suppliers because the tenderer will not want to be bound by contracts to suppliers if the main contract is not awarded to it.

# 2.4.2   Tenders and tendering

Factors that influence a tender will be:

- the complexity and scope of the main project and the decomposition into subprojects
- whether the tender is for the main contract or a subcontract
- whether the tender is being prepared by a consortium or a single organization
- the legal system under which the contract will be drawn up
- incentives to contracting, such as having the resources available, and disincentives, for example a long distance to the project site
- perceived level of risk and perceived level of returns possible
- the balance between gaining adequate profit and making the bid low enough to be successful.

Invitations to tender (commonly also known as *invitations to bid*), requests for proposals or requests for quotations, are the initial communications from a potential client organization to potential contractors (likewise from potential contractors to potential subcontractors). The terms actually used are normally determined during contract negotiations. The invitation to tender signals that a client organization is prepared to be legally bound to another organization in a contract. By tendering, an organization also signals its willingness to be legally bound to the client organization by a contract if the client accepts the terms the tenderer is offering in its proposal.

---

### EXAMPLE 2.13

In English law an important distinction is made between an 'invitation to treat' and an 'offer'. An invitation to treat is an *indication* of the terms upon which a *supplier* is willing to do business, but it does not imply that the supplier will accept what the potential client will offer. Thus in English law a price list is only an invitation to treat and a binding contract to exchange goods for the price indicated does not exist *until* the order has been accepted by the supplier (Marsh, 1994a).

---

An **offer** to do business can be withdrawn at any moment until a contract exists (and note that the legal definition of when a contract comes into existence varies from one legal system to another), unless the offer itself is the subject of a separate contract under which the offer is to be kept open for some specified period. Most tenders in England will specify how long the offer will remain open in the tender document, for example: 'this tender [or sometimes estimate] remains valid for 60 days'. This is known in law as an **option** and cannot be withdrawn within the period stated without incurring some kind of penalty, usually financial.

### SAQ 2.11

Distinguish between an invitation to treat, an offer and an option.

## 2.4.3   Evaluating tenders

Evaluating which tenderer to award a contract to requires assessment of the capability and relevant experience of the tenderers. Where subcontracting is involved, it is not just the main contractor who will require assessment, but all the subcontractors as well.

The headings which follow set out some questions other than price and project definition that need to be asked when evaluating tenders.

*How will the work be managed?*

Recall that in the case of London Ambulance Service's system development, it was unclear as to which of the contractors was actually to be the **lead contractor**, the contractor who has overall project management and quality assurance responsibilities. Furthermore, it was never made clear whether LAS's project manager was undertaking the duties of project management and particularly of project control in the full meanings of these terms, nor what responsibilities and powers he had, nor to whom he was to report. No mechanisms were put in place for regular reports and no rights reserved for the client to inspect work in progress. No common working arrangements, such as methodologies, were agreed.

*How will the client obtain the required level of assurance?*

If the tenderer complies with a national or international quality management standard such as ISO 9000 this can provide, in itself, some measure of confidence in the tenderer. The client may, in fact, demand compliance with such quality standards from all tenderers.

The client may want to obtain assurance from tenderers on a number of different levels:

- the tenderer's financial stability and ability to carry out the work tendered for
- the tenderer's reputation
- the tenderer's experience and management expertise
- the quality of the delivered product, interim products or deliverables
- the application of technical standards.

This may mean that the client will want to reserve rights to audit the contractor's activities and performance.

*How will roles and responsibilities within both the client and contractor organizations be affected?*

Who will be assigned on either side to be responsible for project liaison and project management? Who will be designated to be the person to agree to changes, including changes in timescale and cost? What rights does the client reserve for itself in respect of the contractor? These and a number of other questions need to be answered in order to prevent problems and disputes arising later.

*How will the interface between the two organizations be established?*

Has it been agreed that there will be regular meetings and reviews? Who will attend them? Will regular reports on progress be required? Who is designated as responsible for generating these, and who will receive them? Again, these are key questions to be answered, preferably with actions either already done or to be done early in the life of the contract, in order to ensure the smoothest possible execution of the contract.

### SAQ 2.12

Based on what you have learned so far, draw up an outline checklist of *factors* to be assessed when considering tenders.

## 2.4.4   Accepting a bid

An offer can be accepted, but the acceptance is only valid if it is communicated to the person who made the offer. The acceptance should be stated in the same terms as the offer. If it is not in the same terms, for example if it raises questions or attempts to amend the terms of the offer, it is technically a **counter-offer**, which the other party can either accept or reject, and in rejecting can put forward a counter-offer to the counter-offer!

## SAQ 2.13

You want some work done on your house. You meet with two or three potential contractors and specify that you want the guttering replaced on two sides at the back of the house. You specify that replacing the guttering involves removing the existing cast-iron drainpipes and replacing them with plastic piping. You receive two bids setting out costs for replacing the guttering and three drainpipes at the back of the house. Before accepting one of these, in the course of decorating you discover that one of the drainpipes in the front of the house is damaged and needs replacing. You write to the lower bidder accepting the bid, but state in your letter that you want another drainpipe replaced at the same time. Do you have a contract with the bidder at this point?

Sometimes **letters of intent** are issued between parties to signal an intention to sign a contract or to get preliminary work started or materials purchased. However, the letter of intent has no precise legal meaning; any court case involving a letter of intent will seek to examine the circumstances of the particular letter of intent that is in dispute. Generally, there is no legal obligation on the part of either party to a letter of intent to the other; however, in certain circumstances courts *have* interpreted letters of intent as a binding contract. A letter of intent may also be interpreted by the courts as a legally binding promise to award a contract to one party for the work it describes, and it may also be interpreted as a contract for preliminary work such as design, tooling or the purchase of some items which require long order times; the letter then amounts to a promise to pay.

## SAQ 2.14

Describe the main differences between an offer, a letter of intent and a contract.

# 2.4.5  Summary

Many projects result in the process of specifying parts of the work to be done by other organizations. This means that this work is put out to tender (other organizations are invited to submit proposals for the work). Potential contractors prepare estimates for that work and develop proposals for it that are called tenders. A client organization reviews tenders and decides whether to award a contract, and to whom. If the client awards a contract, it must be stated in the same terms as the offer (tender).

Having studied this section you should be able to:

- define the following terms in your own words:

  invitation to tender, invitation to bid

  tender, tenderer

  contract, contractor, supplier

  client

  parties to a contract

  invitation to treat

  offer, counter-offer

  option

  letter of intent

- state four important questions to be asked when evaluating tenders and give examples in your own words of what these questions address.

# 2.5   *WHAT'S IN A CONTRACT?*

This section discusses the details of a contract, contract administration and some examples of contract law.

In practice, many industry sectors use standard contracts and conditions that have been agreed by industry bodies – typically tribunals – made up of clients, consultants and contractors. These may also be used as 'templates' for drawing up contracts that need to vary somewhat from the standard model.

As we noted at the beginning of the preceding section, a project manager rarely draws up a contract or signs it, yet his or her work is greatly affected by it. We don't expect you to become lawyers, able to draw up contracts or argue clauses in them. However, we do feel that it is very important for the project manager to understand what is or should be contained within a contract so that he or she can plan to meet specific clauses and to negotiate any mechanisms that will ensure the smooth running of the project in the event that these are not included in the contract itself.

## Reviewing the contract

Each contract document should be reviewed by both the contractor and the client. The contractor should review it to ensure that:

- the scope of the contract and the requirements are defined and documented
- the client has the capability to meet contractual obligations.

Each client should review the contract document to ensure that:

- any requirements differing from those in the tender are resolved
- the supplier (contractor) has the capability to meet the contractual requirements
- the contractor's responsibility for subcontracted work is defined.

Both parties should examine the document to ensure for themselves that:

- possible contingencies and risks are identified
- sensitive proprietary information (such as patent applications) is adequately protected
- there are clauses allowing changes to be made if necessary, and clauses specifying the mechanisms for communicating, negotiating and incorporating changes.

Make sure you have specialist legal advice! Some contracts contain 'let out' clauses, for example those concerned with problems that arise due to 'wilful misuse' of a product; and software contracts sometimes contain a clause stating that the contractor is not responsible for any errors 'introduced into the system'. A problem arises when pre-existing faults in the system are triggered by unusual conditions, and there may be arguments about whether a fault was introduced by the buyer or the producer.

Contracts need:

- acceptance criteria: most disputes are about whether or not the contractor has done the work agreed to the standard agreed

- criteria for handling problems detected after acceptance, including quality-related claims and purchasing complaints
- specification of activities to be carried out by the client, especially the client's role in requirements specification and acceptance.

## Purchasing

Purchased products and services may be critical to the quality, cost, efficiency and safety of the services or end-products supplied by an organization. Purchasing of products and services should be given the same level of planning, control and verification as other internal activities. The organization should establish a working relationship with suppliers and subcontractors, including provision for feedback. In this way a programme of continuing quality improvements can be supported and quality disputes avoided or settled quickly.

## Contract terms

Probably the most important part of a tender in many people's eyes is the bid price, though this need not be agreed at the time the order for work or goods is placed if both parties agree to set the price at a later date. If goods have been delivered or work done and accepted by the client even if a price has not been agreed, then the client will be legally obliged to pay a reasonable price for them. In other words, you can't get work done or supplies delivered to you and avoid paying by avoiding making any promise to pay or not stipulating a price you are willing to pay.

# 2.5.1  Financial bases of contracts

A **fixed-price** or **lump sum quotation** in a contract is binding on the contractor. If the cost of carrying out the work or supplying the goods turns out to be greater than the contractor realized when tendering, the contractor still has to meet the obligations of the contract without any additional payment. It is also the case under English contract law that something which was left out of a specification but is necessary to the completion of the work and which is commonly assumed to be a part of such a project must be supplied by the contractor even if the bid submitted and accepted didn't take this specification into account.

---

**EXAMPLE 2.14**

A client's specification for the construction of his house failed to say anything about flooring. The contractor bid for and built the house for the client, but with only under-flooring in place. The client then complained. The court ordered the contractor to provide finished flooring of a specification suitable for the style of house and type of rooms to be floored even though this was never mentioned in the contract, on the grounds that flooring is expected in a normal dwelling house (Marsh, 1994a).

---

A contract can contain a clause, usually called an **escalation clause**, which seeks to protect the contractor against rising prices or wage settlements. A contractor may wish to have an escalation clause included in the contract to protect against inflation: such a contract will specify a formula or index such as the Retail Price Index. In that case the client will be obliged to pay the additional money if the index increases, even if the contractor's costs have not.

**Cost–plus contracts** are contracts in which the contractor's costs plus an agreed percentage are paid to the contractor by the client upon completion of the contract. This type of contract, once common in defence contracts in the USA, is an open-ended one from the client's point of view: *whatever* the cost of carrying out the work, it, plus a percentage, will be due to the contractor upon completion.

**Time and materials contracts** are contracts in which the contractor agrees to carry out the work on the basis that the client pays for the time spent at an agreed rate per hour, day or week, and for any materials. These are more common in the building trades than elsewhere. Normally contractors set a rate that includes some profit margin for themselves, and pass on materials costs with a handling charge included.

Both the above types of contract are known as **cost reimbursement** contracts.

The various forms of contract may be used in combination. For example, a contractor may be willing to tender for most of the work on a project at a fixed price but there may be some element of the work that is impossible to estimate accurately enough until more work is done. A contract could be reached where that element of the work is done on a time and materials basis and the remainder at a fixed price.

### SAQ 2.15

Which form or type of contract would be most suitable in the following situations?

(a) research into a new type of vehicle
(b) installation of lifts and escalators in a large office building
(c) demolishing a redundant brick-works and clearing the site for redevelopment

## 2.5.2 Delivery, the passing of property and risk

Situations may arise during a project when it may be important to know who owns any items involved.

The passing of property in any materials or goods from supplier to purchaser (that is, legal ownership regardless of who physically possesses the materials or goods) is deemed to take place at different points in the process under different legal systems, unless explicit changes to the implied clauses of a contract appear in the contract.

## EXAMPLE 2.15

In English contract law, the passing of property in any materials or goods is judged to occur at the point when generic materials or goods become specific to the contract of sale (a contract comes into existence when the supplier accepts a purchase order). Using 2d nails as an example, 2d nails are considered generic so long as they could be *any* 2d nails, but they become specific when *that barrel of 2d nails* becomes 'attached' to a particular contract. This could occur when a barrel of nails is set aside to fulfil the contract, when a barrel is labelled with the purchaser's name and address, or when a bill of lading directing its delivery is attached to it. While the goods or materials are generic the property in them belongs to the supplier. Once they have become specific, the property in them passes to the purchaser.

This concept is important, because the property in these materials or goods, wherever they are, belongs either to the supplier or the purchaser at a particular moment. If, for example, the purchaser defaults on payment or goes bankrupt once the property in the materials or goods has passed to the purchaser, the supplier is vulnerable because the goods belong to the bankrupt purchaser and will be used to satisfy the purchaser's creditors. This is regardless of whether or not the goods are still on the supplier's premises, or whether or not the purchaser had already paid for them or not. (If the purchaser hasn't paid for the goods, then the supplier becomes another one of the creditors to be satisfied – so far as possible – from the bankrupt's stock.) Risk associated with materials and goods passes from supplier to purchaser at the same time that the law deems the property in the materials or goods has passed to the purchaser. Thus if goods are damaged in transit, who assumes the risk is determined by which party to the contract holds the property at the time they are damaged, which is not exactly the same thing as physically possessing it. Because the passing of property and risk are implied in this way, many contracts will include specific clauses to override this so that it is clearer to both parties who has ownership until what time and who carries the risks. One way to make explicit the passing of property is to specify what constitutes delivery.

### SAQ 2.16

You have an agreement with a supplier of office furniture to supply you with a number of desks, chairs, filing cabinets, tables and bookshelves, and you've paid a 25% deposit. The supplier goes bankrupt before these items have left his warehouse. Do you have any right to take them?

# 2.5.3   Time for completion and incentives

After price, the aspect in a contract most of interest to both parties is the specification of time for completion. A problem can occur when a contractor feels that there is no need to rush to complete a particular contract but the client feels that there is. There are a number of approaches to this.

- Under English law, a client can insert a clause in a contract stating that *time is of the essence*; this gives the client the right to cancel the contract and reject the goods if the contractor is even a single day late. Thus a delivery date (see above) must be clearly specified in a contract containing this type of clause.

- Detailed entries can be made of everything that might delay the contractor in completing the work and require an extension of time. In the UK a standard form of building contract, the JCT80, takes this approach.

- General clauses can be inserted specifying that the contractor is entitled to an extension of the time to complete if the client delays him, if an industrial dispute occurs, or there are circumstances beyond the contractor's control, such as heavy rain flooding a construction site. This approach is common in electrical and mechanical engineering contracts in the UK.

There are various ways of introducing early completion, target cost or co-operation into contracts (see Marsh, 1994b). These are normally associated with cost reimbursement contracts. Contracts of this type require a target estimate to be made, either as a definite sum or as rates in an approximate bill of quantities. In any case, there must be something against which performance of the work can be measured. Actual costs then have to be recorded and compared to the final target cost. The contract arranges to share between the contractor and the client the difference between the target estimate and the actual costs. This creates a very strong incentive for the contractor to keep costs as low as possible, as the difference will then be greater and the contractor's share of this also greater than it would otherwise be. Such contracts also include the payment of a lump sum or a percentage of the target estimate as a project management fee to the contractor. If the contractor overruns the estimate by more than a pre-defined ceiling (the target estimate itself or something somewhat higher than that if the risk is great), then such contracts usually contain a clause indicating that the excess overrun is entirely the responsibility of the contractor. If time is vital, it is possible to vary the amount of savings going to the contractor by the extent to which the contract is completed on or before the target completion date.

---

### EXAMPLE 2.16

Cost reimbursement contracts were used by the State of California to contract work for repair to major highways in the Los Angeles area which were damaged and made impassable by the January 1994 earthquake. In one case, the contract for repair of the Santa Monica Freeway (deemed to be the busiest road in the world) was completed in 90 days, including the complete reconstruction of a number of damaged bridges and a badly damaged roadway and road bed. The work had originally been estimated to take a minimum of 18 months. The contracts specified early completion 'bonuses', with the degree to which the contractor gained being related to how early he could complete the project.

---

Table 2.11 shows an example of varying the contractor's share of cost savings by time so that the earlier the contract is completed the greater will be the reward for the contractor. (Of course, the parties will have to agree in advance how to calculate the cost savings!)

**TABLE 2.11**  One model for early completion incentives

| Period by which contract is finished before or after target completion date | Contractor's share of cost savings (%) |
| --- | --- |
| 6 weeks early | 90 |
| 4 weeks early | 75 |
| 2 weeks early | 60 |
| target date met | 50 |
| 2 weeks late | 35 |
| 4 weeks late | 20 |
| 6 or more weeks late | nil |

(adapted from Marsh, 1994b, p. 97)

SAQ 2.17

Imagine you are in charge of a project in which it is important for the main contractor to complete by a certain date – for example the contractor needs to complete construction of a drilling platform for the North Sea so that it is ready for your team to position before bad weather begins in the autumn. Comment on whether you would stipulate that time is of the essence with a fixed completion date, include an explicit completion date but allow carefully specified delays, or have a contract with early completion incentives.

## 2.5.4  Quality, performance and damages

The law is fairly clear about what constitutes suitable quality for acceptance (which is *not* the same as meeting a quality expectation on the part of the client whether or not it was explicitly stated in the contract). Goods, whether purchased or made as a part of the project, have to correspond to their specification. Normally, goods sold must correspond to the description under which the supplier offered to sell them and the purchaser ordered them, unless the contract specifies otherwise.

*Performance* is gaining greater and more explicit prominence in contracts now than has been the case in the past. Performance means making clear how the delivered product is to be used. While goods in English law are expected to be fit for the main purpose(s) for which they were designed, clients or buyers may want to make explicit in the contract the purpose to which they propose to put them. It then behoves the contractor or supplier to ensure that such goods can meet this purpose. If the client or buyer does not make the contractor or supplier aware of special conditions that might apply to the use of goods, materials or products and the supplier still supplies these in good faith, the risk passes to the client or buyer. Contracts now often specify not only the performance criteria for products, but for services as well. Service levels are pre-determined and enshrined in the contract, and bonus levels for the contractor may be tied to service levels actually achieved.

158

## EXAMPLE 2.17

Marsh (1994a) cites the case of plastic pails exported to Kuwait. These were suitable for all normal uses but could not stand the intense heat and pressures when left standing stacked several tiers high on the dockside in Kuwait. Since the buyer had not made clear to the supplier the extraordinary conditions under which the pails had to perform, the supplier was held not liable for their failure (Aswan Engineering Company v. Lupidine Ltd).

As well as implied quality measures, the client may wish to include in the contract the type of specification to be met or the quality of the processes to be applied in carrying out work so that there is an *explicit, agreed standard* and the work, materials and products can be judged against that standard.

When problems occur, one party of a contract normally loses something. The loss is commonly a financial one or can be quantified in financial terms. The object of **damages** is to place the so-called **injured party** in the *same financial position as would have pertained had the contract been completed properly.* Contracts will often contain a clause specifying damages that can be recovered by the client from a contractor who fails to complete the contract to time or specification as either a sum or a percentage of the contract price; such damages may be made to apply if the contractor overruns the agreed completion date by more than a specified amount (and ceilings are commonly set on damages as well, to avoid bankrupting the contractor).

## EXAMPLE 2.18

A cruise ship needs refitting before the next cruising season. The owners insert a clause in the contracts with their contractors that the work will be completed such that the ship is sailable and the staterooms can be used in the normal way by customers on or before the next scheduled sailing date. Otherwise, damages equivalent to the profits lost because of the unsatisfactory state of the ship will be owed to the client.

A **penalty** can also apply. In law, a penalty is a sum *greater* than the client could anticipate losing and normally has the conditions under which it will be paid specified in detail. Penalty clauses are specifically *excluded* from some types of contract, such as the joint construction trades (JCT) contracts and public sector contracts, as they are often deemed to be unfair in many contracting situations.

### SAQ 2.18
What is the difference between damages and penalties?

## 2.5.5 Payment, guarantees and exclusion clauses

Payment can be in a lump sum at the end, or can occur at stages during the execution of the contract (**stage payments**). In contracts there is no implied time for payment – in other words, the law does not stipulate *when* payment is due if this is not specified in the contract. If the client delays paying, the supplier or contractor does not have the right to terminate the contract. This is particularly a problem where stage payments are involved, because if the client misses a stage payment it will be difficult for the contractor to terminate the contract unless the breach of the agreement is deemed to be large (for example if it were a significant proportion of the total cost) or the failure to pay is deemed to be likely to recur. Contracts also do not contain the implication that interest can be charged on late payments. The contractor can only protect himself if he *explicitly* states within the contract when payment is due and that interest can be charged on late payments.

Ways in which parties to a contract can safeguard themselves with respect to payment are to define precisely what events should trigger a payment and what objective should be achieved when that event occurs. For example, the contract may tie a payment to the delivery of one of the project's deliverables, state the amount due then either in terms of a fixed sum or in terms of a formula by which the amount due can be calculated, and make explicit the time limit within which the payment is to be made. The contract may also provide the contractor with a remedy if the client fails to pay or pays late (such as charging interest or penalties on late payments) and provide the client with the means to recover the value of payments made if the contractor defaults before completing the contract.

Certain guarantees *are* normally implied in contracts, though these can be included explicitly as well. To protect themselves against unknown but implied guarantees, clients or contractors sometimes insert clauses known as *exclusion clauses* in contracts: an exclusion clause states explicitly what one or the other party will not be liable for. However, not all such clauses are legal even if they are made explicit in the contract.

### EXAMPLE 2.19

Parties to a contract cannot insert a clause excluding themselves from liability for death or personal injury due to their negligence. In cases of other forms of loss or damage, a clause can only restrict or exclude liability if the contract meets a legal test of reasonableness. Reasonableness is judged by whether the client sought to negotiate a clause and was given an opportunity to do so, the possibility of insurance against the risk, the level of loss suffered by the client or the difficulty of the task undertaken by the contractor (Marsh, 1994b).

**SAQ 2.19**

If you were very concerned that a contractor erecting a building for you had the building framed and closed in against the weather by mid-September, could you tie some of the payment to this condition in the contract?

## 2.5.6  Why contracts go wrong

Marsh (1994c) lists a number of what amount to failures to use common sense that can ruin a contract. He states that 'the cancer of contracting' is variation in price and time. Change cannot be prevented; few if any projects emerge at the end exactly as they were planned at the beginning. Change must be allowed for. (Controlling change is discussed in Chapters 5 and 6.) As specifications and requirements change, particularly if the changes are not adequately controlled, the changes have a cumulative effect on a project, and on its contract, in terms of the final price of the contract and the completion time. Marsh's list of failures in contracts includes:

1   Inadequate time given to planning and design. Marsh states that this often happens because 'many managements are still not convinced that progress is being made unless holes are being dug on site or plant manufactured'. In software production, many managements like to see code being written and tested and worry when the software engineers appear to be spending too much time simply thinking, or creating documents the management don't entirely understand and which do not appear to make progress towards a working computer system.

2   Inadequate specifications. Many people do not like to commit themselves 'too early' in the process of project specification because they do not wish to be bound later by earlier decisions.

3   Insufficient attention paid to what the tenderer is actually offering, and how close a match it is to what the client is seeking.

4   Lack of disciplined control of change. It is easy for the contractor or project manager to say 'yes' informally to small requests; however, small requests quickly accumulate to have large unplanned effects if the project manager does not insist on proper change control.

5   Technical improvements designed to avoid the creeping obsolescence that occurs to high-technology projects and products even as the project proceeds.

6   Genuinely unforeseen circumstances such as the appearance in a civil engineering project of unsuspected mains services (or the uncovering of a site of archaeological importance) which then have to be excavated and diverted.

Changes of all kinds can result in wasted design work, new design work, cancelling or modifying orders for materials or parts and placing new orders, delay in the project or the incurring of overtime costs in order to keep to the schedule and the need, in some cases, to extend the period as well as the cost of the contract.

**SAQ 2.20**

List ways that changes in the project specification (and thereby the costs and timescale) can be required, and state why this can result in problems.

## 2.5.7  Summary

Contracts, before they are signed, need to be reviewed by the contractor and the client in order that both are certain of what they are committed to once they sign. Contract terms normally encompass price, delivery criteria, time for completion and any incentives, payment, guarantees, penalties and exclusion clauses. Both parties need to check a contract for quality: does the contract contain a complete specification of what is to be done, state any constraints on how it is to be done, include the standards to be adhered to by the contractor, state what is to be delivered and when? Does it allow for *controlled* change?

Having studied this section you should be able to:

- specify items that a contractor should ensure are in the contract document
- specify items that a client should ensure are in the contract document
- define the term *escalation clause* in your own words
- name and briefly define two different bases for determining the contract price
- explain the importance of determining what constitutes delivery and how this relates to the transfer of property and risk
- list ways of specifying the importance of time for completion and what form a contract can take in accommodating reasons for a contractor's failure to complete on time
- describe in your own words one model for early completion incentives
- describe in outline legal definitions of implied quality
- define the terms *injured party*, *damages* and *penalty*, distinguishing between the last two
- distinguish between lump sum payment and stage payments
- describe ways in which parties to a contract can protect themselves with respect to payments
- define in your own words the term *exclusion clause*
- describe six failures that can result in changes to contracts and state why these can cause problems with a contract.

# 3 PLANNING

## *INTRODUCTION*

Estimating and preparing a budget, described in Chapter 2, are only part of the processes of starting a project. Estimating cannot be carried out without concurrently developing a project plan. The activities of planning are described in this chapter, but you should remember as you study it that planning and estimating go hand in hand.

Planning takes place at all stages in a project. It starts in the conceptual phase with outline plans of possible schemes. These are continually refined; planning intensifies as the scope and timing of the project become more firmly established. By the time there is a firm commitment by the sponsor to proceed the plans are developed formally into a project plan. This commitment will be marked by the owner or sponsor (the person or group who will be paying for it) authorizing expenditure on the project, at least up to a certain stage. If the sponsor is having the work done by people outside his or her own organization there will now be a legally binding contract.

Planning is not confined to this initial stage. As the project unfolds it is possible to fill in more and more detail. Towards the end of a project plans are *still* being refined in order to bring it to a satisfactory conclusion. Planning at these later stages is just as important to the success of the project as the initial planning.

For the sake of clarity we assume in this chapter that the sponsor and the contractor are two distinguishable entities, although they may be simply different parts of the same organization. By the time the contract has been made, someone should have been identified to head the project team. We shall refer to this person as the 'project manager' although this will not necessarily be his or her job title. Confusion in job titles may arise because the sponsoring organization will often appoint a 'project manager' from within their own ranks to supervise the contractor. In this chapter the title *project manager* will mean the head of the project team in the contractor's organization.

Planning is more than scheduling. Since much of this chapter is devoted to studying scheduling methods it is important to be clear that much more is meant by planning than producing a schedule of tasks to be performed. Planning means deciding what you need to do to get to where you want to be. This involves:

- having a clear, agreed definition of the goal
- determining what tasks need to be done to get there
- establishing where the resources will come from to perform these tasks – the money, the equipment, the people
- deciding who will do which tasks

- establishing criteria against which the satisfactory completion of those tasks will be judged

- producing a workable schedule for the performance of the tasks

- assessing what might prevent the achievement of the goal and deciding how such risks will be managed

- gaining acceptance of the plan from the sponsor and stakeholders.

In Chapters 1 and 2 you have already studied approaches to the satisfactory definition of the goal of a project and the process by which estimates may be made of the resources needed to get there. You have also studied the assessment of risk and the need for contingency planning. In later chapters we will return to the issue of how you might gain acceptance of the plan from the sponsor and stakeholders (Chapter 4) and establishing criteria against which the satisfactory completion of tasks may be judged (Chapter 5).

In this chapter we will first look at how the project manager should embark on planning to satisfy the client. This will involve initially confirming the goal of the project and continuing liaison between sponsor and project team throughout (Section 3.1). We next study planning 'who does what' – assigning tasks to people (Section 3.2). In Sections 3.3 and 3.4 we will study the scheduling techniques required to produce a workable timetable for the tasks to be performed. Section 3.3 is concerned with producing a feasible schedule without resource limitations and Section 3.4 considers how such practical limits may be handled. Finally, in Section 3.6, we pull together the various elements of planning required to produce the project plan which is needed at formal project initiation.

# Aims and objectives

After studying this chapter you should be able to:

- outline the kinds of plan that the project manager will need to make

- discuss the factors to be considered when setting up the project organization and its administration

- use several techniques for scheduling a project: including milestones, Gantt charts and networks

- compare activity-on-node scheduling with activity-on-arrow scheduling

- produce a schedule and allocate resources in both time-limited and resource-limited situations

- describe a formal project plan and explain its purpose, content, authorship and readership.

# 3.1  *PLANNING TO SATISFY THE CLIENT*

This section is about the plans which a project manager should make to ensure a satisfied client. The scope of work in the project must be properly understood and a co-operative climate established for resolving problems.

## 3.1.1  The project manager's objectives

Consider the problem of attacking a new project through the eyes of the project manager. The primary objective is to complete the project to the contracted quality within the project budget in the contracted timescale. You will notice that this primary objective contains three factors – *quality, cost* and *time*. All of them should be defined in the contract. These three factors have continually to be controlled by the project manager, sometimes trading off one against another. Success requires careful planning.

However, there are other objectives, the most important being client satisfaction. The project manager's client is the sponsor of the project. It is the sponsor who has taken responsibility for initiating this project and is putting up the money. (If money is borrowed it is still the sponsor who is responsible for it.) There are also stakeholders to consider (the involvement of the stakeholders will be discussed in Chapter 4). The project manager will therefore be trying to satisfy not only the sponsor but also the key stakeholders in the project.

Unfortunately, satisfying the sponsor may not precisely coincide with fulfilling the contract to the agreed specification. If the specification included in the contract were so badly prepared that the sponsor received an unsatisfactory product, albeit to the agreed specification, then the sponsor would be alienated and future business relations between sponsor and contractor would be impaired. So part of the project manager's job is to ensure that, as far as possible, within the constraints of the primary objective, the result is a satisfied client. This will usually mean that the originally agreed specification must be *changeable*. A mechanism for keeping track of changes within a project is discussed in Chapters 5 and 6.

The contract will have specified deliverables, the products of the project, to be delivered at several points in the project. (We are using products here to mean the *products of the project* – not any products that sponsors may be selling to *their* customers.) If these deliverables are as specified in the contract then you might expect the sponsor to be entirely satisfied. However, sponsors are not infallible and it is quite common for them not to realize the implications of what they have asked for. It is frequently found that sponsors don't know what they really want until, too late, they see what has been delivered – and don't like it.

---

### ACTIVITY 3.1

A householder contracted a builder for an extension to his house that included a shower room. The customer had asked for a wood block floor in the shower room and this was specified in the plans. The builder, however, had had poor experiences of wood block floors in shower rooms because of the water so to head off trouble suggested that the floor should be tiled instead. This was agreed and the client was satisfied.

Can you think of an example from your own experience where you have specified something that you wanted which turned out to be a disappointment even though it met your specification? How could this problem have been handled so that dissatisfaction was avoided?

### DISCUSSION

As discussed in Chapter 2, it is worth making considerable effort to get the contract right in the first place, but if there have to be changes, the cheapest time to make them is at the planning stage. The implication of this is that the delivered products may differ from the original products contracted for. There is therefore a need to be able to handle changes, a problem that we will return to several times during this course.

Apart from client satisfaction, another objective is the health of the project manager's own organization. When this project is finished the staff who have been involved in it will move on to other projects. Responsible project managers should therefore aim to develop their skills so that after the project the company benefits from their development.

Finally, the organization employing the project manager (the organization paying the wages as opposed to the sponsor paying for the project) will expect to make a profit from this project. The project manager may expect to be called to account for this both during and after the project: it is no good satisfying your client without also satisfying your superiors. (They may be in the same organization but in different departments and the same issue then arises of departmental accountability.)

### SAQ 3.1

What is the primary objective of the project manager?

# 3.1.2 Mutual understanding of the contract

In order for the project manager to have any hope of achieving a successful outcome a necessary condition must be a clear understanding by both the contractor and the sponsor of exactly what is to be achieved. Many of the problems that arise towards the end of a project can be avoided by ensuring that both parties have the same understanding of what is to be done and, furthermore, which of them is responsible for it.

Ideally, the project manager will be involved before the contract is signed to ensure that the separate responsibilities of both the sponsor and contractor are as well defined as possible. If the project manager is appointed after the contract has been signed then his or her first task will be to review the contract to see if there are any undefined areas, and then to reach agreement with the client on how these issues should be resolved. In the ideal contract there are no such ambiguities, but most project managers have to perform in a less than ideal world. Often it is recognized at contract signing that there will be matters that cannot be specified in detail at that stage, simply because the work required to fill in these details has yet to be done.

---

**EXAMPLE 3.1**

A building society asked for tenders to replace existing software with software that extended the range of tasks performed. To make a bid that covered every detail of the existing software would involve each bidder examining the existing software in such detail that the costs to the bidders and to the client in terms of staff time would be prohibitive. In this case the parties agreed some areas of the work would be investigated in detail only after the contract had been signed and that the work would be paid for by the client using a formula related to staff time required. Clearly this is a potentially risky situation where the clients need to convince themselves that nothing in the detail will present an unforeseen hurdle.

---

## Client responsibilities

The naive view of a project is that the client specifies what is wanted and the contractor's job is to provide it. However, this underestimates the client's role in the project team. It is virtually impossible for the contractor to execute a project without continual constructive input from the sponsoring organization. A good project manager ensures that the sponsor understands what will be required from the latter's organization and gets a commitment to provide it. One way of gaining this commitment is to set up a formal liaison committee with minutes of the agreed actions.

What sort of thing might the client be responsible for? The client will normally be responsible for providing data about anything in the client's domain to which the project has an interface. The project may have to deliver a product which works in conjunction with a client's existing system, or with equipment which the client is procuring from another source. Details of the system or the equipment will need to be provided in good time to the project team. The client may also be responsible for training staff to be effective users of the product. Even if the contractor is responsible for this training, the client will be responsible for making the trainees available at the right time as they are unlikely to be under the project manager's authority.

Another client responsibility is likely to be the prompt approval or rejection of intermediate documents produced by the contractor. For example, the contract may have specified that the contractor must submit an outline design for approval before proceeding with the detailed design. Clearly, a timely response is vital if work on the detailed design is to start on schedule; a tardy response would increase the cost and the length of the project through no fault of the contractor.

## Acceptance tests

The client will usually be responsible for performing acceptance tests on the project's deliverables. Remember that deliverables here means all kinds of outputs from the project work: plans, designs, prototypes, equipment, software code, test specifications, training courses, maintenance and operating manuals and so on. Consequently, acceptance tests need not be confined to the last phase of the project. A progressive acceptance by the client of individual deliverables as they become available is likely to unearth problems earlier and establish a better relationship between client and contractor than a single phase of testing at the end of the project.

The criteria for acceptance of all the deliverables should of course be specified in the contract but the client will often be responsible for devising the acceptance tests in detail. If it is the client's responsibility to develop the tests then the project will need a commitment from the client to provide details of the tests in good time, so that the contractor can ensure in advance that each deliverable will pass. Doing this well means that acceptance testing won't be a source of conflict.

It is worth distinguishing between the nature of acceptance testing and the *system testing* that should precede it. During the system testing it may be a good idea to be inventive about different kinds of tests that might be tried. In the software field some developers like to expose their software to a team who try to 'break' it. However, at acceptance it is rather late in the day deliberately to spring new surprises on the contractor. Acceptance testing should be conducted in a more collaborative way, giving the developer every opportunity to anticipate problems that could arise in testing, because otherwise the project will be delayed every time the client discovers some variance from expectations.

### SAQ 3.2

The owner of a small supermarket has decided to install new electronic point of sale equipment in place of older equipment. This will involve physical changes to the workplace for the check-out staff, new wiring, and changes to the way the staff work. The equipment is to be interfaced with an existing stock control system, which will require some modification. An equipment supplier has contracted to design, supply the system, make modifications to the stock control software, train the staff and supervise the initial operation. Make whatever assumptions you think reasonable about the division of responsibilities.

(a) List about half a dozen client responsibilities that the contractor's project manager might identify.

(b) List about half a dozen deliverables that could be specified for the project.

## Timescale

At the estimating stage an outline plan will have been developed showing the timescale of major activities to be performed during the project and especially the occurrence of key events. The timing of key events that affect or are affected by the client or external activities will need to be confirmed so that the outline plan can be established. This becomes the basis for more refined plans that will be drawn up during the project start-up phase. The scheduling aspects of planning will be studied in detail in Sections 3.4 and 3.5 of this chapter.

## Budget

The budget available to the contractor's project manager for completing the project needs to be established not with the client but with the contractor's management. The project budget is the expenditure that the project manager is authorized to incur in fulfilling the contract.

# 3.1.3  Liaison with the client

Frequent and effective liaison between the project manager and the sponsor is essential. This is true even in projects of the turnkey type. A **turnkey project** is one where the client places a contract, the contractor in due course delivers the goods – like delivering a car – and the client then puts the fruits of the project into operation – like turning the key and driving away. You may think that in such a situation there is no need for much liaison between client and contractor but successful project managers rarely hold this view.

To understand why liaison is necessary we have to recognize two important differences between buying a product such as a car and asking a contractor to undertake a project. First, the car buyer understands precisely what he or she is going to get, having seen a similar model and a detailed specification before. Secondly, the buyer knows exactly how the car will be used from previous experience of driving similar cars. Although the client may sometimes think that this also applies to a turnkey project the fact is that only in a tiny proportion of cases do the clients know precisely what they are going to get and exactly how it will be used. Those few examples where this applies are usually repeat orders for a project that has already been performed for this client by this contractor at least once before. (Some project managers will even deny that there is such a thing as a repeat order!)

There are several reasons for liaison between the contractor and client:

- to establish mutual confidence and a co-operative climate
- to exchange technical information
- to report progress to the client
- to control changes while ensuring that the product matches the client's requirements as closely as is practical within time and budget constraints
- to make joint preparations for acceptance testing
- to prepare for commissioning (the transition to normal operation).

Two of these reasons are fairly self-evident: technical information will need to be exchanged and the client will want to know about progress. These need no elaboration at this point. However, let us now consider the other reasons in turn.

## Mutual confidence and co-operation

The project manager must establish a good relationship with the client so that each has confidence that the other is working efficiently towards a successful outcome. Unforeseen problems are bound to arise and each organization will require the co-operation of the other in solving them. Even in a turnkey project the client will want to monitor progress to be sure that the project will be completed on time. For these reasons a channel of communication needs to be set up at the highest possible level between the project manager and the client. One way in which this is done is to establish a steering committee for the project with high-level membership from the client's and the contractor's respective organizations. An alternative is to schedule a series of regular meetings between representatives of both organisations. Written reports will also be required but are no substitute for these face-to-face meetings.

In large projects employing over 100 contract staff, the client organisation will often want to monitor progress more closely by putting members of its own staff into the contractor's offices. These people may have the primary role of providing answers to the contractor's queries, so fulfilling the client's commitment to provide information, but their proximity to the project team allows the client to assess whether the formal progress reports truly reflect the state of affairs in the contractor's office.

---

**EXAMPLE 3.2**

In preparing for this course we spoke with a firm which had contracted a major software development to another firm. While the project had a successful outcome, the client expressed the opinion that the project would have progressed much more smoothly if he had had some of his people actually on the contractor's premises, both to provide information to the contractor when needed and to convey to the client's management their assessments of progress.

---

## Change control

In spite of the best efforts of both client and contractor it is unlikely that the product to be delivered will have been perfectly specified at the time of signing the contract. As the project unfolds dialogue will be needed, not only to clarify uncertainties in the original requirements but also to cater for changes in the client's requirements. The environment in which the project is conducted may have changed or the client may realize that a better match between the proposed product and the real requirements can be achieved by changing the specification. However, change presents risk to both parties. Great care is required to ensure that the effects of any proposed change are properly evaluated before changes to project scope, price and timescale are agreed. The project manager may need to exercise a high degree of diplomatic skill to prevent a project from being sunk in quicksands because of well-intentioned improvements. A formal system for controlling any changes is vital. This will be considered in detail in Chapter 6.

## Preparing for product acceptance

Both parties have to make preparations for acceptance of deliverables. Although it is not the project manager's responsibility to prepare the client for acceptance, it is a good idea to do so. If the client is not ready to accept a deliverable at the agreed time there may be a delay in handing it over and consequent delay in receiving payment. Liaison with the client is therefore recommended to ensure smooth progress of each deliverable through to acceptance. The purpose of this is to avoid surprises. If the tests and timing are agreed well in advance then the acceptance process will go much more smoothly. One way to do this is to set up a joint acceptance committee between the client and contractor, whose purpose is to monitor the progress of both parties towards acceptance of the various deliverables. On large projects an acceptance committee might have a different composition from the project steering committee described earlier. The client will normally be responsible for performing the acceptance tests, using criteria that should have been established before the signing of the contract. Whether or not there are such criteria, an acceptance committee is a forum through which the procedure for acceptance testing can be established.

## Commissioning and further support

Commissioning is often regarded as a project in its own right, with a separate project manager and often an almost totally new project team, although it will usually include some members from the team who designed and produced the system. More often than not commissioning is carried out by a team primarily from the client organization rather than by the contractor. This allows a smooth transition from commissioning into normal operation.

---

### ACTIVITY 3.2

Consider your own project and make notes on your answers to these questions.

- Who was its client or clients?
- Who contracted to do it?
- Was there a good mutual understanding at the outset of the 'contract' between client and contractor?
- Did the clients have a clear understanding of their responsibilities?
- Were procedures set up to establish mutual confidence and co-operation between contractor and client, to control changes on the project and to prepare for the acceptance of the work?
- Did shortcomings in any of these areas lead to a poorer outcome than might have been expected?
- Which aspects of the work might have been better organized?

---

### SAQ 3.3

Why should a project manager want to arrange liaison meetings with the client of a turnkey project, apart from the need to exchange technical information?

# 3.1.4  Summary

The project manager needs to establish a good relationship with the client, the sponsor of the project. The objectives of the project manager are not only to deliver a product to time and cost but also to ensure that the outcome is a satisfied client.

It is important that the client and the contractor (represented by the project manager) share the same understanding of the contract. Responsibilities are not one-sided. The client is responsible for giving timely response to the contractor's need for data, prompt approval or rejection of documents from the contractor, and for preparing for future acceptance testing and commissioning.

Frequent liaison is required between the client's organization and the contractor to:

- establish and maintain mutual confidence and co-operation
- exchange technical information
- report on progress
- exercise change control

- prepare for acceptance
- prepare for commissioning.

Having studied this section you should now be able to:

- define a project manager's objectives and discuss the limitations of a view restricted to delivering a specified product by a given date at a given cost
- explain why the client has responsibilities and give examples
- give reasons why liaison with the client is necessary for a successful project.

# 3.2 ASSIGNING TASKS TO PEOPLE

In this section we consider how the project organization is set up, how
responsibilities are assigned and how a project is administered.

## 3.2.1 Setting up the project organization

During the preparation stages before reaching a contract, the key members of the
project team should be identified and the project manager should check again on
their availability as the likelihood of the project contract increases. A framework for
the project organization should be established. Once the project is sanctioned the
project manager will need to build up the team and give it an identity. (We defer to
Chapter 4 the human aspects of recruiting and managing the team.)

There is no fixed pattern of organization that is applicable to all types and sizes of
project because each organization needs to reflect the job to be done. There are
various ways of organizing a project, as will be discussed in Chapter 4. Figure 3.1
shows a typical organization.

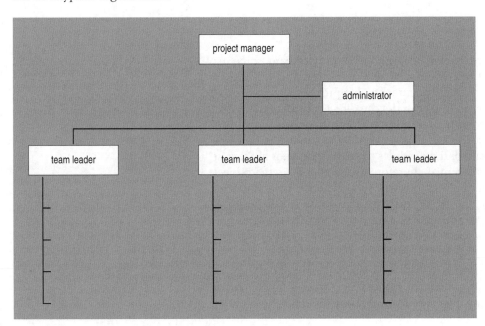

**FIGURE 3.1**  A typical project organization

In a project employing fewer than half a dozen people, each team member could
report directly to the project manager but in a larger project it is necessary to form
groups, each headed by a leader reporting to the project manager. Large projects
need an administrator, shown in Figure 3.1 as reporting directly to the project
manager. The administrator's position on the organizational chart is shown
differently from the group leaders to emphasize the different role: the administrator
has responsibilities which span the whole project. Project administration is
described in Section 3.2.3.

*Terms of reference*

All the people reporting directly to the project manager should be given terms of reference to define their roles in the project.

## 3.2.2 Assigning responsibilities

The basic framework for assigning responsibilities should be the work breakdown structure (WBS). The WBS is a tree structure where the total work to be done is broken down into packages which are further subdivided into elements, and so on for as many levels as the scale of the project requires. Packages are described in work package documents. The lowest-level elements are individual statements of work (SOWs) for someone to perform. (All were introduced in Chapter 2.)

It simplifies the management task if the organizational structure mirrors the work breakdown structure as closely as possible so that responsibilities do not cut across boundaries between the work elements. For example, suppose the project is to install a new plastics manufacturing line: a possible WBS is shown in Figure 3.2(a) and a likely organization to perform the work appears in Figure 3.2(b). Matching the organization and the WBS closely together has the advantage of creating a simple relationship between the people and the work packages.

## Subcontractors

In many projects only part of the work will be done by the project team: some may be done by the client and the rest will be done by subcontractors who will take on a package, as described by a work package document. One problem with work that has been subcontracted is that it is no longer under the direct control of the project manager, yet late delivery or poor performance by subcontractors may jeopardize the whole project. It is not realistic in a large project simply to subdivide the work among the subcontractors and wait for the products to arrive. The odds are that at least one of them will be late. It is essential, therefore, that someone in the project team has responsibility for monitoring each piece of subcontracted work and that the contracts are drawn up so that the project manager has power to take action if a subcontractor fails to progress at an adequate rate or to the specified quality.

### SAQ 3.4

Assuming that the subcontractor is to undertake management of the subcontracted work, what key document would you require a subcontractor to produce at the time of placing the contract (apart from the tender and the contract itself)?

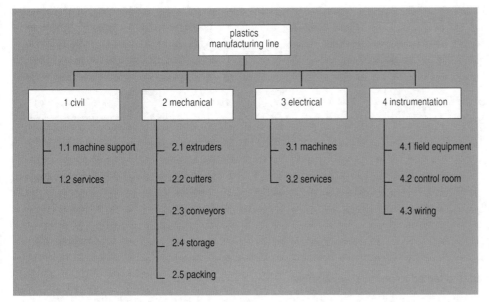

**FIGURE 3.2(a)**
WBS and organization: work breakdown structure for a plastics production line oriented to engineering disciplines

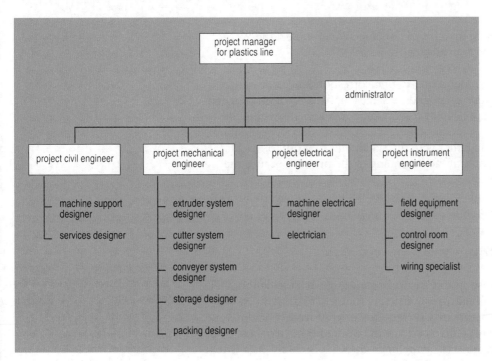

**FIGURE 3.2(b)**
WBS and organization: an organization to mirror the work breakdown structure

Obtaining a good fit between the organization and the WBS may require the WBS to be distorted from the division that the project manager may find more natural. In the case of the new plastics line above it may seem more natural to split the work primarily into the areas associated with each of the main machines, as shown overleaf in Figure 3.3. Here the work to be performed by a given discipline is split even at the highest level of the WBS. Although it may be possible in a large project to make one person responsible for each of the main areas in Figure 3.3 it is likely to be difficult to set up an organization that matches this WBS at lower levels.

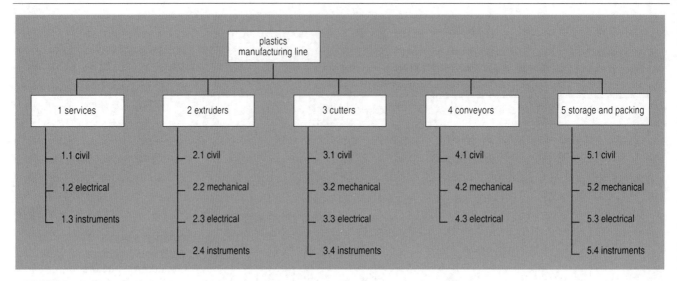

**FIGURE 3.3** Work breakdown structure oriented to physical components

### SAQ 3.5

What is the problem in setting up a project organization to reflect the WBS of Figure 3.3 if the project team is small (say, 10 people)?

Since it is often not possible to produce a one-to-one correspondence between positions on the project organization chart and packages in the WBS, it is normally necessary to give each person responsibility for a number of elements within the WBS, not all contained within the same package. A person's workload would then consist of a list of WBS elements together with the statements of work for each of them. These lists are not known fully at the beginning of the project because the information is not available for such detailed plans. However, as the project progresses the plans should be updated so that the individual work statements can be prepared in time for their execution.

## The responsibility matrix

Often more than one person is responsible for some aspect of each element of the WBS. One person may have the primary responsibility for the work but others may be required to support it and someone may be required to approve it. The different ways in which several people may be involved in each work element can best be represented on a **responsibility matrix** (sometimes known, obscurely, as a **linear responsibility chart**) as shown in Figure 3.4. Each row represents a task and each column a person. In each box within the matrix a letter denotes the responsibility of the person in that column for the task in that row.

### SAQ 3.6

According to Figure 3.4 who has what responsibility for a procurement enquiry relating to a piece of instrumentation?

| $P$ = prime responsibility<br>$S$ = support<br>$N$ = notify | project manager | project administrator | civil engineer | mechanical engineer | electrical engineer | instrument engineer | site engineer |
|---|---|---|---|---|---|---|---|
| civil design | N | N | P | | | | |
| mechanical design | N | N | | P | | | |
| electrical design | N | N | | | P | | |
| instrument design | N | N | | | | P | |
| design review | P | S | S | S | S | S | S |
| procurement enquiry | | P | S | S | S | S | N |
| supplier selection | N | S | P | P | P | P | |
| ordering | | P | N | N | N | N | N |
| installation | N | N | S | S | S | S | P |

**FIGURE 3.4** A responsibility matrix

# 3.2.3 Administration

On any project a lot of administrative work needs to be done if the project is to be kept in good order. In a small project employing fewer than about half a dozen people the project manager will probably look after the administration, perhaps with the assistance of a clerk or a secretary. On a larger project, giving the job of administration to a person equipped with a wide range of skills is more common; that person assists the project manager in controlling the project, and is sometimes called a **project controller** (or project control officer). In a very large project there may be a project control or project support team who are then jointly called the **project support office**. In projects that are too small to justify a full-time administrator a project control officer may be employed on a part-time basis, working on two or more projects. In organizations which have a steady stream of project work there will often be a permanent project support office providing administrative support to an ongoing programme of projects.

Administrative tasks which may be done by the project control officer include:

- scheduling – network analysis and updating
- servicing progress meetings – arrangements and minutes
- supporting client liaison meetings – minutes and briefing documents
- preparing subcontractor contracts and monitoring progress
- monitoring cost, reporting and forecasting
- maintaining the project files
- arranging accommodation – office space for temporary staff or staff temporarily displaced
- providing facilities – phones, photocopying, computer services

- maintaining registers – commitments, deliverables, changes

- controlling document flow – knowing where documents are and keeping them moving through the system

- recording and processing staff expenses

- recruiting temporary staff

- ordering, monitoring and approving payment for equipment.

This list is not exhaustive and those jobs that appear in the list are not necessarily all performed by the project control officer. Nevertheless, all these tasks will be performed by somebody, and if the project manager is not to be overwhelmed by them it is necessary to ensure adequate administrative support.

## Project file administration

A major administrative task is maintaining the project files. In a large project it may be sensible to appoint a **project file custodian** whose sole job is to look after them. The project files contain all project documentation such as the proposal, the estimates, the contract, specifications, minutes, commitments register, schedules, standards, procedures, progress reports, budgets, manuals, reference books and correspondence. By the time the project has been completed the project files could be quite voluminous. It is necessary where large volumes of material result that documents be indexed and the index well maintained. Maintenance of the files and their indexes is complicated by the fact that files may be held on different media: some written, some on magnetic tape or disk and some on microfilm or microfiche. Access to the project files must also be controlled. Some parts may be available to everyone, while other parts may need to have access restricted.

One problem that arises with project files is the need for duplication as insurance against a disaster such as fire or vandalism. Should everything be duplicated and stored in separate locations? How far away should the back-up location be? If the project is overseas, should a copy of everything be shipped 'home'? If duplicates are held, how frequently should the duplicate be updated to keep up with changes in the original? There are trade-offs between the greater administrative burden of duplicating everything and the damage that would be done if the documents were lost. There are no universal rules but these are decisions which the project manager must take before the filing system is set up.

---

### ACTIVITY 3.3

Think about the following and take notes for your project.

- In your project was there an administrator and/or a custodian of the project files?

- If so, was this person used effectively during the project?

- If there wasn't one, were there problems in handling administration or maintaining the files that would indicate a better way of handling such matters in future?

---

## Deputy project manager

The project manager should nominate a deputy. The deputy need not necessarily be shown on the organization chart, but who it is should be clearly defined. The deputy will need appropriate terms of reference defining the limits of their authority. If a project manager tries to work without a deputy – and many do – the danger is that the project manager may become a bottleneck in the project. He or she cannot be absent from the office for any length of time, nor go sick, nor take holidays. With such a full-time commitment it is quite possible that the project manager will collapse under the load and a replacement or deputy will then be required anyway.

One bonus of appointing a deputy is that the job is good training for a potential project manager. The deputy can learn project management without the stress of taking full responsibility immediately and avoids the risk to a subsequent project of management by someone who lacks experience. The deputy needs to keep abreast of the project, taking a wider view than his or her normal job requires. This will absorb time which needs to be allowed for. (This is another example of balancing the cost of insurance against the risk of a hazard: the risk of having to do without a project manager.)

The project administrator may be asked to fill the role of the deputy project manager. The administrator is in a good position to act as deputy because administration is project-wide and the task of keeping abreast of the project in readiness to act as project manager is little additional burden. However, in selecting a deputy there are other factors to take into account, such as leadership and perceived status of the project administrator compared with the team leaders. These factors may be more important than administrative convenience.

# 3.2.4  Summary

At the time a contract is being prepared, the project manager, if he or she hasn't been appointed earlier, is appointed. It is then that person's job to identify key members of the team, particularly if it is to be a large, hierarchically-organized team, and to define a project organization. Terms of reference then need to be drawn up to define the roles each team member will occupy. If work is subcontracted, someone must be responsible for monitoring subcontracted work. The basis for assigning responsibilities is the WBS. Where the structure is complex, a responsibility matrix can be drawn up.

Administration is often key to the success of a project, particularly a large one. Sometimes this is the job of the project manager, but for projects of any size it is convenient and sensible to have a part-time or full-time administrator. Very large projects may additionally benefit from the assistance of a project file custodian, whose job is to keep track of documents. For safety's sake, the project manager needs to consider whether to duplicate documents and how many and how often to do so. Appointment of a deputy project manager is also advisable as 'insurance' and in order to share the load. The administrator is sometimes in a good position to act as deputy.

This section has alluded to many human aspects of project management; these will be discussed in more detail in Chapter 4.

Having studied this section, you should be able to:

- discuss a typical project organization and say when the organization should be set up

- discuss the problems of subcontracting and what needs to be done to monitor progress

- describe the relationship between the WBS, statements of work and the project organization and assignment of responsibilities amongst team members

- state how a responsibility matrix can help where the project organization is complex

- list and describe the tasks of project administration and state who does them in small, medium-sized and large projects

- discuss the necessity of administering project files and state what problems may arise in such administration

- describe the role, advantages and problems of a deputy project manager and state why the definition of such a role is important to the project structure.

You should be able to define in your own words the following terms:

- responsibility matrix (linear responsibility chart)

- project controller or project control officer and project support office

- project file custodian.

# 3.3 *SCHEDULING*

This section describes the use of various scheduling techniques including milestones, bar charts (or Gantt charts) and networks.

Scheduling is one of the main concerns of a project manager. Many good engineering organizations perform projects of high quality – delivered too late. *Time costs money.* These late projects are expensive to the client, to the contractor or to both. Building an offshore oil rig, for example, has only a narrow time 'window' in which the construction phase must be completed before the good weather for the year draws to a close. To help ensure that a project is completed on time it is necessary to prepare a detailed schedule of every activity within the project and monitor progress against this schedule. Preparing and then monitoring a detailed schedule are not sufficient by themselves to guarantee that a project will complete on time.

## 3.3.1 Phases and milestones

The first step in drawing up a schedule is to see whether project work can be broken down on a coarse scale into main phases. For example, when installing new equipment in a factory the main phases might be design, procurement, installation and commissioning. If a project is suitable for such a division into phases this is usually a sensible first step because it allows the large project to be considered as a sequence of smaller subprojects, each of which terminates before the next begins. The key events or main **milestones** in the project are then the points of completion of each phase.

As we noted in Chapter 1, division of a project into clearly distinct sequential phases is often not possible: more usually there are a number of activities which overlap in time. Even when it is possible to divide a project into clearly distinct phases it may be desirable to overlap parts of the phases so that the project is completed more quickly: procurement may be planned to start after design has started but before it has been completed. However, even when phases overlap it is worth identifying significant events that must take place during the project so that there are some fixed markers against which progress can be measured. For example, during the building of a ship there will be a point in the schedule at which the ship will be launched. This represents an easily identifiable, indisputable milestone during its construction.

Ideally, you should identify a number of well-defined key events in a project which can be used as milestones. The characteristic most needed of a good milestone is that there should be no room for doubt about whether it has been passed or not. For example, if you want to use completion of design as a milestone you will have to take great care to ensure that you can define what is meant by the phrase *completion of design.* You need to define precisely what products should have been delivered and how their completeness will be assessed to be able to say when design is complete. Better milestones are those less in need of definition: like the launch of a ship. A good milestone should also have some significance: although the completion of the installation of 1000 metres of cable is *measurable* it is not as *meaningful* as the completion of the cabling of a building.

**SAQ 3.7**

Rate the quality of the following milestones. Suggest improved versions where you can.

(a) equipment drawings 50% complete

(b) extruder installed

(c) building approved ready to receive equipment

(d) 1000 lines of computer program complete

(e) computer delivered to site.

The word **baseline** is used to represent the status of the project or some identifiable part of the project at a particular time. It is the term usually used for the status at the end of significant phases of the work. The next phase then builds upon the *baseline* reached at the end of the previous phase. For example, one possible baseline is that the design of some package of items has been completed and approved. Typically, one would plan that this baseline must be reached before fabrication of those items can start. (Although the word is usually reserved for significant points in the project development it is sometimes used simply to mean the status at any one point in time, a snapshot of the project.)

## 3.3.2  Gantt charts

A very common and effective way of displaying a schedule of activities is to use a bar chart such as that shown in Figure 3.5. Bar charts of this kind are usually called **Gantt charts** in the project management literature after Henry Gantt, who is credited with inventing them during the First World War. The idea is quite simple and probably familiar to you. List the activities down the side of a page and, using a horizontal timescale, draw a bar for each activity to represent the period over which it is to be performed.

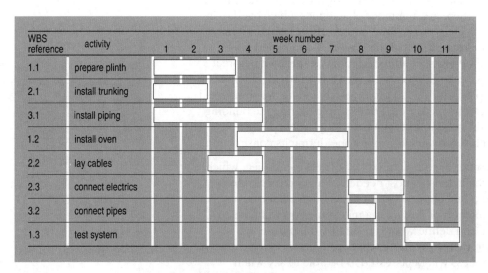

**FIGURE 3.5**  Gantt chart for installing a new industrial oven

Each activity shown on the Gantt chart is an element in the work breakdown structure, so a cross-reference can be made to the WBS to show where it fits in terms of the work to be done and to access other information about the activity. The Gantt chart for installing a new industrial oven, Figure 3.5, makes a cross-reference to the elements of the WBS, Figure 3.6. This cross-reference makes it possible to find the corresponding statement of work for each activity and hence the estimates of cost and time required.

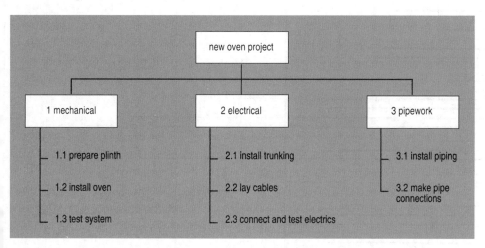

**FIGURE 3.6**  Work breakdown structure for a new oven

The Gantt chart shown in Figure 3.5 is a very simple form. Its simplicity makes it particularly attractive as a way of conveying information about the schedule to the people involved in the project. Its message is clear. It is easy to understand. However, the content of the message in a simple Gantt chart is fairly limited.

There are many variations on the simple Gantt chart which convey more information. For example, colour or shading may be used to show which activities are the responsibility of a particular person or department, or to indicate the current state of progress on each activity. Extra symbols may be inserted to highlight key events, such as the completion of the preparations to install the oven at the end of Week 3, the completion of the installation at the end of Week 7 and the readiness for testing at the end of Week 9.

One useful elaboration is to highlight the chain of sequential activities which determines the minimum time required for the project. These activities are said to be on the **critical path**. (A formal definition of critical path appears in Section 3.3.4.) In this particular project the chain of activities – prepare plinth, install oven, connect electrics and test system – forms the critical path. Delay in any one of these activities would lengthen the project.

An example of the Gantt chart with some of these features added is shown in Figure 3.7. As you can see a Gantt chart can become very complex. This makes it difficult to understand. There is a trade-off between the extra information conveyed to the expert, the loss of understanding by the more casual user and the extra time taken to prepare a complete chart. Computer preparation of the chart may allow it to be tailored more easily to suit the particular audience.

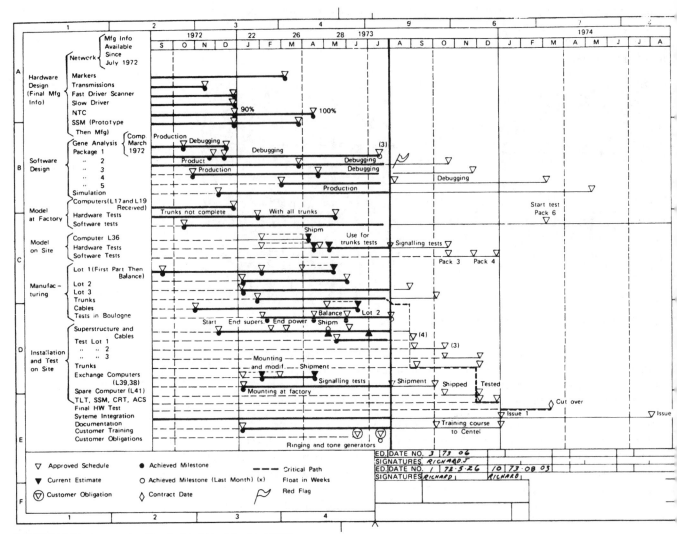

**FIGURE 3.7** A complex Gantt chart (Archibald, 1992)

The main weakness of the Gantt chart is that it is not easy to show the dependence of one activity upon another except by inference. For example, we can see in Figure 3.5 that the trunking is installed by the end of Week 2 and that the activity of laying cables is scheduled to start at the beginning of Week 3. This is unlikely to be a coincidence and we infer that one activity has been scheduled to follow the other. In a small project this may be obvious but in a large project there could have been many activities ending at Week 2 and our inference that it is only the trunking that matters might be wrong. One way of overcoming this is to create lines linking activities that depend on one another. However, this tends to produce a rather cluttered diagram.

Another problem with the Gantt chart in a large project is that many iterations may be required during its construction. The bars representing all affected activities must be erased and redrawn each time the length of an activity changes. To overcome this problem, planners usually use a computer package to help them prepare a schedule so that updating the schedule stored on the computer can be done without the chore of redrawing the chart manually. Computer planning packages can prepare a schedule that takes account of dependencies between activities. The principles underlying these techniques are described in the next section.

## SAQ 3.8

Assume you want to redecorate a moderately sized room, and at the same time you decide to have an electrician move the main light switch and add more power points. The activities, with their durations, are shown in Table 3.1 in the order in which they are to be done. Draw a Gantt chart of this project.

**TABLE 3.1** Decorating a room

| Activity | Duration (days) |
| --- | --- |
| clear room of furnishings, carpet | 1 |
| do electrical work and repair plaster | 2 |
| strip old wallpaper | 1 |
| prepare all surfaces | 1 |
| paint woodwork | 3 |
| hang new paper | 2 |
| restore furnishings and carpet | 1 |

# 3.3.3 Network techniques: activity-on-arrow networks

Network techniques are built into computer planning packages so that even if you know nothing about the technique, the computer can produce a schedule for you that takes account of dependencies between tasks and the availability of resources. Although some computer packages can produce very sophisticated results the principles are straightforward, and you can analyse small networks yourself simply with pencil and paper. This will help you understand what the computer is doing so that you can use computer tools more effectively. The examples that we will use will be limited to very small networks of the kind that are easy to manipulate by hand.

Any project manager ought to be able to produce rough sketches of networks without resorting to a computer. Some would claim that you should always start with rough ideas on a sheet of paper, rather than setting up a project directly on to a computer. Whether you do this may depend on how comfortable you (and others who may be involved in the planning) feel with a particular package. The computer really comes into its own when these rough sketches of a score of activities start to become formalized and need to be kept updated.

There are several variants of the network technique, known variously as **critical path scheduling**, *critical path analysis* and *PERT* (Project Evaluation and Review Technique). The fundamental idea of the network is to represent graphically the sequential relationship between the activities that are to be performed in the project. The aim is to develop a diagram without knowing at the outset the actual time at which activities will be performed (in contrast to a Gantt chart where drawing the bars cannot be done until the dates, or at least the relative order and durations, are fixed). The network diagram of the activities and their dependence on each other need not change significantly even when the estimated duration for activities is altered or new activities added.

To develop a network the planner has to be able to answer two questions for each activity:

1    What must be one before this activity can start?

2    What can be done once this activity finishes?

These help the planner to develop the dependencies between activities. Once chains of dependent activities have been identified, a third question can be asked about each activity:

3    What activities can be done at the same time as this activity?

That is, what activities are independent of this activity, even if these all depend on completion of common 'ancestor' activities? This serves to identify those activities which can overlap in time. At this stage the planner doesn't worry about whether resources are sufficient to allow such an overlap; these three questions serve only to help derive a network of activities that stretch from the start of a project to its completion.

The network is a tool used to arrive at a feasible schedule. There are two families of network techniques, called **activity-on-arrow** and **activity-on-node**. Although the two types diagram look very different the underlying ideas are very much the same (see Figures 3.17 and 3.21 for a comparison). As an activity-on-arrow diagram is rather more compact than an activity-on-node diagram we will discuss activity-on-arrow first and in Section 3.3.5 we will compare it with activity-on-node.

## Activity-on-arrow networks

An example of an activity-on-arrow diagram appears in Figure 3.8. The idea is quite simple. Each activity is represented by an arrow, which starts and finishes at a *node* (drawn as a circle). Each node represents an **event**, a point of zero time duration, which signifies the completion of *all* the activities leading into that node. In Figure 3.8 the activity *find pencil* is independent of the activity *find paper* but only when both have been completed is Event 3 reached and only then can the activity *make drawing* be started.

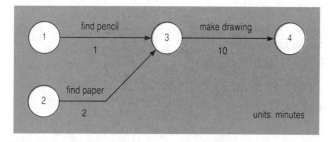

**FIGURE 3.8**  An activity-on-arrow network

We have already noted the convention that circles represent events. The numbers in the circles *identify* events. Below each arrow there also appears a number representing the duration of the activity (in some convenient unit such as hours, days or weeks). The units of time are best chosen so that the numbers are easy to handle, preferably small integers. In Figure 3.8 the units of time are minutes. In a project lasting a year or more the time units could be days or, more likely, weeks. To keep the diagram uncluttered the units are given as a note in the legend of the diagram, and are not repeated on every duration.

Given the estimated duration of each activity, the minimum time necessary for the whole project can be calculated. It is the time taken for the longest path from beginning to end of the project. This longest path is the critical path. This path can be recognized by inspection of Figure 3.8 as the path 2–3–4, which is estimated to take 12 minutes. The path 1–3–4 is not critical because it takes 11 minutes. There may be more than one critical path in a network if there are several paths of the same length.(You will see in Section 3.3.4 how the critical path can be calculated systematically rather than by inspection.)

Unlike the Gantt chart, the physical layout of activities and nodes on the page is immaterial. The event numbers, which merely identify the nodes, are arbitrary, provided that they identify each node uniquely. While the numbers do not have to increase as the project progresses it would be perverse to take no account of any likely order, and usually the numbers are chosen to run in sensible ascending sequences. The pair of event node identifiers at the beginning and end of an arrow may also be used to identify that activity, provided that there is only one such arrow; for example, the arrow *find pencil* may be identified for purposes of drawing and discussing the draft network as Activity 1–3. Best practice is to use the WBS reference.

It is natural (at least for a right-hander) to draw the network flowing from left to right, but when drawing draft networks this is not essential and when you are doing the initial planning you need not feel constrained by this. In a later revision you may take the opportunity to tidy up the layout. In some books you will find arrows drawn at any angle but we recommend you to draw the activity arrows horizontally whenever possible. This helps to keep the diagram tidy and makes it easier to read the activity description.

You may already have an objection to Figure 3.8. You may say that, since you are the person responsible for finding the pencil and you are also the person responsible for finding the paper, then surely the activities cannot be drawn in parallel. What you have identified with this objection is a resource constraint. Don't worry about resource constraints in drawing your network; they will be taken care of later. Assume for the moment that *any number of people* could be available to perform any logically possible activity and therefore pencil and paper *could* be procured concurrently. (We will return to the practical problem of resource constraints in Section 3.4.)

## Dummy activities

If paths through the network are to be identifiable by unique events then it is essential that only one activity joins any pair of nodes. Sometimes, however, the logic of the project requires two activities to occur in parallel joining the same pair of nodes, as shown in Figure 3.9, a project network for developing a computer system.

The activities *develop hardware* and *develop software* would both be identified as Activity 10–20 in the diagram. To avoid this conflict we invent a **dummy activity** to introduce an extra node, purely for identification purposes, as shown in Figure 3.10. The identification of the path 10–20–30 is now distinct from the identification of the path 10–11–20–30. Dummy activities such as Activity 10–11 take no time and are usually drawn as discontinuous arrows to indicate a dependency without duration.

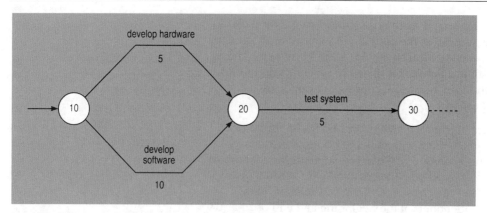

**FIGURE 3.9** Two activities with the same identification

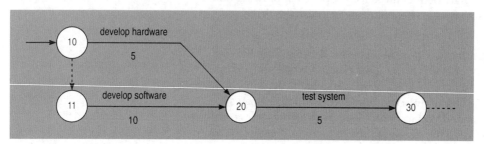

**FIGURE 3.10** The project network of Figure 3.9 with a dummy activity inserted

Dummy activities can be used whenever you wish to show a dependency without a physical activity. The use of dummies will also sometimes improve clarity.

## Multiple starts and finishes

Refer again to Figure 3.8. Note that nodes 1 and 2 in Figure 3.8 both represent the start of the project. Although this is unlikely to cause confusion in such a small network, multiple start and finish nodes ought to be avoided if any confusion could arise. It would be more satisfactory if we could draw the network for any project with a unique starting node. This can best be done by adding a 'start' node, numbered zero, with dummy activities to all the nodes that can start immediately, as shown in Figure 3.11. In practice you may not always want to link up multiple start nodes with dummy activities when the start nodes are clearly identified by their position on the left-hand side of the page, but a dummy activity is particularly useful in highlighting any start nodes that may otherwise be hidden in the middle of a large diagram.

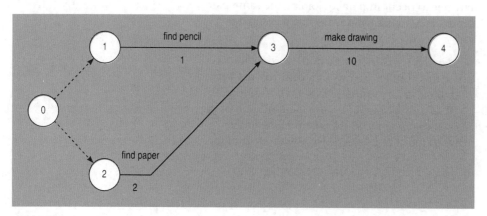

**FIGURE 3.11** A single starting node

## SAQ 3.9

To what extent do the remarks about a unique start node apply to the end of a project?

Any nodes that appear inside a network without at least one preceding activity or at least one succeeding activity are called **dangling events** (or dangles). In a correctly drawn network all dangles should be removed by adding dummy activities if necessary.

# Loops

Project networks are not allowed to contain loops, a cycle of activities where each one requires the completion of its predecessor. This rule prevents us from representing redesign of a component as shown in Figure 3.12.

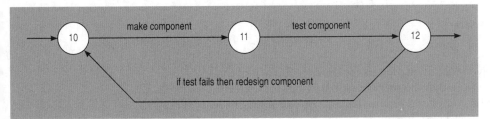

**FIGURE 3.13**   An inadmissible loop

The reason for the rule is that such a network cannot be analysed to show how long it will take. The existence of a loop highlights to the project planner that this project might go on forever. To avoid this catastrophe, some time limit has to be set on the internal iterations so that they can be represented by the more acceptable Figure 3.13.

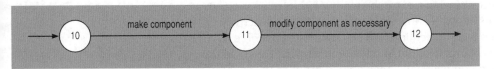

**FIGURE 3.13**   An acceptable finite repetition

Even though Figure 3.13 contains implicit looping in Activity 11–12 it is acceptable because it can be given a finite duration, allowing for the expected number of modifications, so a satisfactory outcome will be reached. This changes the problem to one of estimating how long the iteration implied by Activity 11–12 will take, but at least the network itself is capable of being analysed.

In principle, loops can be handled in a network if the probability of success at each iteration is known or the number of iterations is specified. Networks which allow for probability have indeed been developed, but these seem not to have been popular with project managers. There is some discussion of such networks in the book by Moder *et al.* (1983).

## SAQ 3.10

Draw an activity-on-arrow network to represent the project of digging a well that you studied in Chapter 2, taking into account only the activities shown in Table 3.2.

**TABLE 3.2**  Digging a well

| Activity identifier | Activity | Predecessors | Duration (weeks) |
|---|---|---|---|
| A | clear site | – | 1 |
| B | obtain materials | – | 2 |
| C | obtain pump | – | 4 |
| D | prepare apron | A, B | 2 |
| E | dig well | D | 5 |
| F | install pump | C, E | 1 |
| G | train maintainers | C | 2 |
| H | run trials | F, G | 2 |

(The activities have been given identifying letters for brevity, in place of the more usual WBS reference.) Note that the predecessor activities for a given activity are those that must be completed before that activity can start. Ensure that your diagram has unique start and finish nodes. Number the nodes in any convenient manner. Use dummies as necessary to ensure that all path identification by node numbers is unique.

# 3.3.4  Analysing the network

Once a network has been constructed what use can be made of it? Its main use is to allow the planner to calculate the allowable time span within which each activity must be performed and what the total project time will be. Hence it is possible to determine whether the project as planned will fit into the time allowed for it. On the small examples that we have used you may have been able to produce these answers by inspection, but this would clearly be impractical in a large network with many possible paths to consider. So now we must approach the problem more systematically.

Let's assume that a network such as Figure 3.11 has been drawn and each activity has been given an estimated duration. We first want to find the *earliest* time at which we *could* reach each node. Secondly, at some stage a required completion date will be established and we will want to know the *latest* time by which each node *must* be reached. So, in general, each event node will have associated with it *two* times, an *earliest* time and a *latest* time defined as follows:

- the **earliest event time** is the earliest time at which the node could be reached

- the **latest event time** is the latest time by which the node must be reached if the project is to finish by its required completion date.

*It is important to appreciate that the difference between these two times has nothing to do with the uncertainty of estimating activity durations.* The difference is due to the difference between what *could* be achieved if all activities started at their earliest possible moment and what *must* be achieved if the project is to be finished on time. These earliest and latest times are usually shown in compartments of each node as in Figure 3.14.

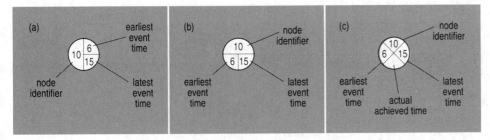

**FIGURE 3.14** Using compartments in a node: (a) British Standard 6046; (b) a common arrangement; (c) four compartments

The convention shown in Figure 3.14(a) is the British Standard system and it is the one we shall use in this course. There are, however, other methods of dividing the node into compartments. The arrangement of Figure 3.14(b) is commonly used and Figure 3.14(c) includes a compartment to show the time at which the node was actually reached when the project was performed. As there are several possibilities it is important to put a key in the legend of any network diagrams that you use so that there can be no confusion. It is also helpful for any reader of the diagram who may not be familiar with the conventions you may use.

## Calculating earliest event times

Calculating the earliest event time for every node is done in a **forward pass** through the network, starting from the unique project start node and finishing at the unique project completion node. The calculations are quite straightforward and it may surprise you to know that you do not need a computer. For large networks you may *prefer* to use a computer, not because the calculations are difficult but because when changes are made to the network later it is tedious to recalculate all the times. The calculations do not involve any iterations.

The time entered as the earliest event time for the project start node can be fixed arbitrarily. We may set it to zero until the time of the project start is known in absolute terms such as a date or a week number on a calendar. Remember that an event time is a *point* in time, not a *period* of time. So if the time is expressed as a week number (which is quite common) there has to be a convention that such a week number appearing in an event node means the *start* or the *end* of the week of that number; if this is vague then team members may interpret the meaning differently. It is not unknown that one member of the team expects to start on a piece of work at the beginning of a given week only to find that a colleague does not expect to complete a predecessor task until the end of that week and both of them believe they are working to the same schedule!

Having fixed the time for the start node you then select *any* of its immediate successors and calculate that node's earliest event time. It does not matter in which order you deal with these successors. The earliest event time at any node is the time at which *every predecessor* activity has been completed. From the start node you then simply pass forward through the network selecting as the next node for calculation *any* node for which you have already calculated the earliest times of *all* its immediate predecessors.

## EXAMPLE 3.3   A forward pass

This example performs the forward pass for the network of Figure 3.15. (You may find it helps to use a pencil to fill in the numbers as we go.)

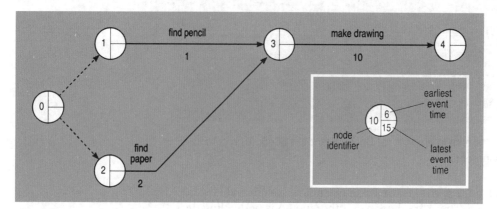

**FIGURE 3.15**   Ready to start the forward pass

We start with the project start node which has been identified as node 0. As we have not been asked to start the project at a particular time we assume that it will start at time = 0 so we fill in its earliest start time as 0. The dummy activities 0–1 and 0–2 take zero time, so the earliest event times of both these nodes can also be filled in immediately as 0. Now you must select Node 3 as the only node for which all data are available. The earliest time corresponds to the completion of *both* the activities leading to it, that is taking the longer of the two times. The earliest event time will be 2 because it takes longer to find paper than it does to find the pencil. Finally Node 4 has an earliest time 12, calculated from the earliest event time for Node 3 plus the duration of Activity 3–4. The earliest time at which this project can be completed is therefore 12. This completes the forward pass. The result is shown in Figure 3.16.

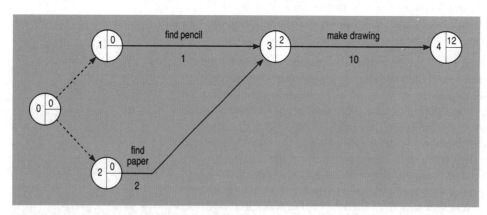

**FIGURE 3.16**   After the forward pass

As the network contains no loops you will always be able to find a 'next' node for which you can calculate the earliest time. There will often be more than one node available for selection as next node, but when you have a choice the order you choose does not matter. Eventually, you will have calculated earliest times for all the nodes in the network, finishing at the project completion node. This completes the forward pass, which in practice presents no difficulty provided the network contains no loops or dangles.

*The earliest event time of the final node in the network is the earliest time it would be possible to complete the project.*

### SAQ 3.11

Redraw the network for the well-digging project (SAQ 3.10) with nodes to allow earliest and latest times to be entered. Do a forward pass through the network and enter the earliest event times for all the nodes.

Deduce the minimum project completion time.

## Calculating latest event times

If we are only interested in how quickly a project could be done then a forward pass would be all that we require. However, given a target finish date, we will usually be interested not only in how quickly the project could be done but also in the latest times that we can allow each event to occur if the project is to be completed by that date. This will tell us the times by which each activity in the project *must* be completed. These times are calculated in a **backward pass**.

Often a project's target date is imposed by external factors but sometimes it is taken to be equal to the earliest time in which the project can be done. (A project might be scheduled to finish at its earliest possible date to begin earning income as soon as possible.) For brevity we shall call such a schedule a **critical schedule**. In general, though, do *not* assume that the target completion date must be the same as the earliest possible completion date.

The backward pass calculates the *latest* event time for each node if the project is to be completed by a given target date. The calculation begins with the latest event time for project completion on a target or an externally imposed completion date and works backwards through the network to the project start node. The method is exactly the reverse of the forward pass. Start at the finish event node and enter the target date for the project. Then work backwards, calculating the latest event time of any node for which *all successor* event times are known. Working methodically backwards you will find that eventually all the times will have been filled in.

### SAQ 3.12

What can you conclude from Figure 3.17 overleaf about the latest times by which the pencil and paper must be found and how long you can sit in your armchair before starting the project?

### SAQ 3.13

Perform a backward pass on the well-digging project. Assume that the well is to be in operation in the minimum time, so the target time is 12 weeks.

# Float and the critical path

Some activities could increase in duration and yet the project could still be completed by the required target date. Such activities are said to exhibit **float**. Float is the excess time available for an activity in addition to its estimated duration. Consequently that activity could either be expanded or started late by this amount and the project would still meet its target date. This float is sometimes called **total float** or **path float**. (A path is any sequence of activities which could be described by following activity arrows from the beginning to the end of the project.)

The term **slack** is sometimes found, particularly in the American literature, with the same meaning as float. British Standard BS 4335 applies the term *slack* to events rather than to activities, meaning the calculated time span within which an event must occur. In practice it is rarely necessary to discuss slack. If you are interested, Lockyer (1984) gives a very full description of the terms *float* and *slack* and shows the relationship between them.

---

## EXAMPLE 3.4   A backward pass

Consider Figure 3.16 once more. Let's suppose that we will be satisfied if the drawing project is completed within 15 minutes. Setting the required latest project completion time at 15 means entering a latest event time for Node 4 of 15. Working backwards through the network selecting available nodes in turn yields a latest time for Node 3 of 15 − 10 = 5 and so on for the other nodes. The result appears in Figure 3.17.

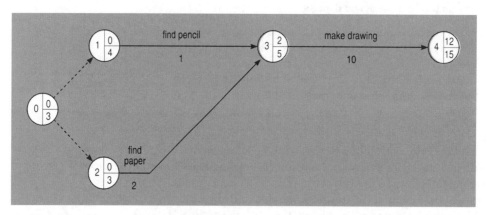

**FIGURE 3.17**   The drawing project analysed

---

The maximum time allowable for any activity may be calculated as the difference between the latest time by which the activity must finish and the earliest time at which it could start. Hence the total float for an activity is given by subtracting the estimated duration from this allowable time, giving the following formula:

total float = latest time of finish event − earliest time of start event − duration

For example in Figure 3.17 the activity *find pencil* has float of 4 minutes, calculated as:

5 − 0 − 1 = 4.

The reason why this kind of float is sometimes called *path float* is that it is *shared* by activities along a *path* from the start to the finish of the project. It is important for you to realize that float is a resource that is *shared* between activities. If any activity uses any of the total float then the other activities on the path have their float correspondingly reduced. If this is not understood then members of the project team may believe that the activity they are working on can safely use the total float which appears in the schedule. In fact if they use any of it then other team members have less room to slip (except as discussed below). The belief that float can be used by an activity without detriment to the rest of the project is a very common misconception.

The concept of float leads to the standard definition of a critical path. *A critical path is a path with least float.*

### SAQ 3.14

Will a delay in an activity on the critical path cause the project to miss its required completion date?

In a critical schedule it is usually easy to spot the critical path because it passes through nodes which have the same earliest and latest times. However, sometimes there is more than one path connecting nodes with equal earliest and latest times and in this case it is necessary to check the actual duration of the activities along each such path to determine which of them is critical. For example, in Figure 3.18 there is an activity *develop software* which might at first sight appear to be critical since it joins two nodes with equal earliest and latest times. The critical path, however, is *ordering and testing the hardware*, path 1–2–3; *develop software* has a float of 10 weeks. So beware the possible trap.

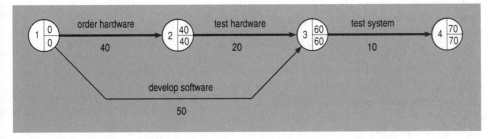

**FIGURE 3.18** Developing software is not critical

Conventional ways to mark the critical path on a network diagram are to use a double bar across the arrows, doubled arrows or broad arrows, as shown on the path 1–2–3–4 in Figure 3.18.

### SAQ 3.15

If in Figure 3.18 the duration of *develop software* had been 60 weeks, then what would you deduce about the critical path?

# Free float

As we discussed above, if one activity takes longer than its scheduled duration then the float available to other activities on that path to project completion will usually be decreased correspondingly. However, sometimes an activity has some float available which it can use without *any* effect on subsequent activities. Such float is called **free float**. Free float on an activity will arise when the node following the activity has an earliest start time controlled by some other parallel activity. It is important to be able to distinguish free float from the float which is shared by activities along a path. For example, in Figure 3.19, Activity B has free float of 10 because the earliest start time of Node 3 is controlled by the path through Activity C. Activity A, however has no *free float* because although there is float along the path 1–2–3, any extension of the duration of A will affect the start time of Activity B.

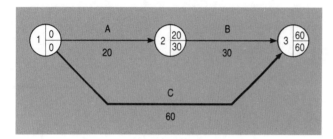

**FIGURE 3.19** Only Activity B has free float

Given a network in which the earliest event times have been calculated the free float of an activity can be calculated using the formula:

free float = earliest time of finish event − earliest time of start event − duration

In this formula dummy nodes are to be disregarded so that the finish event is the start of a successor activity.

If you compare this formula with the one given earlier for the total float you will see that the *latest* time of the finish event has been replaced by the *earliest* time of the finish event. To show why this formula gives the free float for a given activity we argue as follows. Provided that a given activity finishes by the *earliest* time at which any successor activities could start it will not delay any of them. This is the earliest time of the finish event for the given activity. Furthermore, the earliest we expect to be able to finish the given activity is calculated from the time of its earliest start plus its duration. Hence the free float is given by the formula above.

## SAQ 3.16

Below is a description of a computer project for which you are asked to produce and analyse a project network. For brevity we denote each activity with a capital letter which is given in brackets together with its duration.

Some hardware is to be designed (A, 20 weeks), built (B, 20 weeks) and tested (C, 5 weeks). The hardware testing requires a test facility (D, 10 weeks) which can be procured only following the completion of the hardware design. In parallel with the work on the hardware the software is to be designed (E, 30 weeks) and subsequently coded (F, 20 weeks). System testing will require tests to have been designed (G, 5 weeks) following completion of software design. When both the tested hardware and the coded software are available the complete system will be tested (H, 10 weeks). At the end of this testing the project is complete.

(a) Draw the network of the eight activities described above. Perform forward and backward passes to calculate the earliest and latest event times for every node to achieve the minimum possible project time. Enter these times on the project network. (Remember to include appropriate dummy activities.)

(b) Identify the critical path (or paths).

(c) Construct a table showing the (total) float and the free float of every activity.

# 3.3.5 Network techniques: activity-on-node networks

Some project planners prefer a different kind of project network – an activity-on-node network. Essentially, the roles of the node and the arrow are reversed: the node now represents the activity and the arrow the link between activities. There are in fact two distinct varieties of activity-on-node network. One is called **method of potentials** and the other is called **precedence diagram** or **precedence network**. Both allow the links between activities to be assigned a time distinct from the duration of the activity. The method of potentials is the simpler method because it allows links only from the completion of activities to the *start* of other activities, the normal sort of link that you used in activity-on-arrow diagrams. In precedence networks a greater variety of links is allowed, as you will see later. In this chapter we shall use precedence diagram notation.

Each node in an activity-on-node diagram represents an activity and may be drawn as shown in Figure 3.20. There is some redundancy in the information given in these compartments but this has the advantage that all the data on an activity are displayed without needing further calculation.

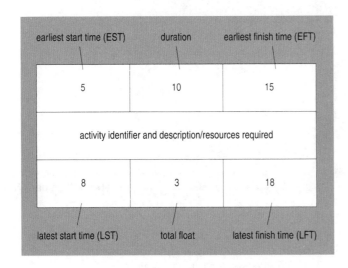

**FIGURE 3.20**
Activity representation in activity-on-node diagrams (using BS 6046)

The representation of the node used in activity-on-node diagrams is more complicated than that used in activity-on-arrow diagrams because the node contains more information. The large compartment in its middle can conveniently be used to contain the activity description and the resources it requires. The top corners show the *earliest* start and finish times. These are produced by a *forward pass* using the same technique as is used in activity-on-arrow network techniques. The bottom row compartments show the *latest* start and finish times and the total float. As mentioned earlier, the *latest* finishing time (LFT) for a project can either be imposed externally, or, if the project is to be completed as soon as possible, can be taken to be the same as the *earliest* finishing time. BS 6046 does not specify how the critical path should be marked in an activity-on-node diagram so we will choose to mark it with broad arrows on the links between the critical nodes. (When using a computer planning package the critical nodes are often coloured distinctively.)

Note that in the main text of this course all times are given as time elapsed from the start of the project, in whatever units have been adopted for that project. You may encounter diagrams elsewhere in which the times for the start of activities are given as the week number in which they *start* but the times for the end of activities are given as the week number in which they *end*. Calculations are not quite as obvious with such a convention and this may cause a little confusion. For example, an activity that takes one week may start at the beginning of Week 1 and finish at the end of Week 1, so a simple difference between these times would apparently correspond to a duration of zero.

## SAQ 3.17

Bearing in mind the methods you have used to produce activity-on-arrow networks, explain how data for the bottom line of the activity node would be produced for activity-on-node networks.

Translating the simple activity-on-arrow network given in Figure 3.17 yields a corresponding activity-on-node diagram, Figure 3.21.

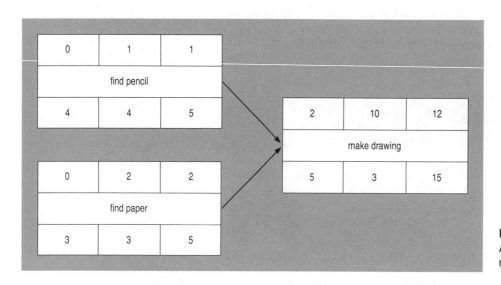

**FIGURE 3.21**
A simple activity-on-node network (compare Figure 3.17)

## SAQ 3.18

(a) Draw the well-digging activity-on-node network corresponding to the activity-on-arrow network given in SAQ 3.10. To save space you may omit a single starting node but your diagram should have a single finish node.

(b) Perform the forward pass and enter the times in the top corners of all the nodes.

(c) Perform the backward pass assuming the project is to be completed in the minimum possible time.

(d) Calculate float for each activity and enter the values in the float compartment of each node.

(e) Mark the critical path on the diagram.

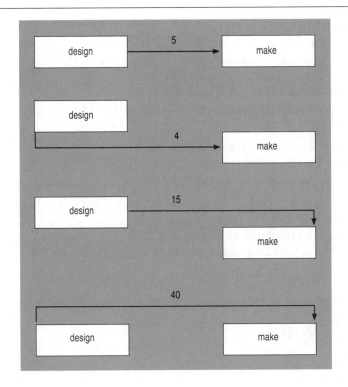

## Types of dependency

So far in this examination of activity-on-node networks there has been a complete symmetry with the activity-on-arrow network. Anything that could be represented on one could just as well be represented on the other. However, the *precedence diagram* or *precedence network* allows abnormal dependencies to be shown between activities. These are difficult to show on an activity-on-arrow diagram. First, relationships can be defined not only between the finish of an activity and the start of succeeding activities (the normal dependency) but also between other combinations of starts and finishes of activities, as we will show below. Secondly, a lapse of time, usually called a *lag*, can be denoted on these relationships. These two features are illustrated in Figures 3.22(a) to (d). The relationship between activities is shown by the positioning of the arrow.

Figure 3.22(a) shows the normal finish-to-start dependency of two activities, designing and making, but with an additional lapse of time, five weeks, between the completion of design and the start of making. This extra lag might represent an allowance for some routine processing and the planner has no interest in showing its details (otherwise the processing lag would be inserted as a normal activity). If more than one activity followed the finish of design then each could have a different lapse of time, or none at all.

Figure 3.22(b) shows a quite different type of dependency from the normal; it shows a start-to-start dependency with a lag between the starts. The position of the arrow is important. It shows that from the moment that the design starts there must be a lag of four weeks before manufacture can start, *regardless of the duration of the design activity*. If the number 4 were omitted, this would mean that manufacture could start as soon as design starts. This sort of dependency would be used when you want to allow some concurrency between the activities but you know that one of them has to have a head start on the other, for example designing and making a number of components.

Figure 3.22(c) shows a dependency from the finish of design to the finish of manufacture, with a time lapse between them. Again, the position and direction of the arrow is crucial. The meaning of Figure 3.22(c) is that manufacture cannot *finish* until 15 weeks after the design has finished. Like Figure 3.22(b) this again allows concurrency between the activities but ensures that due allowance is made for the fact that there is a certain amount of work to be done in the lagging activity that cannot be done until after the leading activity has completely finished.

Figure 3.22(d) shows a start-to-finish dependency. The meaning of this link is that manufacture cannot finish until at least 40 weeks after the start of design. (This seems a rather odd kind of dependency to specify but is given here to complete the picture.)

If the network designer wanted also to show that manufacture could not start until some time after the design had started and could not finish until some time after design had finished, then *both the* links shown in (b) and (c) would be present, as shown in Figure 3.23.

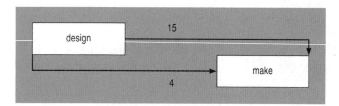

**FIGURE 3.23** Both start-to-start and finish-to-finish constraint

This representation overcomes a problem that is difficult to handle using the activity-on-arrow network technique. Suppose part of a network represents the design and manufacture of a number of similar items. If the making of each item cannot start until its design is complete, but each item is independent of the others, then the making can start as soon as the design of one item is complete and the earliest the making can finish is the time taken to make the last item after all the design is complete.

This situation may be neatly represented in a figure like Figure 3.23 where the link from the start of design to the start of making has a time delay equal to the time taken to design the first item. The duration of the design activity is the time taken to design *all* the items and the duration of manufacture is the time taken to make all the items. The time lag from the finish of design to the finish of making all items is the time taken to make the last item. This is a neater solution than the more complicated one that would have to be used to represent the same situation in activity-on-arrow (Figure 3.24).

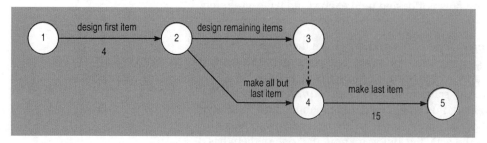

**FIGURE 3.24** An activity-on-arrow diagram equivalent to Figure 3.23

# Analysing precedence diagrams

The presence of links other than the normal finish-to-start links complicates the task of performing the forward and backward passes. Example 3.5 shows the kind of problem that arises.

---

## EXAMPLE 3.5

Consider Figure 3.25. There is a start-to-start dependency from design to manufacture with a lag of four weeks. Handover is the terminal activity of the project. The forward pass is straightforward and yields the number 35 for the earliest project completion time. The backward pass is also straightforward for the handover and making activities. The problem arises in the backward pass calculations for the design activity. What are the values of LST, LFT, and the float, F, for the design activity?

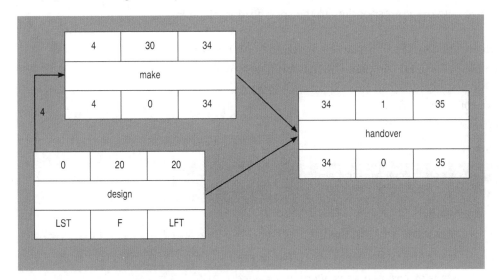

**FIGURE 3.25** Backward pass complications

There is only one dependent activity from the finish of design, handover, which must start in Week 34, so LFT is 34. However, since the design has duration 20 does this imply that the design need not start until week 14? Clearly that would not make sense since design must start four weeks before manufacture starts; in other words, LST must be 0. But if the duration of design is only 20 weeks is it reasonable that it must start at time 0 if it is allowed to finish at Week 34? If so, what is the float?

---

These questions really ask us to consider the meaning of the start-to-start link between design and manufacture. The four weeks represent an initial phase of design, so it must start immediately and there is no float for the initial sub-activity, which takes four weeks. We assume that subsequent stages of design can float provided that design is complete by Week 34. Since the float, F, means the time available for an activity in addition to its duration then it is reasonable to give it the value 14, calculated from:

$$(LFT - EST - 20) = 34 - 0 - 20 = 14$$

We conclude therefore that the numbers to be entered in the design activity are:

LST = 0, F = 14 and LFT = 34.

This method of calculating float implies that float does not necessarily allow an activity to start later than its earliest time. It means only that it has freedom to extend its duration beyond its earliest finishing time. This extension of duration allows an activity to be split into sub-activities, with an inactive period occurring between sub-activities. If such splitting is allowed then the usual rule that the difference between LFT and EFT is equal to the difference between LST and EST breaks down. The calculation of float, therefore, depends on whether such splitting of activities is allowed. We will not pursue this matter any further but, if you are interested, refer to Moder *et al.* (1983) who consider the effects of different computational assumptions: no splitting, splitting always allowed, and splitting allowed for designated activities. They also discuss other precedence diagram anomalies.

### SAQ 3.19

(a) Draw the precedence network corresponding to the specification given in Table 3.3 below.

(b) Perform a forward pass and enter all the earliest start and finish times.

(c) Assuming that the project is to be completed in minimum time, perform a backward pass and enter all the latest finish and start times.

(d) Enter the total float for each activity.

(e) Mark the critical path.

**TABLE 3.3**  Activity data

| Activity | Duration (weeks) | Prerequisites for start and/or finish |
|---|---|---|
| A | 3 | none |
| B | 2 | starts after A has finished |
| C | 6 | starts at least one week after D has finished |
| D | 4 | starts at least one week after A has started |
| E | 3 | starts after C has finished, *and* at least two weeks after F has finished *and* finishes after B finishes |
| F | 3 | starts at least one week after D starts and finishes at least one week after D has finished |

### SAQ 3.20

Draw the activity-on-*arrow* network that corresponds to SAQ 3.18 and analyse it. Your analysis should produce the same results for float as the corresponding precedence diagram. You can decide for yourself which method you find easier to work with.

### SAQ 3.21

Compare the activity-on-arrow representation with the activity-on-node representation by listing the advantages of each.

# 3.3.6 Presenting the schedule: Gantt charts revisited

The network diagram is used by many project managers for communicating the project schedule to the project team and anyone else who needs to know it. This can work well provided that everyone is familiar with networks and with the meaning of the symbols. However, not everyone finds a network diagram easy to read, so it is often a good idea to produce a Gantt chart from the network. As you have already seen, the Gantt chart has the merit of being easy to comprehend. Even people quite familiar with network diagrams usually digest the essential points of a schedule much more quickly when they are presented in Gantt chart form.

Once the network has been analysed, producing a Gantt chart with every activity starting at its earliest possible time is quite straightforward since each earliest start time can be read directly from the network diagram. The earliest finish time of each activity is then just the earliest start time plus the duration. However, it may also be useful to show the *free float* on this chart so that the freedom of movement of each activity can be more readily recognized. Free float is usually indicated by extending the activity bar with a dotted line.

### SAQ 3.22

Produce the Gantt chart for the well-digging project analysed in SAQ 3.13.

## The time-scaled network

An alternative to plotting a Gantt chart is to redraw the network so that it is time-scaled. In this form, the length of the line in activity-on-arrow (or the width of the node in activity-on-node) networks is proportional to the duration of the activity it represents, and the position of the start of an event relative to the left-hand border of the diagram represents the earliest time at which that event can be reached. This doesn't look very neat when using activity-on-node because the nodes become distorted, so in the following example we will use activity-on-arrow.

Consider a project to install a new office system with activities specified as follows:

**TABLE 3.4**  Installing a new office system

| Activity identifier | Description | Staff | Duration (weeks) | Prerequisites |
|---|---|---|---|---|
| A | prepare offices | 2 | 12 | – |
| B | procure equipment | 2 | 8 | – |
| C | design tests | 1 | 5 | – |
| D | install equipment | 4 | 10 | A and B |
| E | test system | 3 | 10 | C and D |
| F | train users | 1 | 5 | A and B |

This can be represented in the activity-on-arrow network diagram in Figure 3.26. (The staff information has been included in this table because we shall use it later when we consider resources.)

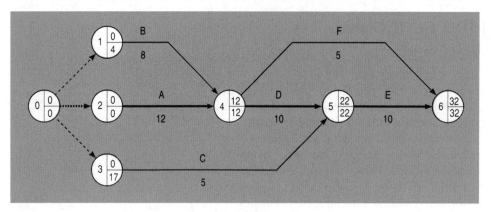

**FIGURE 3.26** A network for a new office system

This network can be drawn as a time-scaled network as shown in Figure 3.27. The difference from Figure 3.26 is that each node is positioned at a time corresponding to its earliest achievement.

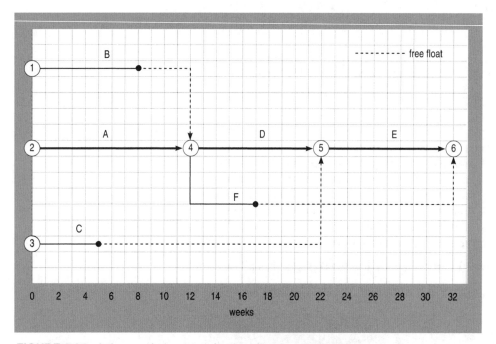

**FIGURE 3.27** A time-scaled network for the office installation.
(Dashed lines extending an activity represent the *free* float for that activity)

The critical path in this diagram is easier to recognize than in a Gantt chart because the critical activities have all been drawn on the same horizontal line across the page. Although this is not strictly necessary it helps to put the message across more clearly. Another advantage of this version of the network is that the free float of Activities B, C and F is easy to see, unlike the usual network diagram where free float has to be calculated from the numbers in the nodes. On the other hand it takes much longer to draw such a diagram: we had to take care in drawing Figure 3.27 that the arrow for Activity B did not clash with the arrow for Activity F.

## SAQ 3.23

Draw a time-scaled network corresponding to the computer project analysed in SAQ 3.16.

## SAQ 3.24

What is the disadvantage of drawing a time-scaled network as the working version of the network?

# 3.3.7 Summary

This section described the use of various scheduling techniques, including Gantt charts, activity-on-arrow networks and activity-on-node networks. The Gantt chart is easy to understand and useful for small projects but cumbersome for larger projects and when modifications are required. It is frequently used as the main way of communicating a schedule that has been produced using a network technique. Forward and backward passes produce schedules including the calculations of float for each activity. The distinction between *free float*, which can be used without delay to subsequent activities, and *total float* which is shared by activities on a path is important. Critical paths are those with least float.

Having studied this section you should now be able to:

- give criteria for the selection of milestones
- construct simple Gantt charts and explain their limitations
- use both activity-on-arrow and activity-on-node techniques to construct networks for small projects
- analyse both types of network completely to yield schedules and floats
- explain the significance of free float compared with total float
- describe a time-scaled network and produce a simple example
- discuss the relative merits of different scheduling methods.

# 3.4  *RESOURCES AND SCHEDULING*

In this section we examine resource issues and discuss how the schedule can be adapted to make the optimum use of the available resources.

Previously we drew network diagrams and derived schedules assuming that any resources needed to perform the activities would be available whenever they were required. Yet in most projects the schedule will be governed to some extent by limitations on the availability of resources: including designers, engineers, tradesmen, shared facilities (such as computers and workshops) and even the constraint of cash flow. If resources are finite it may be necessary to schedule activities not at their earliest date but at a time that makes best use of the available resources.

There are two extreme situations to distinguish: the first is the case of unlimited resources within a fixed project time; the second is the case of limited resources but a flexible project time. The first situation arises where it is so vital to meet the required delivery date that the project manager is prepared to recruit extra staff, pay overtime rates, hire extra services, rent more accommodation, and do whatever is necessary to meet the date. (An example of this is the project to rebuild the Santa Monica Freeway in Los Angeles after it had been destroyed in an earthquake, discussed in Chapter 2. This major traffic artery needed to be re-opened as quickly as humanly possible so any resources needed were made available.)

The other extreme arises where the project manager is not allowed more staff, cannot use overtime, cannot hire more services, and consequently must allow these constraints to dictate a more distant completion date. (We are not, however, talking about a situation where the priority is so low that no resources are assigned at all, but about a situation where the resources assigned are at least adequate to complete the project in a finite period.)

The first situation calls for **time-limited scheduling** – the time is limited and the resources unlimited. The second situation calls for **resource-limited scheduling** – resources are limited and more time must be taken accordingly. If a project manager is faced with limitations on *both* time and resources then one approach is to tackle the problem initially as though it were flexible either in time *or* in resources. If the resources and time constraints are found to be incompatible, *one or the other must be renegotiated* by presenting the options and feasible schedules to the client and/or the project's management.

Often there is no absolute limit to either the time or the resources but there are pressures to contain both within bounds. This situation is somewhere between the time-limited and resource-limited extremes. At the planning stage the project manager will want to explore various possibilities. What if the project is limited to $x$ weeks? What will be the resources required? Varying $x$ and comparing the resulting schedules may yield the best compromise between time and resource limits.

We will consider first the resource implications in the time-limited situation and then look at the resource-limited case.

# 3.4.1 Time-limited scheduling

The objectives of scheduling in the time-limited situation are twofold:

1    to calculate the resource requirements so that they are made available at the right time

2    to schedule each activity so that the resource loading is as smooth as possible.

This is called **resource smoothing**. Although we assume that resources are infinite in time-limited scheduling, the objective is to profile the resource usage as economically as possible, and this almost always means *trying to achieve the lowest peak usage* of all the resources. It is expensive to recruit and train people to work on a project; it would therefore be foolish to schedule the work so that during the peak month twenty people worked on the project when one month later ten of them were idle again.

Optimum resource usage is not necessarily constant throughout the individual project. For example, if resources are shared with other projects then the usage overall may be made smooth by ensuring that peaks on one project coincide with troughs on another. This implies that staff can be moved from one project to another and back again without too much loss of motivation. For simplicity in this chapter we will assume that a level resource usage is optimum.

The first step in planning the time-limited schedule is to use the network techniques studied in Section 3.3 to find the earliest and latest start and finish dates for every activity. Note that the schedule need not be a critical schedule; float may be available even to activities on the critical path. The minimum requirement is that the project *could* be completed before the target completion date when given unlimited resources.

Consider the project network for a new office system given earlier in Figure 3.26. Let's suppose that the target completion time is 32 weeks so that the schedule is, in fact, critical. Next, we require the data for the quantity of each type of shared resource required by each activity. In principle there may be several types of shared resource, such as system designers, electrical engineers, fitters, labourers, workshop machine time. Assume that the only significant shared resource is staff and that this has been estimated for each activity as shown in Table 3.5.

**TABLE 3.5**  Staff required for each activity

| Activity identifier | Description | Staff | Duration | Earliest start time | Float | Latest finish time |
|:---:|:---|:---:|:---:|:---:|:---:|:---:|
| A | prepare offices | 2 | 12 | 0 | 0 | 12 |
| B | procure equipment | 2 | 8 | 0 | 4 | 12 |
| C | design tests | 1 | 5 | 0 | 17 | 22 |
| D | install equipment | 4 | 10 | 12 | 0 | 22 |
| E | test system | 3 | 10 | 22 | 0 | 32 |
| F | train users | 1 | 5 | 12 | 15 | 32 |

It is usual to assume that the resource required remains constant throughout a single activity. If this is not so then the activity can be subdivided into a sequence of components, each having constant resource.

The total staffing effort required, the number of person-weeks over the whole project, is fixed regardless of the schedule of activity. You can easily calculate from Table 3.5 that the total staff effort required will be

$$(2 \times 12) + (2 \times 8) + (1 \times 5) + (4 \times 10) + (3 \times 10) + (1 \times 5)$$
$$= 120 \text{ person-weeks.}$$

Since the project is to be done in 32 weeks we will require $120/32 = 3.75$ staff on average throughout the project. The question is: what is the distribution of staff loading?

On the face of it, if the average requirement is 3.75 staff then it ought to be possible to manage with four people, but we cannot be sure unless we know that the work can be distributed evenly enough over the 32 weeks of the project. To find out, we can calculate the staff required throughout the project assuming initially that every activity starts at its earliest start time. It is possible to construct an initial resource loading chart as shown in Figure 3.28 using the resource requirement and the earliest start times from Table 3.5.

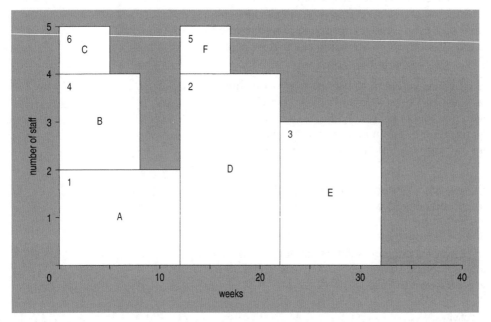

**FIGURE 3.28** Initial resource loading chart. Note: the numbers in the top left-hand corner of each block of work show the order in which that block was scheduled.

This chart has been constructed by drawing areas to represent person-weeks on each activity, starting with the activities that have least float as described below. This initial resource loading is the loading that would be required if every activity started at its earliest date. Clearly this is an unacceptable loading because five staff would be required to meet the peak load. A better distribution is required.

Notice in Figure 3.28 that all the activities that lie on the critical path have been drawn at the lowest level in the chart. This has been done because these activities must be performed at their allotted times as they have no float. So these activities form the *base load* in the schedule. The chart was then built up by adding activities, one at a time, with progressively higher float, laying areas down, one above the other, like slabs on a wall, with their left-hand ends at the earliest start time. (The irregular top surface of the bottom layer will often mean that 'slabs' in layers above the base have to be dislocated to rest on the uneven surface below.)

This method of drawing up a schedule by positioning one activity at a time is called **serial scheduling**. (Later you will meet an alternative method, **parallel scheduling**.) The scheduler lists all the activities in some order, such as increasing float, and then deals with each activity in the list consecutively. The order of activities used in creating Figure 3.28 is shown by the numbers in the activity blocks. These numbers would not normally appear in the diagram: they are simply for your guidance.

There are other ways of displaying the loading. For example, you could use a Gantt chart in which the width of the bars represented the amount of resource, or a Gantt chart with numbers written on the bars for the same purpose. These alternatives may be easier to use when there are a large number of activities to schedule simultaneously, but the technique we have used in Figure 3.28 has the advantage of showing most clearly the overall resource required and the relative ease of rescheduling a block of work.

So far the process has been quite mechanical. If the rules are followed correctly then an initial loading chart can be produced without difficulty. However, now comes the tricky bit. Starting from the (unsatisfactory) initial resource loading the next step is to try to rearrange those activities with float to produce a total resource graph that is as level as possible and does not exceed the resource limit – **resource levelling**. This may not be easy and there are no infallible rules to follow to ensure success. However, by building the initial resource loading chart in the way that we have, the task is made somewhat easier than it would be if this initial chart were built up more randomly. We know at least that activities can only be moved to the *right* from their initial position because they cannot start earlier than their *earliest* start time. Furthermore, the strategy of putting the activities with least float at the base of the chart and those with most float at the top now pays off, because in this example it is easier to see whether any of the more 'floatable' activities can be repositioned to reduce the peak load.

You can move the topmost activities by eye to the right to try to fill up the troughs in the loading chart. It should be easy to see that Activity F can be accommodated *after* Activity D has finished. It would be ideal to make a similar move with Activity C but unfortunately it will not quite fit into the trough after B has finished so the best we can do within the rules that we have set ourselves is to minimize the time for which five staff are required, as shown in Figure 3.29.

The schedule of Figure 3.29, although smoother than the initial schedule, is still unsatisfactory since it requires a fifth person on the project for just one week. This, however, is the sort of schedule that is often produced when working within defined rules. It might conceivably have been produced using a computer. The final step in producing a smoothed schedule is therefore to apply some judgement and bend the rules to suit the circumstances.

In this example, the most likely approach would be to see whether Activity C could be squeezed into four weeks, perhaps by employing a second person on the job for part of the time. Another approach might be to ask staff to work overtime, effectively increasing the capacity temporarily. The point is that in the final analysis the result of the scheduling, particularly computer scheduling, requires the project manager to interpret and consider the options. If you decide that the project cannot afford more than four staff and that overtime and similar measures are ruled out, then your only option is to extend the completion date of the project. We discuss this in Section 3.4.2.

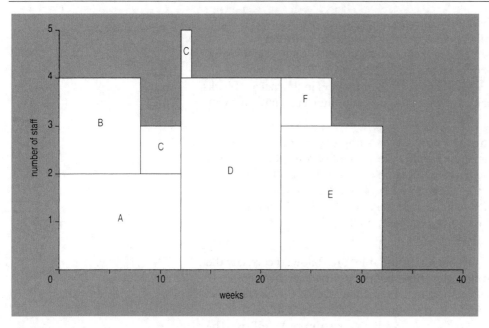

**FIGURE 3.29** A smoother loading chart

Sometimes it is quite difficult to calculate the smoothest loading even when the rules are well defined. In the example chosen here it was a fairly simple task, starting from the position shown in Figure 3.28, to juggle the activities by eye to achieve an optimum within the rules (Figure 3.29). If there had been many more activities it could have become quite complex and it might have been difficult to be sure when the optimum had been achieved. Ideally, what is required is a systematic method that can be computerized. Perhaps surprisingly, there is no known method (at the date of writing) which is guaranteed to produce the best possible schedule in all circumstances, other than to try every possible combination of scheduled times. There are, however, a number of scheduling packages available which can normally be expected to achieve a good approximation to an optimum schedule.

One procedure, attributed to Burgess, is described by Moder *et al.* (1983). In the Burgess levelling procedure the activities are first tabulated in an order of precedence such that the necessary predecessors for the start of an activity are always above it in the table. The activities are first scheduled at their earliest times (corresponding to what was done in Figure 3.28). The levelling procedure then consists of repeatedly cycling through the activity table starting at the bottom and working upwards, adjusting the scheduled time for each activity in turn, using as a measure of smoothness the sum of the squares of the total resource added up over all the time periods.

$$S = \sum x_t^2$$

The only schedule adjustment allowed at each cycle is an adjustment that moves an activity to a later date within its float, never moving back again to an earlier date. The cycle is repeated until no further improvement in smoothness can be obtained. This procedure would be tedious to do by hand but it could be automated and may be used in computer packages.

Note $x_t$ is the resource used in time period $t$.

This procedure uses sums of squares of resource as its criterion for 'best' allocation as this generally leads to a profile that smoothes out peaks and troughs. It is not guaranteed, however, to find the schedule yielding the lowest peak.

The optimizing problem becomes more complex when more than one resource has to be considered. Staff might not be interchangeable and therefore each category of staff needs to be smoothed separately within the same schedule of activities. Furthermore, there might not only be staff to consider but also the amount of workshop time or machine time or space on a factory floor. When several resources have to be levelled together it may be very difficult to decide what constitutes an optimum. Although computer tools will prove invaluable in presenting options to the manager, in the end it is often a matter of personal judgement.

In summary, these are the main steps in manually producing a time-limited schedule of resource loading.

1     Produce the activity network diagram (e.g. Figure 3.26).

2     Produce a table showing for each activity the *resource* required, the duration EST, float and LFT (e.g. Table 3.5)

3     List the activities in order of increasing float (and in order of latest finish time for activities with the same float).

4     Draw an initial resource loading chart with each activity scheduled at its earliest start time, building it up serially in the order of the list produced in Step 3. This produces a loading diagram with the most critical activities at the bottom and those with greatest float at the top (e.g. Figure 3.28).

5     Rearrange the activities within their float to achieve a profile which is as level as possible within the 'rules' (i.e. the duration of activities should not be changed at this step and dependencies must be preserved). This rearrangement may require a systematic procedure, such as the Burgess levelling procedure, if there are many activities. (Output is a diagram like Figure 3.29.)

6     Use judgement to interpret and improve on the loading by changing the 'rules' (i.e. rethink the need for dependencies and consider overtime working at the peak).

When a computer package is used to replace this procedure it is worth noting that judgement is still relevant. The computer can automate only the steps for which rules are laid down.

### SAQ 3.25

Use the procedure outlined above to produce time-limited schedules for the computer project in SAQ 3.16. You have already done the first step of the procedure. (N.B. the minimum project time obtained in SAQ 3.16 cannot be exceeded.) Assume for the purposes of this question that the only resource of interest is the number of staff required, and that members of staff are interchangeable between all the various activities. The staff requirement throughout the duration of each activity is shown in Table 3.6.

Your answer should include the following elements:

(a) the number of staff required if perfectly flat loading could be achieved

(b) an ordered table of the activities

(c) an initial resource loading

(d) an optimum loading within the given constraints

(e) suggestions for measures that you might consider for rearranging the work realistically in order to decrease further the peak load without reducing the estimate of person-weeks required on a given activity.

**TABLE 3.6** Staff requirement for the computer project

| Activity | Duration | Staff |
|---|---|---|
| design hardware | 20 | 3 |
| procure test facility | 10 | 3 |
| build hardware | 20 | 4 |
| test hardware | 5 | 3 |
| design software | 30 | 2 |
| code software | 20 | 4 |
| design tests | 5 | 2 |
| test system | 10 | 3 |

# 3.4.2 Resource-limited scheduling

So far in this section we have assumed that the project *must* be completed by a given date, so we have adjusted the resource allocation within a *fixed time limit*. Now we take the opposite point of view: adjust the time within a *fixed resource limit*. We want to complete the project in minimum time within the resource constraint, so how do we go about finding the best activity schedule?

In the office installation project we found that five staff were required to complete the job in 32 weeks if no activities were redefined. The project manager could have taken a different approach: start with a given resource limit, say four staff, and calculate the time required. This is the approach we take in this subsection.

As in the case for time-limited scheduling there is no known method that is guaranteed to give the best schedule under all circumstances, except for the blockbusting method of enumerating every feasible combination of the scheduled times of every activity. Although this is possible it can consume enormous computer power when there are many activities. There is, however, a commonly used technique called parallel scheduling which, given some rules about priorities, generally leads to acceptable results in reasonable computation time.

Given a set of rules to work to, parallel scheduling is a very straightforward procedure which is easy to use, and can even be done manually when the number of activities is not too large. Parallel scheduling means starting at the beginning of the project and considering *all* the *eligible* activities in *parallel*. Eligible activities are those activities which could be started if resource were available, taking into account the dependency between activities. (Dependency between activities may be expressed by a table such as the first two columns of Table 3.7). If sufficient resource is available to do all the eligible activities then all are allowed to start, but otherwise some decision rule is used to make a selection of those which will be worked on. (We shall return to the decision rule in a moment.) Having selected the activities for the first week of the project, we then move on to the time at which one of the current activities finishes, releasing resource, and repeat the selection process. Eventually all activities will have been completed.

The success of the method depends, of course, on the decision rules that are used to select activities to be worked on. An elementary set of rules that will usually work quite well is set out below:

*Elementary rules*

Rule 1    From among the eligible activities select first the activity that has the *earliest* date for the *latest start time*. If several eligible activities have the same latest start time then select first the one having the shortest duration. If there are still two or more then other finer distinctions such as choosing the activity with the larger resource requirement may follow this.

Rule 2    Always continue with an activity that has been started until it has been completed, i.e. activities are not to be interrupted.

Rule 3    Never allow a resource to stand idle if there is an eligible activity that could be started.

Rule 4    An activity cannot be started with only partial resources.

Notice that, given the set of rules, the computation of a schedule is straightforward and requires no judgement or iteration. This means that unlike time-limited scheduling it is easy to express the rules in a form that a computer package can use. The method is also easily extended to take account of limits on several resources; the computation simply becomes more tedious.

Highly developed computer packages are available which allow the user to produce schedules using various sets of rules. By comparing the best results with each set of rules the project manager can choose the schedule that suits the project best. For example, it may not be essential to retain Rule 2. If the project manager is prepared to have activities discontinued and resumed later it may be possible to achieve a shorter overall schedule. In practice you must remember that activities that are interrupted will take longer than if the people could work on them continuously. So if tasks are to be split there may need to be some judgement made about the increase in duration.

Parallel scheduling is also quite easy to do by hand provided the number of activities is small enough. Let's consider how the parallel scheduling will work for the office installation shown in Table 3.4, given the elementary rules above. For simplicity we will again assume that the only resource to be considered is the number of staff required.

**TABLE 3.7**  Data for each office installation activity

| Activity identifier | Activities depended on | Staff | Duration | LST | Float | LFT |
|---|---|---|---|---|---|---|
| A | none | 2 | 12 | 0 | 0 | 12 |
| B | none | 2 | 8 | 4 | 4 | 12 |
| C | none | 1 | 5 | 17 | 17 | 22 |
| D | A and B | 4 | 10 | 12 | 0 | 22 |
| E | C and D | 3 | 10 | 22 | 0 | 32 |
| F | A and B | 1 | 5 | 27 | 15 | 32 |

The staffing and scheduling times deduced from the network diagram, Figure 3.26, are reproduced in Table 3.7 without resource constraints. Suppose that the resource limit is to be four staff. (If we chose a limit lower than four the project could not be done at all because Activity D requires four staff, but if we chose more than four there would effectively be no resource limit because five staff is sufficient, as we know from Figure 3.28.)

The values given in Table 3.7 for LST, LFT and float will not actually be achievable in the resource-limited schedule because we expect a lack of staff to force some activities to be postponed. However, the values given in the table will serve for the purpose of choosing which activities to assign staff to first. (If you are unhappy with the idea of using values of float and LST that you know cannot be achieved you could add some hefty margin to the required project completion date and recalculate them, but we will not do this as we are only interested in relative values which will not be affected by recalculation.)

Now follow the parallel scheduling procedure, using the rules given above and applying a resource limit of four staff. The scheduling is summarized in Table 3.8, which is discussed line by line below. (N.B. the figures in column 1 of the table are the various points at which resource is released by completion of an activity.)

**TABLE 3.8**  Parallel scheduling for the office installation

| Time | Free staff | Eligible activities in LST order | | | Comment |
|---|---|---|---|---|---|
| | | Activity | Staff | LST | |
| 0 | 4 | A | 2 | 0 | accept |
| | | B | 2 | 4 | accept |
| | | C | 1 | 17 | insufficient staff |
| 8 | 2 | C | 1 | 17 | accept |
| 12 | 3 | D | 4 | 12 | insufficient staff |
| | | F | 1 | 27 | accept |
| 13 | 3 | D | 4 | 12 | insufficient staff |
| 17 | 4 | D | 4 | 12 | accept |
| 27 | 4 | E | 3 | 22 | accept |

At the beginning of the project, time = 0, there are three eligible activities, A, B and C. The other activities are not eligible because they depend on the completion of one or more of these activities. There are insufficient staff to do all three activities so we apply the selection rule, Rule 1 above, and allocate staff to activities with earliest LST. So activities A and B are scheduled to start immediately and C is put aside.

At time = 8, Activity B finishes, releasing two staff. The only eligible activity at this point is C because others depend on A which has not yet finished.

At time = 12, A finishes and there are now three staff free. The eligible activities are D, which requires four staff, and F, which requires one person. Although D has higher priority there are insufficient staff for it (Rule 4), so F is started (Rule 3). This turns out to be unfortunate because one week later C finishes and releases staff which D could use but once F has started it must be allowed to finish (Rule 2).

At time = 13, C finishes and there are now two free staff but the only eligible activity is D which requires four staff and so must wait.

At time = 17, F finishes and D is started as the only eligible activity.

At time = 27, E is started.

The project finishes at time = 37.

The result of this scheduling is shown in Figure 3.30.

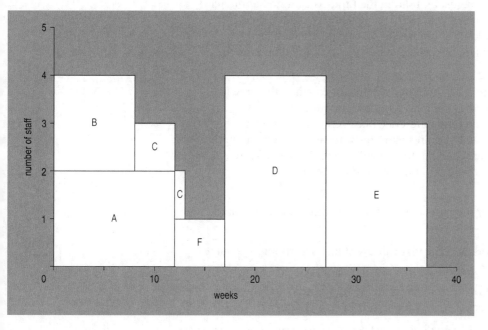

**FIGURE 3.30**
Schedule produced by the
parallel scheduling rules

This schedule was produced by following the rules given on page 219. Normally these rules may be expected to approach closely an optimum schedule within the resource limit. However, in this case we can improve on this schedule by applying a little ingenuity. There was no need to start Activity F as soon as staff became free for it: it has plenty of float. If instead we leave the three staff idle for one week then next week Activity D can start and F can be worked on after D finishes. This produces a better schedule that completes the project in 33 weeks, as shown in Figure 3.31. This is four weeks sooner than the schedule produced by following the scheduling rules.

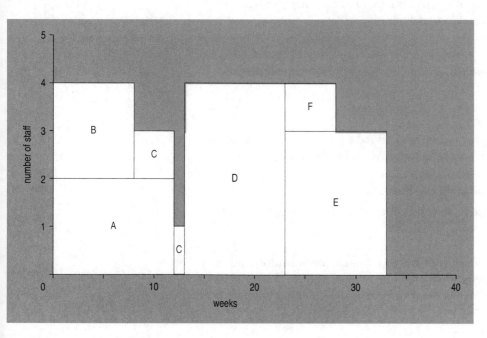

**FIGURE 3.31** Resource-limited
loading chart with strict limit of
four staff

The schedule shown in Figure 3.31 is still not ideal. There is a week in the middle where three staff are idle. Unless these people can be usefully employed on other work the project manager will doubtless want to find a way to avoid this waste. This is where judgement comes in again, just as it did in the time-constrained approach. If Activity C could be shortened by a week, perhaps by using two people on it for a time, then the whole project could be shortened to 32 weeks. This is exactly the time in which we aimed to complete the project when we took the time-limited approach.

It is instructive to compare Figure 3.29, the schedule produced when the time is limited to 32 weeks, with Figure 3.31, the final schedule produced when the resource is limited to four staff. The only difference between them is the way that Activity C is scheduled. In one case it requires extra resource for a week and in the other it simply adds a week to the schedule. In general, however, the schedules produced by the two techniques could differ more significantly, as indeed Figure 3.30 shows.

To summarize, the main steps for the parallel scheduling technique in a resource-limited situation are:

1   Produce the activity network and calculate all event times as though resources were unlimited (e.g. Figure 3.26).

2   Tabulate activity data to show resource requirement, duration and the data such as LST that will be used as criteria for selection (e.g. Table 3.7).

3   At the beginning of the project and then at each point in time where resources are released by the completion of an activity:

- find the eligible set of activities using the dependencies
- select activities successively using the rules.

The resulting schedule will not necessarily be the optimum because the rules are not infallible, but you can normally expect a schedule close to the optimum. A much more detailed discussion of the relative merits of different sets of rules appears in the book by Moder *et al.* (1983). Lockyer (1984) also gives a description of 'branch' and 'bound' methods which, given sufficient time and computational power, yield an optimum. For the practical user there are a number of computer packages available which offer a wide range of possibilities.

### SAQ 3.26

Explain what is meant by parallel scheduling. Very briefly summarize the procedure used.

### SAQ 3.27

(a) Use the rules given in this section to produce a resource-limited schedule for the computer project considered in SAQ 3.25, given the constraint of seven staff.

(b) How long does it take to complete the project?

(c) Is this the shortest possible time, given seven staff? Justify your answer.

### SAQ 3.28

Various kinds of scheduling that take account of resource limitations are provided in computer packages. Which of the two techniques described here, time-limited and resource-limited, do you think would be easier to implement as a computer program? Justify your answer.

## 3.4.3 Summary

We have examined the relationship between the schedule and the requirement for resources. Two extreme situations were considered: time-limited scheduling and resource-limited scheduling. In time-limited scheduling the project completion date is the overriding factor and resources must be found to meet it, at whatever cost. In resource-limited scheduling the reverse is the case: resources are fixed and the schedule must be adjusted to match their availability. Procedures are available for producing an optimum solution in both cases. Project managers need not follow the results of analysis blindly, but should use their judgement to redefine activities whenever necessary in order to achieve a better balance between activities and resources.

Having studied this section you should be able to:

- describe the objectives of scheduling when a project is time-limited
- produce a time-limited schedule from an activity network diagram and list of resources required
- produce a resource-limited schedule using the four elementary rules
- define the differences between serial and parallel scheduling
- use judgement to improve a schedule beyond what the 'rules' allow.

# 3.5 *THE PROJECT PLAN*

This section describes the contents of a project plan. Although a particular structure is described you are not expected to use it rigidly. It is intended to describe the issues that must be addressed in the plan rather than the way that the plan should be organized.

## 3.5.1 Preparing the project plan

In all but the smallest projects the project manager should prepare a formal set of documents called the **project plan**. Usually key members of the prospective project team will help in the preparation. The purpose of this set of documents is to communicate the project manager's intentions to its various readers:

- higher management in the contracting organization
- the client
- members of the project team.

As the project plan has these three distinct readerships there may be some parts of it which are specific to certain people, such as confidential sections for management, but we will ignore these minor differences between versions here.

The project plan is usually developed in at least two stages and passes through several drafts as it evolves. Before the project is sanctioned by the client the plan is initially required in outline form to gain the support of senior management and to establish the client's confidence. (Initial drafts may be used for consultation.) Where a client invites bids the quality of the plans presented by bidders will often be an important factor in the client's decision on whom to appoint. After the project has been sanctioned more detail may be added to the plan as decisions are taken and uncertainties resolved, so that an initial version can be used as a source of guidance to the members of the project team.

During the project the plan should be regularly updated to reflect developments which were either unforeseen at the launch or for which insufficient information was available or which were simply too far ahead to be worth planning in detail.

## 3.5.2 Contents of the project plan

While virtually everyone will agree that there should be a project plan, not everyone will agree on precisely how it should be laid out and exactly what it should contain. There are no rules about this. Nevertheless, there are certain topics that form the core of what most project managers would put in a project plan; these are listed below.

1    Overview or summary

2    Project scope and contract

3    Technical plan

4    Quality and management

5    Organization and personnel

6    Project schedule

7    Resources and facilities (including budget breakdown)

8    Risk assessment and risk management

The content of each of these eight sections is considered in more detail below. The relationship between the various documents in the plan is shown in Figure 3.32.

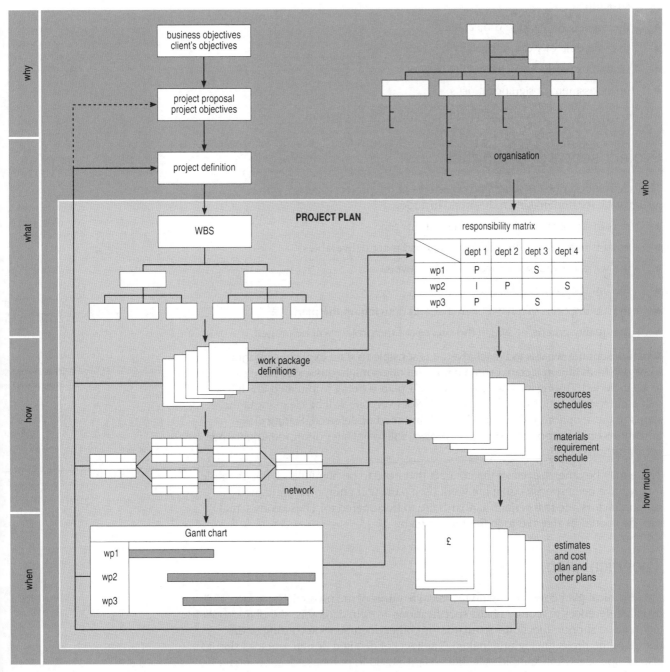

**FIGURE 3.32**   The project plan and its components (courtesy Roy Shepherd)

## Overview or summary

The overview or summary should cover all the essentials in brief. It is a useful introduction to help people reading the plan discern the plan's main structure before examining all the particulars. Some people call this an *executive summary*, based on the notion that a busy executive at the top level will want to spend only a few minutes getting a feel for the project rather than studying all the details. The main points to be summarized are:

- the project's objectives, including the top level of the work breakdown structure

- the organization of the project team

- the schedule of work, especially key milestones

- resources required, including the budget

- an assessment of significant risks.

All these points receive detailed attention in the body of the plan.

## Project scope and contract

This section describes *in detail* the objectives of the project together with a justification for undertaking it. It should include:

- reasons for undertaking the project at this time

- what is to be achieved (requirements and main deliverables)

- the work breakdown structure (higher levels)

- the limits on time and costs

- the assumptions that have been made in drawing up the plan

- the quality criteria by which the success of the project will be judged.

When describing what is to be achieved it is sensible to state explicitly anything *excluded* from the project that some parties involved might otherwise have expected to be included. During the discussions while a plan is being formulated it is likely that a number of options will be proposed. Not everyone will be clear about the status of these options if they have been abandoned or deferred. Stating clear limitations on the scope of the present project will avoid later disappointment and recriminations.

There may be other aspects of the contract that need to be highlighted. For example, it may have been specified that the work uses particular equipment or named subcontractors and that certain standards are to be adhered to. These contractual aspects should be referred to in the project plan.

## Technical plan

The technical plan covers the main technical features of the project. There are usually references to requirements, specifications, system diagrams, site plans, tools, techniques, support functions, standards and other documents according to the nature of the project being undertaken. The level of detailed design required should also be specified: for example, whether it is proposed to purchase or subcontract large modules or to undertake detailed design in-house.

# Quality and management

This part of the plan addresses the issue of how the project is to be managed to achieve the quality expected by the client and the contractor. It will describe, for example, the systems to be used for accounting, authorizing work, change control, the use of configuration management, liaison with the client, reporting and review procedures and safety. (Some of the systems and standards to be employed may be specified in the contract.) A standard methodology such as PRINCE may be specified for the project work.

Some organizations prepare a separate plan, called the **quality plan**, which gathers together in a single document all the activities that are deemed to relate specifically to maintaining the quality of the project, as opposed to those activities essential to project performance. These quality activities concentrate particularly on the maintenance of standards and the testing of deliverables against those standards. (Here we will assume that in the same way that quality is to be built into the project, so the quality activities will be part of the project plans, but they could be contained in a separate document.)

The form that quality planning takes will depend to a large extent on the quality environment in the contractor's organization. In an organization which has already developed quality procedures for performing projects the existing quality manual will already lay down the way in which the project is to be managed. The quality manual, for example, defines what is to be contained in the project plan itself! The quality document will be devoted to considering whether any of those procedures are not applicable to the current project or need modification.

In an organization where there is no quality manual or if the quality manual does not cover projects then the quality section of the project plan will be much longer because it must show how quality will be assured. It needs to cover such issues as:

- how quality criteria will be set for assessing the adequacy of each piece of work
- what measures will be taken to prevent the occurrence of faults
- what will be done to detect and correct the faults that do occur
- what tests will be used to demonstrate whether the quality criteria have been met
- what review procedures will be used
- who will perform the quality control work.

# Organization and personnel

In Section 3.2 we considered how the project organization might be set up and responsibilities assigned. This section of the plan, the organization plan, communicates the results of that work to everyone involved.

The organization plan describes the structure of the project team and the responsibilities of the various people involved in the project. This will include not only the contractor's but also any subcontractor's staff and staff from the client's organization who will have an input to the project. The plan should include an organization chart. If key personnel, such as work-package managers, have already been earmarked for the project their names may be given. If names are not given it is necessary to identify people according to the skills required (for example, 'the project requires three electrical engineers of whom at least one is experienced in designing high-speed drive systems'). If the people are not named then it is also appropriate to say where they will come from, how they will be recruited, what training they will require, and when they will be needed.

## Project schedule

This section describes the schedule of the project in the forms that you have studied in detail in Sections 3.3 and 3.4. It should describe the main phases of the project and highlight all the key milestones. Usually Gantt charts are used in presenting plans such as this because non-experts find them easy to use, but networks are also appropriate if the audience is likely to understand them. The use of activity-on-arrow or activity-on-node will usually depend not on the relative merits of the techniques but on their familiarity to the users of the plan.

## Resources and facilities

This section of the plan summarizes the resources and facilities required in the project, including money, people and services. The requirements for these resources should show not only the total resource required but also the distribution of the requirement over time. For example, the total project budget may be £1 million but that sum is not required at the start of the project. The financial planners will want to know the requirements for cash, probably in monthly or quarterly periods, so that the cash can be made available at the right time. (Provision of cash unnecessarily early costs money.)

Another subject that may be addressed in this section of the plan is the cash flow plan. Given a schedule for the work and estimates of the cost of each element it is possible to calculate the cumulative cash outflow arising from the work. It is normal in a project of some size for the client to pay the contractor at stages throughout the project. These **stage payments** are usually agreed to be due at milestones, representing the completion of recognizable portions of the project. Hence it is possible to calculate cash inflow to the contractor from the schedule of dates planned for these payment milestones together with the amount agreed for each of the stages. Combining the estimates for cash outflow and cash inflow yields the planned cash flow for the contractor.

Similarly, requirements for people and services should be accompanied by the dates when they are needed. While it is natural that a project manager wants to ensure that staff are available early enough, it is expensive to recruit people into a team at the beginning of the project, only to find them waiting to start work that can't be done until later in the project, for example people recruited for installation work when the equipment has still to be procured. (This is an example of balancing the cost of having people idle against the risk that they will not be readily available at the right time.)

## Risk assessment and risk management

This part of the project plan is concerned with risks such as those discussed in Chapter 2. It shows how the project manager plans to manage the risks should they arise. Today this is recognized as being of crucial importance. It often used to be omitted from project plans, perhaps because of its overtones of pessimism: many felt it drew too much attention to the negative aspects of the project. Nevertheless, from the points of view of both the contractor and the client it is vital to know the risks being run and to be sure that the risks will be under regular surveillance so that corrective action can be taken at the earliest possible time. The preparation of the risk management plan is a necessary stimulus to the project manager to take precautions against the dangers. (At this point, many project managers advocate setting up a risk register for use in monitoring risks; however, this does not form part of the project plan.)

## Other components of the plan

The plan outlined above shows the core components which are necessary for almost all project plans. However, it will often be appropriate to have additional plans on matters which do not seem to fit tidily into this structure. In a hazardous environment you might want an entire section dealing with safety matters and for a computer system you often need a security plan.

We do not present the structure outlined above as a universal formula but as a guideline to a minimal set of topics which the project plan should address.

### SAQ 3.29

(a) Who should prepare the project plan?

(b) At what stage?

(c) For what readership?

### ACTIVITY 3.4

Consider your own project and take notes on your answers to these questions.

Was there a document or documents available to the project team that you can identify as the formal plan for the project?

Are there elements within the above description that you think were missing from the plans in your project?

Why do you think this might have been so? Do you think it would have been useful if these missing sections had been included?

Conversely, were there sections in your project plan that we have not thought to mention that you think would be of benefit in any project plan?

### ACTIVITY 3.5

Take notes on your answers to the following.

In your project work was a quality standard used for the preparation of a project plan?

If there was a such a standard, compare it with the outline we have given above. If not, consider whether the introduction of a standard would be beneficial to your organization.

### 3.5.3 Summary

This section has outlined the requirement for a formal project plan, initially to be prepared by the project manager before the project is sanctioned and subsequently to be amplified and updated. Versions may be required for senior management, the client and the project team. The main topics to be addressed in this plan are:

- project scope and contract
- technical plan
- quality and management
- organization and personnel
- project schedule
- resources and facilities (including budget breakdown)
- risk assessment and risk management.

Having studied this section you should now be able to:

- describe the role of the formal project plan
- prepare such a plan for a project with which you are familiar, using documents you have developed during the planning and estimating phases of your work.

# 4 BUILDING AND LEADING THE TEAM

## *INTRODUCTION*

All projects are carried out by people; success is achieved through people working in teams. *People management is the most important element of project management.* All project management is about working with people: it is people who get things done, not objectives, not plans, not machines and not schedules – though all these are important.

This chapter attempts to show the importance of managing in a climate of uncertainty – managing the project team, working with sponsors, senior managers, colleagues and stakeholders. There are many areas we do not cover owing to lack of space and time: in particular there remains much to say about managing people who are difficult, about negotiating techniques, conducting effective meetings and maintaining control of the situation for the duration of the project. These constitute a course in their own right, so we have suggested some further reading on these topics in the 'References and further reading' at the end of the book.

## Aims and objectives

This chapter aims to:

- emphasize the importance of teamwork in projects
- discuss vital interpersonal skills required for projects: leadership; liaison with clients, sponsors and other stakeholders; selecting, building and managing teams
- introduce some of the key techniques for managing project teams.

After studying this chapter you should be able to:

- identify the needs of teams
- recognize the different types of team organization and assess their merits
- understand the different roles needed in teams
- manage 'up'
- build and motivate a team
- lead the team
- negotiate with others and avoid conflict.

# 4.1 PEOPLE AND PROJECTS

## 4.1.1 The project environment

The authors Boddy and Buchanan (1992) see projects as a means of achieving change and note that change means that things will be unfamiliar, uncertain and ambiguous. Managing projects, managing change, is therefore quite different from managing *systems*. A system, once it is in place, is familiar, establishes patterns of work and interaction and generates its own momentum. It is by its very nature long-term. A project, on the other hand, is new and temporary, information may be uncertain, the authority to control may have to be indirect and 'who's in charge' may be ambiguous. Thus, project managers also need to understand their project: not just the technical requirements and objectives that appear on the project documents, but those forces which prompted the project and what will work for it, and the forces that may resist change and will oppose the project.

Project teams need:

- clear aims or goals
- clear objectives
- clear leadership.

The term *aim* is used here as meaning what you intend to do; a *goal* is the desired outcome. *Objectives* focus on achieving the aims – means to an end. Different team members may have different objectives; this is acceptable and occasionally even desirable.

---

**EXAMPLE 4.1**

Consider a professional football team. The team's likely aims are:

- to win matches and trophies
- to bring in paying spectators so the club is profitable.

The team's possible objectives (ways of achieving the aims) are:

- to score goals
- to prevent the opposition from scoring goals
- to play football that is exciting for the spectators
- to win the league, cup or promotion.

The goalkeeper and the striker will have different primary *objectives* but the same *aim*. The striker wants to score, while the goalkeeper wants to prevent the opposition from scoring: both will share the aim of winning the league or cup.

---

Project managers have to provide *leadership*; it is a key role (perhaps the most important role) for project managers. We return to the topic of leadership many times in this chapter, notably in Section 4.2.4. However, let's first consider the various roles project managers have to undertake.

# 4.1.2 The project manager's roles

We use the plural when referring to a project manager's roles because many different roles 'go with the job'. A project manager's key role is to ensure that the team succeeds, and since projects are by their very nature interdisciplinary and cross many organizational lines, routine does not exist and choices have to be made frequently and quickly.

Norris *et al.* (1993) see the job slightly differently – as one of managing the people, the process (the work of the project) and the product (the deliverables, including their quality). This is illustrated in Figure 4.1. In our terms, the schedule and the cost (which were dealt with in Chapter 3), as well as other things such as change and change control (discussed in Chapters 5 and 6), constitute the process, and the standard is expressed in the product. The support given to the project manager by the project team, and the project manager's ability to interact with management, stakeholders, clients and others, constitute the 'people' aspects.

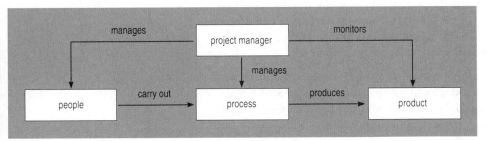

**FIGURE 4.1**  One view of project management (based on Norris *et al.*)

Buchanan and Boddy (1992) identify three models of change, which of course is what the project manager has to manage. Each model applies to different situations and each calls for a somewhat different set of skills from the project manager.

The first model we could call the 'rational-linear' model: it assumes that planned change occurs in a logical, sequential manner and that people do what is expected of them. In software project management this model is drawn as a kind of waterfall and is called the waterfall model of project life-cycles: the problem is identified and analysed before any solution is suggested, planning is completed before any project work starts, design is completed before programming starts, and so on. Gunton (1990) notes that this works well when there are specific and well-defined requirements but poorly in an environment of constant change or where requirements are 'fuzzy'. While the model encompasses deviation from plan, it sees deviation as something that will be noticed and corrected. Several of the techniques you learned in Chapter 3 are aimed at highlighting deviation from plan so that corrective action can be taken. This model of change calls for that kind of skill and technique. However, the model can be regarded as idealized, requiring rationality, near perfect information and clear organization. In reality change may involve many people rather than one 'omnipotent' manager, and different people will have different perspectives on goals, objectives, the use of resources, the desirability of change and so on.

A second model could be termed 'participative': managers of such projects seek to engender a sense of ownership of or investment in the change from all those likely to be affected. It sounds easy, but given life's vagaries such a model can be very difficult to apply. People will often resist change. Markus (1983) identified four types of such resistance:

- resistance arising out of individual attitudes, preferences and personal characteristics

- resistance arising out of system problems like complexity, poor ergonomic features, etc.

- resistance arising from a perceived failure of the change to fit into an organizational context, such as the redistribution of responsibilities after a change, procedural changes, etc.

- resistance arising from political factors: changes in the power structure of an organization, access to important information, new decision-making structures and changes in the ability to exercise influence.

There have been a number of techniques aimed at overcoming resistance, securing participation and encouraging a democratic approach. Broadly, these could be called *sociotechnical* approaches. However, such approaches are difficult to put into practice and often the social issues swamp the technical issues or vice versa; it is not unusual to fail to achieve a balance. And, as events impinge on a project and things may begin to go wrong, trying to maintain collaboration and consensus becomes very difficult.

The third model, which I shall call the 'complex' model, is more in accord with observations of real projects: the model assumes that there may be significant disagreement about ends, means and the use of resources and that there may be politically charged elements of any project, requiring political skills on the part of the project manager.

To manage change a project manager performs a complicated juggling act with the resources available (people, time, money, equipment and information). This means continually making choices about priorities. It follows then that a project manager must be a person who is capable of considering and weighing consequences, and who is unafraid of choosing. For a project to be successful, team members must also be comfortable with this need for decision making. Who but the project manager can ever attempt to shift the team members' thinking towards accepting the need for difficult decisions? This is another dimension of the project manager's role.

Boddy and Buchanan (1992) used a questionnaire to discover the things that practising project managers valued most. The top eight items were:

- getting agreement on goals

- ensuring everyone knows what is expected

- ensuring that resources are available

- improving communications

- being sure that staff understand the reasons behind the changes to be made

- being able to fit all the pieces together

- making sure everyone understands their role, early in the project

- ensuring that benefits are visible to everyone affected.

Most of these items fit well with the socio-technical model of change and show how vital to project success the 'people element' of project management is.

## ACTIVITY 4.1

Drawing on what you have read and from your own experience list what you think are the key leadership skills for project managers.

## DISCUSSION

The key skills that the authors have identified are:

- ability to clarify goals
- ability to clarify team members' roles
- ability to build a team quickly and to gain the team's respect
- ability to motivate staff and to maintain that motivation over long periods
- ability to communicate across all levels
- good interpersonal skills and the ability to influence others
- exercise of political skills
- change management skills
- ability to take a broader view of the project's place in the organization
- ability to maintain progress on work
- but, most of all, *patience*.

You may have thought of others.

## SAQ 4.1

Based on your own experience of projects and what you have read above, list up to six activities that a project manager would carry out, from a people point of view, to get a project off to a good start.

# 4.1.3 Summary

We have discussed the requirement of project teams for clear aims and goals, objectives and leadership, and noted that while all members of a team may share a major aim, they may have different objectives. The project manager has a number of different roles to fill: clarifying goals and roles, providing motivation, communicating to many people, being able to take a broad view of the project. Three models of change were described. Though difficult to apply to any given project, these are useful in understanding the dynamic nature of project work.

Having studied this section you should be able to:

- list the key skills for project managers
- list, from the 'people' point of view, the main activities of a project manager
- describe how some of these skills and activities are used in your own experience
- describe briefly the three models of change, explaining how they apply to real projects.

# 4.2  *DEALING WITH PEOPLE*

Dealing with people – superiors, colleagues, subordinates – requires skill. Skills of this type are normally referred to as **interpersonal skills**. These are skills that we all use to some degree to 'get along' with the people around us: influencing them to do something of what we want, negotiating what we want with them, motivating them to help us, resolving conflict between ourselves and others when it arises. Below we discuss four skills that are particularly important to project managers: influencing, delegating, negotiating and leading.

## 4.2.1  Influencing

Because many organizations constitute project teams in such a way that the project manager is not the line manager of most or all of the team members, project management often involves **influencing** the actions of others, without any direct authority. Persuasion, negotiation and 'marketing' are aspects of leadership and interpersonal skills which require good, if not excellent, communication by the project manager. (This chapter will return to the importance of good communication on a number of occasions, but for the moment we concentrate on influencing skills.)

Project managers often have little formal authority. They therefore get their authority through respect for their experience, good track records, persuasiveness and downright dogged determination – in short, by influence.

The ability to influence the behaviour of others is a very effective form of power. Power most obviously comes from authority, but if the project manager doesn't have formal authority there are other forms of power that he or she can use. Power can be delegated to the project manager by someone very senior in the organization – what Hannaway and Hunt (1992) call *legitimate power*. The project manager may, through force of personality if not through the exercise of legitimate power, be able to coerce co-operation. A project manager who is charismatic or well liked may have authority granted through the wishes of others to be associated with him or her. The project manager may have the authority of expertise: this is especially true when there is a crisis or urgency. Bacon said that *knowledge is power*, and so it is for the project manager, who can obtain *information power*. The project manager can also gain influence from being associated with a more powerful person in the organization: Hannaway and Hunt's *affiliative power*. A group, such as a project team, can also be powerful in its own right; this occurs perhaps best when the group is democratic and works consensually and the project manager is perceived by others as a formal or informal spokesperson. Lastly, a project manager can increase his or her influence through 'political' means, by gaining the support of colleagues and superiors. Project managers need to use those kinds of power most suited both to their subordinates and colleagues and to the situation; having that power and applying it appropriately allows managers to influence where they cannot command.

While we are on the subject of influencing skills, a few words are needed on the importance of personal and work relationships compared with the importance of achieving goals. Project managers must consider if getting what they want in any particular instance is more important than their relationship with whomever they are trying to influence or persuade. A perspective on this is given by the goal–relationship matrix shown in Table 4.1.

**TABLE 4.1**  Goal–relationship matrix

| | Low | High |
|---|---|---|
| **High** | Give way – do it their way (mostly) but remember you are owed a favour. | Use all your skills and patience. Call in any debts. <br><br> Make many but small concessions or compromises. <br><br> Take time to negotiate formally. |
| **Low** | Delegate negotiation to another team member for the experience. <br><br> Walk away – at this level it isn't worth an argument. | Go for it. <br> Dig your heels in. <br> Fight like hell. |

*Importance of interpersonal relationship* (vertical axis)

*Importance of goal* (horizontal axis)

# 4.2.2  Delegating

Like influencing, a key skill for project managers is **delegation**. A project manager should clarify and emphasize the goals and use influencing skills to persuade the team to support them. Delegation then clarifies the roles of the team members in respect of these goals.

The work breakdown structure identifies the tasks that need to be performed; the work package definitions identify the quality; network analysis techniques show the timescale. Deciding who should undertake which tasks is seldom difficult in projects, since members are often included in teams because of the special skills they bring. We suggest a few simple rules for ensuring successful delegation:

1    When delegating a subproject, phase, stage or activity, delegate to the team member who will be responsible for it the *authority* to use resources for that subproject, phase, stage or activity. Having responsibility without matching authority is an invidious position.

2    Delegate, and then avoid 'meddling' subsequently in what the team member does! In practice this means 'selling' the task, discussing approaches with the delegatee, reassuring the delegatee that he or she is capable or can expect guidance. Once discussions are ended, accept mistakes without annoyance or recrimination.

3    Delegate to the lowest level possible, using your knowledge of subordinates to choose those who demonstrate potential for doing the delegated task.

4    People learn from their mistakes, and they need sufficient freedom to make them. They will quickly learn from them, and if they are able to correct them by themselves and without recrimination they will be confident to try

new and different things in the future. (This of course applies equally to project managers and team members.) Clearly, if a team member with responsibility for a particular stage is about to make a serious mistake, the project manager cannot stand by and let it happen. For example, if the chief engineer on a building project sees that a junior engineer to whom he or she has delegated part of the work is about to do something that might threaten safety or cause a serious setback to the project as a whole, then the chief engineer cannot simply stand by and let it happen. But the primary error (and responsibility) lies with the chief engineer for making an unwise delegation in the first place, or for failing to discuss adequately the approach to be used with the delegatee.

5 Make feedback a regular routine: the delegatee reports progress (and problems!) and you must be willing to give guidance or bolster confidence if necessary, and acknowledge success.

You can never delegate all the responsibility. Ultimately you are the project manager, the boss, and you are responsible overall for the project. Example 4.2 illustrates some of these points.

---

### EXAMPLE 4.2: Your way – their way

A project to produce training materials and establish a training system in a country in Eastern Europe was in the mobilization phase. The project manager was not yet engaged full-time on the project because she was winding up an earlier project and only handled the preliminary negotiations with the client. She delegated the set-up work, which involved mainly research and scheduling, learning the protocol and finding examples of the materials to be used to another team member. The team member proposed an early visit to the host country before most of the planning and set-up had been done. The project manager disagreed; she wanted to see more of the research undertaken first. However, she did not interfere except to point out the key activities that must take place before the first visit to Eastern Europe. The planner felt many of these were unnecessary at such an early stage. The project manager gave way, and allowed the early visit.

The project planner soon realized that most of the early activities that the project manager suggested were necessary. He then worked hard to get these done, even working extra hours; however he still had to delay the first visit by a couple of days. The result nevertheless was that the early visit took place successfully and the majority of the activities thought to be needed before the first visit were done after all.

Consider the probable outcome if project manager had not allowed proper delegation, had stamped her authority on the project and not allowed the early visit. Possible consequences are:

- a generally bad atmosphere in the project team (at a key stage of the project)
- a demotivated project planner
- the set-up phase might have taken longer.

---

This scenario is a good example of *positive conflict* – conflict where the outcome is positive in terms of the project and the relationship between the two 'opponents'. Consider also the goal–relationship matrix in Table 4.1; clearly here the project manager considered her relationship with the team member doing the planning to be more important than the goal of detailed project planning before the first visit.

### SAQ 4.2

List five key aspects of successful delegation.

# 4.2.3   Negotiating

**Negotiation** is the process of satisfying a project's (or team's, or department's) needs by reaching agreement or compromise with others. In projects it takes place when, to enable the needs of the project to be met, the project manager has to rely on someone else over whom he or she has no direct authority and who has no direct authority over him or her. Negotiations always take place between two or more parties. Each party will have an initial position (the ideal outcome, from that party's point of view) and a fall-back position (the maximum those who possess or have a call on the resources can give or concede; or, from the project's point of view, the minimum it must get in order to go forward). This is represented in Figure 4.2 below.

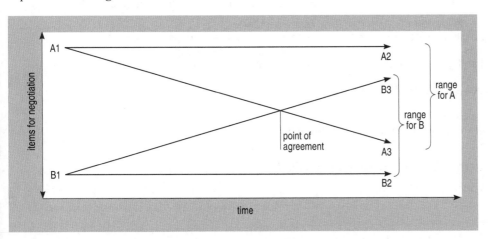

**FIGURE 4.2**   Negotiations. For parties A and B position 1 represents their initial position, 2 their ideal outcome and 3 their fall-back position.

Project managers need to negotiate on the whole range of project issues: resources, schedules, priorities, standards and quality, procedures, costs and people issues. Table 4.2 shows some of the main issues and with whom the negotiation might take place.

Negotiation is not something that takes place only between companies or organizations, or between departments and groups of staff and management.

**TABLE 4.2**   Negotiations in project management

| General areas | Possible issues | Persons/groups to negotiate with |
|---|---|---|
| **Resources** | Cash required<br>Staff time<br>Equipment/rooms, etc.<br>Time span (for phases and overall) | Senior management<br>Line manager<br>Purchasing/IT/estates departments<br>Sponsor/senior management |
| **Schedules** | Order of activities<br>Time for activities<br>Time for stages<br>Deadlines | Team members, sponsor<br>Line managers or their representatives, team members<br>Line managers or their representatives, team members<br>Sponsor, team members, line managers |
| **Priorities** | Over other projects and routine work<br>Between cost, quality and time<br>Of team member work activities | Senior managers, sponsor, other project managers<br>Sponsor, line managers, team members, client<br>Team members |
| **Standards/ quality** | Assurance checks<br>Performance measures and targets<br>Fitness for purpose | Sponsor, project board*, assurance teams<br>Sponsor, project board*, assurance teams<br>Sponsor, team members, assurance teams |
| **Procedures** | Methods<br>Functions<br>Roles and responsibilities<br>Formal reporting<br>Relationships | Team members, advisers<br>Team members, line managers<br>Team members, sponsors<br>Sponsor, project board*, senior management<br>Team members, advisers |
| **Costs** | Estimates<br>Expectations<br>Budgets<br>Expenditure | Various specialists, team members<br>Sponsor, senior management<br>Sponsor, senior management, finance<br>Sponsor, line managers, team members |
| **People** | Getting team to gel/perform<br>Getting/using skills needed<br>Work allocations<br>Effort needed and given (or not) | Team members<br>Team members, line managers<br>Team members, line managers<br>Team members, line managers |

\* Applies when specific methodologies such as configuration management are used.

In life, everyone is negotiating all the time. Within a household, for example, you negotiate on:

- how shared income is spent and general expenses are handled

- who does what tasks and when

- when and where to go out

- what and when to eat

- what to watch on TV

- where to go for holidays.

You probably have a wealth of experience of negotiating, without even knowing it, from your personal life.

## Setting up a negotiation

Every negotiation can be seen as a mini-project. Depending on the relative importance of the issues, each negotiation requires a varying degree of definition, planning, scheduling and control. Some may be highly informal – a few words exchanged in the corridor can be a negotiation. Some may be highly formal. But whether a negotiation is formal, informal or some degree in-between, it is important to consider the questions posed in Table 4.3.

**TABLE 4.3** Important questions to ask before negotiating

| | |
|---|---|
| **Who?** | Who is involved in the negotiation? |
| | Are you dealing with the correct individual(s) (authority level)? |
| | What are the concerns of each individual involved (anxieties, motives, hidden agendas, emotions, etc.)? |
| | Does this negotiation require the sponsor's help? Might another team member do better than you? |
| **Why?** | What is the goal of the negotiation? |
| | Is there a common understanding of this goal? |
| | Is this negotiation important? |
| **What?** | What are the issues? |
| | Can they be established in advance? |
| | What are the needs of both parties? |
| | What must be agreed to? |
| | How much flexibility do you have? |
| | Is there a conflict? |
| **Where?** | 'Their place', 'neutral ground', 'your place'? |
| | If neutral ground, is there a need for an unbiased arbitrator? |
| | Would it help to do something special such as negotiate over lunch? |
| **When?** | How much time do you have? |
| | What is the impact of a delay? |
| | Might later be more favourable? |
| **How?** | What documents are needed in advance? |
| | Are preliminary discussions needed? |
| | Consider: listening skills, communication strategies, objectivity, assertiveness, patience, independence, trust, ability to influence. |

One party will almost always win, or lose, slightly more than the other. Project managers who are good negotiators will manage the outcome of a negotiation such that the differences in what each side obtains are kept to a minimum and conflict is avoided. The ideal situation occurs when both parties to the negotiation gain something significant, a so-called 'win–win' outcome. If this is too difficult to obtain, finding something close to a situation where neither party loses much, a 'no lose' outcome, should normally be feasible. To help obtain this:

...negotiate over lunch

1   Identify and define the problem.

2   Generate various alternative solutions that you are willing to accept (e.g. consider your initial and fall-back positions).

3   Evaluate these alternative outcome solutions.

4   Reach agreement or compromise by selecting the most appropriate solution for both parties.

Then:

5   Implement the result of the negotiation.

Important tactics for negotiating successfully are: adequate preparation (as described earlier), using questions effectively, and not weakening your case inadvertently.

If continuing to make statements that the opposition is unwilling to accept is plainly not likely to change their position, use questions to persuade them (this allows them to think about the issue in a particular way rather than to continue their opposition to a statement). You can also use questions to control the conversation by making your opponents respond to your question rather than lead the discussion with points they want to make. Since using questions well is a key negotiating skill, it is important to plan the questions you will ask and to write them down. If the negotiations become heated, having prepared questions can allow you to reduce the pressure on yourself by giving you time while your opponent thinks of a reply. Signal your intention to ask a question or suggest a solution in order to catch the attention of everyone involved, this has the added effect of putting pressure on the person you are negotiating with.

Keep a good argument strong by not diluting it; concentrate on a few strong points and avoid bringing in more, but weaker, points. A skilled negotiator will spot a weak argument and attack it, putting the other side on the defensive. You may need to write down a few key points that you want to make in order to avoid being drawn into trying to supplement your argument with weaker points. Then stick with what you've written down.

From time to time during a negotiation, whether it is a formal or an informal one, test that both sides understand clearly what is being proposed and at what stage the negotiations are. This keeps everyone on track and on the topic.

Negotiations tend to have one of the following outcomes:

- Your needs are accepted by the other party and little negotiation is required.

- Your needs can be met (or nearly so) but you have to make some amendment or compromise.

- The other party offers some options; you need to make judgements on whether these are acceptable. Further negotiations will be necessary.

- Your requirements are rejected, but normally the other party remains objective; there is a conflict of views and interests – but not normally hostility. You will need to rethink your requirements, and problem solving is necessary.

After a negotiation, summarize the results in writing so that all parties are quite clear about what has been agreed. Build trust with the colleagues with whom you negotiate. Where you have been given a favour or the other party has 'lost' more than you keep a note of this (you owe them a 'favour') – see that they know you remember the occasion. Keep strictly to the agreement, but if this should not prove possible go back and negotiate further (and carefully explain why).

### SAQ 4.3

Read the scenario below and answer the questions that follow.

You are the project manager for a business engineering project in a large service company of about 500 persons. There are six members on your project team; you and three of the project team are full-time and the other three are half-time.

It has become clear to you recently that there is a need for each team member to have a portable personal computer (PC) to enable them to work on project business at home, in their own office or in the project office. You only have a small equipment budget but it is the policy of the company to keep a few portable PCs available for special or occasional use; these are held in the Information Systems (IS) Department for lending. The IS Department also has a moderate range of licensed software that can be loaned as required. You have determined that staff need the standard company word-processing package, a spreadsheet and communications software. You reckon that you must get at least three portables, four would be far better and seven ideal. You know from your own experience that the IS Department tend to have between five and eight portables available at any one time. The project is due to continue for about a further six months, and your need for the portable PCs will build up to its maximum over the next six weeks. You have to negotiate with the IS Department to borrow the PCs.

(a) Jot down a few points on how you would go about planning the negotiation.

(b) What are the main points you would make in support of your case?

(c) What is your hoped-for outcome and (minimum) fall-back position?

# 4.2.4  Leading

According to the dictionary, to **lead** is to:

- cause someone to go with one

- conduct or guide others, especially by going in front

- direct the movements of others

- guide the actions or opinions of someone by argument, induce someone to do something

- to have the first place in something, go first or be first

- direct by example (for instance, an orchestra).

There are plenty of other detailed definitions! Unless you are able to tie some figurative rope around the necks of those whom you need to lead, the only ways to do it are by argument, by inducement, by influence and by example – by going metaphorically 'in front'. Thus most leadership qualities are the personal qualities of the one who would be leader. As has already been said: the leader needs to be convinced of what the goal of the project is and that it is worth achieving, must communicate clearly, use his or her communications skills to influence people, and must keep others motivated to stay with the project until their part of it is completed.

A word needs to be said here about what we might call *negative* ledership skills. We have advocated a positive and open approach to leadership, emphasizing the giving of information and direction, influencing, gaining respect and co-operation. Some authors advocate the use of more 'negative' methods and skills: using, for example, threats, hiding information, blaming others when things go wrong, using delaying tactics to gain advantage or embarrass a rival, sacrificing the future to 'save' a present situation. Kleim and Ludin (1992) mention most of these in their chapter entitled tellingly 'The Political Jungle'. In some organizations the culture is indeed highly politicized and very like a jungle. But bear in mind the drawbacks and hazards inherent in managing relations with people and organizational groups in this way.

Using threat, at least in the first instance, will gain at best only grudging co-operation, and it is possible that a threatened subordinate (or one who perceives him- or herself threatened) will leave, spread dissatisfaction or even sabotage project effort. Concealing information at the very least opens up the possibility that there could be nasty surprises in store should things begin to go wrong; and others, aware of your tactic, may conceal important information from you. A 'culture of blame' can result in organizational paralysis. Delaying tactics, which Kleim and Ludin call *filibustering*, can backfire badly; they note: 'Unless you can attribute the delay to [a believable cause] you may receive blame for the unsatisfactory performance of your project' (p.98). While sacrificing the future to the present is an exceedingly common strategy (one could call it "the quick fix"), someone will have to deal with the consequences later, and it may be you. It is a temporary expedient rather than a solution to a problem, and the passage of time can magify considerably the adverse consequences of even the simplest 'quick fix'.

In any case, the so-called 'Machiavellian' management style not only does not suit every person or situation, it also requires consummate skill to practise. If it's not your natural style, you are best advised to steer clear of it altogether – and we advocate the position that such a style is largely counter-productive.

Specific skills that contribute to effective and positive leadership are mostly based on good communication skills: effective listening and effective talking or writing. Some ways in which a project manager can *lead* individual team members include the following:

### Feedback

Give performance feedback, placing emphasis on positive feedback. Positive feedback – telling someone what he or she is doing right – is motivating. If negative feedback is necessary, it may be far more palatable if it follows some positive feedback. Watch for clues that someone *wants* feedback and try to ensure that any feedback follows an act fairly quickly. Put the emphasis on the action, not on the person, whether the feedback is positive or negative. For example, don't say: 'You're great at writing reports'; say instead: 'That report you wrote last week was very well organized and presented.' If feedback must be negative, make sure the subordinate understands it. Give him or her a chance to discuss how to improve. Needless to say, you should be open to feedback yourself.

### Recognition

Recognize progress and success. According to Robert Townsend in *Up the Organization*, thanks is an under-used form of compensation. If you feel a team member's success is out of the ordinary, *write it down*, either as a memo to their line manager or personnel file, or to your own files for use in their next performance appraisal. Give the person a copy.

### Reward

Reward good performance, even in small ways: buy the person a cup of coffee or lunch, recommend them for a special award, give them a bit more or your time, improve their conditions, for example by reducing weekend working or improving office facilities. Some companies operate award and recognition schemes: consider these if appropriate.

## Encourage

Coach and encourage people to help them improve their own effectiveness. If they perceive this as positive and it comes from you, you will have gained respect and loyalty.

What about having to manage a poor performer? If you have to take someone to task, do so *in private* rather than in a public place or public forum. No one likes to be 'dressed down' in front of others. Be calm; no one likes to be shouted at or intimidated. When you have stated why you judge that a person's performance is poor, be open to discussions with him or her about the job: is it too demanding, does this person have the right sort of training or aptitude, are personal problems impinging on work time? Make suggestions about what might be done, being firm but supportive. Draw up an action plan and get the person to agree to it. Use discipline only as a final measure, bearing in mind that organization procedures and employment legislation have to be observed. Generally, document everything scrupulously.

A good leader knows what's going on. Such knowledge is not solely acquired by sitting in an office waiting for the intelligence to arrive. A most effective technique is to manage by walking around. You will learn what is happening in a way that reports can't possibly convey, your people will get to know you better, and the practice encourages a supportive climate of openness.

---

### ACTIVITY 4.2

In your notebook, write a brief analysis of what you consider to be your personal management 'style'. Are you satisfied with it? Do you feel that people follow you because they must or because they want to? Can you see any ways you might improve on what you currently do?

---

Leadership skills are not necessarily inherent, but they can be developed. They grow out of being able to reason clearly about the project and identify its most important aims (this is often a result not only of the analysis of written documents, but also of *listening* to people who might have a stake in the project). However, the best analysis and reasoning in the world will be worthless unless accompanied by the ability to communicate what the aims are to others and to convince them by well-constructed argument that the project's success is in *their* interest as well as in yours or the organization's. The project manager, like any leader, also needs communications skills to give people a clear and unambiguous idea of what their role will be and how they will be expected to fulfil it. And because projects take time – sometimes a long time – the project manager can't simply play the leader at the beginning and then expect everyone else to follow these initial directions indefinitely. Things will change; even the main aims of a project may change with time. People will become bored or disillusioned or even angry. So the project manager needs to keep exercising the skills of listening, analysing, arguing, giving feedback and resolving conflicts throughout the life of the project.

The whole of this chapter is really about what constitutes leadership.

**SAQ 4.4**

(a) List three 'negative' leadership skills and state their drawbacks.

(b) List three 'positive' leadership skills or tactics and state how they can help a project manager build his or her leadership.

(c) What basic skill underpins leadership skills?

# 4.2.5 Summary

This section has addressed the four main interpersonal skills that a project manager must demonstrate in order to be successful: influencing, delegating, negotiating and leading. These skills include other interpersonal skills such as listening and communicating, as well as the ability to analyse and reason.

Having studied this section you should be able to:

- explain why influence is important in project management

- be aware of the sometimes conflicting importance of goals and relationships

- give five 'rules' for successful delegation

- define what negotiation is and when it is required

- know what questions you need to ask before engaging in negotiation

- explain why it is important to achieve either a 'win–win' or a 'no lose' outcome in negotiation

- list 'negative' and 'positive' leadership skills and state ways in which they hinder or help the project manager develop leadership.

# 4.3 TEAM ORGANIZATION

Different organizations use different types of team. The type affects how that team is managed, what forms of communication the project needs and what aspects of the project the project manager should emphasize. Below we discuss some common types of team. Many teams may not fall clearly into one type, but may combine elements of different types.

Organizations have traditionally been managed through a hierarchical structure. In general the structure has been:

- staff performing similar tasks – together reporting to a single supervisor

- junior managers – responsible for a number of supervisors and their groups

- groups of junior managers – reporting to departmental or unit heads

- departmental or unit heads – reporting to senior managers who are responsible for wide ranging functions such as manufacturing, finance, human resources and marketing.

The number of levels clearly depends upon the size and to some extent on the type of the organization, with the **span of control** averaging about five people, but this can vary widely. This is illustrated in Figure 4.3.

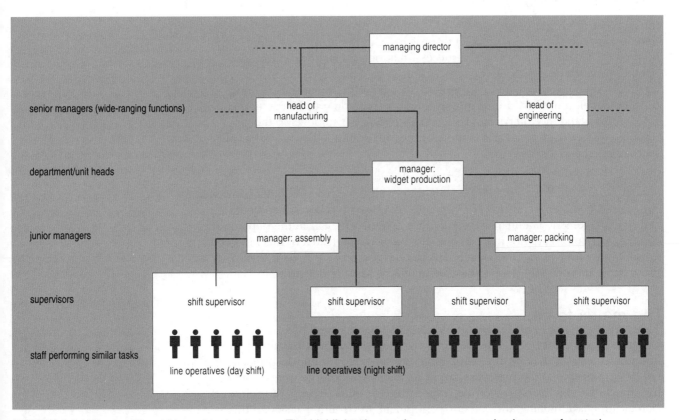

**FIGURE 4.3** The traditional hierarchical structure. The highlighted area shows one supervisor's span of control.

Because projects are primarily concerned with *change* they tend to be organized quite differently in order to respond to that fact. Their organization needs to be more 'fluid' than that of conventional management structures.

# 4.3.1   Four common types of project team

## The functional team

The hierarchical structure described above divides groups of people largely along *functional* lines: people working together carry out the same or similar functions. A **functional team** is one where work is carried on within such a functionally-organized group. This *can* be project work. In organizations where the functional divisions are relatively rigid, project work can be handed from one functional team to another in order to complete the work. For example, work on a new product can pass from marketing, which has the idea, to research and development, which sees whether it is technically feasible, thence to design and finally to manufacturing. This is sometimes known as 'baton passing' on the analogy of a team running a relay race; as one runner completes his or her laps, they pass a wooden baton to the next runner on the team to carry for the next few laps. Needless to say, developing projects using this type of teamwork requires that the project manager with oversight of the entire project must ensure that each functional team hands work over to its successor team in such a state that the successor team can carry on with it without undue problems.

## The project (single) team

The **project** or **single team** consists of a group of people who all work in the same organizational unit on a project or projects, and the team is usually led by the project manager. Such a team, if successful at one project, will often stay together to work on subsequent projects. This is particularly common where an organization engages repeatedly in projects of a broadly similar nature – for example developing software or in construction. According to Norris *et al.* (1993 p. 5): 'Perhaps the most important issue in this instance is to develop the capability of the team since this is the currency for continued success. People issues dominate in a single team.'

The closeness of the dedicated project team should give rise to fewer communication problems within the team than with the other structures. However, care should be taken to ensure that communications with other stakeholders (senior management, line managers and other members of staff in the departments affected, and so on) are not neglected as close-knit single teams of this kind can become introspective and too closely involved with a project to want to 'share' information about it with people they feel might be less committed to it.

## The matrix team

A **matrix team** structure is one where staff report to different managers for different aspects of their work. Matrix structures are often found in projects. Staff will be responsible to the project manager for their work on the project while their functional line manager will be responsible for other aspects of their work such as appraisal, training and career development and 'routine' tasks. In this form of organization staff from various functional areas (such as design, software development, manufacturing, marketing) are loaned or seconded to work on a particular project. Such staff may work full- or part-time on the project. The project manager thus has a recognizable team and is responsible for controlling and monitoring its work on the project.

Many of the project staff will still have duties to perform in their normal functional departments. The functional line manager they report to will retain responsibility for this work and for the professional standards of their work on the project, as well as for their training and career development. Figure 4.4 represents this matrix project structure. In this structure it is important to overcome the problems staff might have with the dual reporting lines (the 'two-boss' problem). This requires building good interpersonal relationships with the team members and regular effective communication.

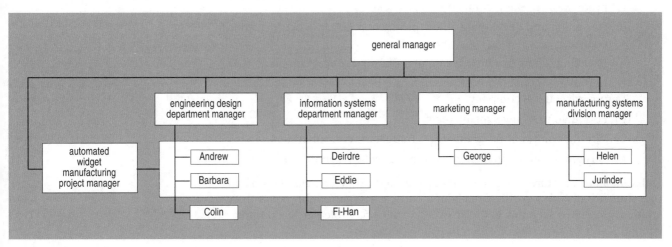

**FIGURE 4.4**   A matrix project structure

## The contract team

The **contract team** is brought in from 'outside' in order to do the project work. Here the responsibility to deliver the project rests very firmly with the project manager, who is the person 'on site' and 'in charge'. The client will, in turn, find such a team harder to control directly. On the other hand, it is the client who will judge the success of the project, so the project manager has to keep an eye constantly on the product aspects.

A variant of this is the so-called **outsourced supply team**, which simply means that the team is physically situated remotely from the project manager, who then encounters the additional problem of distance in managing.

## 'Horses for courses'

It is perfectly possible and indeed not unusual to have mixed teams, where staff who work on the project may be:

● full-time and fully responsible to the project manager

● part-time, responsible to the project manager for their time on the project

● in a matrix arrangement where their work on the project is overseen by the project manager, but are responsible to their line manager for other matters

● in a functional hierarchy, undertaking work on the project under their line manager's supervision, but by negotiation with the project manager.

It is common for the last two arrangements to prevail even on relatively small projects for any specialist work that might be required.

### SAQ 4.5

Consider the following statements of sets of tasks and decide which form of organization would be most appropriate for managing them. Where possible, briefly state the reason(s) for your choice.

(a) Processing applications for entry to a professional society.

(b) Determining an information systems strategy for an organization.

(c) Changing over the production lines in a pharmaceutical company production/packing company each weekend.

(d) Designing and developing a new production line in a pharmaceutical company.

(e) Installing a new production line in a pharmaceutical company.

(f) Improving the methods of research and development in a pharmaceutical company.

(g) Formulating a new suntan cream.

(h) Writing computer programs for a budgetary control system.

(i) Designing and implementing a new budgetary control system.

Different team structures have their advantages and disadvantages. This means that one structure may fit a particular task in a particular organization better than another. You have seen this in the answer to SAQ 4.5. Table 4.4 sets out the strengths and weaknesses of different team structures.

### SAQ 4.6

'Matrix structures are becoming more common and are likely to continue to do so in the future.'

(a) List up to four points why this is (or is not) so.

(b) List three characteristics of organizations where matrix structures and full project structures are likely to be most prevalent.

(c) List up to five likely problems with functional project co-ordination.

## 4.3.2 Summary

This section has addressed the question of how project teams are organized. There are four major types: functional, project, matrix and contract. Teams are also organized from a mixture of these approaches. Each form has strengths and weaknesses that suit it for particular types of project within particular organizational cultures. Having studied this section you should be able to:

● describe the normal hierarchical company organization

● explain how a functionally organized team works and what 'baton passing' is

● describe the organization of the project (single) team

● discuss the matrix team organization and the 'people' problems arising from it

● describe what is meant by a contract team

● given a description of a type of project, state which team organization(s) are most suitable for that type and why.

**TABLE 4.4** Strengths and weaknesses of different structures for project teams

|  | Strengths | Weaknesses |
|---|---|---|
| Functional | Lowest administration costs. | Co-ordination across functional areas is more difficult. |
|  | Reasonably successful in past. | Inflexible. |
|  | Offers more job security and well-defined career paths to staff. | Communication across functional areas is more difficult. |
|  | Pools technical and professional expertise. | Long, slow chain of command. |
|  | Handles routine work well. | Possibly poor communication with client. |
|  | Allows training and apprenticeship in departments. | Tends to push decision-making upwards. |
|  | Line management have control of projects and change. | Novel objectives difficult to fix. |
|  | Easy to set up and terminate projects. | Limits career development outside recognized paths for staff members. |
|  |  | Tends to dampen creative initiatives. |
| Matrix | Acceptable to 'traditional' managers. | Dual reporting lines of project staff. |
|  | Retains functional strengths and control of paperwork. | Staff appraisal and performance measurement difficult. |
|  | Some planning power in project team. | Can cause conflicts of priorities for staff. |
|  | Faster start-ups. | Wider skills required of project manager (e.g. team building more difficult). |
|  | Top management retain control of projects but relieved of day-to-day decisions. | Project manager may not be able to influence who is assigned to the project. |
|  | Flexibility of personnel assigned. | Dilutes the resource available in those functional areas contributing personnel. |
|  | Reasonable interface with clients and customers is possible. |  |
|  | Some team building is possible. |  |
| Project | Greater authority and control. | High administrative costs. |
|  | Team contribute to and share objectives. | Project manager involved in more administration. |
|  | Team building and communication easier. | Difficult to graft on to established organizations. |
|  | Quicker decisions. | Project more difficult to terminate. |
|  | Fewer political problems. | For project staff – lack of job security. |
|  | Good client contacts. | For project staff – feel let down on return to functional job. |
|  | High degree of management skills development. | For project staff – undefined career paths. |
|  | Easier for top management to co-ordinate and influence. | Slow to mobilise. |
|  | Can give career development/change for team members. | Often limited number of good project people available. |
|  | Builds synergy in team. |  |
|  | Clear responsibilities, can be profit centres. |  |

# 4.4  *MANAGING STAKEHOLDERS*

Project managers are almost always very busy people. However, time set aside at the outset of a project to consider who is important and influential to the success of your project is time well spent. People other than the project team who have a stake in your project also have to be managed!

## 4.4.1  Identifying stakeholders

**Stakeholders** are any persons (or groups) who have an interest in your project, are affected by it or who can influence its outcome. Stakeholders will include all the people whose work is changed in any way by a project; those who are affected by it; and all those who can in any way obstruct, block or stall the project, as well as the senior staff who grant the resources. Learning who these people are and understanding their motives is an important aspect of organizational politics. As Hannaway and Hunt (1992, p. 44) note: 'Effective managers are aware of the political reality of their organizations and can act accordingly to achieve their objectives.' They also note that politics in an organization can be a *positive* force.

---

**EXAMPLE 4.3**

A new information systems project that will automatically record and track the progress of production jobs through the organization will have among its stakeholders:

- all those people who record, collate and distribute the data under the old system (e.g. operatives, clerks)
- all those people who receive data under the old system (e.g. planners, accountants)
- anyone who uses the data as information for decision making (e.g. production and warehouse managers)
- those who design and implement the new system, and to some extent those involved in the old system (e.g. information systems and IT specialists, programmers)
- any people who maintain the old system or who will maintain the new one
- senior managers who grant the resources needed for the project

and to some extent:

- those who championed some other project that did not get resources because they went to this project.

---

As you can see, this apparently common, straightforward project has a very large range and number of potential stakeholders. Clearly, then, identifying stakeholders, assessing their interests in the project and then using that information to manage relationships with such groups is an important project management function. Once such stakeholders are identified it is useful to draw up a systematic plan to secure and maintain their support or forestall any trouble. This allows the project manager to concentrate on the most critical groups and reduces the vulnerability of the project when anything unexpected arises. Boddy and Buchanan (1992) advocate a somewhat formal approach to the process of identifying stakeholders that they call *stakeholder mapping*.

A brainstorming or similar technique can be used to identify and list individual stakeholders or groups of stakeholders. Once a list is assembled, a 'map' can be drawn with the names of individuals or groups laid out and connecting lines used to indicate relationships. Next to each name on the list the project manager can note likely reactions. Lastly, the project manager can determine what to do to manage relationships with the identified stakeholders.

In a map drawn for the stakeholders identified in Example 4.3, the project is named and drawn in the middle of a piece of paper and then, for example, clerical and operative staff can be linked to the project by a line, while planners can be linked to the project by another line, and so on. There is no set way to draw up a stakeholder map, so a project manager can develop his or her own conventions to show weak or strong links to a project, whether the group can influence or will be influenced by the project (or both) and so on.

Once key stakeholders have been identified the project manager can draw up a table listing the stakeholders, their goals, their past reactions to the project (perhaps at the proposal stage), what he or she can expect of them now, whether the change embodied within the project will impact the stakeholder in a negative, positive or mixed way, and what their likely reaction is going to be. The last column of such a table can be used to indicate any ideas the project manager has for managing the relationship with that stakeholder, as shown briefly in Table 4.5 below.

**TABLE 4.5**  Example of stakeholder identification

| Stakeholder | Their goals | Past reactions | What to expect | Impact Negative/ Positive | Possible future reactions | Ideas |
|---|---|---|---|---|---|---|
| Production managers | Keep production on schedule | Sceptical of benefits of change, worried about problems with new systems | Likely to be furious if things go wrong at change-over | Could be negative if things go wrong; should be very positive if things work well | Could refuse to switch to new system if they remain sceptical of success | Keep them abreast with progress; involve them in trial runs and testing of new system |

## SAQ 4.7

A newsagent's shop is part of a major national chain. The branch in question sells a wide selection of national and local newspapers, a range of magazines and booklets, books (mainly popular paperbacks) including a wide range of children's books, and an extensive range of greetings cards, plus a few other stationery items such as writing paper, envelopes, notepads and pencils.

The executive and regional management of the chain give the store managers some degree of independence. They select items to sell, decide what stocks to hold and how these are displayed. This branch employs a store manager, two full-time assistants (one of whom acts as deputy manager), four part-time assistants, Saturday helpers and delivery boys and girls. Apart from the main public sales and display area there is a separate office and a staff rest-room. One of the part-time assistants works mainly in the office, acting as stock clerk and book-keeper.

The regional management decide on a project to install a central computer with terminals in each branch. Apart from keeping a basic staff attendance record for computing wages, the store manager is free to decide what use may be made of the new facility.

(a) Who might be the major influences on this branch?

(b) Who are likely to be the stakeholders in existing practices who will be affected by the project, and how might the project affect them?

(c) Draw a stakeholder map like that idescribed above. Using a different coloured pen or pencil, draw in the lines showing the relationships between stakeholders.

---

### ACTIVITY 4.3

Draw a stakeholder map for your project and add it to your project notebook. If you have time, you might like to go on to draw a relationship map like that in the answer to SAQ 4.7.

---

The technique of stakeholder analysis can be applied to many different management situations but is particularly valuable in project management. Identifying the important stakeholders and their relationships enables the project manager to concentrate time and effort where it is most needed.

## 4.4.2 Managing up

The success of a project can, crucially, depend on help and support from senior management. This means not only obtaining resources but also commitment, support and the promotion of the project's goals. To get this, an important part of the project manager's role is to supply both the information that members of senior management need about the project and a sense of 'feeling good' about the project's benefits to the organization.

Your stakeholder map should have identified the project's sponsor and those senior people who are in a position to grant (or have granted) the project resources. It may also have included some senior people who were against the project because they were championing a rival project which did not get the necessary resources. The project manager needs to 'manage' the project's relationships with all of these people. Hannaway and Hunt (1992) suggest that the manager concerned (in this case the project manager) should try to develop relationships, proceed logically and keep others informed, be prepared to explain your decisions, canvass support, develop strong communication channels and recognize the assistance you receive.

Boddy and Buchanan (1992) foresee a problem that can arise with regard to senior managers: they may try to change the direction of a project once it has been defined and resources have been allocated. This is not necessarily due to whim, but because senior managers have other things to think about and know little of the implications of changing focus from a general idea to a detailed and realistic plan. Senior managers are often visionary, and that's their job, but it is easy for them to be only dimly aware of problems of a change in a course of action, or to overestimate the benefits that might acrue from such a change. However, change must also be allowed to happen in a project. If a project is very novel everyone will be learning as the project progresses, and objectives and goals may have to change in light of that learning. In modern business the external environment is also constantly changing: new opportunities or threats may arise. Yet too many changes or changes that appear whimsical or arbitrary cause frustration or demotivation on the part of the project team. The project manager has to strike a balance between allowing for change and protecting the project from too much change by making sure that, as far as is practicable, changes mandated by senior management are not made on the basis of a lack of or poor quality information, and that the senior management also understands fully the implications of any decisions to change. It is the project manager's job to communicate clearly to senior management the costs and benefits of the project, the implications to those costs and benefits of any suggested changes, and to provide full information. As Boddy and Buchanan note (p. 76): "People expect change to be disruptive – so they need to be convinced the pain will be worth it. The project manager has to work with senior management to create and sell [the] vision [of change], to give the change a legitimacy which encourages … support."

Another important aspect of managing up is the need to secure adequate resources for the project. The project manager does this by ensuring that the project's plans are credible and by getting backing for the plans. To do so he or she may need to overcome scepticism or may need to make moderate changes in goals and plans. Getting resources from 'the top' helps the project by showing that senior management have given firm support and by giving the project some prestige.

## Managing the sponsor

To make this work the project manager must consider what the sponsor needs, and what is needed from the sponsor. For example, sponsors need to:

- feel comfortable with and confident in the project manager and project team
- know that they and the project manager share a vision of the project's aims
- see motivation and commitment on the part of the team
- be kept informed about progress, successes and difficulties
- have more knowledge about the project than other senior managers.

Project managers need from sponsors (among other things):

- active interest
- a very clear view about the sponsor's expectations for the project
- clarity about the parameters and constraints the project has to operate within
- advice and help with managing relationships with other senior managers
- early warning of any changing goals at the organizational level.

Project managers also need to be able to modify the sponsor's expectations about the project as changes are introduced.

## Managing the resource providers

For most projects the sponsors will not be solely responsible for allocating the resources for a project; project managers must therefore also think about managing any other resource providers.

Other senior resource providers need:

- to know what is happening in the project generally: quick, easily assimilated information, as they have little time to spare for projects not their own

- no surprises – for senior managers to hear news about a project through the 'grapevine' rather than from the project manager or sponsor suggests that the project manager's communication channels are poorly established

- early warning of trouble and difficulties; senior management will want to feel they are influencing the finding of solutions.

...no surprises

### SAQ 4.8

Consider an accountancy and management consultancy business with about 170 employees. About half the employees are accountants or professional consultants and the remainder are support staff. The firm has four departments which handle customers' business, with one department responsible for each of the following areas:

| | |
|---|---|
| Public sector | 39 staff |
| Small commercial businesses (under £1 million annual turnover) | 40 staff |
| Large commercial businesses (over £1 million annual turnover) | 40 staff |
| Charities and other not-for-profit enterprises | 25 staff |

The Large Businesses Department has traditionally been the major department, but in recent years the main expansion of the business has been in the Small Businesses Department, for retail businesses in particular. There is now a proposal to split the Small Businesses Department into two new departments, dealing with retail and non-retail respectively. The new Retail Small Businesses Department will be formed from about half of the Small Businesses Department's current staff with staff numbers expected to rise to 35 through new posts. This new department will be housed in new premises (yet to be found) but within one mile of the current offices. A project is being set up to:

- find premises
- agree the requirements of the section for the next five years
- plan and estimate the costs of the move
- procure all the equipment, including the IT equipment
- occupy the new premises in stages.

The firm is run by an executive board consisting of the managing director (who is a partner), the four heads of departments (also partners), the human resources manager, the information systems (IS) manager and the financial director (also a partner). The sponsor for the relocation project is the head of the Small Businesses Department. The financial director has been very keen on setting up the new department, but the managing director took some persuading to support the split and the move. The IS manager sees the move as an opportunity to extend the use of IT in the company and to begin a move to a 'state of the art' IT platform. Currently there are information systems on job-progress, company accounts and payroll. The IT platform is a fully networked system allowing file sharing and transfer and electronic mail. A leading and respected consultant from the Small Businesses Department has been designated project manager and the project should be completed in eight months.

(a) How much contact, and of what type, would you expect between the project manager and sponsor?

(b) Who are the *key* stakeholders on the executive board, and what contact would you expect between them and the project manager?

(c) What other special considerations are there for the project manager when 'managing up'?

(d) What formal reporting might be expected?

# 4.4.3 The organization as a network

While the interest and support of senior management can be crucial to the success of a project, an organization, to function properly, is more than a simple hierarchy with reporting lines going up and 'directing' lines going down the levels. It tends to be a network in which co-operation amongst people on the same or broadly similar levels is very important to getting things done. 'Politics' also tends to be played across the organization as well as up or down it. Ignoring those stakeholders who are not senior but who are colleagues in other departments, fellow contractors on a multiple-contract project and so on, can seriously imperil a project. A project manager's tasks include maintaining good relationships with these other stakeholders, and negotiating with them to get things done, share resources and solve problems.

Here again conflict between departments can arise and the project manager needs to manage it. For example, one department which will benefit greatly from the completion of a project may be eager to press ahead with great speed, while another, where the project will cause great changes that will require considerable adjustment, may be just as eager to proceed slowly and deliberately. The project manager will have to balance these conflicting demands on the project. Negotiation skills come into play here, as well as conflict management skills. The project manager needs to know (from the stakeholder map) which departments or functions the project depends on and which will be affected by the project results and how. If the project manager knows how committed each department or function is to the change represented by the project he or she can then begin to undertake negotiating between the conflicting requirements of the two departments.

Negotiation techniques were described in Section 4.2.3.

---

### ACTIVITY 4.4

Check the stakeholder map you drew up in Activity 4.3. Does it include everyone, and have you considered how to deal with their interests?

---

# 4.4.4   Building the project team

Unfortunately project managers rarely have the opportunity to select members for their project teams. For the occasions where they do there is a wealth of management literature about personnel selection, covering:

- interviewing skills
- job definition
- psychometric testing
- assessment testing

to name but a few of the techniques.

Selection for project teams, particularly matrix structure teams, is normally a pragmatic process of finding who has the skills required and who is available. Often there is little choice. *Project managers should, however, seek to influence this process.* They will need to consider the mix of skills required and when the particular skills are needed. An effective team can usually be built (with patience and skill) from the most diverse set of characters. However, there will be times when someone who is likely to be more of a liability than a help is the person available, so the project manager should also obtain the 'right of veto' to use when they feel a particular individual is wrong for the team they are building. Overuse of this veto will be resented by line managers: use it wisely and cautiously.

Accepting this, project managers must still exert influence by first defining the common functions of the group or team they are to lead. These functions can be divided into *task* and *maintenance* functions (see This, 1974). These are, of course, team and group working functions, rather than technical skills.

Common task functions are:

- Initiating: someone on the team must initiate ideas, solutions, etc.

- Information or opinion seeking: if a team member asks for information, others will be happy to supply it or give an opinion. In most teams more people will be happy to respond than will be willing to ask.

- Clarifying or elaborating: team members who ask for clarification of ideas others have presented are valuable because this leads to common understanding when the point is clarified.

- Opinion giving: stating a particular view or belief in reply to a range of suggestions is valuable.

- Consensus testing: people are needed who will test to see if the team is ready to reach a decision or come to an agreement.

- Summarizing: someone who will attempt to summarize what the group has discussed and where they are at the moment is useful.

Common maintenance functions are:

- Encouraging: furthering group participation by encouragement.

- Harmonizing: reconciling disagreements.

- Compromising: the amendment of conflicting ideas to make them acceptable to both parties.

- Expressing group feelings: sensing the team's feelings and mood so the team can deal with them.

- 'Gate-keeping': sensing when others are not getting the opportunity to participate because of the more extrovert and talkative members of the group.

- Setting standards: expressing or applying standards to evaluate the group process.

Project managers may be able to supply some of these but should not try to supply them all. In participative, well-functioning teams different members should be able to sense when these are needed and be able to step in and supply them. The project manager's role is to ensure that all these are provided; they should influence the building of the team to obtain the right balance.

In determining task and maintenance functions, the project manager has gathered the basic information necessary for undertaking a bit of job design. While job design is commonly a function of a personnel department (usually in consultation with line managers) the topics considered in designing a job can be a very useful tool for the project manager trying to set up a team. To 'design' a successful team, the project manager should:

- list all of the activities and tasks of the team (what do members need to do)

- group these logically or naturally

- remove any duplications and redundancies

- organize the items on the list into 'jobs' – what you expect a person to do

- relate the 'jobs' to those skills required to complete the job

- relate the 'jobs' to the degree of autonomy that the job holder will need to exercise to complete the work successfully.

The first three points should emerge naturally from the WBS and related documents.

What you are left with is a list of jobs and a related list of tasks and activities that constitute a specification for the persons required to fill them. These lists also form the basis for drawing up a detailed description of each job which can be discussed and then agreed with the person who will take that job. (Having a clear and agreed description of each job which both parties sign is a very useful communication tool between manager and subordinate: it eliminates misunderstandings.) The written description should include the following items:

- who the manager is for the purposes of *this* job (remembering that in a matrix team structure this will probably not be the person's line manager)

- who the person is who will be doing the job (once the person has been identified – early on it may be the ubiquitous 'A.N. Other')

- a descriptive title, which may have nothing to do with the person's actual job title

- the purpose of the job

- the main duties, responsibilities, tasks and activities

- a statement of what authority the person will have (e.g. signing off for quality assurance checks, authorizing expenditures)

- any conditions, such as travel, location, hours of work, which don't comply with ordinary assumptions or the person's main contract

- any agreed feedback mechanisms such as regular progress reports or progress meetings

- any training needs identified at the outset.

Successful project managers also consider the interpersonal mix of the team. Effective teams usually have a majority of staff who work well together. A few independent 'free spirits' are also likely to be included, and perhaps one or two dependent characters who are good team players but who need more direction from the manager or from someone more integrated into the team's way of working.

To be able to assemble a team with the right work skills *and* the optimum personality mix, the project manager should draw up a specification of the person(s) required for the team, even if the manager has little actual input into who will be selected. Even where the project manager has little say, having drawn up a specification at least gives a clear picture of the discrepancies between the ideal person and the individual who will actually fill the post. (A common saying is that any person who fulfills 75 per cent of a description is as ideal as one can normally expect, and someone who fulfills half of a description is going to be quite useful in that post.) A specification of the person should contain:

- ideal educational qualifications, but note if these are necessary or simply 'good to have'

- whether professional qualifications are needed (bearing in mind that for some jobs a licence may be necessary)

- ideal experience, described in terms of years of doing a particular kind of work (e.g. "will have programmed in C or C++ on major systems developments for at least three years"); note instances where less experience is acceptable and don't forget to include verbal skills and numeracy where these are needed (someone may be an excellent programmer but not capable of giving the necessary presentations to management)

- personal characteristics: these may include physical characteristics if certain characteristics are part of the job (e.g. heavy lifting is required), but be *certain* that they are a genuine requirement and that they are described in terms of what needs to be done, not in terms of, say, 'muscular physique'); personality traits also should be included where these apply, but again be *certain* that 'a sunny disposition' is actually a requirement of the job and not just something you desire for your own peace of mind

- special requirements such as willingness to travel.

In terms of personalities Boddy and Buchanan (1992, p. 109) indicate some less obvious but nonetheless important clusters of characteristics to look for. A project manager should attempt to find these clusters for any team he or she assembles. These are:

- team-building skills: people who are facilitators, natural negotiators, who work well with others and are able to carry the 'individualists' of a team along with them

- awareness of the process of getting things done: people conscious that the *way* things are done can be as important as *what* is done

- time and commitment: people willing and able to give the time and commitment to ensuring that the team works effectively

- someone able to see the broad picture (the 'helicopter view')

- someone aware of progress and status of the project and how that relates to project completion

- an administrator with the knack of keeping orderly records and documents, organizing meetings, informing people of dates and deadlines and processing the paperwork (often a person is brought in especially to occupy this role and no other).

Other authors noted by Boddy and Buchanan advocate varying numbers and definitions of roles. Handy (1990) lists four: the 'captain', the administrator, the driver and the expert, while Belbin (1981) lists eight: the co-ordinator; the shaper; the creative person; the critic (who is better at analysis than creativity); the networker who keeps a team members in touch with each other and the outside world; the person who turns ideas into action; the popular person who contributes encouragement, understanding and support; and the person who, with relentless follow-through, ensures that deadlines are met.

If the project manager is in the enviable position of being able to select some or all of the members of the team, either by making new appointments or by interviewing and selecting from amongst a pool of eligible employees, then both the job descriptions and specifications of the person can feed into job advertisements, interviews and any other selection procedures that might be used (for example, psychometric testing). Otherwise, the project manager can use the information gathered and formalized as a basis for negotiating who should and shouldn't be appointed to the team.

## ACTIVITY 4.5

Evaluate briefly the team you are working with at the moment (or one you've worked with in the recent past) in terms of the roles mentioned above. Were any missing? How has the presence or absence of these roles affected the way the team has worked?

## When the team has been selected

Where the project manager has had little or no involvement in the selection of the team, he or she should:

- ascertain why each person was selected for the project team (for example, there may be no one else available with the right skills)

- not accept members on reputation alone but give them a chance to show their mettle

- meet separately with each team member; find out what their aspirations are

- ask the client, sponsor or senior management for extra staff on the project if there is some key skill missing

- look for any member of the team who may be more destructive than constructive (for example, someone who is unduly aggressive with others); if any are found talk privately and constructively to the person involved about the problem

- try to get the team to set the detailed objectives, plans or schedules collectively (their 'ownership' of what they are going to do is important)

- try to find a quick 'win' for the team (e.g. extra person, more resources, extra time) to gain the team's confidence and establish a position of leadership

- use all the team-building skills and techniques possible.

...talk privately and constructively

Project managers are likely to find with a new team that members are confused about their roles, that there may be understanding about the project's overall aims but not necessarily a consensus supporting these. Team members are normally pleased to be on the team (but often don't say so). Members usually have the required technical competence and experience, and they are usually ready to let the challenge of the project draw on these.

*Project managers tend to neglect relationships with and between team members at the early stages because their attention is on the early tasks.* Project managers who neglect to address the early difficult relationships and role confusion may find that by the time such issues surface, putting right the relationships and team processes may be very costly in time and endeavour. Hence, time taken at the beginning of a project to examine collaboratively how the team is going to work together is well spent. This can include methods, procedures, any training or briefing requirements, work relationships and the priority concerns of team members. The reward is that the team works effectively more quickly and has fewer interpersonal problems. Use the job descriptions and specifications of the person to aid this process.

## ACTIVITY 4.6

You are a newly-appointed project manager. In one week, you must have your first team meeting with your new matrix project team, and your project is scheduled to begin in about one month. You can assume that the project has been separately justified and approved but you now have to run it.

Take a few minutes to list all the things you might want to consider, learn, or accomplish before meeting with your team for the first time. Include your specific plans for the first team meeting.

## DISCUSSION

Amongst your answers we hope you included at least some of the following:

Pre-meeting:

1   Establish what the objectives for project are, find out any other information about the background to the project (definition, main objectives, etc.).

2   See the sponsor/client or senior person responsible for initiating the project.

3   Find out the timescale, resources available and any major milestones.

4   See all the team members separately to: establish what special skills they can bring to the project; determine what their commitment to the project is, and any hidden agendas they have; find out about their other work commitments; give them information about the project and its aims and milestones, etc.; determine what they hope to get out of being on the project (i.e. their wants and needs).

5   Talk to the line managers of the team members.

6   Find out all you can about the resources available for the project (e.g. people, cash, equipment, rooms, time). Is each satisfactory, or could more be obtained if justified?

7   Set up the first team meeting: decide its objectives and fix the agenda (or items of business if you wish the meeting to be informal); determine if anyone other than team members should be present; arrange for someone to take notes.

8   Give plenty of notice for your meeting, and ensure all the necessary staff can attend.

First meeting:

1   Plan the meeting carefully.

2   Decide how you will introduce yourself and the project, and your role generally.

3   Ensure you explain the goals and objectives and that you show your commitment to them.

4   Try to do something special for the first meeting, e.g. coffee, biscuits, lunch, cocktails, wine flowers - whatever is appropriate in your organization (and try to leave enough in the budget to do something similar at the very last meeting!)

5   Make sure that all those present participate and are able to express their views and feelings about the project.

6    See that team members are clear about their roles and responsibilities on the project and about what their 'pay-off' for being on the project might be.

7    Discuss how progress on the project will be monitored and measured, and what your expectations as the leader are.

8    Share any anxieties or concerns you have about the project (if you judge this to be valuable and appropriate in the circumstances).

9    If the project has a matrix structure or is not full-time, discuss how you and the other team members are going to communicate.

10   Ensure that appropriate notes are taken. Generally, action points are better than formal minutes, but at the first meeting a bit more than simple action points will be needed. Decide who the notes will be distributed to outside the project team.

11   Ensure that any problems which need resolving are recorded for subsequent action.

12   Finally, make sure all the team members know what happens next.

# 4.4.5   Summary

This section has addressed the managing of stakeholders in a project – those who are 'up' the organization, those who are less directly involved but have concerns about the project, those on the project team. Stakeholder mapping is an important technique for identifying all the stakeholders and thereby being aware of their concerns and likely impact on the project. In particular, the project manager needs to be able to manage the project's sponsor and resource givers and to operate successfully within the network of the organization. While the project manager may not be able to pick and choose members of the project team, he or she needs to ensure that there are people on the team who can fill certain non-technical functions such as initiating ideas, testing consensus, encouraging, compromising and setting standards. Once the team has been selected, the project manager has to get to know each member in order to help that member contribute most effectively to the team. As initial impressions are important, the section has emphasized planning the first team meeting.

Having studied this section you should be able to:

- identify stakeholders who are key to the project's success
- draw a stakeholder map for a project
- explain what the information needs of the sponsor are and how the project manager can fulfil those needs
- describe the main task and maintenance functions that the project manager must ensure are available within the project team
- explain how to assess the likely relationships in a team and how to get the team off to a good start
- state how you would prepare for and conduct an initial team meeting so as to establish your leadership.

# 4.5  *KEEPING THE TEAM MOTIVATED*

## 4.5.1  Theories of motivation

The question of why people are motivated to behave in a particular way is clearly of fundamental importance and there are many approaches to studying this. Our approach to the topic is not comprehensive and we limit ourselves to a consideration of aspects which in our judgement are relevant to project management. In particular, we confine our attention immediately to very brief introductions to Maslow's theory of needs, Herzberg's motivation–hygiene theory and expectancy theory as described by Porter and Lawler (1968). We then briefly discuss two theories of work which try to answer the question: 'Why do people work?'

### Maslow's hierarchy of needs

Maslow (1943) suggested that the behaviour of individuals, which includes members of a project team, is determined by their strongest needs. His model was of a hierarchy of needs, as shown in Figure 4.5, which could be filled up from the bottom; that is, a lower level need would have to be satisfied before a higher level need could come into play. The levels are:

- physiological needs – basic needs for food, drink, sleep and air
- safety – security, predictability and order
- relationships – affectionate relations with other people, such as family and friends, and for being part of a social group
- esteem – self-respect and the esteem of others
- self-fulfilment – development of one's potential.

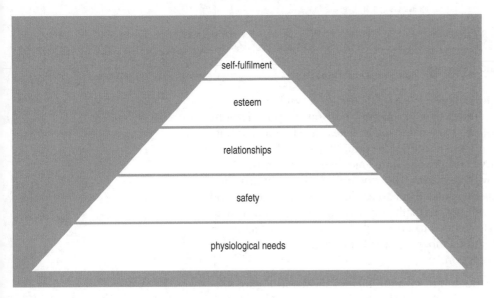

**FIGURE 4.5**  Maslow's hierarchy of needs

The hierarchy is of limited value: it does not rigidly apply to everyone, nor does it apply to any one person all the time. For example, some people are willing to take risks – to jeopardize basic safety needs – in order to achieve self-fulfilment (people engaging in dangerous sporting activities come to mind here). Circumstances mean that most individuals will at some time in their lives 'sacrifice' a more fundamental need to fulfil a higher one (like the hungry mother who sees to it that her baby eats, even at the expense of her own needs). However, it is worth noting that within a narrow context like a project it is relatively easy to spot manifestations of these kinds of behaviour. Thus, a member of staff on a short-term contract (who may feel 'unsafe' as a result) may react differently in some circumstances from one who has a permanent contract. The former may be less willing to put family needs before work requirements and may work longer hours (but resent it) than the latter, who will feel 'safer' leaving at the normal end of the working day to go home to family or friends.

## Motivation–hygiene theory

Herzberg (1959) suggested that broadly there are two categories of need which are essentially independent and which affect behaviour in different ways. These categories are called *hygiene* or *maintenance factors* and *motivators*. Details of the factors and the relationship between them are shown in Figure 4.6.

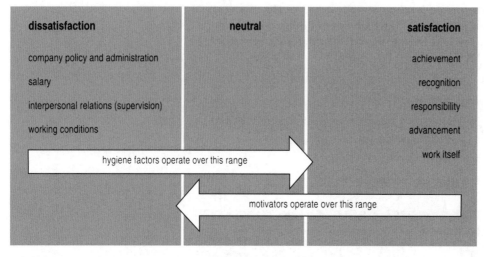

**FIGURE 4.6**   Hygiene factors and motivators

The hygiene factors influence the degree of dissatisfaction of a worker. The quality of these factors could neutralize a team member's dissatisfaction *without* leading to any satisfaction in the job. Poor company policies can demotivate but very good ones will not contribute much to employee motivation: advancement is a good motivator, but poor salary can outweigh any enjoyment of it. Thus, hygiene factors are concerned with *necessary but not sufficient* conditions for a satisfied worker. (The term *hygiene* comes from an analogy with medicine: good hygiene can prevent illness but will not normally improve health.) To motivate a worker, Herzberg suggested that we need to ensure that the motivator factors are present. These factors affect a team member's level of satisfaction or the position on the scale from neutral to satisfaction.

Inspection of the particular hygiene and motivation factors shown in Figure 4.6 reveals the relationship between Maslow's and Herzberg's theories. Hygiene factors such as company policy and administration cater for low-level needs in the hierarchy. In contrast, motivators such as responsibility and advancement cater for high-level needs.

# Expectancy theory

The essence of expectancy theory is that individuals are seen as rational beings who have views and expectations about their lives. In particular, they have views about the *outcomes* (or consequences) of their behaviour. Expectancy theory was first used as an approach to work motivation by Georgopoulos *et al.* (1957) and related to workers in a household appliances company. Their theory was termed 'a path–goal approach to productivity' because they assumed that motivation to work depended essentially on two factors:

- the specific needs of an individual
- the expectation of fulfilling those needs through productive behaviour.

Productivity is viewed as a path to valued goals. Behaviour or performance depends on the outcomes that an individual values and the expectation that a particular behaviour will lead to these outcomes. Given that an individual perceives clear links between greater effort, improved performance and attainment of valued outcomes, he or she will make a greater effort. The situation is as shown in Figure 4.7. The links in the figure shown as dotted lines indicate that they may not be real but are *perceived* by the worker as being highly likely to exist.

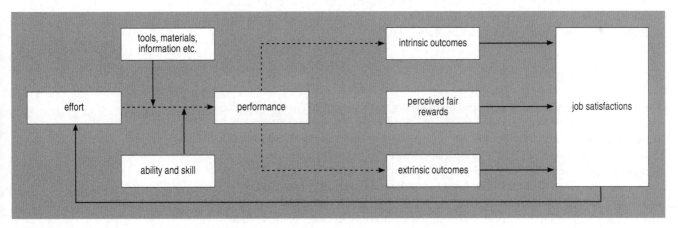

**FIGURE 4.7**  Perceived links between effort, performance and outcomes

Broadly, there are two types of outcome: *intrinsic* and *extrinsic*. Intrinsic outcomes are those which result directly from the job. A sense of achievement is an intrinsic outcome. It does not have to be 'given' to a worker by anybody else. It is generated by the performance of the task itself. Another intrinsic outcome might be a feeling of having learnt something. Sometimes praise from a second person may generate these feelings but often the job itself can provide the feedback. In contrast extrinsic outcomes are caused by someone else. Praise and pay are examples of extrinsic outcome.

## The humanistic theory of work

The humanistic theory of work is closely allied with humanistic theories of education and social organization and is broadly libertarian in nature. Work is deemed a natural, even a physiological, way of expending accumulated bodily energy. Work is basically healthy and productive both in societal and personal terms. Overwork is defined as work "supplying the few with luxury – not for the well-being of all" (Kropotkin, quoted in Russell, 1919). This view perceives work as valuable in itself. The theory has a venerable pedigree, going back to the Medieval notion of the 'joy in labour'. People work because they enjoy work, because it's a healthy and fulfilling thing to do, because they seek through work to create a higher form of society.

## The commodity theory of work

A contrasting view is that labour is no more and no less than a commodity to be sold on the market for maximum return. In this view work has no intrinsic value other than obtaining the means whereby to afford consumption of goods and services produced by others. The main assumption behind this is "I am what I am because of what I own and use up" (Chomsky, 1991). Life's primary aim is to accumulate and consume and the underlying assumption is that work is repulsive and no one would undertake it if it weren't for the fact that paid work affords the opportunity to exercise freedom as a consumer. This view of labour also has a long pedigree; the ancient Greeks considered work to be abhorrent, to be done by someone else if at all possible, but perhaps necessary in order to produce the goods (food, etc.) necessary to sustain a person in the life of the mind or of politics, which they perceived as a far higher calling.

## So which is it?

For many people, work will combine elements of both theories. The more choice and autonomy an individual can exercise in doing work, the more that work approaches, in its basic characteristics, productive leisure, and the more likely it is that those people will enjoy work for itself and feel it a natural and healthy thing to do. As one looks further down the hierarchy in which work is organized, the more likely it is that people will have less or no choice and autonomy and the more their approach to work will resemble the commodity theory: they will feel that work is something they do only in order to be able to do other things in life - to satisfy as best they can the different levels of Maslow's hierarchy of needs.

The more a person's job contains elements of choice and autonomy, the more control they have over their working conditions and environment, the more likely they are to feel that the work they do gives *intrinsic* satisfactions; the less choice, autonomy and control they have the more *extrinsic* satisfactions become necessary.

Some people find considerable comfort in having a job which is well-defined and circumscribed – one where they are not in charge and therefore don't have to worry nights about eventual outcomes – provided that there are not other pressures put on them. For example, the job ends at normal quitting time and no one expects the employee to carry the problems of the job home. Such people often 'live' for productive leisure and see their jobs simply as enabling them to enjoy such leisure. These people find little intrinsic satisfaction in their work but generally don't feel this to be a problem so long as work does not impinge on their 'real' lives outside the workplace. Others find that a job calling for creativity, risk-taking and challenge - a job which is not closely defined and leaves them plenty of room to choose how to meet the challenges it presents - is as important to their sense of themselves as anything else they may do in their lives. Their jobs come to resemble a model of productive leisure to them and they look to work for its intrinsic pleasures and satisfactions. Motivating people involves trying to make the job, the work, fit the person's own expectations of what work will yield for them personally, and it will be different for everyone.

### SAQ 4.9

Using either the theories of motivation or the theories of the nature of work, explain the likely motivations suitable for the following jobs:

(a) a job involving the routine processing of insurance forms

(b) industrial design work

(c) an architect.

## 4.5.2  Influencing the team's motivation

The various theories of motivation suggest that performance can be affected by expected outcomes, the motivators or by the fulfilment of some need. These can, to some extent, be influenced or even controlled by the team project manager. Project managers can ensure that:

● staff have clear objectives and know clearly what they need to do

● the right tools, conditions and environment are available

● staff are well-informed

● the staff members' motivations have been matched as well as possible to the work and its expected outcomes.

The manager can also influence rewards and attempt to see that they are fair. He or she can also give *praise*, which – remember – comes absolutely free to the manager and the organization! As Robert Townsend said so succinctly in *Up the Organization* (1971): 'Thanks – an undervalued form of compensation.'

To be able to fulfil needs with rewards the project manager must be able to measure efforts towards the expected outcomes, focusing on the measurable and reportable results. It is a project manager's duty to see that staff are duly rewarded in some way for their efforts, whether it's a public thank you, a lunch, a letter of commendation, a recommendation for promotion or monetary compensation beyond the salary. Good interpersonal relationships between manager and team are like a bank account; the manager can't continue to 'draw on' them without making some 'deposits'.

...a public thank you

## SAQ 4.10

Compare the needs of Alan, a permanent employee of a bank working in a 'traditional' functional hierarchy who has been seconded part-time to a matrix project team, with the needs of Sally, hired as an individual contractor for that same project team. Limit your answer to Maslow's and Herzberg's theories.

# 4.5.3  Summary

This section has looked at what motivates people to work from three perspectives: the hierarchy of needs, hygiene factors and motivators, and expectancy theory. The hierarchy of needs assumes that needs range from the basic physiological needs to needs for safety, relationships, esteem and, at the highest level, self-fulfilment; and that if a lower-level need is not being met, then meeting it becomes a stronger motivation than meeting a higher-level need. This theory has serious limitations but within those it can be useful. The theory of hygiene factors and motivators assumes that the hygiene factors influence the degree of dissatisfaction of a worker, and the motivators influence the degree of satisfaction. Expectancy theory assumes a link between effort, performance and outcomes.

In addition, we have looked at the humanistic theory of work and the commodity theory of work, and have seen how, for many people, their motivation to work has elements of both theories, depending on levels of autonomy, choice and control.

Having studied this section you should be able to:

- classify a person's needs according to Maslow's hierarchy

- understand the limitations of Maslow's hierarchy in explaining behaviour

- classify factors surrounding a job and state which, in a particular situation, are likely to be hygiene factors or motivators

- give a brief explanation of expectancy theory

- describe two theories of work and explain how the nature of a job is reflected in these theories

- list some ways the project manager can influence the motivation of team members.

# 4.6 *PEOPLE, PROJECTS AND MANAGERS*

Managing projects is different from managing systems. Projects represent unfamiliar territory while the system is familiar. Projects are temporary and systems are long-term. Projects are task-oriented and systems are process-oriented. Projects need a lot of negotiation while systems generally exist in an environment of established relationships and co-operation. Projects are usually managed by people with little direct authority while systems are usually managed on clearly established hierarchical lines.

What, then, do project managers need to do to manage successfully with respect to people in a project environment?

1   Know those involved, their motivations and needs (identify stakeholders).

2   Know what the project's objectives are and be able to communicate these clearly to *all* stakeholders.

3   Build in feedback systems and go intelligence gathering throughout the project's lifetime (talk to people, listen to people, build in good reporting mechanisms).

4   Establish clearly identified roles for the participants. Part of this will emerge from stakeholder mapping, part from job definition, part from developing a specification for the person, part from knowing who is doing what, part from understanding individuals' motivations.

5   Build a team. Define what skills you need and what kind of person you want. Try to get what you need. Establish yourself as a leader in an open and supportive working environment. Amplify people's skills through delegation, practice, training, feedback and coaching. Recognize progress and success, and reward good performance even if in small ways.

6   Build a network of supporters, keep them informed but don't bother them too much; try to win over those who might feel threatened by your project or reduce their capacity to cause problems.

7   Communicate, communicate, communicate. Remember that communication is two-way: it requires active listening as well as talking and writing. Remember that too much can be as bad as too little and try to obtain a balance between telling enough and telling too much. Make sure that you have clear lines of communication with everyone necessary.

In the end, all projects end. It's in their very nature, and more will be said about the formal closure of projects in Chapter 7. So don't forget that in the end you, the project manager, also have a life to live and it isn't confined to your current project. Bear in mind that at some point you will have to let go of the project because it stops being a project and becomes a product, a procedure or a system. You will then move on to something else. There will probably be a psychological wrench at ending the project, and you may have some worries about what you will do afterwards. The time to begin thinking these thoughts is not at the very end but during the course of the project, and perhaps even as early as its outset. Then you will be well-placed to let go gracefully and you will have determined what or where you want to move onto next.

# 5 MANAGING AND CONTROLLING PROGRESS AND COST

## *INTRODUCTION*

The scope of the project has been defined, the project plan has been produced, the organization has been set up, the resources have been allocated and the project has been sanctioned. Now we are concerned with what the project manager has to do while the project is executed. The term 'execution' is used here to mean all the activities in the project following the initial planning, organizing and authorization, until the project is finished.

You have already studied in Chapter 4 the issues that arise in managing the project team so these chapters concentrate more on the techniques that may be used to ensure that the project is monitored and controlled and brought to a successful conclusion.

## Aims and objectives

The aims of this chapter are to describe the monitoring and control of the progress of a project and its cost against the plan.

We describe the earned value system for monitoring cost and progress.

After studying this chapter you should be able to:

- outline the project manager's duties during the main execution phase

- describe and criticize techniques for measuring the project status

- explain how an earned value system works and use it to produce measures of progress against the plan and of expenditure against the budget

- compare and contrast several methods used for monitoring progress, including milestone tracking, earned value and an updated project network

- discuss methods for avoiding slippage.

# 5.1 *MANAGING THE INITIAL STAGES*

## 5.1.1 The project manager's activities

The activities of a project manager throughout a project may be considered to fall under the following headings:

- initiating
- planning, organizing and staffing
- monitoring and controlling
- directing
- communicating.

### Initiating

The most significant initiating actions by the project manager will normally occur during **project mobilization**. Project mobilization is the first major activity once the project has been authorized. Mobilization consists of all the activities needed to get the project up and running. It is not sufficient to make plans and obtain authorization – the project has to be pushed into action.

This will typically require the following activities:

- hold the project launch meeting(s)
- clarify roles and responsibilities
- identify training needs and arrange workshops
- hold start-up meetings with work package managers and stakeholders
- obtain agreements for work commitments from project staff (and their managers where appropriate)
- set up the change control procedures
- ensure that the project support infrastructure is in place
- set up or invoke existing quality assurance mechanisms
- agree a timetable for monitoring and control meetings and reports
- ensure that the initial critical activities are started.

You might think that once this mobilization phase has been completed the project manager will have no more initiating to do. Although major unplanned initiatives are often unwelcome, you must be alert to the need for fresh action to grasp a profitable opportunity or, more often, to head off trouble before it becomes serious. Nevertheless, excessive initiative at later stages may be counterproductive because the project team already has a plan to work to, and it will be disruptive if the manager continually produces new ideas about the direction of the project. Initiative has to be used sparingly to avoid confusion about objectives and the loss of productive time in considering alternatives to the current plan.

# Planning, organizing and staffing

Once the project has been mobilized the peak of the planning activity may have passed, but planning is an evolutionary process that continues throughout the project. Harrison (1992) uses the term 'rolling wave' to describe the way that planning evolves through a large project. In a large project there will be a planning hierarchy with coarse plans at the top, Level 1, and more detailed plans at lower levels as shown in Figure 1.1 overleaf. Harrison describes how the planning wave rolls through the project:

> Hierarchical planning normally incorporates the rolling wave concept of planning. In many projects it is not practical or possible, because of the lack of the necessary information to plan the complete project in any level of detail in its early stages. Often the necessary information to plan the later stages of the project in detail is actually generated in these earlier stages. In such projects the use of the rolling wave concept overcomes this problem.

> At the start of the project it is generally possible to create only a Level 1 summary plan outlining the complete project, with more detailed Level 2 or 3 plans for the early stages of the project. Then as more information is generated by these earlier stages, it may be possible to create a Level 2 plan for the complete project, and a Level 3 plan for the middle stages of the project. Later, as the middle stages generate more information, the Level 3 detailed plans for the final stages can be created.

> This can be likened to a rolling wave, moving from left to right, that is from the start of the project to its finish. The work in front of the rolling wave is only planned in coarse detail to Level 1, or perhaps Level 2, with the crest of the wave being the development of Level 3 or 4 plans. Within cost accounts, or larger packages of work, the same concept can be used. The earlier activities are fully developed work packages or job cards, and the later are larger 'planning packages' in which the work is not fully defined and detailed.

> (Harrison, 1992, pp. 151–154)

You may remember the phrases *work package level* and *cost account level*, which represent levels within the work breakdown structure (WBS) described in Chapter 2. Harrison emphasizes that planning is not a once-and-for-all operation, rather that as the project moves forward there is a planning wave that rolls ahead of activity execution and elaborates the detail of the work about to be done. We therefore have to modify our original model of a simple life-cycle where there was a planning phase followed by an execution phase.

Similarly, organizing and staffing are continuing activities, although the bulk of this work will have been completed when the project is mobilized. However, a project organization is much more fluid than the long-lasting organizations appropriate to the other operations of a business, so occasionally you may want to reassign responsibilities, especially when the project team is expanding or contracting. It may often be appropriate to reorganize completely as the project enters its closure phase, as we will discuss in Chapter 6.

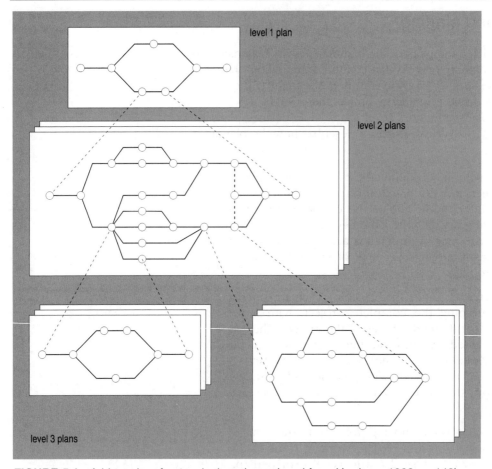

**FIGURE 5.1**  A hierarchy of network plans (reproduced from Harrison, 1992, p. 148)

### ACTIVITY 5.1

Give three examples of areas of a project for which plans are made only in outline at project start-up, and explain why detailed plans cannot be made at that stage.

### DISCUSSION

There are many possible examples because this applies to almost all areas of a project beyond the mobilization activities. For example, construction plans, test plans, commissioning plans, and project closure plans are all necessarily only outline plans initially because the detailed plans for these activities depend on the completion of earlier activities, such as design.

## Monitoring and controlling

Monitoring and control are the project manager's predominant activities during the main execution phase. Meredith and Mantel (1989, p. 373) define project monitoring as follows: 'Monitoring is collecting, recording and reporting information concerning any and all aspects of project performance that the project manager and others in the organization may wish to know.' The same authors define control rather succinctly: 'Control is the act of reducing the difference between plan and reality.' (*ibid*., p. 427).

Monitoring is a necessary prerequisite for control. Any effective control system must have a desired status (the current plan) and a measurement of the actual status before you can take action to make changes. We shall develop the subject of monitoring and control in Sections 5.2, 5.3 and 5.4.

## Directing

In simplified terms, directing is *ordering* something to be done. The distinction from controlling is that a directive does not require a previously set objective or a measurement of the current status.

For example, the following are directives:

- In this project quality standards X, Y and Z will apply.
- No overtime will be paid for unless it has been previously authorized by your supervisor.
- There will be a progress review every Monday morning at 9.00 a.m.
- Frank Smith will take charge of the design of the conveying system.
- All the section leaders are to study the Open University course in Project Management this year.

There are a number of managerial activities which might be considered to be part of 'directing' a project: supervising, delegating, motivating, counselling, co-ordinating and setting standards. All these activities will be required from time to time during the execution of the project. You have already met most of them in Chapter 4.

## Communicating

High on the list of skills needed by a project manager is the ability to communicate. As discussed in Chapter 4, this means not just the outgoing half of communication, talking and writing, but also the incoming half, listening and reading. All too often the phrase 'good communicator' is used wrongly to describe someone who is good at putting his or her case across but is deaf to the words of others.

As you have seen in Chapter 4 the people with whom the project manager has to communicate form a wide spectrum:

- senior management – to keep their continuing commitment
- client – to facilitate collaboration and to prepare for acceptance
- senior members of the project team – to co-ordinate their activities
- all team members – motivating, training, supervising, listening
- heads of functional departments – to avoid conflict over resources
- suppliers and subcontractors – to help select and monitor them
- prospective operations/maintenance staff – to achieve smooth handover.

The project manager must not only be a good communicator but must also encourage good communications *between* the team members. Although the work breakdown structure attempts to break work into components which are as self-contained as possible, in practice there must be a good deal of give-and-take on the interfaces between the work elements. A good network of lower-level, informal communications is invaluable.

### SAQ 5.1

You may have encountered managers who hold the view that staff should be told only what they need to know to do their job – nothing more, nothing less. Such managers believe that information should be disseminated on a 'need-to-know' basis. Give three advantages and three disadvantages of such an approach. In what circumstances would you use it?

# 5.1.2 Problems, problems

In the earlier stages of a project people are usually optimistic – sometimes to excess – and plans are developed and estimates prepared in a spirit of enthusiasm for the new venture. When the project moves into execution a more mature realism, even pessimism, is likely to prevail. Where before there were challenges there are now only problems. These problems will filter up through the team to the project manager with whom the 'buck' finally stops. As project manager you should expect *most* of the following to occur during your project:

- technical design problems will arise
- there will be difficulties in meeting quality or reliability specifications
- the original specification will prove deficient
- equipment will cost more than estimated
- some items will have been overlooked in the estimate
- activities will take longer than expected
- in the design phase it will be found that part of the requirements cannot be met within the planned time and cost
- the selected technology will fail to deliver the expected performance
- key staff will leave the project
- changes will increase the workload
- other projects will be given priority over yours
- suppliers will be late delivering equipment
- a supplier may go bankrupt
- change in the market makes the original objectives obsolete
- installers may go on strike
- a subcontractor's work will be below standard
- new legislation may prohibit a planned course of action.

Dealing with some of these problems is routine for the project manager during execution. You will probably have anticipated many of them by performing a risk identification and analysis and have contingency plans. Contingency planning will prove essential if the disruption caused by the problems is to be minimized. Having a contingency plan will mean less time is lost in consultation and deciding what to do next, and it will also mean that an appropriate budget can be invoked quickly. Nevertheless, some problems will be unexpected, considered low risk, and will now eat into your reserves of time and money if you still have any. A project manager needs resilience not to be depressed by them and to maintain a balanced view.

## ACTIVITY 5.2

Here is a typical problem for a project manager. You are halfway through the design phase of a fixed-price project to design and supply a robotic manufacturing system when the design engineers reach the conclusion that the level of reliability specified in the contract cannot be met. The reliability of the robots that had been envisaged at the estimating stage had been overestimated by the supplier who now will only guarantee some lower performance. Further discussion with your designers reveals that a route to higher reliability is uncertain. There may be alternative suppliers but costs and timescales are uncertain and would require further research.

Consider the following questions:

(a) Would you prefer to keep this news from the client?

(b) When should your own management be informed?

(c) What steps could you take to recover from this blow?

## DISCUSSION

This kind of situation is not unusual.

(a) If this is a significant problem the client must be told as soon as possible. You may recall from Chapter 3 that one of the first tasks of the project manager is to establish mutual confidence with the client. Secrecy will undermine your credibility. Nevertheless, give yourself time to prepare an outline of options so that you are prepared for some difficult negotiations. It is better to have a discussion with the client armed with a range of potential answers than just with a nasty problem.

(b) Your own management should be informed at once – and before the client. (You may need to fend off the suggestion from your management that there is no need as yet to talk to the client.)

(c) Ask the engineers to produce an outline of the options, within the time constraint of a few days. (No detailed research is possible.) Ask them to include the option of using the robot originally envisaged with an estimate of the reliability now expected. Then arrange a meeting with the client with the aim of negotiating either for reduced reliability or for a delay in delivery and an increase in the price to pay for the additional work and perhaps higher cost equipment that may be needed as well. As the contract is fixed-price you may expect some tough bargaining ahead, but remember also that the client has to be realistic. The client presumably still wants the project to be completed. If you are put into a position where future costs will be more than the fixed price you may have to recommend abandoning the project.

Although we have taken the supply of a robotic system as an example here you could apply the same sort of problem to any project. Perhaps it has occurred (or will occur) in your own project and you will have had to take similar actions.

# 5.1.3  Summary

Most activities with which the project manager is concerned during execution fall under the headings: initiating, planning, organizing, staffing, monitoring, controlling, directing and communicating. Although the first four of these activities are primarily performed at earlier stages of the project they continue at a reduced level throughout its execution.

An important initiative after project authorization is the activity of mobilization. This means getting the project up and running. Planning continues after mobilization. We described Harrison's concept of the rolling wave in which detailed planning runs ahead of the activities that are about to be performed.

The main activities in the execution phase of a project are monitoring and control. These rely heavily on the communication system used by the project team. We listed typical problems that the project manager may have to face during the project. These are the sort of problems that most projects present during execution and which therefore have to be watched for so that the project can be brought back under control.

Having studied this introductory section you should now be able to:

- list the main types of activity that the project manager performs

- explain what is meant by mobilization

- list typical problems likely to be encountered during execution and explain how monitoring and contingency planning are likely to help overcome them.

# 5.2 PROJECT MONITORING AND CONTROL

This section shows you what is meant by controlling a project. Techniques for measuring the status of the project, including the use of milestones, periodic reports and reviews, are discussed.

## 5.2.1 Elements of project control

A classical control loop, such as the equipment for controlling temperature in a room, consists of measuring the value of the parameter you want to control, comparing that value with what is wanted and taking appropriate action if there is any discrepancy. Controlling a project is somewhat similar, though more complicated, as illustrated in Figure 5.2.

What is controlled is the project itself. Unlike a simple control loop the project has many variables contributing to its status. Because work progresses on a number of activities simultaneously its status is multidimensional, and what you would like to know about it may be difficult to measure.

In principle, the project manager compares all the current status measurements with their desired values (as set out in the project plan documents). If there is any discrepancy the manager signals the project team who take actions, and so change project status to bring it closer to what is wanted.

Unlike the classical controller which simply increases any corrective action according to the difference between the desired state and the actual state the project manager must use a great deal of skill and judgement in deciding what actions to take. There is a similarity with the automatic controller which we want to emphasize – before taking action the project manager must compare the *desired* and *actual* states. The control loop cannot work unless the project manager knows *both* these quantities.

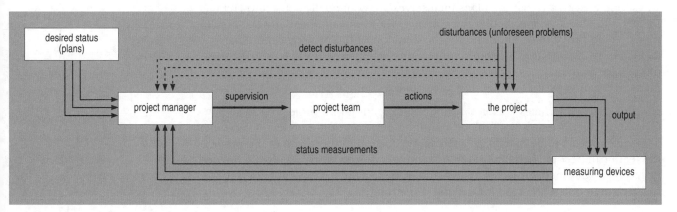

**FIGURE 5.2** Project control loop

The desired status is of course continually changing as the project progresses, and is the *planned* status at the *current* moment. So, for example, after six months' work on a two-year construction project you would compare the construction achieved with the planned status at six months before deciding on the appropriate signals to the constructors. The plans themselves will be continually evolving and the revised plans will be part of the communication to the project team. At the end of the project the desired status is fulfilment of the contract requirements.

Actual status may be measured through such devices as reports and progress meetings, and these will be discussed in more detail later. As in many control loops there are problems with accuracy and time delays, so some measurements of status are exceedingly difficult to make.

## Anticipation

A feedback control loop is good enough for most purposes but control engineers can do even better with a technique called *feed-forward control*. This amounts to detecting sources of disturbance, such as draughts in a room, and taking action in *anticipation* of their effect, such as raising the heat input *before* the temperature has dropped. Project managers can do the same.

A project manager using feed-forward control tries to counteract disturbances on the project or on the project team by anticipating the effect of those disturbances and taking action early. This is more difficult than feedback control because it requires timely awareness of impending trouble. This is a technique that has been in use for centuries, as the following passage from Machiavelli (1513) shows:

> When trouble is sensed well in advance it can easily be remedied; if you wait for it to show itself any medicine will be too late because the disease will have become incurable. As the doctors say of a wasting disease, to start with it is easy to cure but difficult to diagnose; after a time, unless it has been diagnosed and treated at the outset, it becomes easy to diagnose but difficult to cure.

## Changes to the plan

The control scheme outlined in Figure 5.2 is an over-simplification in several ways, one of which is that the plans themselves are continually subject to change. Ideally, the objective specified in the contract would remain fixed and the initial plans would prove to be adequate for the duration of the project. Unfortunately this is rarely, if ever, true. Changes in the plans will almost always occur because of changes in the client's requirements, because of imperfections in the original plans or because of unforeseen difficulties in executing them.

No project manager likes changes during the execution of a project because any change usually increases both the cost and the duration of the project. Even when a change appears to be beneficial, such as a reduction in the scope of the project, the team can become demoralized, for example if design work already completed has to be abandoned. Project managers therefore usually have good reason to resist change unless the case for making it is strong.

Some people hold the view that a contractor may actually welcome requests for change from a client because changes represent an opportunity to charge the client extra. The client is often unable to obtain competitive bids because the contract has already been placed, so the contractor is apparently in a good position to make profit on the work involved. While recognizing the validity of this point when the scope of the changes is sufficiently small for the contractor to accommodate them easily, it is the authors' view that the cumulative effects of numerous changes will often be disastrous to the execution of the project. The effects of large numbers of changes are well illustrated by the Channel Tunnel project in which the contractors claimed that they had ended doing a very different job from the one originally contracted for, from which arose much of the delay in the tunnel opening.

In spite of the disadvantages, changes are inevitable if a project is to take advantage of new opportunities, to adapt to changing circumstances or to avoid problems arising from unforeseen events. Consequently, the project manager must set up procedures by which all proposals for change, whether originated by the client or by the project team, are carefully examined for their impact on the project. Such changes are then only accepted if on balance they are predicted to be beneficial when account has been taken of all the consequences. We shall return to consider this in detail in Sections 6.3 and 6.4.

# 5.2.2 Measuring project status

## Gathering the information

A large part of what a project manager has to do is to gather information about the status of the project so that the appropriate control actions can be taken. There are many ways to do this: team meetings, regular reports, small meetings on specific topics and informal casual discussions. These methods complement each other in giving the information in different ways but vary in reliability and accuracy.

The project manager wants information to be:

- timely
- clear
- relevant
- accurate.

Not all the methods of acquiring information will be equally good on all these points. The periodic reports may be designed to be clear and accurate, but if something happens just after a periodic report has been submitted the project manager needs to know it; it is much more relevant and timely to hear about this informally – though perhaps not entirely accurately – from a communicative member of the team. This communication can then be followed up by more purposeful enquiry.

The need for full up-to-date information has to be set against the provision of that information imposing too heavy a burden on the project team and, indeed, on the project manager who could become overloaded with too frequent and too detailed reports. Ideally all the information received is relevant to the impending decisions and actions.

## Improving accuracy: milestones within activities

One way to improve the *accuracy* of progress reporting is to use activity-level milestones. We noted before that at the planning stage it is necessary to identify milestones applicable to the project as a whole. We are now talking about a lower level of detail: milestones *within* an activity. Activity-level milestones allow finer resolution when measuring the position and improve the accuracy of the report. They may be defined shortly before the activity is started or possibly as the first step within the activity rather than at the outset of the project. Example 5.1 illustrates typically why these intermediate milestones are necessary.

---

## EXAMPLE 5.1

An engineer was to design a piece of equipment, a task that she estimated initially would take four months. She was issued with a work assignment at the beginning of the year which specified the scope of the work quite precisely in terms of the deliverables which she was to hand over at the end of April. At the end of the first month she thought that as she had estimated four months for the total job she had probably completed about a quarter of the work. Her subsequent monthly progress reports appeared as follows:

| January: | Design 25% complete |
| February: | Design 50% complete |
| March: | Design 75% complete |
| April: | Design 90% complete |
| May: | Design 95% complete |
| June: | ? |

Presumably the job was eventually completed! The point of this story is that the engineer had no *yardstick* against which to measure her own progress. She was not being fraudulent but, like many an engineer, optimistic. Only when the well-defined delivery point approached did she realize that the design was less than 100% complete. It is exceedingly difficult to determine when a piece of work is 25% or 50% complete.

It would have been preferable if the work could have been divided into several phases, not necessarily four equal months' work, but phases which the engineer could recognize as finished or not finished. The monthly reports would then have been able to show which of these phases had actually been completed. The estimating by the engineer concerned is virtually eliminated.

---

There is an additional productivity advantage to having these activity-level milestones because it is human nature to work a little harder as a deadline approaches. *Deadlines concentrate the mind.*

> Depend upon it, Sir, when a man knows he is to be hanged in a fortnight, it concentrates his mind wonderfully.

> (Dr Samuel Johnson, in a letter to James Boswell, 19 September 1777)

This might lead you to decide that all work must be broken down into as many identifiable stages as possible, each with well-defined milestones, preferably with deliverables specified. Indeed, why stop at monthly stages? Why not split the work into weekly or even daily tasks? But clearly this can be taken too far. Consider the disadvantages of excessively detailed breakdown. Close monitoring may be so irritating to the engineer that she hands in her resignation. The monitoring itself costs time and effort, and it may well be impossible to plan such detailed milestones.

Probably the optimum is just enough milestones to enable corrective action to be taken if slippage occurs. As a general rule each individual assignment should not exceed more than about four weeks and some project managers would prefer less. For junior staff the optimum period between milestones is probably about a week.

---

### ACTIVITY 5.3

Suppose the project manager anticipates the problems of monitoring the four-month assignment in Example 5.1 and asks the engineer to provide a more detailed breakdown of the work to be done. She replies that as she has not yet started the design she cannot yet give such a breakdown. How might the problem be resolved?

### DISCUSSION

Probably the best way forward is to schedule the first task within the design activity as the top-level design, from which one of the deliverables is the plan for the remaining detailed design. When this top-level design has been completed the engineer may need to discuss the plan with the project manager so that the subsequent milestones can be identified. The essential point is to achieve some early partitioning of the work into recognizable modules.

---

# Periodic progress reports

The traditional tool of management for measuring the current position is the periodic written report made monthly or weekly. The project manager needs such routine reports on the cost, the effort expended and the progress of each element in the work breakdown structure. Gathering the data for cost and effort reports is a routine function in most organizations when managing continuous operations but particular attention to these reports, and especially their timeliness, is more necessary when managing a project.

To be immediately useful the reports need to be presented to the project manager classified under headings that correspond to the work breakdown structure. This may or may not coincide with individual staff assignments. A collating job may be necessary, so that you do not waste valuable time chasing reports, extracting the relevant data and fitting them together. Keeping the reporting system relevant and timely is a part of the job of a project administrator or project control officer.

*Timeliness*

Timeliness cannot be overemphasized. The purpose of the periodic reports should be to help the project manager to become aware of problems early. (Remember the advantage in the control loop of feed-forward control.) Reports are often submitted too late and processed too slowly to be useful.

*Reporting by exception*

You need to make the reporting requirements clear at the beginning of the project. One way to encourage useful reports is to prescribe a standard report form with suitable space allocated to what the project manager really wants to hear about. Essential items on the report are not only what the expenditure, effort and progress have actually been but also what they were *planned* to be. (Remember that control requires comparison with the desired value.) The best kind of report will highlight those items which differ significantly from the plan. This is called *reporting by exception*: 'Everything is on schedule/within budget except ...'. Forecasts of future problems are particularly useful.

Progress reports are often uncommunicative. Their authors usually regard them as an extra chore and a burden that they would rather not have, and their purpose is not recognized: they become bland statements of business-as-usual, phrased comfortingly to stop questions being asked. The reporting process can also be seen as threatening and cause team members to exaggerate the work done. To overcome these problems it is essential that the report writers should not feel threatened and should get helpful feedback.

If the writers think that the reports are just filed for the record then naturally they regard them as an annoying overhead activity, preventing them from getting on with their real work. If, however, you show some response such as, 'I see there are problems with the design of the communications system', or 'Glad to see the conveyor looks like coming in under price', then the team member is likely to write future reports more willingly, especially if it is seen as a way of gaining help with problems and recognition of good work. It may be helpful to discuss issues arising from the reports at review meetings (which we will discuss shortly). If this is to be done then you need to arrange the timing of meetings so that there is a recent set of reports available.

### SAQ 5.2

List six uses to which a project manager might put the regular reports.

### *Electronic reporting*

It is worth considering whether *written* reports are needed at all. Access by all team members to an electronic information system can alleviate some of the drudgery associated with preparing a written report, especially if that report needs to be combined with others and edited for senior management. Shared access to a project management information system has the advantage of providing much quicker communication than is normal with periodic written reports and still allows the report to be formally recorded in the system when such formality is needed.

An electronic system makes it much easier to process the information in different ways. One way to organize the reporting system is to have a database of status information which can be updated by authorized users of the system and interrogated by all the team members (not necessarily all having access to all the data). A less formal way is to use electronic mail for the reports. Reports can still be combined and edited more easily than with written reports but need not adhere to a standard that might be imposed by an information system.

### ACTIVITY 5.4

Consider whether electronic communication, formal or informal, could help you in your project work. Are there likely to be advantages in reduced paper handling and subsequent processing? Is it practicable to use a shared database of status information? What disadvantages are there? Make notes to this effect in your project notebook.

# Progress review meetings

The project manager will require progress review meetings so that key members of the project team can communicate regularly with each other as a group. The progress review meeting allows the team to hear how other parts of the project are progressing and to decide how problems affecting more than one section may be resolved. (A progress review meeting is distinct from a quality review of the work, discussed later in Chapter 6.)

The progress review not only helps to highlight problems but also to establish the commitment of the team to work together to achieve a successful outcome. A good project review meeting fosters a team spirit; a bad one increases rivalry and induces pessimism.

Review meetings are expensive. There may be half a dozen highly paid people in attendance, so it is important to avoid spending too much time on routine reports, or on matters which are of concern to only one or two members of the group. The project manager, who normally chairs these meetings, should organize the business so that routine reports are dealt with quickly and sectional concerns are discussed outside the meeting. All papers should be circulated to participants some time before the meeting.

A good progress review meeting consists not just of a series of dialogues between the manager and individual team members but involves discussions amongst several of the team members on each topic. If a dialogue seems to be developing to the exclusion of others, discussion of that topic should be cut short and continued outside the meeting.

An important outcome of the progress review is that a number of actions should be agreed by the team and specifically by individual members of the team responsible for carrying them out. The *public commitment* to these actions in a progress review meeting is a significant element. These commitments are recorded in the minutes which should be circulated promptly after the meeting. The next meeting should review actions to see what progress has been made. A useful technique is to arrange for the issue of an *actions* list for each person along with the minutes so that the actions are less likely to be overlooked.

In a large project, review meetings are required at lower levels to review progress on the activities of different groups or sections within the project. Often these are conducted by the members of the progress review team, so this is an opportunity not only to review progress within the section but also to report on higher-level meetings to ordinary team members. The lower-level review meetings are often more informal, and may not necessarily use minutes. Even if minutes are not taken, it is beneficial to record the actions and decisions in some way, perhaps by a note pinned to the section notice board.

An issue that may arise is whether it is good for the client to be represented at the internal progress meeting which the project manager holds with the team. Some clients insist on being present, but if they do not, should the project manager encourage them to come? The advantage is that it closes the communication gap between the team and the client so that the client has a better understanding of what is going on and the team will get a quicker reaction to questions raised. The disadvantage is the danger of suppressing problems and inhibiting open discussion. The balance may depend on the personalities of the people. Given the right client representative there is everything to be said for it.

## Informal discussions

Informal, casual discussions are a vital source of information to the project manager. A manager who is sufficiently approachable will get to hear of problems much sooner than one who relies only on regular reports and reviews. An approachable manager who regularly makes informal contact with all members of the project team will have much better knowledge of the true state of the project than one who gathers information only through formal channels. This takes time, however, so you must take care not to become so overloaded with routine business that there is no time left for these invaluable informal contacts.

# 5.2.3   Closing the loop

Gathering the information about the project status is only half the job required for control. The other half is:

● evaluating the information

● taking action

● checking that the action has worked.

The action required will usually be to get some member(s) of the project team to *do* something. This was the thrust of much of Chapter 4. If something is wrong then the next step is to decide, perhaps with the team, what to do about it. And then do it!

To quote from a comment given by an engineer responsible for project work in Matthew Hall Engineering in a case study for an Open University course:

> Progress monitoring can be achieved in many ways according to the scale of the contract, but the objective is always to provide management and supervisors with the information they need to control that task. Monitoring must never be confused with control nor knowledge be mistaken for action. It warns management of deviations from plan so that corrective action can be taken, but successful control relies on the skill and experience of the project manager and supervisors.

The control loop is closed by taking action and then monitoring again what has happened to the project. The regular cycle of *monitor–control–monitor again* is the control loop of project management.

# 5.2.4   Summary

The control of a project can be compared to a feedback control loop. Control requires both a definition of the desired status (a plan) and also a measurement of the actual status. Control may be improved using a feed-forward technique: anticipation. Project managers need status information that is clear, accurate relevant and timely. Activity-level milestones improve accuracy. Techniques for measuring the project status include periodic reports, written or electronic, progress reviews and informal day-to-day contact with members of the project team.

It is not enough merely to gather data. The data must be evaluated to check for its reasonableness, and when necessary control action must be taken.

Having studied this section you should be able to:

- describe the elements of project control
- explain in what ways the project manager improves on the simple classical controller
- describe several ways in which the project manager gathers information about the state of the project
- explain what is meant by 'closing the control loop'.

# 5.3 *MONITORING AND CONTROLLING THE COST*

This section concerns measuring the current cost of the project and relating it to the achievements so far, so that an estimate is continuously available for the cost of the project at its completion. We introduce a number of cost control terms and describe the use of an earned value system to relate cost to achievement.

## 5.3.1 The earned value method

The accounting systems commonly used in a business are rarely adequate for monitoring project costs. We saw in Chapter 2 that there might be a conflict between the cost classifications used in a project and an organization's standard accounting practices. For example, in most businesses material and labour costs are not usually recorded in the precisely attributable way that is required for project control, and often the reports from the accounting system are not available in time for the manager to exercise any control. Furthermore, it is rare in a non-project business to record the value of work *achieved* alongside the *cost* of achieving it. Measurement of expenditure alone is almost useless: it is essential to know what has been achieved as a result of this expenditure.

The consequence of these deficiencies of standard accounting systems is that many project managers have to set up their own system for monitoring and controlling project costs and achievement. The system that we describe here is called an **earned value** system, because it seeks to show the manager not only the cost of the work performed so far but also the *value earned* by that work. Such systems are now quite common among project performing organizations. Some clients may insist on the use of such a system.

The earned value of the work performed on a project is the cost that the estimator attached to that work when the project budget was defined. Another term for it which is rather more explicit is **budgeted cost of work performed**, or BCWP. This is the term we shall employ in this book but it is interchangeable with earned value. The budgeted cost of work performed at any stage during the project can be calculated by adding up the component values of the elements of work that contribute to the project, taking account of the fractional completion of each element.

The use of the word *work* might be taken to imply that we are only interested in the labour aspects of the cost of a project. However, the budgeted cost for an element of the WBS will often be subdivided into categories such as labour, materials, equipment and subcontracted work. Each of these categories can be analysed separately if the data are available so that, for example, cost overruns can be identified as due to higher equipment costs rather than staff costs. To keep the following discussion simple, we shall not keep referring to each category separately but you should appreciate that project costs would probably be broken down so that, where we consider the work done on a project as a whole, the same arguments would normally apply to these individual categories separately.

Note that the earned value required in these calculations should *not* include any profit or loss element. The values should represent costs in a way that will be consistent with the reported actual costs. So, for example, if staff costs are to be reported at standard rates regardless of actual salaries then these are the costs that should be used in calculating BCWP. Similarly, if staff costs are expected to rise with inflation then the values of BCWP should be similarly inflated. For simplicity we will not include the complicating factor of inflation in any of our calculations.

In addition, if they were based on the agreed budget for each element of the WBS, they could easily amount to several pages of tabular calculations. However, to show the principle, let's take the new office system considered in Sections 3.4 and 3.5, broken down into only six activities. (The activity identifier would normally be the WBS reference but for brevity we have used the letters A to F.) Suppose the budgeted values of each element, agreed at the estimating stage of the project, are as shown in the middle column of Table 5.1. The budgeted cost of the work performed on each element is then calculated by multiplying the budgeted cost of the element by the fraction of the work that is complete. The BCWP for the whole project is the sum of the individual elements.

**TABLE 5.1**  Calculating BCWP for a new office system

| Activity identifier | Description | Budgeted cost of element (£000) | % complete | BCWP (£000) |
|---|---|---|---|---|
| A | prepare offices | 100 | 50 | 50 |
| B | procure equipment | 200 | 50 | 100 |
| C | design tests | 50 | 25 | 12.5 |
| D | install equipment | 20 | 0 | 0 |
| E | test system | 30 | 0 | 0 |
| F | train users | 10 | 0 | 0 |
| | **total** | **410** | **–** | **162.5** |

If milestones have been passed corresponding to 50% completion of the office preparation and equipment procurement and 25% of the tests have been designed then the BCWP is calculated in Table 5.1 as £162 500. (Although no breakdown has been shown within these elements we are assuming that milestones have been defined to allow satisfactory estimates of percentage completion to be made.) A more complete version of Table 5.1 would show work packages subdivided into work elements, most of which would be either 0% or 100% complete, leaving the partial progress on only a minority of elements to be assessed more subjectively.

It may be argued that subjective assessment of the fraction complete is so unreliable that the only valid approach is to report work as being in one of only three states: not started, started but not complete, completed. From this it is then possible to calculate the lower and upper bounds for the value of BCWP. The lower bound, the minimum value of BCWP, is calculated by taking zero as the value of fraction complete for all partially completed elements. The upper bound, the maximum value of BCWP, can be calculated by taking the fraction complete as 100% for the partially completed elements.

## SAQ 5.3

Assume that progress on the computer project (introduced in SAQs 3.16 and 3.25) is as shown in Table 5.2, where we have used the simple three-state method of reporting described above.

(a) Calculate the range within which BCWP must lie.

(b) Is it reasonable to take the average of the lower and upper bounds as the actual value of BCWP?

(c) What additional milestones will be required in the partially completed activities if BCWP is to be known at this stage to within 10% of the total cost of the project?

(d) What will be the value of BCWP at the end of the project?

**TABLE 5.2**   Status of elements in the computer project

| Activity identifier | Description | Budgeted cost (£000) | Status |
|---|---|---|---|
| A | design hardware | 20 | completed |
| B | build hardware | 40 | completed |
| C | procure test facility | 10 | completed |
| D | test hardware | 4 | partially completed |
| E | design software | 30 | completed |
| F | code software | 26 | partially completed |
| G | design tests | 5 | not started |
| H | test system | 15 | not started |
|  | **total** | **150** | |

# Estimating the cost at completion

As the project progresses, the **actual cost of work performed** (ACWP) can be monitored by collecting data on the incurred costs of the labour and materials used by the project. (Note that schedule slippage also affects the cost, but we will deal with this issue in Section 5.5.) These costs must be on the same basis used for the estimate of BCWP. So, if the labour cost in BCWP included an overhead factor for office accommodation and administration then the costs presented in ACWP must either include the same factor or include the costs of accommodation and administration if that has been measured directly. The ACWP can then be compared to the BCWP as shown in Figure 5.3.

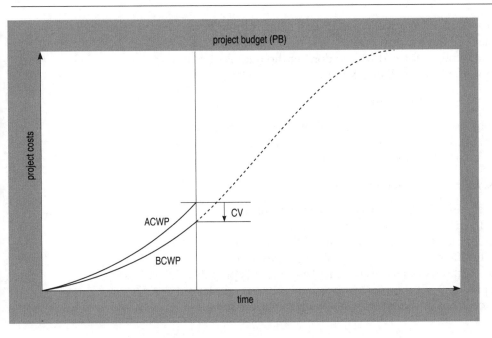

project budget (PB)

project costs

ACWP

CV

BCWP

time

**FIGURE 5.3**
Comparison of actual and budgeted costs of work performed

The **cost variance** (CV) is a value that will be regularly updated throughout the project and is the difference between BCWP and ACWP:

CV = BCWP – ACWP

(In the example shown in Figure 3.1 the value of CV will be negative because the actual cost exceeds the budgeted cost.) At the end of the project BCWP will reach the agreed budgeted cost at completion, the project budget (PB), and the value of ACWP will be the total costs incurred on the project. So the cost variance at that time will, if positive, be the cost underrun of the project. A negative value of CV will represent a cost overrun.

This definition of CV is the usual one used in project reporting but you may find the term *variance* used the other way round, i.e. a positive variance will represent actual costs over budget. You therefore need to be careful not to take a stated variance at face value, but ensure that the term is being used in the sense that you expect. To remember the way round that the term is being used in this book you may find it helps to think of a positive CV being a good thing and negative CV being bad.

I WAS DOING FINE UNTIL I LET MY C.V. SLIP!

The **estimated cost at completion** (ECAC) will depend on what assumption the project manager chooses to make about the cost of work still to be performed. One assumption is that the work still to be performed will be done at the budgeted cost, the original estimate. In this case the ECAC will be given by:

$$ECAC = PB - CV \qquad \text{(Assumption 1)}$$

A more realistic assumption may be that the remaining work will be performed at the same cost/budget factor that has been observed in the work performed so far. In that case the estimated cost at completion will be given by:

$$ECAC = PB \times (ACWP/BCWP) \qquad \text{(Assumption 2)}$$

The ratio BCWP/ACWP is sometimes called the **cost–performance index**, CPI. Early in the project, when the fraction of work completed is small, the cost–performance index may be an unreliable guide to the costs of the rest of the project because it is based on insufficient data, so it is probably better to use Assumption 1 until at least 30% of the work has been done. Later on, it is probably more appropriate to use Assumption 2. As the project approaches 100% completion the two estimates approach each other so then it does not matter which assumption is used.

Another item frequently required in a monthly cost report is the **cost to complete** (CTC). The cost to complete (as opposed to the cost *at* completion) is the estimated cost of the work still to be done. Since the cost so far is ACWP, the relationship between the cost to complete and the estimated cost at completion is:

$$CTC = ECAC - ACWP$$

Should you ever be in a position of having to decide whether to continue a project or cancel it and cut your losses the CTC is the most relevant figure to know. Costs that represent money or time already spent are water under the bridge, called **sunk costs**, but the CTC is the money still to be spent. You may decide that it is best to cancel a project if the CTC is greater than the benefits likely to be obtained if you were to continue. In this case you will have to write off the sunk costs and 'chalk it up to experience'.

A number of cost control terms have now been introduced and it may be useful to summarize the ones that we have introduced so far in Table 5.3. (This table will be augmented and summarized again at the end of Section 5.4.)

**TABLE 5.3** Cost control terms

|  | Term | Meaning |
|---|---|---|
| ACWP | Actual cost of work performed | Actual costs incurred in performing work so far |
| BCWP | Budgeted cost of work performed | The budgeted (planned) cost for work performed so far |
| CPI | Cost–performance index | The ratio of the budgeted cost of the work to the actual incurred cost: CPI = BCWP/ACWP |
| CTC | Cost to complete | Cost of work still to be done |
| CV | Cost variance | A measure of performance in cost terms: CV = BCWP – ACWP |
| ECAC | Estimated cost at completion | The projected completion cost of the project |
| PB | Project budget | The budgeted cost of work to be performed to complete the project |

## SAQ 5.4

Which of the terms in Table 5.3 vary throughout the project and which terms remain constant?

## SAQ 5.5

In a one-year project with a budget of £200 000 it is found that the actual cost of work performed is £110 000 and the budgeted cost of work performed is £100 000.

(a) What is the estimated cost at completion if you assume that the cost–performance index remains constant?

(b) What is the estimated cost at completion if you assume that the remaining work is performed to budget?

# 5.3.2   Controlling the project cost

*Controlling* cost is much more difficult than *monitoring* cost. It is almost impossible to prescribe how it should be done. There are numerous books on cost control which, in spite of optimistic-sounding titles, are really mostly about techniques for cost monitoring. Cost monitoring is, of course, an essential prerequisite for cost control – without it the project manager is left in the position of one who can only exhort the team to do their best but does not know whether to praise them or blame them for their past performance. It comes back to the project control loop, Figure 5.2: status measurements are essential for control.

One axiom should be stated at the outset:

> *You cannot control the cost of an item when the money has already been spent or irrevocably committed.*

A consequence of this axiom is that cost control is all about controlling *future* commitments, not about controlling *past* expenditure. So the main element of cost control is the *authorization* to spend money, which we discuss below. If control can only be exercised over future commitments, what then is the point of cost monitoring – gathering and reporting the costs of historical spending? Some would argue that such monitoring is done purely to satisfy the accountants about where the money has gone, and is useless as a tool for controlling cost. It isn't, so how does it help?

The answer to this is threefold. First, there is the effect upon the attitude of the project staff towards spending. The fact that the project manager is cost conscious must be strongly communicated to the project team so that their attitude towards expenditure reflects this. This attitude can be either fostered or neglected according to the mechanisms which are instituted by the project manager for authorizing expenditure and for calling staff to account for their spending. Secondly, the cost monitoring system gives feedback so that the project manager knows whether the authorization controls are working. Thirdly, if costs do overrun, it gives the project manager advance warning to seek more funds before the cash runs out.

## Authorization

During the execution of the project cost control is mainly exercised by authorizing only those commitments which are detailed in the project budget breakdown with some margin, perhaps 10%, to allow for inaccuracies in the estimate.

In some companies each order for external expenditure will carry a code so detailed that it can be checked against the estimate for that individual item before the official order is placed. More commonly the code embraces a number of component orders because the cost account is set higher in the work breakdown structure (WBS) than the component level. Even so, the person responsible for initiating the order will be expected to ensure that the cost of all the components within the cost account does not exceed the estimate by more than the tolerable limit.

Similar control is required for the expenditure on staff time. For close control a system is required in which every unit of time is booked against a cost code representing an activity within the WBS. Authority to book against a given code has to be given in advance. The only difference from the system of monitoring commitments for equipment is that the units of measurement are usually days or hours rather than money. The translation of time into cost charged against the project is usually based on some formula according to the grade of the employee, and includes a factor to cover all the overheads such as the provision of office accommodation, heating, lighting and phones (as we saw in Sections 2.3.4 and 2.3.5.

## Timing

A project manager's power to influence the final cost of a project diminishes as the project progresses. The most effective time in the project at which to exercise control is at the conceptual stage when the scope of the project is being defined. At each successive stage, the scope for exercising control diminishes until at the finishing stages the project manager is almost powerless to affect the outcome.

In the definition phase there has been little expenditure and it is still possible, by cancelling the project, to save nearly 100% of the project budget. Although this may seem to express a rather pessimistic attitude there is no doubt that it would have saved a great deal of money for many project sponsors if some projects had been aborted at an early stage. Think of the Euro Disney project, where, rather than cancelling it, a rescue package was put together when it turned out to be unprofitable because the investment had already been made. Huge sums would have been saved if this outcome had been foreseen earlier. (Of course this is easier to see with hindsight, but it shows the importance of getting the concept right.)

The next most effective stage at which to save money is the feasibility study when the scope of the project is defined. Perhaps some parts are less valuable than others. The cost of each function needs to be carefully estimated to ensure that each piece of the project is worthwhile. The specification may need pruning to get the best value for money. (Very occasionally the reverse is true: the scope needs to be expanded to achieve better returns.) To minimize risk it is better to start with a smaller scope and add to it at a later phase. Value engineering (see Chapter 1) is used to examine each part of a system to see if there is a better or cheaper way to achieve the desired result. This may be applied at various times but is valuable particularly in the design phase where it can have a significant impact. You may remember that the inquiry into the London Ambulance Service project suggested that value engineering could have been applied profitably.

Once the scope has been defined the most important of all documents for cost control can be produced: the project budget. This will give a detailed breakdown of the cost of the project showing the budgeted cost of every item to be ordered and every activity to be performed down to the lowest level of detail that it is economically possible to achieve given the knowledge available at that stage. This is the level at which cost control is exercised.

## Knowing when to 'pull the plug'

Sometimes the most cost-effective action that a project manager could take would be to 'pull the plug' - to get the project closed down. Unfortunately, it is very difficult for a project manager or the initiators of a project to see matters in a clear-sighted way. Staw and Ross (1987) have pointed out a number of reasons why it may be very difficult for the manager of a project to decide that it needs to be abandoned. These reasons are:

- The nature of the project itself may have led to the expectation that there would be temporary problems, so when these arise they may be dismissed as nothing other than expected difficulties.

- A project with high closing costs and little salvage value may be difficult to abandon because of the exit costs.

- Commitment may have been established too well to allow closure to be contemplated.

- Psychological factors are important. It's hard for those who have been rewarded for their previous tenacity now to be seen to be giving up.

- Intermittent rewards encourage the hope that things may improve.

- People perceive only what accords with their established beliefs. Consequently they may bias the data to favour these beliefs and undermine the credibility of contrary evidence, especially if data are ambiguous.

- Bad news in a project may be interpreted as a personal failure, so the project manager may want to persist and prove that the project is in fact a success.

- Social pressures lead us to admire people who are tenacious in the face of adversity.

- Organizational inertia may make it easier not to 'rock the boat'.

In summary, Staw adn Ross are saying that it may be difficult for the managers of projects to pull the plug on them because they are over-committed to them. To counteract over-commitment it is necessary to find ways of getting an objective view of the future of a project. One way is to encourage managers to stand back from time to time and ask them to view the project as though they were seeing it for the first time. Would they invest in it starting from this point?

This may be difficult for a committed project manager to do, so another approach is to bring in some genuinely new people to make a judgement. An audit may be the best way. In really difficult cases it may be necessary to replace the management.

One obvious difficulty that project managers face is that they will be deemed to have failed if the project is terminated. Staw and Ross point out the need to establish an environment where the project manager and the seniour staff face reduced penalties than is normal when projects fail. This is contrary to the usual attitude that success is to be rewarded and failure penalized. Instead, reward the honest recognition of problems and the courage to cut losses.

# 5.3.3 Summary

The section has described an earned value system for comparing the current cost of a project with its budgeted cost. It is necessary to split the work into elements, each having a budgeted cost, which may be expressed in cash terms or in hours of work. The budgeted cost of the work performed can be calculated by summing the achievement over all the elements. CV is the cost variance and is a measure of the cost under- or overrun for the same amount of work, a measure of how well you are doing financially compared with the budget plan. The cost control terms are summarized in Table 5.3. All the elements of Table 5.3 except for the project budget vary throughout the project.

Cost control requires a system of cost monitoring coupled with appropriate authorization to members of the project team to spend money or book time to individual cost codes. The power to influence the final cost diminishes as the project progresses.

Some projects ought to be closed early. This can be difficult both for the organization and personally for the project manager.

Having studied this section you should now be able to:

- describe the earned value system for monitoring costs
- define and explain the significance of all the terms listed in Table 5.3
- discuss ways of controlling costs
- discuss the effect of control actions at different stages of the project
- describe some ways of recognizing 'problem' projects
- describe ways of dealing with overcommitment, organizational inertia and fears of the risks of failures.

# 5.4  MAINTAINING THE SCHEDULE

In this section we review several methods used by project managers to monitor progress against the schedule. These methods include updating the project network, milestone tracking and using the earned value curves.

Just as it is important to track actual expenditure and compare it with the project estimate, it is important to track actual progress on activities and compare that with the project schedule. As tasks are completed late, on time or – more rarely – early the schedule needs to be amended. Tasks not foreseen in the original plan must be incorporated into both schedule and budget. All this will tell us *where* we are and help us to keep advancing toward our goal. Such tracking also gives us early warning of problems, thereby allowing us to take corrective action.

## 5.4.1  Updating the schedule

The preferred method for estimating the date at which a project will be completed is to update the project network to reflect the current position. Using current data on the progress of each activity the calculations of all the earliest event times can be repeated, but starting from the position as it is now known to be. This requires only the durations of activities to be updated and need not involve redefining the network unless there has been a change in the logic of dependencies.

If a computer planning package is used it should be a fairly straightforward task to update the durations and recalculate all the event times. In this chapter the extent of completion of an activity is shown by doubling the normal activity arrow appropriately – along the whole length of a completed activity or along a proportional part of its length for a partially complete activity. Completed activities could, of course, be deleted from the network and replaced by a start node representing the present time. This could be worthwhile at a late stage in a project to simplify the resulting diagram. However, it is often convenient to retain the historical part of the network to show the complete picture and to avoid redefining it.

The results of updating the network could of course be presented in the form of a Gantt chart, which is more understandable to most people. A technique of showing completed work by a different colour or shading of the bar can be used.

### SAQ 5.6

Consider the project of installing a new oven with an original planned schedule based on the earliest start dates from the network shown in Figure 5.4 overleaf. Suppose that after 10 weeks' work all the activities are on schedule except the installation of the plinth. This activity is only half complete and its total duration is now estimated to be 10 weeks instead of the original five weeks.

Revise the network calculations to produce a new estimate of the project completion date. Use a double arrow to represent completed or partially complete activities.

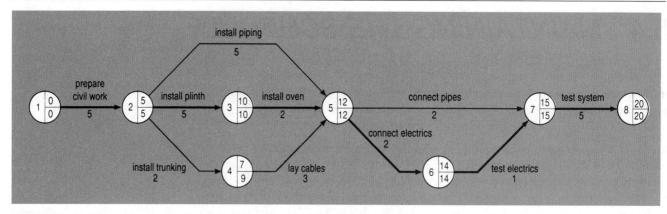

**FIGURE 5.4**  Planned schedule for installing a new oven (earliest starts)

## 5.4.2  Milestone tracking

Senior management may prefer to be given a less detailed picture of progress that concentrates on recording the rate of progress past the milestones. Milestone tracking is a way of removing the detail and recording how dates for the milestones have evolved during the project. This method has the advantage of being able to show at a glance not only the present status of milestones but also the evolution of that progress over the life of the project so far.

Let's see how milestone tracking would work on the oven project. If you look at Figure 5.4 you will notice that all paths through the network pass through events 1, 2, 5, 7 and 8. These seem therefore reasonable candidate milestones. Suppose that they have been well defined and that, in conformance with an earliest starts schedule, their planned dates are as shown in Table 5.4, where we have assumed that the project is due to start in Week 10 of the calendar year.

**TABLE 5.4**  Planned milestone dates for oven project

|   | Description | Network identifier | Scheduled date |
|---|---|---|---|
| A | project start | 1 | 6 March |
| B | civil work complete | 2 | 10 April |
| C | installation complete | 5 | 29 May |
| D | ready for testing | 7 | 19 June |
| E | project complete | 8 | 24 July |

During the project there will now be regular reports showing the dates at which milestones were actually passed and giving revised predicted dates for those which have yet to be passed. A milestone tracking chart as it would appear at the end of the project is shown in Figure 5.5.

The chart evolves line by line during the life of the project. At the beginning of the project the dates have been set for the milestones as in Table 5.4. The positions of the five planned milestones have been plotted across the chart as shown by the inverted triangles containing the letters A, B, C, D and E. For example, letter E is positioned at 24 July, the scheduled completion date of the project.

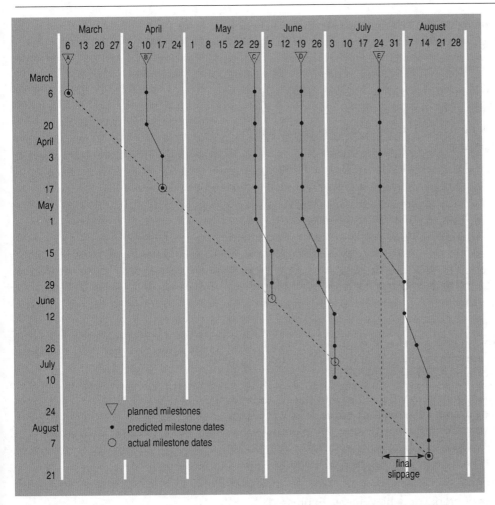

**FIGURE 5.5**  Milestone tracking chart for the oven project (after Archibald, 1992)

To follow the evolution of the chart take a piece of paper and cover up everything in it below the line of planned milestones. Now imagine that there are reports at fortnightly intervals showing new milestone dates. The dates of the reports are listed down the left-hand side of the tracking chart. If you move your piece of paper down one row at a time you first uncover the report for 6 March which might say that the project had been started and that the predicted dates for all the other milestones were on schedule. This is plotted on the chart by the black dots showing the new dates for each milestone as at 6 March. Now move the paper down to expose the report on 20 March. All milestones remain unchanged. But if you uncover the next report, on 3 April, you will find that milestone B is now predicted to be delayed by one week – the dot representing its position has moved one week to the right, to 17 April. All the other milestones are predicted to be at their original dates. Uncovering further reports you will find that Milestone B is duly passed. It was last predicted to be passed at 17 April and the ringed dot at milestone date 17 April for the report of 17 April confirms that it is duly passed.

There will be no further reports on Milestone B after 17 April, which explains why the chart has a diagonal line running across it. Clearly there can be no change in the status of a milestone at reports made after the finally achieved milestone date. If you continue to move your paper down to expose further reports you will find that further slippage of other milestones is reported on 15 May and at other dates later on. The final milestone report on 21 August shows the project to have been completed when Milestone E was passed at 14 August.

### SAQ 5.7

(a) In the report for 1 May, what is the date predicted for passing Milestone D? When is this milestone actually passed?

(b) For this milestone tracking method to work is it necessary that reports are given at regular intervals?

(c) What might you think of the status as reported on 12 June?

### SAQ 5.8

What are the particular advantages of a milestone tracking chart?

# 5.4.3 Calculating slippage from earned value S-curves

You have seen in Section 5.3 how an earned value system can be used to calculate cost overruns. The same system, using the same data and the same curves, can be used to estimate the overall performance against the schedule.

To be able to compare achievement with plan we need to introduce a term for the planned achievement: the **budgeted cost of work scheduled**, BCWS. BCWS represents the planned cumulative achievement by plotting the planned values of BCWP (budgeted cost of work performed) against time. Remember that BCWP represents the accumulation of work done; it is not a *rate* of working.

Although both BCWP and BCWS are usually measured in terms of cash they are really measurements of quantities of work (or achievement) expressed. An equally valid unit of measurement would be person-days if this chapter were applicable to *all* the work done on the project. (The trouble with person-days is that this may not be costed the same for all persons, but you may be prepared to tolerate such an inaccuracy if it is more convenient to measure days.)

BCWS represents the accumulation of *scheduled* work while BCWP represents the accumulation of *performed* work. The graph of BCWS against time can be plotted at the outset of the project once the cost of each activity has been estimated and a schedule has been produced showing when each activity is to be performed. By adding together the rates of expenditure on all the activities each week, the total rate of expenditure on the whole project can be predicted from start to finish of the plan. These weekly or monthly rates of planned work can be accumulated to give a scheduled cumulative achievement, the budgeted cost of work scheduled (BCWS) as shown in Figure 5.6.

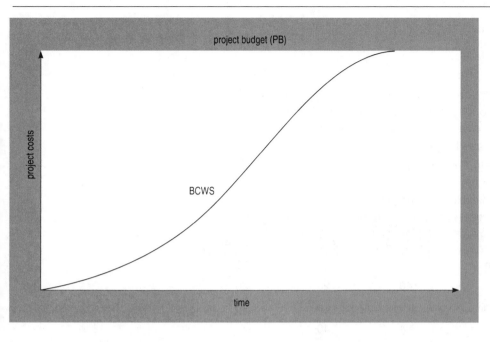

**FIGURE 5.6**
Scheduled work performed
against time

To calculate BCWS we need to know three things: the budgeted cost of each activity, the time at which that activity is scheduled to be performed and the spend profile within each activity. The budgeted cost should be available from the estimate and the scheduled time can be found once each activity has been given a *scheduled* start time, not necessarily the earliest start time. It is necessary to know the spend profile during the performance of each activity. Assuming that the rate of expenditure is constant during the activity, this will often be accurate enough, although a different profile could be used if this was believed to reflect the nature of the activity better.

The planned schedule need not necessarily correspond to starting activities at their *earliest* start. We noted in Chapter 3 that the smoothest possible resource profile will often require activities to be postponed. For planning purposes it is possible to calculate two extreme BCWS curves, one assuming earliest starts and one assuming latest starts, as shown in Figure 5.7. These two extremes show the limits between

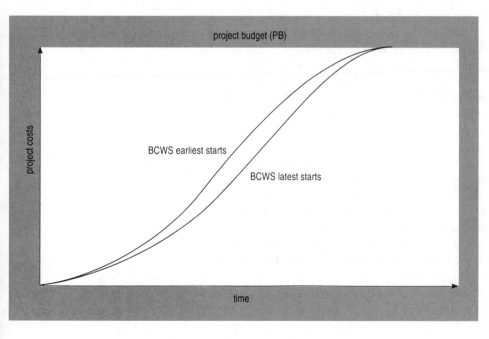

**FIGURE 5.7**
Range of possible BCWS
schedules within which the
planned BCWS must lie

which any chosen BCWS curve must lie. The actual BCWS will depend on what schedule the project manager chooses.

### SAQ 5.9

(a) Use the data given in Table 5.5 to compute the value of BCWS at 5-weekly intervals throughout the project. Assume that the rate of expenditure on each activity is constant throughout its duration.

(b) Plot the graph of BCWS against time.

(c) Why can the slope of the BCWS curve never be negative?

**TABLE 5.5**  Scheduled expenditure on computer project

| Activity | Description | Budgeted cost (£000) | Start time* | Duration (weeks) |
|----------|-------------|----------------------|-------------|------------------|
| A | design hardware | 20 | 0 | 20 |
| B | build hardware | 40 | 20 | 20 |
| C | procure test facility | 10 | 20 | 10 |
| D | test hardware | 4 | 40 | 5 |
| E | design software | 30 | 0 | 30 |
| F | code software | 26 | 30 | 20 |
| G | design tests | 5 | 30 | 5 |
| H | test system | 15 | 50 | 10 |

\* N.B. These are times measured in weeks from the start of the project (not the same as week numbers). The problem of denoting time in week numbers rather than elapsed time was discussed in Chapter 3.

## Schedule variance, schedule–performance index and estimated completion date

By comparing the planned work performed with the actual work performed it is possible to arrive at a measure of how far the current achievement differs from expectations. The term used in the earned value system to measure this is the **schedule variance**, SV. The schedule variance may be rather difficult to understand when you first meet it. It is a measure of the work performed compared with the plan expressed in cash terms (or whatever units are used for BCWP), not in terms of a length of time as you might possibly have expected:

SV = BCWP – BCWS

The SV measures in cash terms how far work has progressed compared with plan: a positive value means it is ahead of plan, a negative value means it is behind plan. You can remember which way round it is defined if you think that, as with the CV, 'positive is good, negative is bad'. The value of SV measures how much work has been achieved at a given date compared to what was scheduled; it does not immediately reveal how far the project is ahead or behind plan in terms of time. However, you can see that such a time measure can readily be obtained from the graphs of BCWP and BCWS.

The scheduled rate of completion of the project is represented by the BCWS curve, the budgeted cost of work scheduled. Remember that the term *budgeted cost* is really a measurement of work, but is presented in cost terms in order to have a standard unit of measurement. So BCWS represents the accumulated value of the work which should be achieved at any date if all is performed to schedule. However, we also have available, through the earned value system, a measurement of the budgeted cost of work performed (BCWP) which measures the work actually done in the same cost units. The time lag of one curve behind the other at any date in the project is a measure of the slippage.

Figure 5.8 shows a typical situation. At the end of June the value of BCWP has reached the value scheduled for the end of May. The current slippage is therefore one month. It is important to appreciate that, as BCWS and BCWP are both *budgeted* and not actual costs, there is no need to take any account of cost escalation in making this calculation. This has been taken care of by using budgeted cost in both curves.

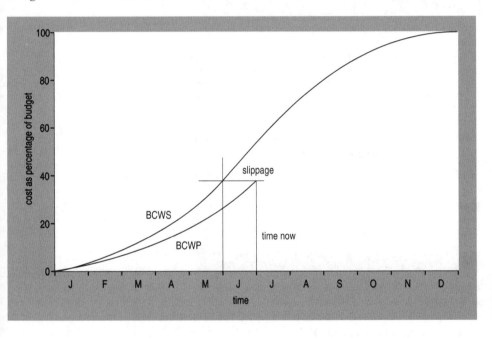

**FIGURE 5.8**
Slippage deduced from BCWS and BCWP

## Schedule–performance index

Some reports on project progress show an index somewhat similar to the cost–performance index, called the **schedule–performance index** (SPI). It is defined as:

SPI = BCWP/BCWS

The attraction of this index is that it is easy to compute from values which have already been obtained without the need for drawing a graph to see how far behind schedule the current value of BCWP is. The value of SPI will be greater than unity when the project is ahead of schedule and less than unity when the project is behind schedule. However, you probably already realize that the ratio of BCWP to BCWS at a given time is *not* the same as the ratio of the time taken to achieve the same amount of work, which is what you are primarily interested in. (If you require to be convinced of this then try drawing some typical S-curves.) In particular, as a project approaches completion the value of BCWP will, by definition, approach BCWS and hence the value of SPI will always eventually approach unity regardless of the length of time that the project took. So, although this index is given here for completeness you should treat its value with some care.

### Estimated completion date

We are now in a position to introduce our last earned value term in this course, the **estimated completion date**, ECD. This date will depend on what assumption you make about the rate of working for the remainder of the project.

### SAQ 5.10

Suggest two alternative assumptions that might be made similar to those used for predicting the cost at completion.

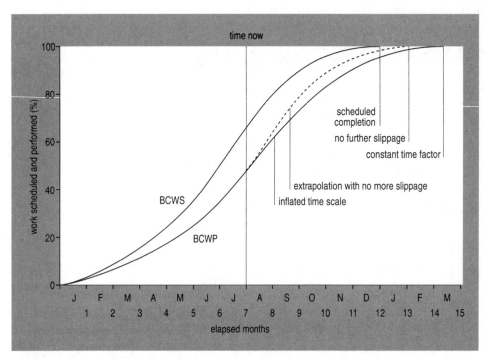

**FIGURE 5.9** Alternative assumptions for predicted achievement

The effect on the estimated completion date of making different assumptions is shown in Figure 5.9. If it is assumed that all remaining work is performed at the scheduled rate, then the projected completion date will be one month behind the original scheduled completion date. If, however, it is assumed that the timescale for the outstanding work has to be multiplied by the same factor as for work performed so far then the projected slippage is much greater. The work scheduled to be done in five months has taken six months, so the time scale inflation factor is 1.2. The scheduled one-year project will take 1.2 × 12 months, i.e. the estimated completion date is 14.4 months from the start of the project. The projected slip is 2.4 months.

As the effect of different assumptions is so large you need to choose between them. You must decide whether the factors that have affected progress so far are likely to persist or whether they are factors that belong only to the past. You must exercise your judgement according to the apparent cause of the previous slippage.

## SAQ 5.11

Suppose the main cause of slippage has been identified as given below. For each case, which of the two assumptions for completion of the remaining work do you think more reasonable? Justify your answer.

(a) The original estimates of timescale were optimistic.

(b) Staff recruitment took longer than expected.

(c) There have been several changes requested by the client.

(d) The software design, now complete, took longer than planned.

## Significance of S-curve slippage

The slippage estimated by the time difference between BCWS and BCWP is a measure of the delay in the *overall* rate of work on the project. If the slip between two curves is one month it cannot necessarily be inferred that each individual activity is now one month behind schedule. The aggregation of all the components that make up the earned value means that we may have reached this earned value by being ahead on some parts of the work and behind on others so that the total achievement is as reported. The value represented by BCWP is an *overall* measure of work done and does not distinguish between work that it is critical to perform to reach the final target and work that is less critical. The only way to find out whether the critical activities are on schedule is to update the project network.

## ACTIVITY 5.5

Consider again the project of installing the new oven with an original planned schedule based on the earliest start dates from the network shown in Figure 5.4. Assume as in SAQ 5.6 that after 10 weeks' work all the activities are on schedule except the installation of the plinth. This activity is only half complete and its total duration is now estimated to be 10 weeks instead of the original five weeks.

(a) Plot the BCWS curve for the original (earliest starts) schedule assuming the budget values in Table 5.6 for each activity and assuming a constant rate of work on each.

(b) Calculate the budgeted cost of work performed after 10 weeks (when the plinth installation is only half complete).

(c) Use the earned value method to predict a completion date.

(d) Compare the date obtained assuming that all subsequent work is of planned duration with the value obtained in SAQ 5.6 by updating the network. Should you expect the two figures to be the same?

### DISCUSSION

(a) The plot of BCWS is shown in Figure 5.10 overleaf.

(b) The budgeted cost of work performed after 10 weeks is

5000 + 2500 + 5000 + 2000 + 3000 = £17 500.

(c) Reading from the BCWS curve in Figure 5.10 the value of work performed should have reached £17 500 after about 9.2 weeks. So the project is nearly one week late so far. If no further slippage occurs the project is expected to be complete after nearly 21 weeks. If however, we assume the same time factor slippage in the second half of the project then the project should be complete after nearly 22 weeks (20 × 10/9.2).

**TABLE 5.6**
Budgeted costs for the new oven project

| Activity | Budgeted cost (£) |
|---|---|
| prepare civil work | 5000 |
| install plinth | 5000 |
| install piping | 5000 |
| install trunking | 2000 |
| install oven | 2000 |
| lay cables | 3000 |
| connect pipes | 2000 |
| connect electrics | 2000 |
| test electrics | 1000 |
| test system | 5000 |
| **total** | **32000** |

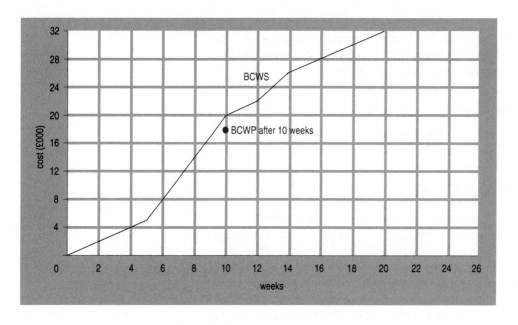

**FIGURE 5.10**  BCWS for oven project

(d)  The date obtained in SAQ 5.6 was 25 weeks yet the earned value method implies that with remaining work at planned duration the project should finish at the end of 21 weeks. In general you should not expect the two estimates to be the same.

In Activity 5.5 we calculated, using the earned value method, that the project cannot now be completed before the end of Week 21. Yet the project completion using the critical path was found to be at the end of Week 25. So how has this discrepancy come about and which estimate is likely to be correct?

To answer this we must consider the meaning of the calculations that have been performed. The estimate using the network calculation depends only upon the length of the critical path. Provided that the durations of activities on the critical path have been correctly estimated, and provided also that activities off the critical path are not so delayed that they become critical, then the network method should give an accurate estimate of the completion date. The earned value method, based on the S-curves, takes no account of the critical path and yields a result based on the *overall* amount of work performed.

In the particular example of SAQ 5.6 and Activity 5.5 the work that has been delayed is all on the critical path; the activities *off* the critical path are all up to schedule. Hence the earned value method has underestimated the consequence of the delay for the critical activities and given an optimistic completion date. However, the reverse could have been the case. Suppose for example that at the end of 10 weeks the plinth has been installed but only just over half the piping has been installed and there is still two weeks' work to do on cable laying. It is possible that the network method would show an unchanged finishing date and yet there has been considerable loss of time in uncritical activities, so that work on all three paths at this point has become critical. This will not matter if they can all be progressed to meet the date of 12 weeks for Event 5 and all the subsequent work can be kept up to schedule. Nevertheless, the earned value method would show up this loss of time and forecast a delayed completion date. This would be a warning signal that the project was not really progressing as smoothly as an unchanged critical path estimate might suggest.

Focusing only on the critical path the network method may mislead the project manager into believing that the schedule is being maintained when in fact progress off the critical path has been slow, and float is being consumed. Unless this consumption of float is monitored, it could transpire that later in the project the amount of work outstanding on previously non-critical activities turns out to be greater than can be achieved with the available resources, and a number of new critical paths materialize. The estimate based on the earned value method is therefore a useful measure of project progress, to be considered probably as a secondary measure alongside the critical path calculations.

# 5.4.4   Combined cost and schedule graphs

The effectiveness of a cost and schedule control system can be greatly enhanced by displaying the combined results graphically. You have seen in Section 5.3 that the relative positions of the curves for ACWP and BCWP tell you how well you are doing financially and in this section you have seen that the relative positions of BCWP and BCWS tell you how well you are doing in terms of achievement against the schedule. If all three curves are given in the same diagram you should be able to deduce both these measures.

### SAQ 5.12

Given the earned value curves for a project as shown in Figure 5.11 deduce the cost and schedule variances and hence describe the situation as you would have seen it:

(a) at the end of May

(b) at the end of September.

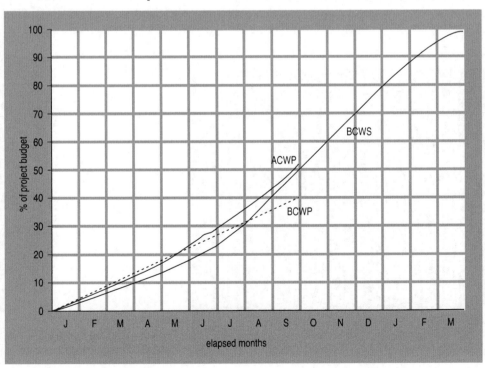

**FIGURE 5.11**
Some earned value curves

Since we are particularly concerned with the final cost we might find it useful to display the progress of the estimated cost at completion (ECAC) against time, as each monthly cost report becomes available, as shown in Figure 5.12 below. If the estimates were really unbiased then you would expect to see a random walk progress across the page. This means that there should not be any particular trend detectable except by chance. However, as shown in Figure 5.12, successive estimates of the cost at completion tend to rise as costs seem almost invariably to exceed forecasts. The final destination of a graph such as Figure 5.12 seems likely to be rather higher than any of the estimates plotted so far.

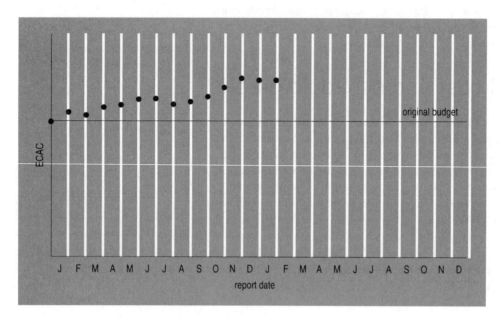

**FIGURE 5.12**
Project estimated cost at completion (ECAC) against report date

Similarly, it is informative to plot successive estimates of the completion date, as shown in Figure 5.13. Like cost estimates, the expected completion date will often show a tendency to drift.

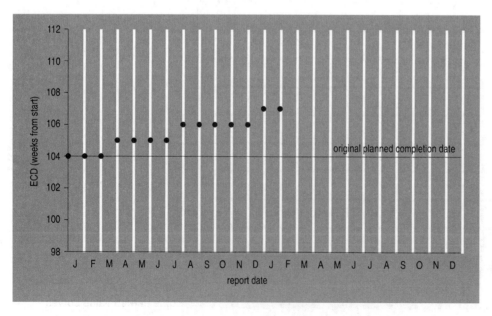

**FIGURE 5.13**
Project expected completion date (ECD) against report date

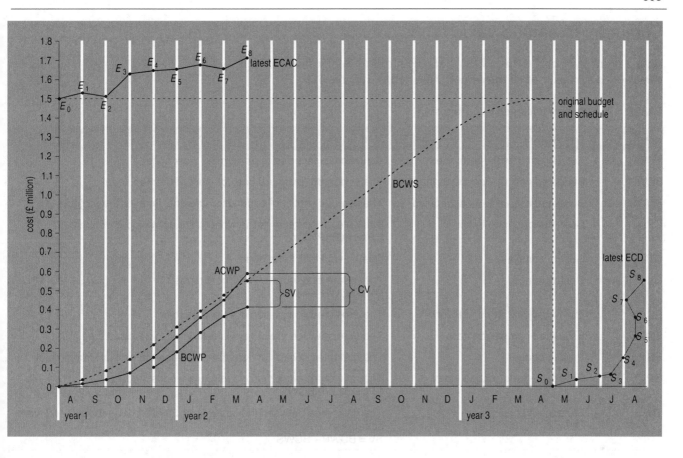

**FIGURE 5.14**
Cost and schedule performance
chart (Archibald, 1992)

Archibald (1992) devised an informative way of combining the usual earned value graphs with graphs showing the estimated cost and the completion date. This combination is shown in Figure 5.14. Although this appears to be a fairly complicated graph it contains a great deal of information.

Across the middle of the graph is shown the progress of the usual three earned value curves, ACWP, BCWP and BCWS. Superimposed above is the plot showing the progress of the estimated cost at completion. (The numbers $E_0$ $E_1$, $E_2$, $E_3$, etc. represent the successive revised estimates.) Similarly, superimposed at the right-hand end of the graph is a plot of the estimated completion date, ECD. (The numbers $S_0$, $S_1$, $S_2$, $S_3$, etc. represent the successive revised schedule estimates.) To make the graph of completion date more readable, each successive ECD is plotted at a height corresponding to the actual cost of work performed at that report date and similarly with the ECAC plots across the graph. Plotted in this way the graphs of ECAC and ECD will eventually meet at a point which corresponds to the actual cost at the actual completion date.

### SAQ 5.13

Suppose you happened to be the fortunate manager of the ideal project in which the estimated cost and completion date remained constant throughout the project. What would the graphs look like when presented as an Archibald cost and schedule performance chart? (Assume an initial budget of £100 000, project duration of one calendar year and an arbitrary shape for the BCWS curve.)

## Summary of earned value terms

With a number of new terms added to those introduced in Section 5.3, it is useful to present a summary of all the earned value terms in Table 5.7.

TABLE 5.7   Summary of earned value terms

| Term | Description | Meaning |
|------|-------------|---------|
| ACWP | Actual cost of work performed | Actual costs incurred in performing work so far |
| BCWP | Budgeted cost of work performed | The budgeted (planned) cost for work performed so far |
| BCWS | Budgeted cost of work scheduled | The planned profile of expenditure against time for the project |
| CPI | Cost–performance index | The ratio of the value of the work to the actual incurred cost: $CPI = BCWP/ACWP$ |
| CTC | Cost to complete | Cost of work still to be done |
| CV | Cost variance | A measure of performance in cost terms: $CV = BCWP - ACWP$ |
| ECAC | Estimated cost at completion | The projected completion cost of the project |
| ECD | Estimated completion date | The date at which the project is estimated to be completed |
| PB | Project budget | The budgeted cost of work performed when the project is completed |
| SPI | Schedule–performance index | The ratio of the work performed to the work scheduled: $SPI = BCWP/BCWS$ |
| SV | Schedule variance | The difference between the budgeted cost of work performed and work scheduled: $SV = BCWP - BCWS$ |

# 5.4.5   Avoiding slippage

> How does a project get to be a year late?
> … One day at a time.
>
> (Brooks, 1975, p. 153)

In *The Mythical Man-Month,* Brooks has an essay entitled 'Hatching a catastrophe'. It happens that Brooks was writing about software but there is little in what he says that does not apply to any kind of project. Consider the following extract:

> When one hears of disastrous schedule slippage in a project, he imagines that a series of major calamities must have befallen it. Usually, however, the disaster is due to termites, not tornadoes; and the schedule has slipped imperceptibly but inexorably. Indeed, major calamities are easier to handle; one responds with major force, radical reorganization, the invention of new approaches. The whole team rises to the occasion.
>
> But the day-by-day slippage is harder to recognize, harder to prevent, harder to make up. Yesterday a key man was sick, and a meeting couldn't be held. Today the machines are all down, because lightning struck the building's power transformer. Tomorrow the disk routines won't start testing, because the first disk is a week late from the factory. Snow, jury duty, family problems, emergency meetings with

customers, executive audits – the list goes on and on. Each one only postpones some activity by a half-day or a day. And the schedule slips, one day at a time.

(*Ibid.* p. 154)

Brooks identifies three remedies in particular that help the project manager to keep what he calls the 'termites' under control. He stresses the importance of having a schedule. The milestones in the schedule 'must be concrete, specific, measurable events, defined with knife-edge sharpness' (p.154). (We discussed in Section 2 the problem of the 95% complete syndrome.)

A second remedy is to use a critical path schedule to concentrate the effort on the critical activities and to counter the excuse that 'the other piece is late anyhow.'

A third problem to overcome is the lower-level manager who doesn't want to worry his boss about the small slippage that he hopes to be able to make good later. Brooks suggests that this problem is partly due to the lower-level manager's fear that his boss will over-react and so prefers to sweep the problem under the rug. Two solutions are proposed to overcome this problem: one is to reduce the 'conflict' and encourage the sharing of information openly, the other is to 'yank the rug back' using reviews and reports. Brooks recommends the use of a watch-dog group to handle the administration of plans and controls.

## Adding extra resources

When a section manager reports to the boss that the schedule is slipping the boss will often respond with the question 'How many extra people do you need to get back on schedule?' This question is often unanswerable because of 'Brooks's Law':

Adding manpower to a late software project makes it later.

(Brooks, 1975, p. 25)

The 'law' could be expected to apply not only to software projects but to any technically complex project where there is strong interaction between the workers.

Brooks's Law is based on the fact that when work is partitioned there is a communication effort that has to be added to the work to be done. Part of this communication is due to the training and familiarization required when a new member joins the project team. Another part is the intercommunication which is proportional to the number of pair-wise links in the team. Adding a new member to a team decreases the effort available from the existing members by the amount required from each of them for communication with the new team member. As the team size increases this loss will eventually more than offset the extra effort added by the new recruit.

## Some causes of slippage

The question of extra resources is not the only question to consider if a schedule is slipping. If the project is slipping you will want to know *why* it is slipping. Here are some questions you might consider based on issues that have already been raised in earlier chapters (especially Chapter 4):

*Are the section objectives clear to the team?*

If the objectives are not clear then time will be wasted on irrelevant activities. Furthermore, when this waste becomes clear to the person involved, he or she is then likely to be demoralized about the work and feel less committed to future tasks fearing that they too will turn out to be a waste of time.

*Are the team members committed to the project?*

This commitment should have been gained early in the project by their involvement in the planning stage, but it needs to be nurtured throughout.

*Do the staff accept their targets as realistic?*

By involving staff in the estimating stage the manager should have arrived at targets that are accepted as realistic. If their estimates were disregarded the staff may be unwilling to accept targets that are difficult to achieve. The targets must also take account of the technical skills.

*Do the staff believe their work is valued?*

If they do not think that the job they are doing is worthwhile they are unlikely to perform enthusiastically. If they think that no one notices the work they do then they will see less purpose in doing it well. People need rewards for good work – not necessarily financial. You may be surprised at the effect that buying someone a cup of coffee can have!

*Is training required?*

Many managers will be reluctant to 'waste' valuable project time training staff when they are needed on the job. Naturally, it would be better if the training requirement had been foreseen. Nevertheless, if the skills of the team are inadequate for the task in hand it is better to get them trained earlier rather than later. It is better to sacrifice a few weeks effort early in the project and have an effective team member for the whole life of that project than recognize the need too late and lose the same number of weeks at a later date and have an effective person for only half the project.

## Are technical standards set at an appropriate level?

If the standards are unnecessarily high then productivity may suffer. Worse still, standards may be disregarded if they are not respected as appropriate.

## Are people working on other things?

If there are other interesting activities to be done and there is no one to notice who is doing what, then members of the team may be doing things which are quite irrelevant to the project. Some policing is unfortunately necessary.

## Should more work be subcontracted?

Possibly too much of the work on the project is being undertaken directly in-house. The extent of subcontracting will have been decided at the planning stage but if the project is slipping then perhaps more could be subcontracted. There are communication problems here, as when adding any extra staff, but if the subcontracted work can be identified as packages which are as self-contained as possible it may relieve the burden on other staff. This is offset by an additional administrative burden.

## Should the scope of work be reduced?

The scope of work may include optional items, or items that could be delivered as a second stage. The contract with the client may be negotiable. Perhaps a phased delivery can be agreed.

## Are changes being made too frequently?

Changes during the project are very necessary to ensure that the client's requirements are met as closely as possible, but they can be a great hindrance. Perhaps the review procedures, discussed in Chapter 6, should be tightened so that only changes that are absolutely necessary are accepted.

You might notice that very few of these questions can be answered by a manager who uses only written reports and formal reviews to assess the situation. Most effective managers spend at least half their time in less formal ways, talking to the people working on the project, discussing their problems, helping them plan how to overcome them, fostering co-operation between team members and showing appreciation of their efforts. The project manager needs to find out what the members of the team think are the reasons for slippage and whether they have any remedies. Remedies that come from the team itself are more likely to be acceptable than remedies imposed from outside.

If the answers to the above questions suggest that very little can be done to improve matters then the project plan will have to be updated. Perhaps the project is slipping because of factors outside the manager's control, such as late deliveries from suppliers or subcontractors. Possibly the original estimates were too optimistic. This is not an unusual situation but, as discussed in Chapter 2, you should try to see that the mistake is not repeated by ensuring that data from this project are used to improve the estimates for future projects.

## 5.4.6  Summary

The methods that are available for maintaining the schedule include: updating the project network diagram to show completed and partially completed activities; milestone tracking to show how the dates of milestones move throughout the project; calculating slippage from earned value BCWS and BCWP curves. The value of combining all BCWS, ACWP, and BCWP on a single graph was demonstrated together with other graphic displays such as graphs of ECAC and ECD.

Having studied this section you should now be able to:

- show how to use an updated network to estimate a new project completion date

- describe and use a milestone tracking graph

- use earned value curves to compute a schedule variance and deduce slippage

- interpret the meaning of a set of earned value curves and interpret other forms of graphic display.

# 6 MANAGING QUALITY AND CHANGE

## *INTRODUCTION*

Chapter 5 looked at two major aspects of project execution: managing progress – measuring how much work has been done and how much money has been spent – and controlling progress – comparing what *has* happened with what *should* happen and making adjustments in order to keep on track.

This chapter looks at two further major aspects of project execution: maintaining quality and dealing with the inevitable changes that arise during the life-cycle of every project.

Perhaps we should start with a reminder of the definition of quality, as used in such standards as BS 5750 and its international equivalent, the ISO 9000 series. The following definition is given in BS 4778 and used in subsequent standards:

> quality: The totality of features and characteristics of a product or service that bear on its ability to satisfy stated or implied needs.
>
> (BS 4778)

*Change* is, as we have said, inevitable. It can involve substitution, for example of one component for another; alteration, for example change made to a design for the purpose of improving marketability of a product; additions, where the client may want more features or functions; or deletions – as costs mount the client may decide to eliminate a desirable but not strictly necessary feature or function in order to save money. The need to make changes can also arise due to unforeseen circumstances revealing themselves in the course of project work – new legislation, for example.

Chapter 5 ended with a discussion of creeping slippage on schedules: the sort that accumulates one day at a time until, if unnoticed, it can reach substantial proportions. Change can behave in the same way. Minor changes can accumulate quickly, and if not controlled properly, can have a serious – even disastrous – impact on schedules, cost or even the ability to complete the project. This chapter addresses the problem of controlling change.

## Aims and objectives

After studying this chapter you should be able to:

- explain the purpose of a quality review and how it is conducted
- describe the mechanics of auditing a project
- explain the reasons for requiring change control

- explain how the conduct of a project is affected by the use of configuration management
- explain the terms configuration control, configuration identification, configuration status accounting and configuration auditing
- identify the components that need to be handled in a formal manner to avoid uncontrolled change
- ask questions of a designer to identify likely change control problems
- outline the functions necessary to maintain adequate change control on a project.

# 6.1  *MAINTAINING THE QUALITY*

This section is about maintaining the quality during the execution of the project. It is the first of three sections on quality issues. Sections 3 and 4 are concerned with the causes and effects of change on a project and a method of handling it called configuration management.

We assume that plans have been prepared as described in Chapter 3. We now want to examine the quality activities after the project launch and see how they might be performed. In the first part of this section we will try to keep the discussion general, giving principles that you might expect to apply to many kinds of project, but especially to those that include a 'design' element. The second part of the section will illustrate quality principles as applied to software production. Although this second part is based on software there are lessons to be learnt from it for many other types of project, particularly those that deliver a 'soft' product, such as a new system, a document or a service. The section concludes with a discussion of auditing methods.

## 6.1.1  Monitoring quality

Quality is monitored by reviewing and testing what has been produced. A **quality review** is a review of the quality of some part of the work. Earlier in the project there will have been quality reviews of the requirements, the estimates and the plan. (These reviews could have been conducted using any of the methods listed here.) Once into execution there will be reviews of the work in progress and testing of finished products. A prime example is the design review, described below, necessary in all projects that have a design phase.

Less formal methods are walk-throughs and inspections. In a **walk-through** the originator of a product such as a design document or program code supplies copies of the product to reviewers for familiarization and then 'walks them through' it at an informal review. The reviewers make comments to the originator about any errors or problems they discover in the course of the walk-through. These are then discussed by the group. In an **inspection** a colleague or colleagues of the producer of some product inspect the product in detail and pass their comments directly to the originator. This course, for example, used a team of critical readers to comment on drafts of the materials as they were produced. This is a form of inspection.

Most products may be tested directly to see if they do what they are supposed to do. Often it is possible to test components of the final product at various stages. Software is a good example: a high proportion of the effort that goes into a software product will go into its testing, described in more detail in Section 2.2. 'Hard' products or components can be tested, using those methods and tests most suitable in each case. These can range from visual inspection of materials and components to the use of elaborate simulations, test 'harnesses' and 'beds' and highly technical inspection methods using sampling, X-ray, ultrasound or tomography. What is required will be dictated by the material, component or product, by the technological risk if it fails and by cost and time constraints.

# Design review

> A design review is a formal documented, comprehensive and systematic examination of a design to evaluate the design requirements and the capability of the design to meet these requirements and to identify problems and propose solutions.
>
> (BS 4778)

The primary function of the **design review** is to provide the client and the contractor's management with information about design status and identified problem areas. With this information, the client and the contractor's management can make decisions about approving production or can explore alternatives; project staff can use the information to evaluate changes to specifications and establish test programmes.

We see from this that a design review is a distinct type of meeting with a different purpose from the regular progress review meetings. Its purpose is to test the technical quality of the work done.

Design reviews are usually conducted as a series of formal meetings during the design phase of the project. In addition to the primary objective of ensuring that requirements will be met and no design weaknesses will jeopardize the project, there are some more specific objectives to be borne in mind. Design reviews should attempt to confirm that the optimum (or at least a perfectly satisfactory) design approach which will meet the requirements will be achieved. They should also attempt to identify and confirm the final design as a basis for later production and seek to avoid errors that will cause problems in later fabrication or use of the product.

A design review is held at the end of an important phase of the design work, before the next phase begins. It will probably start with a presentation by one or more team members, describing their work. Criticism and comment from other team members will then be used to examine the quality of the design.

Reviews can range from simple to complex and expensive – from two or three key people meeting semi-informally to a highly formal meeting involving a dozen or more people. The outcome of a design review will be a summary showing which aspects of a design have been accepted as satisfactory and which problems have still to be resolved, specifically:

- a list of design items approved
- lists of tasks to be completed
- preparation of data for design changes
- reports of action items to correct deficiencies in design.

The design review *may* suggest approaches to solving the outstanding problems but the reviewers should be discouraged from spending too much time finding solutions during the meeting. Rather than finding solutions the meeting should identify people who will be responsible for solving the problems.

## Who should attend?

The project manager should attend and probably chair the meetings. If the project is so large that it has to be partitioned into subprojects then this role would probably be taken by the manager of the subproject. A design review co-ordinator may be appointed where the meeting is large, or where smaller meetings are frequent. The other attendees constitute a design review board: the person(s) responsible for the design and other specialists in design, testing, producibility, quality, reliability, logistics. It is preferable that they have contributed in some direct way to the aspect of design under review.

The presence of peers from other project teams can often be used as a catalyst for a fruitful exposure of deficiencies. Many project managers regard the presence of these outsiders as essential.

The satisfactory completion of a thorough design review is a signal that the project can proceed to the next phase. Therefore, an important aspect of any design review is the corrective action items that result. To note this in an unambiguous way, the minutes of such a meeting must be recorded carefully and completely, and identify clearly individuals and dates for action items, and be distributed to all interested parties.

In addition to minutes, the person chairing the meeting should write and distribute a *design review report* after each design meeting. The writer should include a list of attendees, a synopsis of the decisions or results of the review, any corrective action items and the names of those responsible for them, and a schedule for completing action items. This should also be sent to all participants.

### SAQ 6.1

What are the differences in the timing, the team composition and the subject matter of a progress review and a quality review?

Probably second only to getting the requirements right, the design phase of a project is critical to the success of the project. Getting the design phase right greatly increases the chances of producing a satisfactory, indeed, 'good' product. A careful and frequent review at all stages and in all phases of design greatly increases the chances of ending with the 'right' and 'good' product at the end of the project.

It is at the design phase that value engineering becomes crucial. Each item of the design needs to be examined to determine whether it gives optimum value. Is this aspect over-specified, given the parameters of the requirements, or will it produce a satisfactory product? Is this the *best* option here, or is there a better one? The answer to questions like these depends, of course, on what the requirements specify and what options are available to the designers.

Finally, the early review of design is likely to reduce the possibility of intractable or difficult problems arising during later phases of the project. It is easier, and cheaper, to correct a fault at the design stage than it is to carry out the same correction later, when considerable rework may be required.

### SAQ 6.2

What aspects of a project is a preliminary design review likely to look at?

# 6.1.2 Software quality

The previous subsection outlined a general approach to assuring quality in the execution phase of any kind of project. In this section we will illustrate these general principles by showing their application to software projects. We will discuss first what we mean by software quality and secondly how we might ensure that we get it in a project.

# The meaning of 'software quality'

The standard methodology approved by the British government for the management of software projects is called PRINCE. We shall be reviewing PRINCE in more detail in the final chapter of this book but it is appropriate to anticipate what it says about quality at this point. The PRINCE quality guide expresses quality entirely in terms of the *user's requirements*:

> A product of an acceptable (or high) quality will conform to all of the [user's] requirements; a product of an unacceptable (or low) quality will conform to only some or none of those requirements.

(CCTA, 1993)

It seems to be commonly agreed that the quality that matters is what the user requires. However, this still leaves room for a lot of acrimonious debate unless the requirements are well specified in the first place. Some quality definitions use the word 'expectations' in place of requirements. Clearly such a definition will work very nicely from the client's point of view but it is virtually impossible for a project manager to commit to fulfilling expectations unless those expectations can be made explicit in terms of precise requirements that can be tested. This is not to say that requirements cannot be changed. The requirements specified at the contract stage may not be the same as the client's real requirements at the end of the project. This need for change will be discussed later in this chapter.

The problem of how to measure software quality is discussed by Wesselius and Ververs (1990). Wesselius and Ververs identify three components of quality: part which is objectively assessable, part which is only subjectively assessable and part which cannot be assessed at all. Clearly it is desirable from everybody's point of view that as many as possible of the user's expectations should be defined in terms of objectively assessable requirements.

Requirements may be classified into two types: functional and non-functional.

*Functional requirements* express what the software will do. For example: 'the supervisor must be able to retrieve from the employee database the hours worked for all staff reporting to him/her'. Such requirements may be at various levels of detail and should be hierarchically broken down, so that more detailed functional requirements are components of higher level functional requirements such as: 'records must be accessible based on a number of staff parameters'. Functional requirements may be easier to express in precise terms than non-functional requirements.

*Non-functional requirements* are requirements such as the need for the software to be easy to maintain. These are more difficult to pin down, but help in specifying these requirements may be provided by using **software metrics**. A metric is a numerical measure of some quality of the software which might otherwise seem subjective. For example, you might wish to specify that software should be easy to maintain, but ease of maintenance is not something we readily attach a number to. Instead, you could specify it in terms of measurable quantities that you know to be correlated with it, such as complexity. Complexity metrics *do* exist. A complexity metric might be measured by a software tool that applied certain defined tests to that software.

---

## ACTIVITY 6.1

Suggest how you might devise a metric for ease of use of a piece of software.

## DISCUSSION

A metric for *ease of use* might be specified by measuring the performance of users of the software in comparison with their performance on other software with similar capability. For example you might measure the time taken for experienced operators to perform a given list of operations on the system.

The subject of 'usability' metrics for software is now a rapidly expanding one, and is an area of active research.

---

# Testing for software quality

Testing is an integral part of software development. It needs to take place at all stages so that faults are found as early as possible and the cost of rectification is minimized. Bennatan (1992) lists the following types of test that are applied to software:

- unit testing
- integration testing
- subsystem testing
- system testing
- regression testing
- alpha testing
- beta testing
- acceptance testing

These tests have been listed roughly in the order in which they will occur. This is also an order that represents an increasing size of scope of the test being conducted.

Software testing is complicated by the fact that four distinct aspects need to be tested:

- it functions as required
- it is as correct as possible (errors are found and eliminated – 'debugging')
- it performs as required: it is robust enough, fast enough and efficient enough to meet requirements now and for the foreseeable life of the product
- it is usable by its intended users.

These may seem self-evident, but it is perfectly possible to have software that is logically correct but doesn't function as required, or to have software that functions as required but isn't robust or doesn't operate fast enough. An example is provided by the London Ambulance Service case study in Chapter 1. Although the developers had trouble getting the function right they largely solved the problem. However, the system contained a very simple error that caused it to fail disastrously after a few days, nor was it robust enough to withstand the failure of one of its components: the file server. It was also too slow for peak requirements and had very serious usability problems.

### Unit testing

Unit testing is the testing that a programmer performs on his or her own code during the development of a unit or module. As far as possible the programmer will want to ensure that the unit behaves as required and conforms to good programming practice. A unit test is limited in scope because it requires a test harness to artificially represent the software with which it will eventually be combined. The unit test is the lowest level test and therefore the most detailed. The programmer should be able to ensure that as much of the code within the unit as possible is exercised. This testing may require special code to be added to the unit for diagnostic purposes that is later removed or rendered inactive (a practice called *instrumenting*).

### Integration testing

Integration testing is the testing that takes place when units or modules are combined with other modules to make larger modules. This testing concentrates on the interfaces between the units to ensure that they work correctly together. It is worth noting that a mismatch between what one unit expects of another should have been identified at the design review stage. Integration testing will nevertheless reveal those occasions when the review has inadvertently allowed a mismatch to slip through.

### Subsystem testing

Subsystem testing is the testing of definable parts of the whole system which are sufficiently self-contained for their functions to be realistically tested in the absence of other subsystems. Not all software is developed in subsystems but where they have been specified it is likely that different subsystems will have been produced by different teams of people. Each subsystem has a formal set of requirements to meet and tests at this stage concentrate on whether each subsystem meets its own specification.

### System testing

System testing is the first testing of the completely integrated software and hardware. It can be fully tested against the requirements specification using the tests that should have been developed during the project in conjunction with the users. Robustness and speed of execution will be measured at this stage. These are factors that are difficult to estimate with precision at earlier stages. Once all software and hardware has been integrated it is possible to ensure that the speed of response to an operator is adequate, that the rate of working overall will meet the requirements and that the system is robust enough for its intended peak loads and is unlikely to fail catastrophically.

### Regression testing

Regression testing means going back over tests that have been performed satisfactorily at an earlier stage but which now need to be redone because of changes that have been made either to the module itself or to modules with which it interfaces. It is useful to have a range of automated standard tests which can be very rapidly repeated when it is expected that virtually every test should be passed without trouble.

*Alpha and beta testing*

Alpha testing is the final stage of system testing before the system can be released for real users to try. Beta testing is the stage where the system can be used by real users but in an exploratory way, to ensure that they are happy with its behaviour before they become committed to using it in routine fashion.

It is at this stage that 'usability' is most severely tested. Typically there would need to be special support for trials at this stage so that in the event of faults appearing the user has expertise available to overcome the sort of teething problems that may be expected.

Acceptance testing is the formal testing against agreed criteria for the fulfilment of the contract between the developer and the client. These tests are not expected to find further faults but are expected to confirm that the developer has fulfilled all obligations.

### SAQ 6.3

Why might it be necessary to perform regression testing of units after they have been integrated with others?

## Validation and verification

The terms *validation* and *verification* are used to distinguish two rather different kinds of activity in quality assessment. Validation is the process of checking that a product is what the client requires, whereas verification checks that the product produced at one stage conforms to the specification that was supplied to it, not necessarily in the form of a user requirement. For example, one validation activity may be to invite the client to send some typical users to check that they are happy to work with some particular method of inputting data. A verification activity at this stage would check that the way the data was to be put in accorded with the design specification.

Boehm translated these terms into:

Verification: 'Are we building the product right?'

Validation: 'Are we building the right product?'

(Boehm, 1981, p. 37)

## Planning for testing

The tests that are to be conducted, the purpose, the people, the procedures and the resources all need to be planned for in advance. As testing has a high user involvement the availability of users to specify or perform the testing needs to be planned with the client. Ince, Sharp and Woodman (1993) suggest that the following information should be contained in most test plans:

- the objectives of each kind of test
- the criteria determining when a particular testing phase is complete, e.g. when integration testing is complete
- the test schedule
- individual responsibilities

- resources required:

  support software, including testing tools

  hardware configuration

  the amount of computer time

  personnel

- testing strategy, including procedures for:

  identifying, generating and documenting test cases

  tracking progress

  stress testing the software

  reporting and correcting detected errors

  regression testing

- documentation produced

- test procedures

(Ince, Sharp and Woodman, 1993)

This list may raise a few questions. Why should we need criteria for when to regard a particular testing phase as complete? The obvious answer might seem to be that testing is complete when no more faults can be found. The trouble with this answer is that it is *impossible* to say when the last fault has been found because you cannot know that another will not be found tomorrow. Hence some criterion is needed which reflects the importance of diminishing the estimated number of undiscovered faults to as few as possible, balanced against the likely testing effort required to find another fault. Testing to ensure perfection is impossible.

Another item needing explanation is **stress testing**. This kind of testing means subjecting the software to stresses beyond the performance required in normal use. If an enquiry system is intended to be able to respond to 10 requests per minute the tester might subject it to a request rate of 20, 50 or 100 requests per minute to see whether it behaved acceptably. An orderly queue building up might be acceptable but random acceptance of the requests might not be. Severe stress testing (until the software fails under the load) will indicate what are the maximum parameters under which it will operate in an acceptable way and what behaviour it will exhibit when it fails.

## Who does the testing?

There are several candidates for the job of testing: the software designer, the programmer who wrote the code, other members of the software development team, an independent test team and users, or technical people from the client's organization. You might use these different candidates in different ways at different phases of the testing.

At the unit testing stage it is usually the programmer who does the testing initially, especially while the code is still subject to frequent correction as a result of the testing. The programmer knows the structure of the unit and can devise tests that will exercise the program to the fullest possible extent. Also, the efficiency of detecting a fault, correcting it and retesting is likely to be higher at this stage if just one person is involved. Then there is a human factor to consider: the satisfaction to the programmer of producing tested units rather than units which have faults which someone else will discover.

However, the programmer lacks independence and the same weakness that caused an error to exist in the program may also cause that error not be tested for. There is also the problem that, unconsciously, many programmers design tests to show that the module they have written *works*, and such tests tend to find fewer errors than if the tester sets out, instead, to 'break' the module in order to reveal as many errors as possible. So once the programmer believes that the software is ready for integration it is advisable to scrutinize it independently. This scrutiny is ideally supplied by someone who has been trained for this purpose. An independent team of testers will develop skills in testing so that they will find more of the errors more quickly. They should also have been trained to present their test results in a way that will not cause ill-feeling in the programmer concerned. Whether such a team is available to the project or not, someone with a quality assurance role (not necessarily in a QA department) should sign off the documents that show which tests have been performed and the outcome of those tests. The documentation should be so arranged that those same tests can be replicated if necessary.

### SAQ 6.4

(a) Complete Table 6.1 below by indicating whether a particular type of test will certainly or possibly test that aspect of software quality. We have completed one column using two ticks (✓✓) for certainly, one tick (✓) for possibly and a cross (✗) for not at all to show you what is wanted.

**TABLE 6.1**  Test type and quality aspect

| Quality | Unit test | Integration test | Subsystem test | Alpha test | Beta test |
|---|---|---|---|---|---|
| function | ✓✓ | | | | |
| correctness | ✓✓ | | | | |
| performance | ✗ | | | | |
| usability | ✗ | | | | |

(b) We have left regression testing out of Table 6.1. Can you think why?

## Preserving the quality

There is a danger that further modifications to tested software undermine the quality of that software. Any modification, no matter how trivial, invalidates the testing to the item, so that it is no longer possible to guarantee that this software passes the tests. To avoid this danger the tested software, whether at the unit level or after integration with other modules, should become an item under **configuration management**. This means that it is an identifiable object that will subsequently be changed only after proper procedures have been carried out. We will discuss configuration management in detail in Section 4.

## 6.1.3  Auditing a project

*The main aim of an audit is to reduce uncertainty.*

An **audit** is an official examination. Although the most commonly known type of audit is a financial audit – an official examination of the accounts of an organization – this is not the kind of audit with which we are concerned here. In project work we are most often concerned with two types of audit: a general project audit to determine the status of the project and a quality audit to determine how closely the processes adhere to standards and how closely the products match the user's requirements. (The term *audit* implies a degree of formality. However, an incoming project manager taking over an existing project would normally need to conduct an informal audit of the project to check its status.)

A **project audit**, in contrast to a financial audit, is an appraisal of the technical status of a project, or a specified part of a project, and will most usually be performed during a project rather than at its end. A project audit is performed by an independent auditing body external to the project team, it is conducted in a formal and systematic manner, and its object is to assess the project's current status and future prospects in comparison with the project requirements.

The **quality audit** is a planned examination of all or part of a project by:

- determining whether practices conform to specified standards
- critical analysis of the deliverable that is the result.

It differs from a project audit in that its focus is on adherence to standards and the QA aspects of the project. It is usually carried out for the specific purpose of checking that quality standards are being applied when:

- a quality problem is suspected, and a manager would appreciate a fresh look at the area by an impartial observer
- a company's business requirements are such that it must be registered as conforming to an external standard (e.g. the BSI). This may be to conform with the client's requirements, such as conditions for tendering for government contracts. In such cases internal audits are necessary to prepare the company for audits by the registering body.

In what follows we shall not distinguish between a project audit and a quality audit because, although the quality audit is aimed specifically at quality standards, *both kinds of audit contribute to quality*. The purpose of the project audit is, in the end, to ensure that the project achieves quality by producing the correct end-product for the agreed price, with work completed according to the agreed schedule. It takes a wider view than design or progress reviews, looking not just at one deliverable or one aspect of the project, but at the totality of work carried out up to the time of the audit, the work that *ought* to have been done and the work remaining to be done. It compares what it finds to what it expected, based on the contract and its supporting documents and makes recommendations on how any deviation can be corrected. Thus a project audit helps ensure that the project produces what it should.

## Who does the auditing?

Auditors must be *independent* from and *external* to the group being audited so that there can be no accusation of bias nor temptation to justify the *status quo*. Their function is to discover the truth. Auditing usually requires a small team, typically about three or four highly skilled people, but the team may be larger if the audit is a big one or it may consist of just one person, say the quality manager. Although auditors must be external to the *group* being audited they need not be external to the *organization*. Audits can be either internal or external.

The auditors need to be mature people who will be convinced only by arguments supported by evidence. Yet they need to be sensitive to the feelings of the people whose area is being audited. It is very uncomfortable for the people being audited to have their work examined so closely by outsiders. The auditors therefore have to be able to gain co-operation and respect.

Chilstrom (1983) suggests requirements for prospective members of an auditing team. Criteria in the selection process would generally include but not be limited to the following:

- specialist or generalist (an audit team needs a good mix)
- must have professional acceptance at all levels
- technical competence in specialized areas
- analytical mind, articulate, and personable
- writing ability
- listening ability
- maturity and adaptability
- line or staff supervisor experience
- no project involvement – to increase objectivity
- enthusiasm for and support of the audit assignment.

In addition to Chilstrom's list we would add that, above all, the auditors must have the determination to uncover the truth and the integrity to report it honestly and impartially.

## When to audit

An audit is usually a short, sharp exercise. It could take as little as a day but more typically takes about two weeks of investigative work together with another week or so for preparations and for reporting afterwards.

The audit may arise in various ways. It may have been planned at the outset of the project. If a project is technically or managerially complex the need for an audit may have been identified at the contract stage to satisfy both the client and the contractor that the project is not exposed to excessive risk in its later, usually more expensive, stages. Alternatively, an audit may not have been planned but arises when the requester wants to establish project status, perhaps because the project appears to be in difficulty, or because of a change of ownership, or perhaps because the project manager feels an audit is required. The request will often come from a concerned client, worried that a late project will mean financial loss, but may also be requested by other parties who have some stake in the outcome. The right of a party to call for an audit may be written into the contract.

The project is usually in progress. An audit is more useful as a tool for assessing the progress of a current project than for reporting on the achievements of a completed one. Unlike a financial audit, project auditors are often expected to make recommendations or at least to clarify the status. The future conduct of the project may be materially affected by the auditors' actions.

The timing of an audit depends very much on the circumstances. If it is a planned audit it will probably follow the end of a key phase of the project. An unplanned audit may be required at any time. The only general rule seems to be that an early audit of a project is likely to be much more useful than a late audit because there is then much more time in which to make use of the auditors' work. Note the contrast here with the usual financial audit that might be expected at the end of a project. This does not mean that an audit, or evaluation, at the end of a project may not be useful for the future conduct of other projects (see Section 5).

An audit is expected to reveal not only *current* status but also likely *future* prospects so that the recommendations of the report can influence the future conduct of the project. An essential feature of the audit is the *comparison* with project requirements; the auditors have to consider not only the current status but also the project's expectations as expressed in the contract.

## How is auditing done?

An audit is *formal* and *systematic*. It will be initiated formally and conducted with a prescribed scope, to produce a report within a given time. Systematic methods ensure that the conclusions of the report are properly justified as confirmed fact, free from subjective judgements.

- The audit must be focused on a particular topic (a process, procedure or deliverable).

- The criteria against which the audit is to be made must be identified.

- The audit team must be properly briefed and must be given access to all relevant documents and personnel.

- The audit team must be given adequate time and resources to produce a proper report, but reports should be prepared within an agreed timescale.

- There should be no prior indication from management as to what results they expect.

- The report from the audit team should be reviewed with the relevant managers (project manager, general manager, quality manager).

- Any disagreements should be recorded in the report or, if these are a result of error, the report should be corrected.

An audit may be considered to consist of the following six phases (described in more detail in Chilstrom's paper):

- Phase 1: initiation and planning – agree the purpose, constraints, terms of reference.

- Phase 2: establish project baseline – what was expected at this point according to the contract and all agreed changes.

- Phase 3: investigation – gather the facts and record where they have come from.

- Phase 4: analysis – try to draw conclusions from the data.

- Phase 5: report and present conclusions – report to the requester of the audit and other parties as agreed at the outset.

- Phase 6: termination – evaluate the audit.

### SAQ 6.5

What are the features of an audit that distinguish it from:

(a) a visit by senior management

(b) a major design review

(c) a progress report

(d) a project evaluation after termination?

# 6.1.4 Summary

This section concerned the actions that the project manager and others can take to maintain the quality of the project during the execution stage. (At an earlier phase a quality policy and quality activities were put in place, ensuring well-defined requirements, sensible estimates and good planning.)

At the execution phase we are concerned with products that are being or have been produced. The most important activity is the quality review, of which the prime example is a design review. Other activities include testing, walk-throughs and inspections.

The conduct of a design review was described in detail. Maintaining the quality of software production was used as an example.

Auditing a project was described: a general audit determines the status of a project and a quality audit determines how closely the products match the user's needs.

Having studied this section you should now be able to:

- outline the activities performed to maintain quality during the execution phase of a project

- describe the conduct of a design review

- differentiate between a progress review and a quality review

- illustrate quality monitoring with specific examples on software quality

- explain the value of a metric

- outline the various kinds of testing that may be performed for software (and similar products)

- describe a project audit and a quality audit, explain how they differ, how, when and why they are done and by whom.

# 6.2 CHANGE: CAUSE AND EFFECTS

This section discusses two kinds of change: those that have obvious external impact and those that appear to be internal to the project. Changes may be called external if they directly affect the contract with the client: the need for their control is self-evident. Changes which are internal affect the working relationship between members of the project team. This section establishes the need to control not only the first kind of change but also the second.

The consequences of a change can be out of proportion to the actual change made. A small change in the user's requirements late in a project may mean a radical rethink by a top-level designer. The consequence of a change of design at the top level is amplified in the lower-level design and construction work. An experienced designer should perhaps be able to anticipate some requests but there is a limit to how much tolerance to change can be built in. Later in the project it may be necessary to make changes at a low level in the design very quickly so that the project meets it schedule.

If there is a large amount of uncontrolled change the result is lost effort. This contributes not only to overspending on the project but also to poor morale in the project team. Change for which no plans or provision of resources have been made can also adversely affect the allocation and utilization of resources, for example by causing unexpected and expensive reworking.

The effects of some changes may not be apparent until long after the project has been completed. An undocumented change can lead to chaos later.

All this sounds depressing and some project managers may react by attempting to ban all change. However, in spite of the difficulties, it is impractical to prevent change, whether external or internal. The answer is to organize the management, development team, testers, the users' representatives and the client in some way in order to cope with the effects of change and to minimize its disruptive impact; this is **change control**.

A change control system should include the following elements:

- a *base*, defining the current state of the item, to which any change is referred
- a means for submitting proposals for change
- a mechanism for evaluating the impact of the change, including cost, time and effects on others
- a decision-making authority to approve or reject
- a method of recording the approved (or rejected) change
- a method for publishing the change
- a means of monitoring the implementation of the change.

The use of change control is appropriate to all projects concerned with developing products, particularly those that are large or complex or both. All projects will employ *some* kind of change control, even if it is not known by that name, with varying degrees of success. However, it is important that the correct type and amount of change control be employed: for large projects extensive, strict and formal control will be required; for smaller projects a minimal amount of control may be indicated, conducted informally.

# 6.2.1 Changes to project deliverables (external changes)

Proposals for changes to project deliverables will usually arise because the client now wants something different from what was previously agreed. The proposal for change may come from within the project team because a team member thinks that the client's needs have changed or because the original proposal is not cost-effective.

Initially, neither those who want the project performed nor those who undertake it fully understand each others' needs. Furthermore, despite efforts to keep fixed what the project is to achieve, new facets requiring development are always uncovered during its execution. These two factors naturally lead to changes in the project's aim, which in turn result in changes to its design and implementation. Often the designers and clients understand the requirements fully only when most of the deliverables have been produced. At this late stage the effects of changes can be enormous.

It is quite common for some change in the project's external environment to occur: the market for the product changes, a new technique or a new component becomes available, resources required may not materialize, a machine that was to be purchased is no longer manufactured. The changed environment may imply a changed aim, a change in the design, a change in the way of working or even cancellation.

Nearly all project managers recognize the need to cater for these changes because they have an obvious impact on the project scope and the payment to be received from the client. A mechanism for handling them should be agreed between client and contractor as part of the contract.

There is usually a standard form for the purpose of requesting and approving changes to a project, such as that shown in Figure 6.1. The form has space allocated for subsequent stages of the approval process. Harrison says that it should contain the following information:

1. It identifies the change, describes it and gives the cost account, work package or cost control number it affects.

2. It gives the reason for the change.

3. It identifies who is initiating or requesting the change and provides for that person's signature.

4. It gives a first descriptive appreciation of the consequences of the change and the segments of the project it affects.

5. It gives a rough estimate of the effect on the project schedule.

6. It gives an order of cost estimate of its effect on cost.

7. It can optionally give a code number to identify the cause of the change for post-project analysis, for example: customer request, late design change, error/omission in design, legal, environmental reasons, increase in economic return.

(Harrison, 1992, p. 206)

```
┌─────────────────────────────────────────────────────────────┐
│ CHANGE REQUEST                                                │
│ PROJECT:                      Number: _____ │
│                               Revision: _____ │
│                               Date: _____ │
│                                                               │
│ ITEM AFFECTED:                Name: _____ │
│                               Work package: _____ │
│                               Item no(s): _____ │
│                               Change requested by: _____ │
│                                                               │
│ DESCRIPTION OF CHANGE:                                        │
│                                                               │
│                                                               │
│                                                               │
│ REASON FOR CHANGE:            Code: _____ │
│                                                               │
│                                                               │
│                                                               │
│ ITEMS/AREAS AFFECTED BY CHANGE:                               │
│                                                               │
│                                                               │
│                                                               │
│ INITIAL ESTIMATE OF COST/SAVING* _____  FIRM ESTIMATE: ___ │
│ Effect on schedule:                                           │
│                                                               │
│                                                               │
│ REMARKS:                                                      │
│                                                               │
│                                                               │
│                                                               │
│ CHANGE APPROVED/REJECTED*                                     │
│                                                               │
│ Contractor's signature: _____  Date: _____ │
│ Client's signature: _____  Date: _____ │
│ *Delete one                                                   │
└─────────────────────────────────────────────────────────────┘
```

**FIGURE 6.1** A typical change request form (Harrison, 1992, p. 207)

Once approved the change needs to be incorporated in the plans and budgets. For example the earned value system discussed in Chapter 5 will need an amendment to the BCWS otherwise the work performed will be compared with an inappropriate plan. Too often you see exaggerated reports of projects which have overspent, with the implied criticism that the project management has been ineffective. These reports may be unfair to the project manager if it is the client who has decided that new requirements should be introduced and a revised budget has been agreed. It has to be clearly on the record that the impact of the change on cost and time has been approved by the client.

# 6.2.2 Internal changes

Internal changes are often not as tightly controlled as external changes. By internal changes we mean changes that are confined to the internal work of the project: apparently not requiring consultation with the client because the agreed deliverables are unaffected. For example, it may be found necessary to correct mistakes or desirable to make improvements in designs that may have been thought complete.

Consider for example a software project that uses a 'top-down, stepwise refinement' method of development. This means that the aim of the project is defined first, the outline design is produced next (high-level design), followed by successive design levels down to the detailed technical information before construction begins. In principle, the top-level designers conceive the whole design at once and divide it up with well-defined boundaries between all its components. But these top-level designers are fallible, and it is likely that revision of at least one level of the design will be needed for a project requiring more than a few months of effort. So the members of the development team generate change themselves as they realize, when attempting to expand a lower level of the design, that deficiencies in a higher level must be corrected before they can make progress.

Another internal change is simply the correction of earlier mistakes. It may not always be appreciated that correcting a mistake *is* making a change. The extent to which control over the correction of mistakes is required depends on how far the original defective item may have affected the work of others.

There are always interfaces between individual work areas and some overlap is unavoidable as a result of the interaction between components even in a hierarchical design. This leads to constant negotiation of the boundaries between the various work areas and difficulty in providing each team member with exactly the information required to carry out the job efficiently.

Design reviews help to keep a design coherent, but in order to keep the review team manageable, only the designers whose work area is under investigation will be involved. It would be a waste of people's time for the whole team to attend every review. Consequently, no one has a full understanding of the entire design. Changes will result from errors detected in the reviews and also during development work.

Change control is a form of communication. In a small project this can be informal and unstructured without undue risk of the message (the change) being lost or misinterpreted. However, a large project will require a formal, structured and documented method of communication. Even in the smallest projects it is essential that a record be kept of agreements between team members where the work of one affects another. Communication using electronic mail is good for this sort of agreement because of the ease with which a record is kept.

To illustrate the need for control over internal changes, Example 3.1 overleaf describes the progress of a typical software project in an organization which employed change control only over project deliverables.

## EXAMPLE 6.1  A defective internal change control procedure

The project was well defined, with a change control board to authorize all changes to the project deliverables. In the early stages, each team member was supplied with all the available information about the project, as the team was composed of only four people working in together to devise the initial, highest level of the project design. Frequent reviews of this top design level took place, using peer group review. At this stage, interaction between team members was personal, so the originator could communicate all that was known about the project to each team member and reviewer.

As the work progressed into successively lower levels of the design, the job became more complex as more components were developed and more information on both new and existing components was generated. More designers were assigned to the team (as planned) but consequently the personal interaction between all team members became difficult because of the greater number of people involved. No single person kept track of all the components being developed.

The project manager realized that communication between designers can absorb large proportions of productive time so he told them to keep control of their own work area and to disseminate information about the changes they made to other designers only as necessary. With pressing deadlines, the designers became less concerned with the performance of their colleagues and failed to communicate adequately with them about the changes they were making. They naturally put first priority on meeting targets for their own deliverables.

As the work progressed, there were about a dozen people working on the project, each of whom was responsible individually for ensuring that the changes they made did not adversely affect other people's work without prior agreement. However, in such an environment, nobody was quite sure what everybody else was doing or which version of each item of the design they were using. As the communication paths are numerous in any team of a significant size, the team spent a great deal of time communicating!

### A change co-ordinator

It soon became apparent that the team members could not retain a knowledge of their own work and disseminate it effectively to others, so frustration grew and lack of progress was blamed on changes by certain team members which affected others. The project manager asked for a volunteer to co-ordinate design changes by acting as a link between those requiring change and those from whom agreement was required. As the new co-ordinator could not possibly understand the entire system completely and the ramifications of each change, she could not present a full account of the requirements of each change to either party, which resulted in arbitrary and distorted decisions. Several months passed with no improvement and in consequence the unfortunate co-ordinator bore the brunt of all complaints. At this point she collapsed under the strain and left the project.

The point to note from Example 6.1 is that trying to communicate the effects of any change *after* it has taken place is insufficient: it is important that the effect of a change is understood before it occurs. The development team involved in that project would have had to go through a traumatic reorganization in order to re-establish control over changes that affected the project's internal conduct.

### SAQ 6.6

Do you think that the change control board proposed for change to project deliverables could have had its remit extended to include internal change? Justify your answer.

### ACTIVITY 6.2

Consider how changes are handled in your own area of work. Focusing on a particular piece of work, write down in your project notebook how a particular change is handled, including who initiates it, how its effects on cost and timescale are assessed and how approval is given to proceed. Assess the suitability of this process and whether it could be improved in the light of the previous discussion of the effects of uncontrolled change.

### ACTIVITY 6.3

How will a change in project scope affect the earned value system? Consider in particular what needs to be done about the value for the project budget and values for budgeted cost of work performed and scheduled, and hence the cost and schedule variances.

### DISCUSSION

The impact of the change on the cost and the timescale will have to be estimated before the change is approved. These changes will therefore be reflected in new values for the project budget and for all budgeted values and timings of components affected. Actual costs and progress are only fairly comparable with these new estimates.

When there are horrific reports in the press about amazing overruns in cost or time of a substantial project the comparison is often being made with the original project scope and timescale. Although such comparisons may be of interest politically, they more usually reflect the amount of change to the scope of the project that has occurred rather than the management of the project. This is not to say that the escalation of scope is not of interest, but the distinction needs to be made in fairness to the project manager.

# 6.2.3 Summary

Changes create problems for project managers but it is impractical to prohibit them. Changes that affect the project deliverables (external changes) are more often recognized than changes that affect only the internal conduct of the project (internal changes). Merely monitoring change is insufficient. External changes are often handled by setting up a change control board, with membership from both client and contractor, to agree the changes before implementation. Handling internal changes is often more difficult, partly because of the potential volume of internal change as designers see better ways to do things and partly because of the problem of knowing exactly how to apply change control procedures.

Having studied this section you should now be able to:

- explain the reasons for needing a system for change control
- list the elements which any change control system needs to contain
- outline the content of a suitable change control form and its purpose
- explain why internal changes affecting the interfaces between team members need just as much attention as external changes.

# 6.3  CONFIGURATION MANAGEMENT

This section outlines a formal method of change control called configuration management. This is a way of conducting a project so that changes from all levels can be handled.

## 6.3.1  An outline of configuration management

The term configuration management (CM) was originally applied to hardware systems such as the production of an aircraft. It is now increasingly used in change control systems for software and today this is probably the most significant area of its application. The phrase configuration management means the use of a management discipline designed to ensure that a system retains consistency between its components when parts of it are subject to change. Bersoff *et al.* (1980) give the following definition:

> ...the discipline of identifying the configuration of a system at discrete points in time for purposes of systematically controlling changes to this configuration and maintaining the integrity and traceability of this configuration throughout the system life cycle.

(p. 20)

Some people use the term *configuration management* as though it applied just to the specification of some product *after* it has been tested. The techniques of configuration management are then confined to ensuring the integrity of that product during its useful life. This is only a limited use of the techniques of configuration management. The definition given above includes the phrase 'throughout the system life cycle' and implies a much earlier introduction of configuration management into the process. If CM is used *throughout the life-cycle* it means that it starts as soon as there is any agreed document that will be used as the basis for later development work. It is this wider ranging use of the term configuration management that we will be assuming in this course.

The basic idea is that the components produced during the development of a project form a **configuration** of identifiable items which may be changed only in a systematically approved and recorded manner. The items can be sets of requirements, specifications, manuals, outlines for modules of software, drawings of pieces of hardware, plans for testing – in fact anything that can be identified and that contributes in any way to the end use of the project. The word *configuration* means the totality of these components and the interrelationship between them.

A key concept of configuration management is knowing which items in the configuration are dependent on a given item, as in Example 6.2.

## EXAMPLE 6.2

In the design of a refrigerator it is likely that the specification of the door handle is dependent on the specification of the door but is independent of the specification of many other parts of the refrigerator, such as the motor. Knowing this dependency will define the scope of the effects of changing any one item. Notice that in this example we have the used the phrase 'specification of the door handle' rather than just 'the door handle'. This is because we are usually interested in documents describing or defining an object rather than in the particular object itself.

The configuration is progressively built up as components are developed. At the beginning of a project the configuration consists of the documents specifying the scope of the project: the requirement specification. By definition, once this specification has been authorized as a component of the configuration it becomes subject to the change control procedures. (In a large project the requirements may consist of a set of items rather than a single item so that the requirements themselves can be subdivided.)

Notice that the configuration does not include components which are still in the process of formation. The burden of applying change control to a component while it was being actively developed would be too heavy. Thus, during the development process, the 'configuration' forms only part of all the existing design, as shown in Figure 6.2. The large box contains the items that are inside the configuration. These have been identified and their subsequent progress will be recorded. No changes to them will take place without authority. But outside the box there are components which are not yet part of the configuration because they are changing day by day and have not yet reached sufficient maturity to make change control appropriate.

We shall call the items *outside* the box **design objects** and the items *inside* the box **configuration items**. From a change control point of view we shall be concerned only with the configuration items: the designer still has freedom to manipulate design objects at will. It is the designer's own responsibility to keep track of changes to design objects, but no one else need know about such changes.

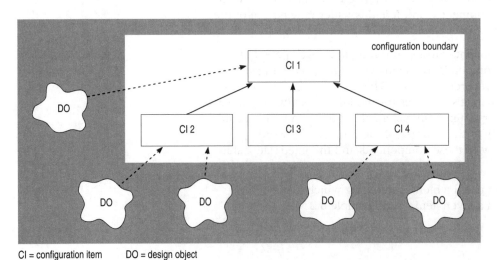

CI = configuration item     DO = design object

**FIGURE 6.2** Configuration items and design objects

It is particularly useful to have any interface agreements between members of a project team defined as configuration items. In the case of the refrigerator, if the door and its handle are being designed separately it would be sensible to get agreement first on exactly how the handle will fit to the door so that both the handle designer and the door designer can proceed independently. This agreed interface specification would become a configuration item that both designers could rely on not to be changed without their common agreement. The specification might need to be added to if other issues arose that needed agreement before design of one or other of the dependent components could proceed.

## Freezing?

Some people like to think of the transition from design object to configuration item as 'freezing' the object. It rightly conjures up the idea that the object is no longer fluid. However, freezing is a little *too* strong a term. Configuration items may *still* need to change, and under the discipline of configuration management they may still do so. The more appropriate phrase to describe their state is that they are 'under change control' rather than 'frozen'. For example, the refrigerator door handle designer may subsequently realize that the specification of the fixing interface gives a problem when she comes to select from a range of standard products. With the agreement of the door designer the interface specification can be changed provided that no other designer has since declared that they too are relying on that specification. All the designers who had declared that they relied on an item would need to be consulted.

### SAQ 6.7

(a) What is the difference between a design object and a configuration item?

(b) What is the advantage of allowing design objects to exist in the project system?

(c) What is the advantage of having an interface specification recorded as a configuration item separately from the complete specification of one or other of the components that use that interface?

(d) What is the latest stage at which you expect the requirements specifications to change from being design objects to being configuration items?

In answering SAQ 6.7 above you will have realized that a configuration management system must be set up at a very early stage in the project: ideally from the outset. It should then remain in existence throughout the life of the system which it describes, so that it can be used for maintenance until the system is dismantled.

## Constructing the configuration

Most projects are constructed hierarchically from the top downwards; that is, the highest-level design of the project is generated first, then divided into lower levels which are themselves subdivided. This method of design and construction applies to most physical objects and systems. Within each subdivision on each level of the hierarchy, items should be identified whose concept and implementation can be grasped by individual members of the project team. The design structure of the project is a natural basis for the choice of configuration items.

For example, Figure 6.3 shows the configuration hierarchy of an Open University course on project management. At the top are the course requirements which specify such things as the subject of the course, its aims and objectives, the overall length, its academic standard and position in the study programme. At this level there need be no mention of how individual topics are to be treated or what the structure of course should be. At the next level comes the course specification (produced by the course team) – it shows the structure of the course, the documents to be prepared and the topics to be covered within each unit. The arrow from the *course specification* to the *course requirements* shows that the *specification* is dependent on the *course requirements*. This means that if the course requirements were to change then there is a potential impact upon the specification. The meaning of an arrow from an item X to another item Y in Figure 6.3 means that item X 'uses', 'invokes' or 'relies upon' item Y, so that any change to Y potentially affects X.

The configuration below the course specification fans out into outline descriptions of each unit, typically documents of about a dozen typed pages, showing the proposed structure of the unit in terms of the topics to be considered in each section. Below this the structure fans out even further into the actual text for each section or a software item. The arrows from these outlines to the specification again mean that they depend only on this specification.

This purely hierarchical structure is an ideal which may not account for all the dependencies between items. For example there might need to be a dependency of the software package upon the text of Unit 3. This would be shown by as additional arrow from the Software Guide to the Unit 3 text. A dependency could be in both directions, which would mean that the two items depend upon each other. The complete configuration diagram could look very complicated with a large number of extra arrows showing the non-hierarchical links as well as the underlying simpler structure.

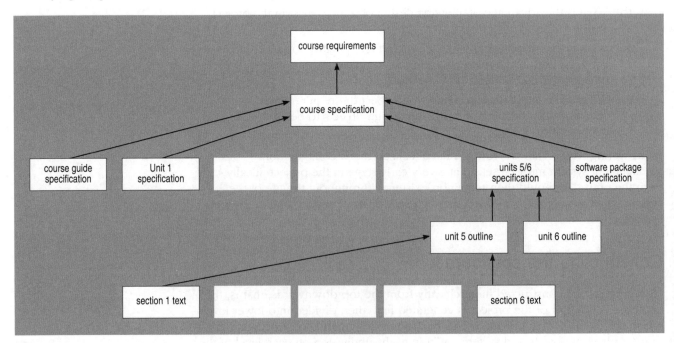

**FIGURE 6.3**  Configuration hierarchy for an Open University course

In practice a database rather than a diagram is required to record the structure. There are normally too many items to make a diagram intelligible. Computer tools such as Lifespan are available which not only can hold the data equivalent to this diagram but also provide the services required for change control, status accounting and auditing which we describe later. If we continue to use the term *configuration diagram* it is to be understood that the term embraces the equivalent information held in a database.

## SAQ 6.8

What is the implication of a dependency link upon the order of development of the items linked?

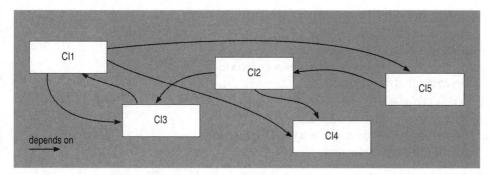

**FIGURE 6.4**   A non-hierarchical structure

The use of a design hierarchy such as Figure 6.3 is not a prerequisite for configuration management. Configurations can be set up in which there is no particular pattern to the structure, so that the relations are amorphous, as shown in Figure 6.4. The relationship between components in an amorphous structure is more difficult for a design team to comprehend, so some easily understood underlying structure, such as the tree of Figure 6.3 is preferred, even if this has to be supplemented by additional relationships.

When assessing the impact of change, the primary concern will naturally be with the effect on those items that directly depend on the change. However, if in consequence any of these dependent items themselves have to be changed, the effect will extend to all the items that depend on those items, and so on. The most satisfactory design from a change control point of view is one that reduces the interfaces between items to a minimum.

Subdivision of items has advantages and disadvantages for configuration control. The advantage of subdividing configuration items into smaller identifiable items is that any request for change can be focused more precisely on the area affected. However, below a certain level of detail it becomes counterproductive to subdivide items further. The advantage of greater precision in identifying the item is outweighed at low levels by the volume of items and the difficulty of interpreting requests for change when focused on too small a detail.

For example, suppose for the purpose of precise configuration management the design of this course were to be subdivided further than Figure 6.3. Each unit could have been specified in terms of the sections that it would contain. This precision would allow one author to request approval for change to an individual section from the other team members. This might be tolerable. However, if the sections were further subdivided into paragraphs, the requests for change would be too numerous, too trivial and not easy to interpret. The degree of subdivision of configuration items needs to be judged to minimize the overall effort involved.

## The mechanics of configuration management

There are four main elements that make up the discipline of configuration management: configuration identification, configuration control, configuration status accounting and configuration auditing. In brief these elements serve the following purpose.

- **Configuration identification** identifies uniquely all the items within the configuration.

- **Configuration control** is a system through which changes may be made to configuration items.

- **Configuration status accounting** records and reports the current status and the history of all changes to the configuration. It provides a complete record of what happened to the configuration to date.

- **Configuration auditing** is the audits performed to ensure conformity between the items in the configuration and their specifications. Audits ensure not only a match between what is delivered and what was requested but also consistency throughout all the project documents.

These elements will be discussed in greater detail in the rest of this section.

### SAQ 6.9

(a) What is the scope of configuration management when it is used throughout the project life-cycle?

(b) What are the four principal elements of configuration management?

# 6.3.2   Configuration identification

## Identification conventions

In order to establish a successful method of requesting change, a clear identification scheme must be adopted within the configuration. Therefore, once the structure of the configuration and the unit of control has been chosen, each item must be identified so that it is unique within the system and recorded in a register. The activity of registering names is called configuration identification.

The exact identification scheme chosen is not significant as long as the identification given to each item within the configuration is *unique* and *always remains the same*: several people will be involved with the item in various capacities and confusion will arise if its identification is changed. It is usual to split the identification into a 'name' which remains fixed throughout the life of the item and a 'version reference'. For example, a course unit could be called 'Planning unit' and to distinguish the second version we could say 'Planning unit: draft 2'. It would be difficult to keep track of the item if its name were changed every time it was modified. In most discussions about the item its name would be used by itself without the version reference.

## Choosing item names

Names are best kept reasonably short but unique and meaningful: a name is tedious to remember if it consists of a paragraph of text, but meaningless if it is merely a single letter. It is tempting to make an item's name correspond to its position in the hierarchy, but this is not recommended because then the item's position will be fixed permanently. For example, if instead of the name 'Planning unit' we had used the name 'Unit 3' during the development of this course, it would be rather inconvenient if at a later date we had wanted to rearrange the units so that 'Planning' became the second unit of the course.

Another disadvantage of names based on the current structure is that in order to use the item in another application it would have to be renamed. Once it is renamed it becomes a different item and any changes to the new item will have no effect on the original, as the relationship between them will have been broken. Generally, schemes which attempt to make names correspond to position work well for a short time, but degenerate into confusion as the design is developed further. The naming scheme may also inhibit sensible rearrangement of the design.

In large projects the naming convention must be planned early so that problems do not arise later with name clashes. For example, if a project employs several subcontractors it is necessary to ensure that names used by one subcontractor cannot replicate names used by another. The name of an item should be chosen so that it will be unique in the largest configuration ever expected for it.

### SAQ 6.10

Judge the quality of the following names for configuration items:

(a) 'names section of change control unit'

(b) 'motor bearing'

(c) 'Y37'

(d) 'door'

(e) 'module 4'.

## Labelling the items

Every configuration item needs to be physically labelled in some way to proclaim its identity, in other words a label that says that this physical item is the item recorded in the configuration register. For documents, the label is usually just the name and version number written in some prominent place. For a physical item it may be an identification tag or an identifier etched into it during manufacture. The point is that the label is required to identify this object unambiguously as the item referred to in the configuration register.

In the days before word processors it was easier to recognize a master document because of the way it was produced, with corrections and amendments (sometimes initialled) clearly visible. The use of word processors and computer-aided design techniques has made it much more difficult to be sure a document is what it claims to be, because it may have been copied and unauthorized changes may have been made to it. Careful consideration must therefore be given to how the rightful owner of the item name will be recognized. It may, for example, be necessary to produce a physical document and have it signed and safely stored after it has been approved or to 'lock' the item in such a way that it can be replaced only by an authorized person.

When a change is required, such as a modification to a piece of equipment already operating in the field, there must be a simple mechanism for indicating that the change has been carried out. For example, a circuit card may be etched with numbers which can be scored out as each change is made. Although this is not so easy with software it should be possible to identify which version of a piece of software is actually installed. Ideally the identity label should be protected so that the version number cannot be changed without authorization.

### Identification of software items

Software poses some particular difficulties for identification. One problem is that any one item of software may take several different forms, and another is that it may be quite difficult to label the item visibly without the risk that the label is later detached from the item. Let us consider these two problems in turn.

Once the program for a module has been written, compiled and tested it may be available in several different forms, or *representations* as they are sometimes called. For example, there may be any number of the following:

- source code listing on paper
- source code held on a disk
- source code held on a magnetic tape
- source code in the memory of a computer
- assembly language representation on the same four media as above
- machine code representation on the same four media as above.

The identification system should distinguish between these various representations so that when a change is made to an item it is as clear as possible just which representations of the item have been changed. This brings us to the second problem, the labelling of the software item. Labelling source code is not too difficult. The source code listing should contain a title or comment to identify it. When printed on a piece of paper it may carry an authorization with a signature, preferably in a coloured pen, to label it as the master. However, when the source is held in the memory of a computer it requires considerable discipline to ensure that any change to the code is reflected in a change in the identifying label.

Once the source has been compiled and a machine code representation produced, the labelling problem becomes extremely difficult. Titles and comments are stripped away in producing the pattern of bits that is held in the memory of the machine that will execute it. Probably the best solution to this problem is to use an automatic system of code generation in which the state of the machine code version is kept updated by the system.

### SAQ 6.11

Suppose there has been a hazardous incident in a computer-controlled plant. The investigator finds that some of the software was delivered to the control room on disk in machine code form. The investigator would like to carry out an audit of this software to identify the source code and hence the design from which it was derived. What problem could arise in doing so?

## Baselines

In a large project the development of numerous configuration items in parallel may lead to a sense of chaos even though each individual item is fully under control. A technique favoured by some project managers and clients to bring the development into order is to impose a structure of **baselines** into the development. A baseline is the state of the configuration, or a defined part of the configuration, at a particular point in the development, usually at a major milestone in the system life-cycle. A baseline may be defined as a set of known and agreed configuration items under change control at a discrete time from which further progress can be charted.

The baselines to be used in a project may be defined in advance in consultation between client and contractor to give greater visibility to the status of the project. A typical set of baselines is shown in Figure 6.5. Each of the baselines shown in Figure 6.5 marks a plateau in the development of the system. Briefly, these are:

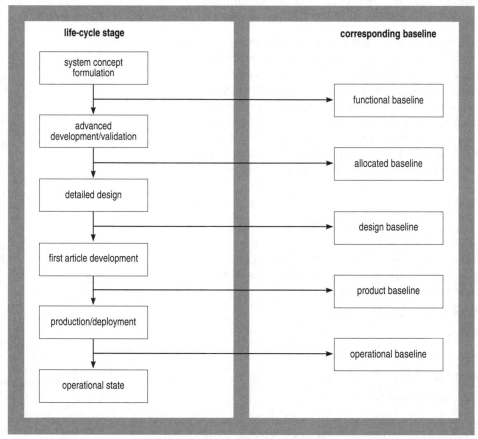

**FIGURE 6.5**
The system life-cycle and associated baselines (Bersoff *et al.*, 1980)

- *Functional baseline:* requirements documents defining what the system is expected to do.

- *Allocated baseline:* after initial outline design. Records what functions will be performed by which parts of the system.

- *Design baseline:* after detailed design. All the detailed documents and drawings show how the product will be built. Good basis for a design review.

- *Product baseline:* after developing the first article. The documents that describe it.

- *Operational baseline:* after testing and improvements. The baseline defines the product in operation.

Not all projects need conform to these baselines. It may be more appropriate to define a different set in a particular project to reflect the circumstances. For example, at the end of a review of the status of a project the project manager may wish that status to be on record as the baseline as at the review.

Note that a baseline need not apply to a whole configuration: it may apply to a defined part of it. For example it is possible to select a particular component of a system and to baseline all the configuration items that are relevant to that component. This gives greater flexibility so that not all parts of a system need reach the given baseline at the same time.

Any given baseline must be identified uniquely so that anyone investigating the baseline has a definite starting point. This means that the full status of the whole configuration at that baseline needs to be stored and identified so that it is possible to retrieve it later. The current state of a project can then be determined as the baseline plus all the implemented changes.

You may think that once a baseline, such as the design baseline, has been established the design ought to be frozen. This baseline design would then act as a firm platform on which to base the further development. However, this could seriously devalue the worth of the project since proposals for amendment often arise from the omission of a valuable function from the original design or from an incorrect initial design. If it is impossible to gain permission for change, progress will be held back. Nevertheless, the impact on the project of a change to the design at the baseline should be carefully considered, particularly if it entails change to a high-level area of the design structure at a late stage in the development plan.

### Software project baselines

In a software project it is particularly difficult to track the cost and progress of the project, owing to the lack of well-defined intermediate stages in its design. Change control baselines, over and above the standard baselines that were mentioned above, can be used to establish progress points for each level of a hierarchically constructed software system. For example:

- completed and approved requirement specifications
- completed and approved design
- tested modules of code ready for integration
- integration testing complete and approved
- system testing accepted complete by customer.

These additional baselines give the project management more reference points from which to track the cost and progress of a project. Subsequent modifications can then be performed under control. Note that the above baselines are unlikely to apply to a complete system, but only to some defined part of it, otherwise none of the units could be baselined as 'coded ready for inspection' until all the units were in that state.

### SAQ 6.12

(a) What is a baseline?

(b) What is the purpose of using baselines?

## Multiple configurations

It is often necessary for more than one configuration of hardware or software to co-exist. For example, if you were developing a refrigerator you might want one version for use in Europe and another in the USA. These parallel configurations are usually referred to as **variants.** One variant does not supersede the other. Both are available simultaneously.

Another way that different versions arise is when a product is improved or otherwise changed over time. The new version supersedes the old but nevertheless if the old product is still in existence its configuration has to be maintained. You will almost certainly be familiar with this situation when trying to obtain a spare part for a broken piece of equipment. The replacement may not fit if the supplier has not kept careful track of the configuration of your equipment.

### SAQ 6.13

Consider the configuration management of the production of this course, i.e. the configuration shown in Figure 6.3.

(a)  Suggest one way in which another variant could arise.

(b)  Suggest how a different version of one variant could arise.

## Protecting the configuration

Once an item has been identified as a configuration item it requires protection: protection from unauthorized change and protection from accidental destruction such as in a fire. The usual way to provide this protection is to set up an **archive** or **configuration store**, a physical store of the configuration items with duplicate copies held in a physically remote location so that an accident that destroyed the master would be unlikely to destroy the copy. The archive requires a **custodian** (archivist or librarian) to ensure that items are changed only after authority has been granted to do so, using the proper consultation procedures.

You may wonder whether it is really necessary to centralize the configuration store. Would it not be possible to appoint the designers as custodians of their own configuration items? Informally this may work but the trouble with such a democratic system is that it may fail for one of the following reasons:

●    the whole system fails if even one designer abuses the procedures

●    designers will be tempted to make small unauthorized changes

●    designers prefer technical work to security work

●    the security activities are time-consuming and tedious.

For these reasons it is better in a formal system to appoint a custodian of the store or alternatively to use an automated tool that will not allow designers to make changes until the proper authority for change to an item has been granted. An advantage of using an automated tool as the custodian is that the use of word processing has made it more difficult for a custodian to recognize the difference between the master version of an item and a duplicate copy. An automated tool may not be so easily fooled.

If a mistake in a configuration item needs correction then the change control procedure still needs to be invoked before the correction can be made. This may seem pedantic and frustrating to the person who made the mistake. Nevertheless there needs to be a publication of the proposal to correct the mistake and a record of the change. It would of course be sensible to minimize the bureaucracy associated with matters like this, which is a reason not to insist that all changes are approved by the project manager.

### SAQ 6.14

Why should mistakes not be rectified immediately by the item controller without any fuss?

Last week a designer was developing a component and was allowed to make changes freely. The component then became a configuration item. This week the designer notices a silly mistake and wishes to correct it. The custodian tells her that she cannot do so without authority. The designer says this is crazily bureaucratic. Is it? Justify your answer.

# 6.3.3   Configuration control

Procedures should be set up to ensure that the configuration control system works as intended. It is necessary to establish a change control procedure so that no change is made without assessment of its impact by people potentially affected by the change or without approval by an appropriate authority.

## A configuration control mechanism

A mechanism is required which can handle a wide range of requests for all sorts of change, ranging from minor details of implementation to radical changes of system function. The requester may be a senior manager or a junior designer, and may be well informed about the structure of the project or almost totally ignorant. Not every request will be supported by convincing argument. The problem is to find a mechanism in which the work of assessing impact and the work of approving the change are performed by the right people in the project. This is the advantage of a system which allows individual **item controllers** rather than referring everything to a top-level **change control board** (or **configuration control board**).

The essence of change control is that all change to configuration items requires prior approval by a recognized authority for that item, the item controller. There is an important distinction to be drawn between the role of the item controller and the custodian mentioned earlier. The item controller authorizes change to an item and the custodian ensures that no changes take place without that authorization and according to approved practices. The item controller may be a person or a committee and it is often appropriate to have various authorities appointed, according to the position of each item in the project. For example, it has already been noted that some items will require approval for change from both client and contractor, while others are matters of detailed design, internal to the project.

A typical authority for change control for items at the top of the project hierarchy is a change control board consisting of:

- client technical representative
- client commercial representative
- project manager (contractor organization)
- senior designer.

There may also be someone to give the maintenance and operational points of view. It is not usually appropriate to submit every proposal for change to this top-level committee for approval as the composition of this board is unsuitable for minor amendments. Possibly the project manager or administrator could handle all internal changes within a small project, but in a large project it is necessary to delegate authority. In general, when each design object becomes a configuration item someone will be appointed as the item controller and given the authority to approve changes to it.

### SAQ 6.16

Would it be feasible to appoint a single person, say the project manager or a senior engineer, as the controller for all items below the top level? What would be the advantages and disadvantages ?

A **configuration administrator** is useful as the person to whom all requests for change are sent in the first place. The administrator routes the request to the appropriate controller.

The basic steps in a mechanism for change control using configuration management are as follows:

1   A requester sees the desirability for a change and sends a change request, giving reasons for the change, to the configuration administrator.

2   The administrator records the request and sends it on to the named item controller.

3   The item controller appoints someone to assess feasibility and the impact of the change unless this has been done by the requester already.

4   The assessor consults the designers and users potentially affected and submits an assessment to the item controller for decision. To ensure that the consultation is performed properly the assessor should place on record the responses from all the people affected.

5   The item controller approves or disapproves.

6   The administrator records the decision and reports it to all concerned.

7   The project manager or team leader appoints someone to implement the changes (if any).

8   The implementer reports completion to the administrator.

9   The item controller authorizes the new version.

10   The administrator records and publishes the new status.

There are some points to notice about this mechanism. Several people seem to be involved: a requester, an administrator, an item controller, an assessor and an implementer. These are not necessarily separate people, but are simply names for functions to be performed. The impact of the change must be assessed before the decision to make it is made. All significant events are recorded and published.

### SAQ 6.17

Suppose the lead designer of an item is also registered as the controller for the item (a reasonable practice). If this designer sees the need for a change, is it sensible to cut the bureaucracy, implement the change and then perform steps 9 and 10 of the procedure ? If not, why not? What would prevent this?

## Assessing the impact of a proposed change

Who is needed to assess the impact of a proposed change depends very much on the scope of the change, which is usually reflected by the position of the item in the configuration hierarchy. For example, to assess the impact of a change on the functions to be performed by the system may require the participation of several senior people in the client and contracting organizations. In contrast, if the change is merely correcting a minor fault in a low-level item it may require only a junior designer to assess its impact.

Each component, or at least each design area within the configuration, is normally the responsibility of an individual designer. It is therefore best to use that designer, who has a detailed knowledge of a particular area, to assess the impact of change upon that item. This is better than asking an outsider to do the work because an outsider will take much longer to investigate and may overlook a vital factor.

As a result of a request for change to one item, consequential change to other items may be required. The configuration dependency diagram can be used to stimulate designers of affected items to provide details of the effects of the change on factors such as cost or performance for their own items. These can then be aggregated to provide the overall effects of the original change request.

To decide whether a change ought to be carried out, it is necessary to:

- estimate the benefits of making the change and the consequences if the change is not made
- predict and assess whether the change will affect the overall system and what any such effects are likely to be: the viewpoints of all the users of the system are often of particular concern
- estimate what will need to be changed elsewhere in the design as a result of the original change and what the ramifications of the change are likely to be at all levels within the design hierarchy
- estimate the consequences on the cost and time taken to complete the project.

Gathering this information requires the estimating skills discussed in Chapter 2.

### SAQ 6.18

(a) How can the configuration diagram or the equivalent database be used to help in impact assessment?

(b) Suggest two advantages and two disadvantages if a project manager were to decide that all requests for change should be accompanied by an assessment of the impact of the change.

## Active controls

Configuration management is unlikely to work if it is purely a passive system. The project manager needs to exert active control, first to ensure that design objects are brought under change control at an appropriate time, and secondly to ensure that other team members are using the latest approved versions of items as soon as possible. These two issues are considered below.

### Timing

Consider the problem of a designer working on some aspect of a project within a team of other designers with whom she will need to co-operate to produce a complex piece of equipment. Assume that a specification has been produced for her module and registered as a configuration item. It has specified the interfaces which affect other modules and she now has to develop a detailed design.

Before producing a final version, she will need to experiment a great deal, incorporating ideas into the area, testing them and correcting or replacing them if they do not work. She may have to repeat this trial-and-error cycle several times before finding a solution and may produce a huge quantity of data and intermediate work in the process. However, these experimental cycles have no relevance for the rest of the project team: providing them with details of this intermediate work would only serve to confuse. At this stage all that is required is for her to keep careful track of her own versions privately. Change control is inappropriate.

However, at some point she will reach a stage where fairly firm conclusions have been reached and she is able to record a first draft design for the benefit of her colleagues and subsequent stages of the work. This is the time to submit her work to change control. This need not prevent her from making further changes, but any such changes will require prior approval and will be on the record. The design object has become a configuration item.

The timing of the application of control to a component is critical.

- Applied too early, change control will slow down the development of the item by introducing restrictions on change.

- Applied too late, the lack of change control will lead to confusion at the interfaces between components.

The project manager must judge the optimum time at which to bring a component under change control, taking account of the rate of change of the component and the requirements of other members of the team.

### SAQ 6.19

Name one item which should be placed under change control as soon as a contract is agreed between client and contractor.

## Checkpoints

The initial registration of an item as a configuration item under change control is only the start of the change control process. Normally, work will continue on an item and this means that the changes produced by this process should be regularly submitted for approval. Left to themselves, designers tend to continue development without submitting the changes for approval. This means that the registered version gets more and more out-of-date compared with the version that designers are currently using in their own private work space. This does not contradict the principle of configuration management but it keeps work private for too long. This tendency may be overcome by instituting **checkpoints**.

The ideal arrangement is that a designer should agree with the project manager on a number of stages during the development at which the latest controlled version will be updated. This has two advantages: first, less work will be lost if this designer is unable to complete all the development work and, secondly, other team members benefit from using updated versions.

At a minimum there should be a checkpoint at the completion of any module of work and at the completion of any agreed change. However, if too many checkpoints are imposed the designer concerned will have to spend too much time ensuring that the work is under control. If control checks are applied every six days it will be expensive, whereas if control checks are applied every six months there is a risk of losing all intermediate work if some unforeseen, disastrous event occurs. There is a trade-off between the reduction in efficiency caused by enforcing too many checkpoints and the risk of losing work if there are too few.

*Use of out-of-date versions by others*

Suppose a designer has implemented a change and tested it, and it has been declared fit to replace the previous version. At what stage should this new version be adopted by the other members of the project team? Immediately? Within some time limit? Or at the designer's discretion?

The most straightforward course of action, from the project manager's point of view, is to insist that only one version of any item is in use at a time and that everyone should adopt the new version immediately it has been approved. By this means, the project manager can be more confident that each item will interface satisfactorily with the latest versions of all other items in the design hierarchy.

Unfortunately, this strategy makes progress difficult. If a change is made to a particular design environment, other designers working in that environment will naturally be suspicious about how it has affected their work area. For example, if they are developing software and are forced to use a new version of a subroutine developed elsewhere they may blame the change for any subsequent failures, regardless of whether the change has had any impact on their work; consequently it will be difficult to re-establish confidence.

However, as soon as someone is allowed to continue to use an out-of-date version the introduction of the new version is delayed and it is possible that, in the extreme case, the new version will never be adopted by all the designers. Clearly, this is not acceptable in the development of a system where all the parts must eventually work together. Some procedure is required to ensure that new versions are adopted within a reasonable time.

If latest versions are to be adopted within a reasonable time it is necessary to establish some kind of checking procedure on the versions in use. Consider the following three possibilities:

1    Set a time at which the whole project team must adopt the latest approved version, in synchronism, for example 'every Thursday at 7 pm'.

2    Inspect the versions which people are using and implement a time-out rule such as, 'you may not use versions which have had a successor for more than two weeks'.

3    Inspect the versions which people are using and judge whether it is reasonable for them to be used, depending on the prevailing circumstances.

The first of the three options is the easiest to implement, but requires people to terminate their hypothesis-forming and testing cycle at the same time: this will not always constitute the most efficient use of personnel. (In a software project it might also consume significant computing resources on Thursday nights.)

The time-out option is practical but relies on the project manager's ability to persuade the development staff to be disciplined in their approach. It can be implemented with reasonable ease but you can never be sure that everyone is in synchronism.

The last option is the most friendly but also the most difficult to implement as it relies heavily on personal interaction and wise decision making. It could take a lot of the project manager's time unless this checking can be delegated to someone else.

The mechanism chosen for a given project will depend upon the project manager's confidence in the development team and the importance of maintaining synchronism for the task. It will also depend on how much time the project manager can afford to devote to the task.

## SAQ 6.20

A project manager on a large job insists that work should be entered into the change control system at the end of every day and that everybody must use only the latest versions of all components. Give two major flaws in this procedure.

# 6.3.4 Configuration status accounting

The purpose of configuration status accounting is to keep a record of all the events that have happened to a system under development to allow comparison with the development plan and to provide **traceability**. It should be possible to answer questions such as: 'What is the current status of development of area $X$?' 'By what route did it reach this state?'

As we have discussed in Chapter 5, control of a project requires both a plan and a measurement of status. Status accounting is a contribution to the second of these two requirements.

To answer questions about status and history it is necessary for the system to record all transactions affecting each configuration item from the time that the configuration management system is established for the project. This means that meticulous records must be kept. Although it would be possible to keep such records manually this is obviously an area where a database is invaluable for assembling the relevant facts, so we will assume that such a system is employed. Most of the input to it probably goes via the administrator who handles the change requests, but the precise mechanics of who physically enters the data are immaterial.

The records that are accumulated in the database include:

- the creation of new configuration items together with the name of the change control authority
- incident reports (i.e. faults reported that may produce change requests)
- change requests
- change approval/rejection decisions
- change notices (issued when items have been changed)
- updates to items stored in the system itself
- baseline configurations.

Using these data the status accounting system should be able to produce reports on the status and history of any item or collection of items, such as a baseline. Such reports may be scheduled to be released periodically, for example before regular project review meetings, but may also be required on an *ad hoc* basis to respond to queries from members of the project team or project auditors or later by people maintaining the developed system.

Some typical queries could be:

- What is the history of development of the power supply unit? Why is it now handling 10 amps when the original specification only called for 5 amps?
- How many incident reports have there been in the last month? What proportion of these have led to change requests?

- Who needs to approve any changes that are proposed for this software module?

- On what items have changes been approved which have not yet been implemented?

- What items in the design baseline have been changed since it was approved?

- Has our new system of checkpoints reduced the incidence of spurious change requests?

The project manager can also use the status accounting reports to assess the present state of achievement in all areas within the project. The current state of progress can then be compared with the plans for each area, and appropriate corrections can be made. Thus the status accounting system can be used not only as a record of change but also as a record of progress to help the project manager to make decisions during the execution of the project.

### SAQ 6.21

(a) What are the main purposes of configuration status accounting?

(b) Describe briefly how it is done.

# 6.3.5 Configuration auditing

Configuration auditing developed from the aircraft industry's need to be sure that each aircraft was constructed exactly as the designers intended it to be. It ensured, for example, that an outmoded component was not replaced by a new one without proper consideration and a record of that decision being made. The same method is now used to check that every item delivered by a project has been developed and produced as agreed.

The aim of configuration auditing is to check that, in spite of changes that may have taken place in requirements and design, the items produced conform to the current specification and that all the quality assurance procedures claimed to be in place have actually been performed satisfactorily. This is done by verifying that when any item is produced it conforms to the specification produced for it at the previous stage. That specification will itself have been verified for conformity with the project requirements. Clearly, the introduction of changes can lead to a breakdown in this evolutionary chain unless great care has been taken to ensure that the changes are applied consistently, not just to the item finally constructed but also to its antecedents at the earlier stages.

Auditing does not necessarily involve the auditors in performing the verification themselves: it is a matter of *ensuring* that the verification has been done and that the records are complete and satisfactory. The verification process could be carried out at any time but in particular, when a baseline is to be established, an audit is required to ensure that the configuration at each successive baseline has been verified as conforming with the items in the configuration at the previous baseline.

If auditing is to be feasible then each item produced must be identified and all the activities undertaken to make that item must be recorded. For example, the name and version reference must be etched into a circuit card or stamped on to a metal component. This makes it plain to everyone what the object is supposed to represent. By reference to the status accounting system it should be possible to recreate its history precisely.

Audits should also be carried out to make sure that changes have been implemented and recorded correctly. How often and to what depth such audits are undertaken will depend on the importance of ensuring that a component conforms to its specification. For an aircraft component it will be extremely important for safety reasons but for a domestic appliance it may be less important (although safety may be a factor in some cases). Sometimes a configuration audit can only be thoroughly carried out by taking the finished product to pieces, but this could be an expensive procedure, so most verification will need to be built into the design and construction activities, checking for conformity at each stage. The auditor can then examine the records that show that this verification was indeed carried out, usually from a document signed by the person who did the checking.

The use of manual change control procedures often results in discrepancies between the finished component and the specification, which the auditing procedure should discover. However, if automated change control procedures are used it is much more likely that the discrepancy will not be allowed to occur in the first place.

# 6.3.6   An example of configuration management

This example is intended to illustrate how configuration management affects the conduct of a project by following through a project to develop a 'green' refrigerator. While the example, and the design team involved, may seem too small to warrant the application of full configuration management, we have chosen it because it illustrates principles which are appropriate in larger and more complex projects.

A small but increasingly successful firm has built a good reputation for its products, refrigerators and freezers. The management are now convinced that there is a developing requirement in the market for a 'green' refrigerator. Since the company is small, they feel that it is possible to fill this expanding niche in the market with a good product, quickly. After much consultation a product requirements definition document is agreed and this becomes the first configuration item.

**Configuration  item**

| | |
|---|---|
| *Item name:* | Requirements definition |
| *Created:* | 10/1/97 |
| *Change authority:* | Engineering Division manager plus Marketing manager |
| *Description:* | Master copy held in Engineering files ref Green/1/1 |
| *Items depended on:* | Nil |

This information is held on a database under the control of an administrator in the Engineering department. The description is a pointer to show exactly which document is being referred to, the requirements definition itself being held securely in a file. This item depends on no items already in the system – there aren't any others yet!

The design team has two lead designers, who decide that one will be responsible for the refrigeration unit, the controls and the motor, and the other for the carcase, the interior fittings, and the door. Together they draw up a top-level design and submit it to a meeting chaired by the marketing manager at which it is confirmed that this design conforms to the requirements definition. This now becomes the second configuration item.

**Configuration item**

| | |
|---|---|
| *Item name:* | Top-level design |
| *Created:* | 25/1/97 |
| *Change authority:* | Lead designers with project manager |
| *Description:* | Master design held in Engineering files ref Green 1/2/1. |
| *Items depended on:* | Requirements definition |

The point here is that this item is dependent on the requirements definition, an item already in the configuration. Any request for a change to the requirements definition could affect this second item. As the design of individual components proceeds other configuration items are stored in the database – the designs for the carcase, the motor, the interior fittings etc. As each item is added to the database it is necessary to record precisely where that design is held and it must be held in such a way that no changes take place without authority. Some items spawn others (the door design, for example, has a fastening design which is dependent on the carcase and door designs). The configuration after a month or so looks like Figure 6.6.

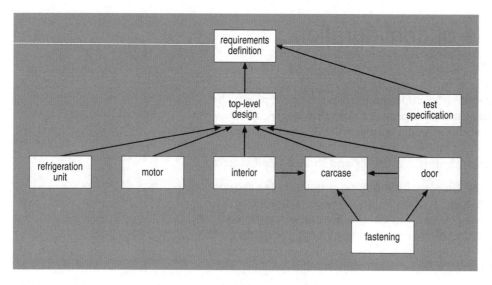

**FIGURE 6.6**
Refrigerator configuration

Change requests start to appear. The designer responsible for the refrigeration unit undertakes some research on non-CFC refrigerants. He discovers that this will require some changes: the coils have a different geometry from the one specified in the top-level design. Consequently there needs to be change request not only for the refrigeration unit itself but also for the top-level design.

**Change request**

| | |
|---|---|
| *Originator:* | Abel Baker, designer |
| *Date:* | 15/2/97 |
| *Item(s) to be changed:* | Top-level design and refrigeration unit design |
| *Outline of change:* | The refrigerator will use liquid propane as a coolant, and will require a design for the refrigeration coils and a motor suitable for this coolant. |
| *Reason for change:* | Liquid propane is presently the most effective non-CFC coolant available for domestic refrigeration. |

The administrator checks the database to find out what other items are recorded as *directly* dependent on any of the items for which the change is requested so that the full impact of the effect of a change can be assessed. Notice that in the first instance there need be consideration only of items that have been declared dependent on the items for which change has been requested. There could be lower-level items that depend *indirectly* on the top-level design, via say the carcase design, but there is no need to consider them unless a change is necessary in the carcase design itself.

The designers meet at the project manager's instigation, and determine that the changes required by using liquid propane will affect the refrigeration unit and the top-level design but not the carcase. So there is no need to worry about items dependent on the carcase design. Nevertheless, the fact that there has been a change is notified to all the design team in case someone working on the design of something which is not yet part of the configuration is relying on the earlier designs.

All the change requests, the impact assessments and the decisions of the item controllers are recorded by the administrator using the database. Occasionally the administrator is asked questions by the designers, such as 'How do we come to be using this size motor?' The administrator uses the database to recall the history of its design from the original document identified as the motor design and all subsequent changes to it.

The quality manager also asks questions to ensure that the product is meeting the intentions of the managers of the Marketing and Engineering Divisions.

- Is there a record of all the configuration items, uniquely identified, with records of all requests for change and the outcome of each?
- Have all changes been properly authorized?
- What evidence is there of verification that the detailed designs conform to the top-level design?
- Is there a record of management agreement to the top-level design?
- Are there any outstanding requests for change to the designs?
- Is there a specification of the tests which will be conducted before the refrigerator design is approved for manufacture?
- Overall, if a refrigerator were constructed to the detailed designs, would it meet the sponsor's requirements?

Everyone in the department who had anything to do with the development of this refrigerator is affected by the decision to use configuration management. The project manager finds that he has quite a 'selling' job to ensure that everyone adhered to the system even if they don't really like it. Some found it onerous and were irritated by the extra administration and the delays caused by the change control procedures. But others find it useful that nobody changed things without letting them know and liked the way that they can get information about the reasons for past decisions.

## SAQ 6.22

Find examples in the description of the development of the refrigerator above of the use of:

(a) configuration identification

(b) configuration control

(c) configuration status accounting

(d) configuration auditing

# 6.3.7 Summary

Section 4.1 outlined configuration management. Following Bersoff *et al.* we have defined it as: 'the discipline of identifying the configuration of a system at discrete points in time for purposes of systematically controlling changes to this configuration and maintaining the integrity and traceability of this configuration throughout the system life cycle'.

We introduced the four components of configuration management: identification, control, status accounting and auditing. Identification means knowing exactly what is in the configuration at any one time. Configuration control means the processes which are used to protect the configuration so that items are changed only through procedures that ensure a proper assessment of the impact of the change. Configuration status accounting means keeping records of everything that affects the system so that reports can be produced showing what happened and when. It provides traceability. Configuration auditing means checking that the items produced have been tested and inspected for conformity with the requirements and that the hardware or software delivered conforms to the documentation which purports to describe it.

Having studied this section you should now be able to:

- explain what is meant by the terms configuration identification, control, status accounting and auditing

- distinguish between design objects and configuration items

- propose a suitable identification scheme for a given project

- explain what procedures you might use for configuration control

- outline the benefits of configuration status accounting

- explain the roles of a configuration custodian and an item controller.

# 7 CLOSING THE PROJECT

## *INTRODUCTION*

This chapter is mainly about the particular difficulties that arise as a project approaches completion and presents techniques that can be used to overcome them. The final section is concerned with the review of the conduct of the project that is needed for the benefit of future projects and the review of the business situation that is needed to ensure that the planned benefits are being reaped.

# 7.1 *HOMING IN ON THE TARGET*

Right from the beginning the project manager should focus on the target: successfully closing the project. The project will have a finite duration and the project manager will want to ensure not only that the project has been completed technically to good quality, within budget and schedule, but also that the ongoing business after the project has been completed is as healthy as possible. As the project progresses, the plan for its closure will need to be developed. This is sometimes called a *phase-out plan*, a *close-out plan* or a *termination plan*.

There are several factors for you to bear in mind:

- the future of project staff
- handover and maintenance
- documentation
- contract completion
- financial accounting
- project review.

Some of these tasks are rather unexciting, even downright tedious, compared with the tasks being undertaken at the project launch. Spirer (1983) presented the problems of closing the project in the form of a tree as shown in Figure 7.1.

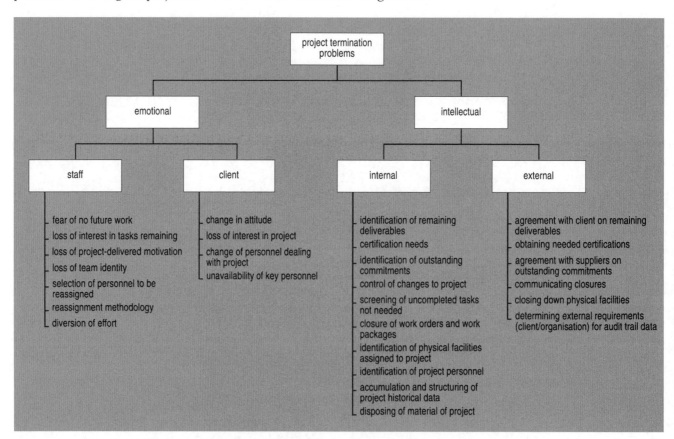

FIGURE 7.1  Project termination problems (Spirer, 1983)

To overcome the loss of interest in the project that is likely to come in the closing stages, Spirer (1983) proposed that 'project termination' should be treated as a project. This is a psychological trick, perhaps, but it may be necessary to try to produce that same enthusiasm that marked the beginning of the project. Specifically, Spirer proposes:

> Make it clear that close-out has its own project identity. Some project managers give the close-out its own project name. Start-up meetings for the beginning of the termination phase help to establish the concept that there is a well-defined goal to be met – closing out the job properly.

(p. 251)

Once termination has been made a project, there are a number of suggestions for encouraging the project spirit:

- Provide a team identity – New project name? Newsletter?
- Hold frequent informal team meetings.
- Keep in touch with members personally.
- Plan the re-assignment strategy – keep the best people until last (if you can!).
- Set objectives for good closure – documents and spares for trouble-free maintenance.

Under the 'intellectual' heading Spirer lists the actual work to be done and under the 'emotional' heading he lists the human problems to be overcome. Both the staff and the client may be affected. Let's consider some of the problems.

## Future of project staff

The approach of the close of a significant project may be a very uncomfortable time for the project staff. If people are not assured of their future, then it may be very difficult for the manager to maintain the project's impetus over its final stages. A hitherto successful project may become sluggish and difficult to manage. Sometimes this uncertainty is unavoidable – a business cannot always guarantee continuity of employment, but if possible the manager should try to ensure that each member of staff knows his or her own future prospects as closure approaches.

The timing may be delicate. On the one hand the manager wants to reassure the staff that they will not be unemployed after the project, but on the other hand the manager also wants to ensure that the staff complete the current project before getting too enthusiastic about the next one. Once a team member has started work on the next project it will be exceedingly difficult to get that person back to tie up any loose ends, so the project manager must make sure that any outstanding work is taken care of properly. The manager may of course be concerned about his or her own future. Towards the end of a large project it would not be surprising if thoughts of the next job were distracting. Hopefully, the manager's manager will be preparing a plan for this!

The problem of the effect of the approaching closure of the project on staff attitude is of course easier to handle if the team have been well motivated towards a successful outcome throughout the project. If the team building has gone well then it is likely that, in spite of concern over the future or the attraction of a novel assignment, the strongest factor will be the satisfaction of seeing the present project succeed.

The project manager needs to plan with the business management how the staff will be phased out. This plan would take account not only of the needs of the project itself but also the other needs of the business (other projects) and the development of the staff. If there is no plan then what can easily happen is that staff are redeployed in a piecemeal fashion as it becomes noticed that the staff are under-employed. This is likely to lead to unplanned re-allocation of tasks and hence to reduced morale.

Re-allocation of tasks is indeed quite likely to be necessary as the end of the project approaches. If some staff are to be transferred to other work then quite often the unfinished work of the leaving staff has to be taken on by somebody else. The ideal of a person fully employed up to the moment of leaving, and the tasks all nicely tidied up at the same time is unlikely always to be achieved. Negotiating skills are called for, perhaps arranging with the next 'employer' for some allocation of the leaver's time so that they can return to the project for brief periods over the next month or so.

One advantage of the matrix organization discussed in Chapter 4 is that the redeployment problem is much less severe than in an organization in which staff are primarily allocated to project teams. In the matrix organization the staff do not have to develop a new relationship with their line manager when they change projects. It is also much easier to make transitional arrangements at the start and finish of projects.

Staff performance on the project needs to be suitably rewarded. If the project has been lengthy then it is quite likely that senior management will want a report anyway on the performance of the staff on the project from the project manager. However, even if no formal reporting procedure is demanded by the management it is good practice to ensure that high levels of performance are duly recognized, and poor performance noted too. The way that this is done depends very much on the personnel policies of the employer, but most will have some means of recognizing good performance and counselling staff about their future. In a smaller, less formal, situation a public thank-you may be more appropriate than a written report.

## Handover and maintenance

The outcome of many projects is a working system to be handed over to some other organization to operate. For example, at the end of a factory construction project there is a manufacturing plant to be operated. The ease of future operation and maintenance of such a plant is specified among the objectives for the project manager at the outset but as the project approaches completion the prospective operation and maintenance managers are likely to take a progressively greater interest. If they do not do so of their own accord then the project manager needs to activate them.

The operating and maintenance staff need to be trained. Maintenance procedures need to be established and this may require an input from the project personnel. It can be helpful to involve some of the future maintenance and operations staff in testing and commissioning. These people are then well placed to write the operations and maintenance manuals or at least provide input to them.

# Documentation

Allied to the maintenance issue is the need to complete the project documentation. All phases of the project should already have produced documentation but this needs to be reviewed to ensure that it is complete, indexed and accessible. Copies may need to be archived for future reference. Seen through the eyes of maintenance staff the project documentation may not appear as satisfactory as the project staff believed. It is a good idea to expose the maintenance manuals to the staff who will have to use them long before the project closes. The maintenance staff may well assist in preparing the manuals.

The documentation includes complete lists of all the project deliverables, showing how they fit together and how they were designed and tested. Furthermore, the documents should show how it was intended that the product should be used and maintained. This applies just as much to software as it does to hardware.

# Contract completion and acceptance

The manager needs to obtain from the client a formal acceptance that the contract has been fulfilled. This could be a sticky point unless you have taken care to ensure that acceptance criteria and project deliverables have been well defined. The greatest problems are likely to occur where the specification is so loose that there is room for wide disagreement over the interpretation of what constitutes completion. All this should have been foreseen at the time that the contract was placed. (Informal contracts between departments of the same organization are likely to produce the worst problems of this kind.)

Ideally, it should be possible to refer to a document produced at the project launch which specifies precisely the criterion for acceptance – but of course there will have been changes. This is where the documentation of those changes may prove to be vital. The agreed changes should have included the impact on the acceptance criteria.

Acceptance need not necessarily be 100 per cent. The client may accept that the project has been completed, but with 'reservations'. The reservations will list the items still outstanding, and these may then be dealt with by the project team over some agreed time-scale. It may not make economic sense to fulfil every aspect of the agreed scope of work, even with the changes agreed so far. Using the Pareto principle, it is foolish to spend huge resources on work that is of only minor interest to the client. Negotiation is the sensible way round this problem. Hopefully, unless the client is unhelpfully stubborn, an agreement will be reached between the contractor and client that payment for the work is adjusted to take account of those elements of the work that cannot be tackled economically.

The project manager in a reversed role as the client of the subcontractors will in turn ensure that all subcontracts have been fulfilled correctly and authorize final payments to subcontractors and vendors. There may be a number of minor matters that have to be handed over to a post-project administrator to tie up after the project has closed.

# Project closure checklists

Checklists are useful at all stages of a project, including project closure. Archibald (1992) suggests that at project closure the benefits of a checklist are to:

- Clearly indicate the close-out functions and responsibilities, reducing ambiguity and uncertainty.

- Reduce oversight of important factors.

- Permit close-out progress to be monitored.

- Aid project team members with little or no experience in closing out a project.

- Inform other project team members about the activities of other projects during the close-out phase.

(p. 364)

### SAQ 7.1

Archibald's checklist is designed for a large project where a project office is involved. Produce a shorter checklist, say about a dozen items, that might be used in closing a smaller project.

## Financial accounting

The project manager is responsible for the preparation of a financial statement of the project. How much did it finally cost compared with the original sanctioned budget? The discrepancies will need to be explained. Often the scope of work will have changed during the project but if all changes have been documented, justified, and the costs agreed with the client there should be little argument. You will want to find out where the money went so that the estimating on future projects is improved.

Problems will arise, however, if expensive changes have been made without adequate consultation and recording. The client may well be reluctant to agree that so many changes were actually requested, and the project organization may stand to make a loss. The client's memory of requested changes is invariably short. Clients are often horrified to discover how many changes they have made, so it is essential to have a formal record of all changes and their costs. Remember the heated public arguments over the responsibility for the extra costs of the Channel Tunnel project?

# 7.2  PROJECT REVIEWS

Project reviews may take various forms, one being the final report of the project manager, a second form being de-briefing meetings and a third being a more independent assessment or audit of the project. The aim of these various reviews is fundamentally to answer some questions about the conduct of the project for the benefit of future projects. Was the project completed to quality, time and cost targets? If not, why not? Are there lessons to be learnt? Are there any follow-up actions on this project? Answers to these questions should be documented and presented to the management.

Meredith and Mantel (1989), in discussing the form of the project manager's final report, conclude that although the report may take a variety of forms the following issues should be addressed:

- project performance – compare achievement with plan

- administrative performance – review administrative practices within organization

- organizational structure – recommendations for changes to structure

- team performance – confidential report to senior management on the team members' effectiveness

- techniques of project management – review the methods used for estimating, planning and cost control.

Meredith and Mantel make the following remarks about the use of the final report:

> For each element covered in the Final Report, recommendations for changing current practice should be made and defended. Insofar as is possible, the implications of each potential change should be noted. Commonly ignored, but equally important, are comments and recommendations about those aspects of the project that worked unusually well. Most projects, project teams, and PMs develop informal procedures that speed budget preparation, ease the tasks of scheduling, improve forecasts, and the like. The Final Report is an appropriate repository for such knowledge. Once reported, they can be tested and, if generally useful, can be added to the parent organization's list of approved project management methods.
>
> (p. 538)

## After the project is over

After a project is over the benefits of doing it need to be reaped. The project was done for a purpose and the sponsors ought to make sure that they are getting value for money after all the work that has been put in. A formal way of doing this is to hold a post-completion review.

A **post-completion** or **post-implementation review** is conducted to find out whether the planned benefits are actually being realized and to identify any actions required to ensure that they are. This is rather a high-level review, not of the *conduct* of the project itself but of how appropriate the outcome has been to the needs of its sponsors.

The best time to hold such a review is as soon as possible after the project has had time to start showing the planned benefits. If it is held too soon it may be difficult to know whether the project will actually realize its benefits. On the other hand if it is delayed too much the potential benefits will also be delayed and may even be lost altogether if an atmosphere develops of thinking that the project has been a waste of time.

A key issue is whether the products of the project have been accepted by the users, operators and maintainers. The project may seem to have gone well from the contractor's point of view, with all the agreed products delivered to the specified quality criteria and yet the sponsor will not get the benefit unless the products are being put to good use in the business.

This review should therefore concentrate not on the *performance* of the project but on the *delivery of benefits* to the business.

The outcomes of such a review may include actions to make the products more usable. This might mean ensuring that the users are given fuller training in the best way to use the products or it might mean more attention to the usability of the products. (One advantage of an early review is that project personnel may still be available to help bridge gaps between product potential and product performance in the hands of the users.)

Other outcomes will be the identification of areas for further improvement of the project products. Possibly this is already in hand as part of a phased development in which case the review is an aid to the definition of a successor phase. Alternatively, this may be may be the start of something new: the life-cycle starting a new project with a recognition that more could be done. The next project starts here.

### SAQ 7.2

Distinguish between the primary purposes of the Project Manager's Final Report and a Post-completion review.

# Summary

At the end of a project two kinds of problem have to be coped with: technical problems and emotional problems. One of the more difficult problems is arranging a smooth transition for the project staff so that they contribute effectively to the project until they leave it. Technical issues include handover and maintenance, documentation, contract completion, the financial account and a project review. Checklists are recommended to ensure that nothing is overlooked.

After the project has been completed it is necessary for the project sponsor to ensure that the benefits for which the project was authorized actually materialize.

# The last act

To bring this book to a conclusion we can do no better than to quote the speech of Lord Bardolph from Shakespeare's *Henry IV Part II* (Act I, Scene III, lines 41–62). Thought to date about 1597-8; this would have been during the great period of Elizabethan theatre-building, and it is likely that Shakepeare would have been at least passingly familiar with the process of designing and building a theatre. Shakespeare himself was part-owner of the Globe in Bankside (Southwark), which was re-erected there in 1599 after the main parts of it had been disassembled in its original site in Shoreditch, Middlesex in an overnight 'flit' from the leaseholder. This is not to say that the theatre was portable, but that it was, in our parlance, system-built at the master builder's site, moved in pieces to the levelled theatre site and then assembled. The 'flit' involved disassembly, transport of the members across the river to the new site, and re-assembly.

*Lord Bardolph*

> ... When we mean to build,
> We first survey the plot, then draw the model,
> And when we see the figure of the house,
> Then must we rate the cost of the erection,
> Which if we find outweighs ability,
> What do we then but draw anew the model
> In fewer offices, or at last desist
> To build at all? Much more, in this great work –
> Which is almost to pluck a kingdom down
> And set another up – should we survey
> The plot of situation and the model,
> Consent upon a sure foundation,
> Question surveyors, know our own estate,
> How able such a work to undergo,
> To weigh against his opposite; or else
> We fortify in paper and in figures,
> Using the names of men instead of men[1]:
> Like one that draws the model of an house
> Beyond his power to build it, who, half through,
> Gives o'er and leaves his part-created cost
> A naked subject to the weeping of the clouds,
> And waste for churlish winter's tyranny.

---

1 Or else we make plans that we cannot carry out – good-looking plans that we substitute for the actions necessary to carry them to fruition.

# APPENDICES

# 1 *EVALUATING PROPOSALS FINANCIALLY*

## Checklist of costs

### 1 Land and building costs

- Purchase, site clearance, provision of access and workroads
- Alterations, extensions, civil engineering work
- Provision of services and associated control systems:

    Air conditioning
    Heating
    Lighting
    Plumbing
    Air, gas and fluids supply
    Waste disposal and general drainage

- Partitioning, insulation (for noise, heat, vibration and draughts), decoration, floor covering and treatment
- Fixtures and fittings, furnishings
- Fire prevention, e.g. sprinkler systems
- Environmental controls
- Use of temporary premises
- Security systems
- Disposal costs:

    Dilapidations
    Renovations
    Book value write-offs
    Site clearance

- Professional charges:

    Agents' fees and costs
    Solicitors' fees and costs
    Architects' fees and costs
    Consultants' fees and costs

- Hire of special equipment
- Depreciation costs
- Rent and rates

### 2 Plant and machinery costs

- Purchase or leasing costs
- Site preparation, civil engineering work
- Provision of services, associated processes
- Installation costs
- Dismantling, renovation, relocation
- Hire of special equipment
- Retooling
- Maintenance charges
- Depreciation costs
- Machine utilization and downtime
- Professional charges
- Provision of safety systems
- Insulation, i.e. noise, vibration, heat, etc.
- NBV write-offs in event of disposal

### 3 Working capital costs

- Increased inventory values:

    Raw materials
    Consumables
    Components
    Assemblies
    Finished stocks

- Inventory write-offs
- Increased work-in-progress levels, debtor levels
- Increase in provision for bad and doubtful debts
- Stockholding and financing charges
- Space requirements, fixtures and fittings for inventory and work-in-progress
- Transport and/or relocation of inventories

## 4  Personnel costs

- Redundancy payments
- Payment in lieu of notice
- Retention incentive payments
- Productivity bonus payments
- Overtime payments
- Shift and working conditions premium payments
- Salary and wage costs and related overheads
- Changes to remuneration systems
- Changes in working practices
- Use of contract labour
- Use of temporary staff
- Replacement costs
- Relocation costs
- Training costs
- Travelling and accommodation charges
- Special clothing
- Time recording systems

## 5  Business disruption/ protection costs

- Temporary build-up of inventories
- Extended supply/manufacturing lead-times
- Increased work-in-progress
- Use of alternative sourcing
- Loss of sales during changeover
- Narrowing of profit margins

- Reduced customer service levels
- Fall in process yields and/or productivity
- Materials wastage
- Shortfall of skills availability
- Publicity measures
- Security measures

## 6  Other potential cost factors

- Market research work
- Feasibility studies, pilot studies
- Project planning and control
- Transitional control systems
- Changes to management and administrative systems and procedures
- Promotion and publicity costs
- Design work
- Patenting of new products
- Transport and other costs arising from geographic changes
- Insurances
- Trade subscription
- Stationery
- Communications systems
- Professional fees and costs
- Taxation charges
- Commission payments and royalties
- Costs of raising capital
- Increased production lead-times

# Checklist of savings

## 1 Land and buildings

- Sale of land and buildings
- Vacation of land and buildings (i.e. saving of rent and rates)
- Subletting of land and buildings
- Reduction in services costs (heating, lighting, etc.)
- Reduction of maintenance costs
- Better utilization

## 2 Plant and machinery

- Sale of plant and machinery
- Reduction of power and other services requirements
- Improved machine utilization
- Reduced maintenance costs
- Increased working life, i.e. lower depreciation
- Termination or reduction of leased items and leasing charges
- Improved handling methods
- Use of less expensive plant and machinery
- Reduction in space needed for plant and machinery

## 3 Working capital

- Reduced inventory values
- Reduction of work-in-progress levels
- Reduced debtor levels, decrease in incidence of bad and doubtful debts
- Reduction of space and equipment requirements for inventories
- Reduced financing charges
- Improved credit terms from suppliers
- Disposal of surplus stocks

## 4 Materials

- Reduction in usage of direct materials
- Reduction in usage of indirect materials
- Reduction of wastage

## 5 Personnel

- Reduction of manning levels
- Improved productivity
- Reduction of overtime
- Reduction of lost time
- Improved working conditions

## 6 Other

- Increases in sales and/or profit margins
- Grants, subsidies
- Increased tax allowances
- Improved process yields
- Reduced packing and transport costs
- Improved quality, fewer rejects
- Insurances, savings on premiums
- Trade subscriptions
- Reduced stationery costs
- Better communications, reduced communications costs
- Geographic factors
- Savings of scale
- Marketing and sales considerations
- Improved environmental control, reduction of pollution, etc.

# Average gross annual rate of return method

This method concerns itself entirely with profitability and completely ignores the pattern of cash flows and the payback period! This at least brings it into line with the usual object of proposal evaluation.

The method calculates the *average* proceeds (positive net cash flow) *per year* over the life of a project and expresses this average as a percentage return per year on the project investment. This can be demonstrated by looking again at Proposal A to invest £100 000 described above:

The initial project investment (I) = £100 000

The total positive net cash flow (NCF) over the five years of the project life (L) = £135 000

Annual *average* proceeds (AAP) $= \dfrac{NCF}{L}$

$$= \dfrac{£135\ 000}{5}$$

AAP = £27 000

Return on initial investment $\quad = \dfrac{AAP}{I} = \dfrac{27\ 000}{100\ 000} \times 100 = 27\%$

In comparing proposals we may find that the payback period and the annual rate of return methods give us completely opposite results, hence the recommendation never to use either of these methods alone. Use both and then decide what is your main objective – is it quick payback or high rate of return in the longer term?

Having arrived at the average gross annual rate of return for a proposal, compare that rate with the financing cost rate which you believe you will have to pay on the funds needed to finance the proposal. If the rate of return exceeds the financing cost rate, go ahead. If it does not, either try to find a cheaper source of finance or refrain from implementing the proposal.

With this method you could, if you wished, include depreciation costs on fixed assets as cash outflows in the cash flow statement, but the normal way to allow for the writing-off of fixed asset values is to use instead the average net annual rate of return method described below.

# Average net annual rate of return method

This is no more than a variation of the average gross annual rate of return method but it assumes full recovery of the whole proposal investment (including fixed asset costs) out of net cash flows *before* calculating the rate of return on the investment. Because of this, the average annual rate of return is expressed as a percentage of the *average* capital employed instead of as a percentage of the original investment.

This can be illustrated using two examples, which we will call Proposal A and Proposal B.

*Proposal A*

Initial proposal investment = £100 000

Total positive net cash flow over life of proposal (five years) = £135 000

*Surplus* total net cash flow (NCF) after recovery of initial investment = £35 000

Average net cash flow (ANCF) per year (over five years)

$$= \frac{NCF}{L}$$

$$= \frac{£35\ 000}{5} = £7000$$

This is then divided by the average capital employed (ACE) which in this case is calculated on the basis of an initial outlay of £100 000 and a final outlay of zero, i.e. ACE = £50 000.

Average *net* annual rate of return =

ANCF  = £7000 ÷ £50 000 × 100%

= 14% a year

*Proposal B*

Initial proposal investment = £100 000

Total positive net cash flows over life (five years) of proposal = £160 000

*Surplus* total net cash flow after recovery of initial investment = £60 000

Average net cash flow per year =

$$\frac{£60\ 000}{5} = £12\ 000 \text{ per annum}$$

Average *net* annual rate of return = £12 000 ÷ £50 000 × 100% = 24% a year

If you use the average *net* annual rate of return method as described above then make sure there are no depreciation costs in the cash flow statement, otherwise you will be trying to recover fixed asset expenditure twice over.

Both the average annual rate of return methods suffer from the same disadvantage: namely that cash flows over the life of a proposal are 'smoothed out' as a result of averaging – the *pattern* of the cash flows is completely ignored.

In both these methods, the cash flows used are those *before* taking the effects of corporation tax into consideration. The reason is to allow comparison of the results (the rates of return) with the expected financing cost rates on the funds needed to finance the proposal. These financing cost rates (which depend upon where the funds come from) will probably be *gross* rates, i.e. before tax is taken into consideration. It is, of course, essential to compare like with like!

# 2   *DEPRECIATION COSTS*

The cost and expense of purchasing and installing assets is *capital* cost and expenditure.

With a few exceptions assets lose their original value as they get older and more used (quite independently of the costs incurred in repairing and maintaining them). Anyone who has purchased a new car and then tried to sell it or trade it in a few years later will understand exactly what this means! The older an asset gets and the more it gets used, the less it is worth in general.

Eventually, assets have to be replaced because they are worn out, obsolete or no longer economic to maintain and at that point an organization has to find funds to finance the replacement. It is therefore common (and prudent) business practice to set aside out of profits (usually at the end of each financial year) the estimated decreases in asset values due to increasing age and usage to provide a cash flow for the purpose of financing asset replacement when this becomes necessary.

This practice is called *depreciation*. The amounts set aside are called *depreciation costs* or *charges*. They are revenue costs and are additional to the revenue costs incurred in repairing and maintaining the assets concerned.

The principal methods by which depreciation is calculated are:

- the straight line method
- the constant percentage on reducing balance method
- the annuity method
- the current replacement value (CRV) method.

These methods are now described briefly.

## The straight line method of depreciation

This is the most commonly used method. The formula is:

Original cost of asset (A) minus residual value of asset (R) divided by the estimated useful life (L) of the asset (in years)

$$\text{Depreciation} = \frac{A - R}{L}$$

In other words simply divide the expected diminution in asset value $(A - R)$ by the number of years over which that diminution will take place $(L)$; this gives the depreciation cost per year. The original cost of the asset will include installation charges that have been capitalized as well as the purchase price of the asset itself. The residual value is what you think the asset will be worth at the end of its estimated useful life (net of any dismantling charges).

# The constant percentage on reducing balance method

This method is also in very common use and is the method applied by the UK's Inland Revenue tax authorities when they assess the profits of an organization for corporation tax purposes. The annual depreciation cost is quite simple: the latest net book value (NBV) of the asset is multiplied by a constant (fixed) percentage depreciation factor.

If we apply this method to plant of, say, £200 000 (assuming a depreciation factor of 20% per year), the calculation is as follows:

|  | Depreciation cost | NBV after depreciation |
|---|---|---|
| Year 1 | £200 000 × 20% = £40 000 | £160 000 |
| Year 2 | £160 000 × 20% = £32 000 | £128 000 |
| Year 3 | £128 000 × 20% = £25 600 | £102 400 |
| Year 4 | £102 400 × 20% = £20 480 | £81 920 |

and so on.

With this method the asset never gets written down to a zero residual value and the depreciation charge becomes less each year during the life of the asset (though this is usually offset by rising repair and maintenance costs in later years).

The percentage factor used in this method will depend upon the nature of the asset, an estimate of its expected useful life and what residual value you think it might have at the end of that life. It simplifies things considerably to adopt the percentage rates used by the tax authorities for corporation tax calculation purposes.

# The annuity method

This method is based on an assumption that as depreciation costs are written off each year, funds of the same value will be invested at compound interest to build up to the replacement cost of the asset (less any residual value it may have) at the end of the asset's life. It therefore involves estimating the life of the asset, the replacement value required and the expected rate of interest on funds invested. Compound interest tables are then consulted to ascertain the annual investment needed and this is then the annual depreciation cost.

# Current replacement value (CRV) method

In times of continual inflation it is a realistic assumption that when the life of an asset has expired the replacement asset will cost more to purchase and install than the original one did. The CRV method recognizes this problem and aims to write off sufficient depreciation each year out of profits to build up to the eventual higher replacement value of the asset when the time comes.

There are a number of different formulae used. The most common method is:

1  Calculate (from price index tables or latest price lists) the CRV of the asset.

2  From the calculated CRV, deduct the latest estimate of the asset's residual value (R) and also deduct the total cumulative depreciation (D) written off to date.

3  Divide the result of calculation (2), i.e. the remainder of asset value still to be written off, by the *remaining* number of years of estimated useful life (L) to give a new annual depreciation charge:

$$\frac{CRV - R - D}{L}$$

# 3   BEAMA CONTRACT PRICE ADJUSTMENT FORMULA

The contract price shall be subject to variations in accordance with the BEAMA Contract Price Adjustment Formula (January 1979). If the cost to the contractor of performing his obligations under the contract shall be increased or reduced by reasons of any rise or fall in the rates of wages payable to labour or the cost of material or transport above or below such rates and costs ruling at the date of tender, or by reasons of the making or amendment after the date of tender of any law or any order, regulation or by-law having the force in the United Kingdom that shall affect the contractor in the performance of his obligations under the contract, the amount of such increase or reduction shall be added to or deducted from the contract price as the case may be, provided that no account shall be taken of any amount by which any cost incurred by the contractor has been increased by the default or negligence of the contractor.

Variations in the cost of materials and labour shall be calculated in accordance with the following formula

## (i)   Definitions: for the purpose of this formula:

'Contract price' means: the total sum certified in each Interim certificate less the total sum certified in all previous certificates in respect of the Plant Works.

'Contract period' means: the period between the date of acceptance of the Contractor's tender or the date of any earlier written instruction to the Contractor to proceed with the work and the date of the Contractor's application for the individual Interim certificate concerned.

## (ii)   Labour element

45% of the Contract Price will be regarded as the Labour Element and will be varied proportionately to the difference between the Basic Labour Cost Index and the Mean Labour Cost Index expressed as a percentage of the Basic Labour Cost Index. The Labour Cost Index will be the BEAMA Labour Cost Index for the Mechanical or Electrical Engineering Industry as appropriate to each section of the works. The Basic Labour Cost Index will be the Labour Cost Index at the base date; the Mean Labour Cost Index will be the average of the Labour Cost Indices published during the second half of the Contract period.

## (iii)   Materials element

45% of the Contract Price will be regarded as the Materials element and will be varied proportionately to the difference between the Basic Materials Index and the Mean Materials Index expressed as a percentage of the Basic Materials Index. The Materials Index will be the Department of Trade and Industry Price Index Order VII (excluding MLH 342) – Table 1 – Mechanical Engineering Industries: Materials Purchased or the equivalent Index for Electrical Machinery as appropriate to each section of the works (1970 = 100) published monthly in *Trade and Industry*. The Basic Materials Index will be the Materials Index *last published* before the base date: the Mean Materials Index will be the average of the Materials Indices so published during the middle three-fifths of the Contract Period.

(Harrison, 1992)

# 4 *PROJECT CLOSURE CHECKLISTS*

**TABLE 1** How to use the project closure checklist (Archibald, 1992)

| PROJECT TITLE | CUSTOMER | COST TYPE |
|---|---|---|
| _____ | _____ | _____ |
| CONTRACT No. | COMPLETION DATE | PROJECT MANAGER |
| _____ | _____ | _____ |

THE PROJECT CLOSE-OUT CHECKLISTS ARE DESIGNED FOR USE IN THE FOLLOWING MANNER:

COLUMN I (ITEM No.) Each task listed is identified by a specific number and grouped into categories. Categories are based on functions, not on organizations or equipment.

COLUMN II (TASK DESCRIPTION) Task descriptions are brief tasks that could apply to more than one category and are listed only in the most appropriate category.

COLUMN III (REQUIRED, YES OR NO) Check whether the item listed applies to the project.

COLUMN IV (DATE REQUIRED) Insert the required date for accomplishment of the task.

COLUMN V (ASSIGNED RESPONSIBILITY) insert the name of the man responsible to see that the task is accomplished on schedule. This may be a member of the Project Office or an individual within a functional department.

COLUMN VI (PRIORITY) A priority system established by the Project Manager may be used here, e.g. Priority # 1 may be all the tasks that must be accomplished before the contractual completion date, Priority # 2 within 2 weeks after the completion date, etc.

COLUMN VII (NOTES, REFERENCE) Refer in this column to any applicable procedures, a government specification that may apply to that task, etc.

**TABLE 2**  Project closure checklist (Archibald, 1992)

| Item No. | Task description | Required yes/no | Required date | Assigned responsibility | Priority | Notes, reference |
|---|---|---|---|---|---|---|
| **A** | **Project Office (PO) and project team (PT) organization** | | | | | |
| 1 | Conduct project close-out meeting | ___ | ___ | ___ | ___ | ___ |
| 2 | Establish PO and PT release and reassignment plan | ___ | ___ | ___ | ___ | ___ |
| 3 | Carry out necessary personnel actions | ___ | ___ | ___ | ___ | ___ |
| 4 | Prepare personal performance evaluation on each PO and PT member | ___ | ___ | ___ | ___ | ___ |
| **B** | **Instructions and procedures** | | | | | |
| | Issue instructions for: | | | | | |
| 1 | Termination of PO and PT | ___ | ___ | ___ | ___ | ___ |
| 2 | Close-out of all work orders and contracts | ___ | ___ | ___ | ___ | ___ |
| 3 | Termination of reporting procedures | ___ | ___ | ___ | ___ | ___ |
| 4 | Preparation of final report(s) | ___ | ___ | ___ | ___ | ___ |
| 5 | Completion and disposition of project file | ___ | ___ | ___ | ___ | ___ |
| **C** | **Financial** | | | | | |
| 1 | Close out financial documents and records | ___ | ___ | ___ | ___ | ___ |
| 2 | Audit final charges and costs | ___ | ___ | ___ | ___ | ___ |
| 3 | Prepare final project financial report(s) | ___ | ___ | ___ | ___ | ___ |
| 4 | Collect receivables | ___ | ___ | ___ | ___ | ___ |
| **D** | **Project definition** | | | | | |
| 1 | Document final approved project scope | ___ | ___ | ___ | ___ | ___ |
| 2 | Prepare final project breakdown structure and enter into project file | ___ | ___ | ___ | ___ | ___ |
| **E** | **Plans, budgets and schedules** | | | | | |
| 1 | Document actual delivery dates of all contracted deliverable end items | ___ | ___ | ___ | ___ | ___ |
| 2 | Document actual completion dates of all other contractual obligations | ___ | ___ | ___ | ___ | ___ |
| 3 | Prepare final project and task status reports | ___ | ___ | ___ | ___ | ___ |
| **F** | **Work authorization and control** | | | | | |
| 1 | Close out all work orders and contracts | ___ | ___ | ___ | ___ | ___ |
| **G** | **Project evaluation and control** | | | | | |
| 1 | Assure completion of all action assignments | ___ | ___ | ___ | ___ | ___ |
| 2 | Prepare final evaluation report(s) | ___ | ___ | ___ | ___ | ___ |
| 3 | Conduct final review meeting | ___ | ___ | ___ | ___ | ___ |
| 4 | Terminate financial, manpower and progress reporting procedures | ___ | ___ | ___ | ___ | ___ |

| Item No. | Task description | Required yes/no | Required date | Assigned responsibility | Priority | Notes, reference |
|---|---|---|---|---|---|---|
| **H** | **Management and customer reporting** | | | | | |
| 1 | Submit final report to customer | _____ | _____ | _____ | _____ | _____ |
| 2 | Submit final report to management | | | | | |
| **I** | **Marketing and contract administration** | | | | | |
| 1 | Compile all final contract documents with revisions, waivers and related correspondence | _____ | _____ | _____ | _____ | _____ |
| 2 | Verify and document compliance with all contractual terms | _____ | _____ | _____ | _____ | _____ |
| 3 | Compile required proof of shipment and customer acceptance documents | _____ | _____ | _____ | _____ | _____ |
| 4 | Officially notify customer of contract completion | _____ | _____ | _____ | _____ | _____ |
| 5 | Initiate and pursue any claims against customer | _____ | _____ | _____ | _____ | _____ |
| 6 | Prepare and conduct defence against any claims by customer | _____ | _____ | _____ | _____ | _____ |
| 7 | initiate public relations announcements re contract completion | _____ | _____ | _____ | _____ | _____ |
| 8 | Prepare final contract status report | _____ | _____ | _____ | _____ | _____ |
| **J** | **Extensions – new business** | | | | | |
| 1 | Document possibilities for project or contract extensions, or other related new business | _____ | _____ | _____ | _____ | _____ |
| 2 | Obtain commitment for extension | _____ | _____ | _____ | _____ | _____ |
| **K** | **Project records control** | | | | | |
| 1 | Complete project file and transmit to designated manager | _____ | _____ | _____ | _____ | _____ |
| 2 | Dispose of other project records as required by established procedures | _____ | _____ | _____ | _____ | _____ |
| **L** | **Purchasing and subcontracting** | | | | | |
| | For each Purchase Order and Subcontract | _____ | _____ | _____ | _____ | _____ |
| 1 | Document compliance and completion | _____ | _____ | _____ | _____ | _____ |
| 2 | Verify final payment and proper accounting to project | _____ | _____ | _____ | _____ | _____ |
| 3 | Notify vendor/contractor of final completion | | | | | |
| **M** | **Engineering documentation** | | | | | |
| 1 | Compile and store all engineering documentation | _____ | _____ | _____ | _____ | _____ |
| 2 | Prepare final technical report | _____ | _____ | _____ | _____ | _____ |
| **N** | **Site operations** | | | | | |
| 1 | Close down site operations | _____ | _____ | _____ | _____ | _____ |
| 2 | Dispose of equipment and material | | | | | |

# ANSWERS

## SAQ 1.1

The answer is shown in Table A.1.

**TABLE A.1** Project management versus operations management

| Projects | Operations |
| --- | --- |
| significant change | any changes small and evolutionary |
| limited in time and scope | never-ending |
| unique | repetitive |
| resources transient | resources stable |
| goal-oriented management | role-oriented management |
| transient | stable |
| attempt to balance performance, time and budget | performance, time and budget usually fixed and balanced |
| need to balance objectives | management generally in state of equilibrium |
| more exciting (perhaps!) | 'steady as she goes' feel |

You may have listed other aspects.

## SAQ 1.2

It is more likely that such a suggestion will fit with the *mission* of a catering firm but not with the mission of other types of organization.

## SAQ 1.3

(a)   In Figure A.1 we have drawn columns showing the cost of each category of fault and the percentage of total production that this represents, but this problem is simple enough for you to be able to manipulate the figures directly. The order is:

> 500 scratched and gouged
>
> 350 incorrect size despatched
>
> 200 out of round
>
> 50 substandard polishing
>
> 5 burring

(b)   This suggests that the greatest value improvement can be obtained by addressing the scratching and gouging problem, and then by correcting problems in the despatch of orders.

In reality the Pareto analysis may produce different results as other factors are certain to have an effect. Rectifying the problem of the incorrect size of widget will probably entail only the cost of taking the 350 wrong ones back into stock and despatching the right ones. The 200 widgets that were out of round will have to be scrapped and replaced by new ones at twice the cost of the faulty 200.

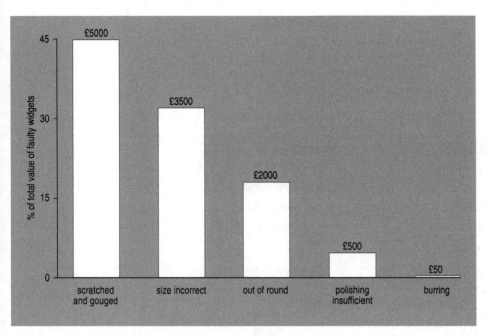

**FIGURE A.1**   Pareto analysis of widget problems

## SAQ 1.4

The purpose of a scenario is to provide a general statement of an idea of what is involved in order to meet an objective. This provides a basis for subsequent assessment. Scenarios are developed from ideas, by any method for generating ideas and selecting those that are possible or reasonable.

## SAQ 1.5

(a)   Main steps are:

1   Identify important features.

2   Identify the constituent elements of each feature.

3   List the elements.

4   Attach a point value to each depending upon its relative contribution to the feature. Ensure that the sum of all the points for the elements of a feature adds up to 1.00.

5   Assess the features using the constituent elements and assign the point values for each constituent assessed.

6   Sum the point values.

7   Multiply the sum of point values for each feature by the weight factor for that feature.

8   Sum these for all features to obtain a figure of merit (FOM) for the candidate product.

Products can then be compared using their figures of merit.

(b)   The value of doing a features analysis is in taking an objective view of the features identified in the requirements as key or important, then establishing a ranking system and applying it in an attempt to find the product whose features most closely meet the requirements.

## SAQ 1.6

The calculation of payback period for Proposal A is simple:

Payback period = 20 000/3200 = 6.25 years

Proposal B is slightly more complex, as shown in Table A.2 below.

**TABLE A.2**  Net cash flows for Proposal B

| Year | Flow in year £ | Cumulative cash flow at year end £ |
|------|------|------|
| 0 | −20 000 | −20 000 |
| 1 | −2000 | −22 000 |
| 2 | 2675 | −19 325 |
| 3 | 3200 | −16 125 |
| 4 | 4550 | −11 575 |
| 5 | 6550 | −5025 |
| 6 | 7000 | 1975 |
| 7 | 8000 | 9975 |

Proposal B will recover the initial project investment some time before the end of year 6, at which point it would have achieved a surplus of £1975. If we assume that the £7000 net annual **cash inflow** for Year 6 occurs in 12 equal monthly cash inflows, it will be nearly the ninth month of the year before payback is achieved: approximately 5.75 years.

Therefore it seems that Proposal B is likely to pay back its investment sooner than Proposal A. However, when reaching this conclusion it is necessary to consider the accuracy of the estimates. In this case a difference of 6 months in payback may be significant.

## SAQ 1.7

(a)  This is a discounting problem. At the end of the period your money will be worth £215.65 in present-day terms. This was found using the discount table, looking down the 3% column and across the 5 year row to obtain the factor 0.8626 and multiplying the £250 by that factor.

(b)  This is a compounding problem. At the end of the first year you will have £250 × 1.03 = £257.50. That is multiplied by the same factor to obtain the second year's total of £265.23. Likewise, the third year is £273.18, the fourth year is £281.38 and the fifth and final year is £289.82 (all rounded to the nearest penny).

(c)  This is both a compounding and discounting problem. Intuition should tell you that if the rate of inflation is the same as the rate of compounded return on your investment, you will break even – your money will be worth £250 in present day terms at the end of five years.

## SAQ 1.8

The answer appears in Table A.3.

**TABLE A.3** NPV of Proposal B using 12%

| Year | Net cash flow £ | Discount factor | NPV £ |
|------|-----------------|-----------------|-------|
| 0 | −20 000 | 1.0000 | −20 000 |
| 1 | −2000 | 0.8929 | −1785 |
| 2 | 2675 | 0.7972 | 2132 |
| 3 | 3200 | 0.7118 | 2277 |
| 4 | 4550 | 0.6355 | 2891 |
| 5 | 6550 | 0.5674 | 3716 |
| 6 | 7000 | 0.5066 | 3546 |
| 7 | 8000 | 0.4523 | 3618 |

Total net present value of proposal: −£3605

## SAQ 1.9

A trial and error method is required to establish the value of the discount rate that gives a value of NPV equal to zero. We have already tried 12% and found a large negative NPV so next we might try 6%. You would find that this gave a positive NPV. Successive trials between these values show that at 7% the NPV is still positive, (£867), and at 8% it is negative, (−£137). You should therefore conclude that the Internal Rate of Return of this proposal is just under 8%.

## SAQ 1.10

(a) The value of IRR is independent of project size.

(b) The value of NPV would be doubled.

## SAQ 1.11

The decision tree is as shown in Figure A.2. The values of the outcomes at each leaf are the net benefits of the whole path from decision to the end of the path. Note that the value of an outcome can be negative. The values of the EMV for each decision are also shown on the figure, £9400, £4000 and £7000.

## SAQ 1.12

Controlling changes by managing them (change control), a vital function in all projects other than the most minor.

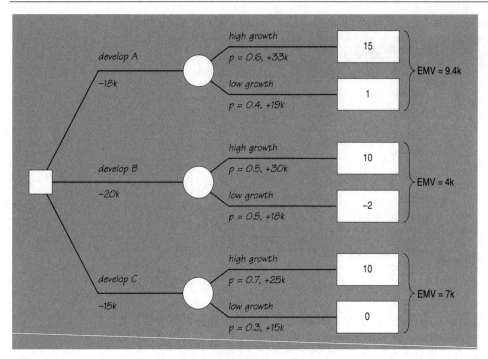

**FIGURE A.2**   A decision tree for three products

## SAQ 2.1

Work breakdown structure

Statements of work

Product breakdown structure

Cost breakdown structure

## SAQ 2.2

To describe what tasks make up a project and then to organize these tasks in a logical way for use elsewhere in planning and monitoring.

## SAQ 2.3

Both types of document identify in detail work to be done and may state the standard to which the work is to be done. The statement of work also indicates what *inputs* are necessary to that work. Both types are not only a specification of what is to be done but an aid to estimating and to establishing clear understandings between client and customer or manager and employee.

## SAQ 2.4

To describe complexes of machinery and equipment for two purposes: to allow comparisons to be made between elements from different suppliers or manufacturers in order to determine the optimum choice of elements, and to aid in the estimating of the costs of the entire complex.

## SAQ 2.5

It describes the categories for estimating and helps to ensure that nothing is left out of the estimating process. Its categories serve as a cross-reference to items in the WBS, the product breakdown structures and statements of work.

## SAQ 2.6

The answer is shown in Table A.4 below.

**TABLE A.4** Risk, strategy and type

| Risk | Strategy | Type |
|---|---|---|
| Supplier goes bankrupt | Identify and approach alternative supplier | Contingency plan |
| Supplier does not deliver on time | Penalty clause in contract with supplier | Risk transfer |
| | Add extra time to project plan after date told to supplier | Risk reduction (leave yourself a 'cushion' of time) |
| Specification of components must be met as they interface with items from other suppliers | Stipulate exactly what specification must be met in the contract with supplier | Risk reduction and risk transfer (supplier risks getting it wrong, not you) |
| Key expert in supplier's organization may leave | Watch this situation | Risk acceptance (you will need to review situation from time to time) |

## SAQ 2.7

To give the project a total cost in which you and others can have a defined measure of confidence.

To discover what the requirements are and evaluate them.

To identify those factors that will need to be controlled and discover which measures can be applied to monitor these factors during project execution.

To communicate with the contractor's management and the client about the costs and risks (and costs of risks) of the project.

To allow those concerned with the project to make decisions about it and about alternatives within the scope of the project.

## SAQ 2.8

(a)  The 'similar project' approach compares the project or task to actual costs and times for similar projects or tasks and uses these as a basis for the estimate, applying judgement as to how the present project or task differs from the baseline project or task.

(b)  The component method uses the work breakdown structure extended as necessary. The estimator looks in turn at each of the lowest level tasks to be carried out, estimates times for each, totals them and can then apply a rate for the work to obtain a cost estimate.

(c)  The standardized method assumes the existence of a body of actual data large enough to be statistically analysed in order to derive a formula for estimating.

## SAQ 2.9

(a)  There are two ways. The estimator can either use the organization's median rate for the expected grade and type of employee or prepare three estimates using the highest, median and lowest rates for the employee type. This results in a range within which the actual value is *likely* to fall.

(b)  A common method is to add a fixed percentage, typically 10%, of estimated costs as a contingency reserve. Another is to add 5% of committed but unspent costs plus 9% of planned but uncommitted funds plus 1% of all outstanding costs. (Actual figures should depend on assessed risk.)

(c) The base date estimate is a means of measuring performance against original estimates while taking into account the effects of inflation. Actual costs are either inflated or deflated (depending upon the changes in the value of money) before being compared with the original (base date) estimate. Figures for changes in the value of money over time must be available in order to use this method.

## SAQ 2.10

- Organize.
- Draw up a task list (e.g. WBS or other).
- Draw up a product breakdown structure if needed.
- Draw up a cost breakdown structure and cross-references.
- List materials, supplies, component parts, etc.
- Gather data.
- Estimate.
- Classify and consolidate.
- Prepare and present to management or the client.
- *Always* apply checks at each step.

## SAQ 2.11

In English law an invitation to treat is simply a suggestion of the terms under which a potential contractor or supplier is willing to *consider* doing business.

An offer constitutes the terms under which a contractor or supplier will do business if this is accepted by the client.

An option is a clause that specifies how long a tender or estimate will remain valid.

## SAQ 2.12

- Experience of tenderer for this type of work
- estimation of quality of work done previously by tenderer
- financial soundness of tenderer's organization
- likely working relationship between tenderer and client
- the level to which the work, quality, risks and schedule have been specified in the tender document
- whether the tender appears to set out achievable objectives (do estimated costs and schedules appear to be achievable?)
- whether the expectations of the tenderer and client about the work are in harmony with each other
- what type of contract will be signed.

(The first three items can be ascertained in part by asking for and taking up references from previous clients, the tenderer's bank, etc.)

## SAQ 2.13

Not in law. You've made a counter-offer, in which you've specified something that was not part of your original discussion with the potential contractors.

## SAQ 2.14

An offer is a statement of the type, standard and cost of work that a contractor is willing to undertake.

A letter of intent does not have the legal strength of a contract. Whether or not the terms agreed in a letter of intent are enforceable depends upon a case-by-case examination of the letter and its circumstances by a court.

A contract contains terms which are legally enforceable. Disputes may arise as a result of changes to the work or standard specified and to the resulting cost and time elements, but the terms of a contract must be met by the contractor and if they are the client must pay.

## SAQ 2.15

(a)   Because research tends to be 'open ended' work where it is difficult to specify precisely what is to be delivered, it is likely to involve a cost–plus contract or a time and materials contract.

(b)   This type of work would usually be contracted using a fixed-price contract, unless there was some very novel aspect to the work.

(c)   This type of work could employ any of the three types of contract depending on the degree of uncertainty.

## SAQ 2.16

This depends on whether or not the supplier, before going bankrupt, in some way indicated *which* desks, chairs, cabinets, etc., were to be used to fill your order. If he did so, then these items are your property, but you will have to pay the remaining 75% to the supplier's receivers. If he did not, then you do not have property in any furniture in his warehouse and can only attempt to recover your deposit from the receivers.

## SAQ 2.17

A 'time is of the essence' contract may not be acceptable to the contractor because delays due to weather, suppliers being late or industrial disputes cannot be ruled out. You could have a contract that listed these and allowed for delays – but could the contract be worded so that you still had your platform available by, say, no later than 15 August? You could specify a contract with early completion incentives to minimize the chance of an extremely expensive delay if you had to wait through the winter and spring before positioning your platform. This might be the best option, because the contractor could use the knowledge of the cost savings to pay extra to more reliable suppliers and to forestall industrial disruptions through bonus incentives for the workers.

## SAQ 2.18

Damages reimburse a party to a contract for financial loss incurred as a result of problems in completing that contract. A penalty is a punitive sum to be paid in addition to any damages.

## SAQ 2.19

Yes. You could stipulate a stage payment to be due upon completion of the framing and closing in of the building. You could include a formula reducing the payment if the contractor is late, or you could include a formula increasing the payment if the contractor is early.

## SAQ 2.20

Ways in which changes can be required are:

- unforeseen circumstances arise
- the technical imperative ('keep up with changes in the technology!')
- inadequate specifications
- inadequate planning and design, perhaps due to the management imperative ('Let's see people out there sweating!')

Changes have a cumulative effect on a project; even a modest number of apparently small changes can make a project overrun its budget or schedule. If changes are not properly agreed, estimated and the likely effects communicated to all parties, disputes can arise as a result of the project not adhering to the contract.

## SAQ 3.1

The primary objective is to complete the project to the contracted quality within the allocated budget and the agreed timescale.

## SAQ 3.2

(a)  The following list of possible client responsibilities is not exhaustive:
- provide details of the interface to the stock control system
- provide details of the physical environment for the equipment, dimensions of the space available, details of existing cabling
- allocate some of the supermarket staff to answer the contractor's queries
- make staff available to facilitate the installation of new equipment
- provide accommodation and facilities for installation staff
- provide storage space for equipment and materials during installation
- provide training facilities and allocate time for supermarket staff to learn how to use the new system
- have staff available for testing at times when the supermarket is closed
- provide details of acceptance tests
- prepare the user manual for the staff.

(b)  Deliverable items could include many items of which the following is a selection to show the scope:
- system requirements specification (analysis of contractual requirements)
- project plan (updatable)
- design specification (hardware and software)
- blueprints (floor plans)
- software listings as tested by software house

- physical equipment, installed and commissioned
- installation procedure specifications
- maintenance manuals (hardware and software)
- vendor documentation (for equipment procured from any third party supplier via the contractor)
- system test criteria, testing plan, results
- training for staff.

## SAQ 3.3

There are four main reasons:

- to establish mutual confidence and a co-operative climate
- to report progress face-to-face
- to control changes
- to prepare for joint activities (e.g. acceptance, commissioning).

## SAQ 3.4

You would require the subcontractor to produce a plan for the subcontracted part of the project. You would then need to evaluate this plan to ensure that it was feasible and that it fitted in with the overall scheme.

## SAQ 3.5

The problem is that each package in Figure 3.3 requires a team of mixed disciplines: civil, mechanical, electrical and instrumentation. For a small project this could be difficult because it requires five civil engineers to fill the five civil design functions and similar numbers in other disciplines. If the project requires only one or two civil designers then each of them would have to fill more than one position in the organization.

## SAQ 3.6

According to Figure 3.4, the prime responsibility is the project administrator's. Support could be obtained from the instrument engineer or indeed from the civil, mechanical and electrical engineers. The site engineer needs to be notified.

## SAQ 3.7

(a) This milestone is very poor because it is difficult to measure '50% completion'. It might be improved if it were possible to define several packages of drawings, preferably with an action following completion, e.g. 'extruder drawing package approved for construction'.

(b) This milestone is quite good, but the word 'installed' could be open to various interpretations. An improvement would be 'extruder installed and ready for first production trial'.

(c) This milestone is good. The word 'approved' tightens its definition.

(d) This milestone is poor because although the number of lines is measurable we cannot interpret the significance. If this represents a number of modules it is better to itemize those modules that have been coded and are ready for testing.

(e) This milestone is quite good. It is easily testable unless there is dispute about what constitutes 'the computer'. If the computer consists of several modules, the milestone could be improved by specifying that it means all of them, including any peripheral equipment, and that it is ready to be installed.

## SAQ 3.8

Our answer is shown in Figure A.3.

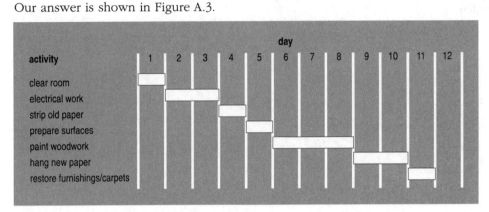

**FIGURE A.3** Gantt chart for decorating a room

Best practice would use WBS references as activity identifiers on Gantt charts and other planning documents. Certainly the WBS references should be used once a document ceases to be a draft and becomes 'official'.

## SAQ 3.9

Projects should also have only one finish node. If at some point in the network there is a node which represents the completion of some part of the project from which there is no further activity, then this node should be linked to the unique project completion node with a dummy activity. The purpose of this is to highlight all the points of completion.

## SAQ 3.10

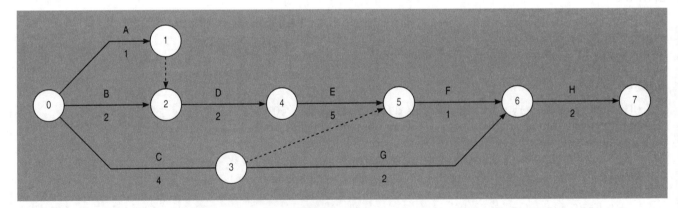

**FIGURE A.4** The activity-on-arrow network for well-digging

The network that you have produced should be logically equivalent to Figure A.4. If your network has extra arrows or more event nodes than ours then you are probably making it too complicated. Try not to introduce dummy nodes unnecessarily.

## SAQ 3.11

The earliest event times for each node are shown in the top right-hand corners of the nodes in Figure A.5. At the end of this forward pass we can conclude that it will take a minimum of 12 weeks to complete the project.

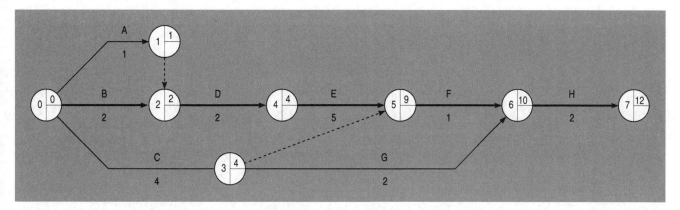

**FIGURE A.5**   Network for well-digging after the forward pass

## SAQ 3.12

The pencil and paper must both be found within 5 minutes (latest time for Event 3) and someone must start looking for the paper within the next 3 minutes (latest time for Event 0).

## SAQ 3.13

The solution is shown in Figure A.6. The critical path is marked with broad arrows.

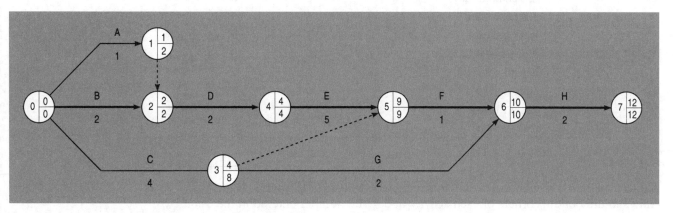

**FIGURE A.6**   The fully analysed well-digging network

## SAQ 3.14

Not necessarily! Even the activities on the critical path may have float if the project does not have to be completed by its *earliest* possible date. (It *is* true that any delay in an activity on the critical path will delay the project beyond its *earliest* possible completion date. It may still meet its target date if that is different.)

## SAQ 3.15

Path 1–2–3 and path 1–3 would *both* be critical.

## SAQ 3.16

(a)  After the forward and backward passes the project network should appear as in Figure A.7. (You may have chosen different node identity numbers.)

(b)  The critical path is the path through Activities E, F, H, or using our node identifiers: 0–2–6–8–9.

(c)  See Table A.5.

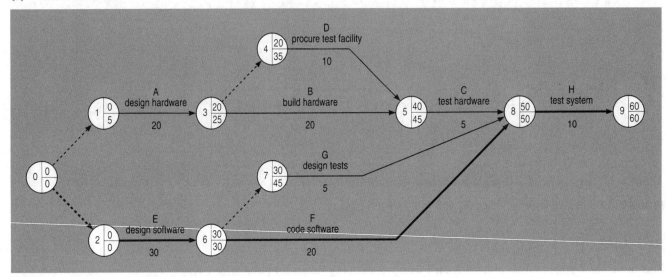

**FIGURE A.7**  The computer project analysed

**TABLE A.5**  Float and free float for each activity

| Activity identifier | Description | Total float | Free float |
|---|---|---|---|
| A | design hardware | 5 | 0 |
| B | build hardware | 5 | 0 |
| C | test hardware | 5 | 5 |
| D | procure test facility | 15 | 10 |
| E | design software | 0 | 0 |
| F | code software | 0 | 0 |
| G | design tests | 15 | 15 |
| H | test system | 0 | 0 |

## SAQ 3.17

A *backward pass* through the network, starting at the final node, produces the entries in the bottom corners of each activity node. The number entered in the bottom right-hand corner of a node is the latest finishing time, LFT, for this activity and is deduced by examining all the links from this node to immediate successor nodes. It will be set equal to the earliest of the latest start times of all the successor nodes. The latest start time (LST), in the bottom left corner, is calculated from LFT by subtracting the duration of the activity. Float can be calculated using the formula for total float given earlier in Section 3.3.4. Float is entered in the middle compartment of the bottom row.

## SAQ 3.18

The solution appears in Figure A.8.

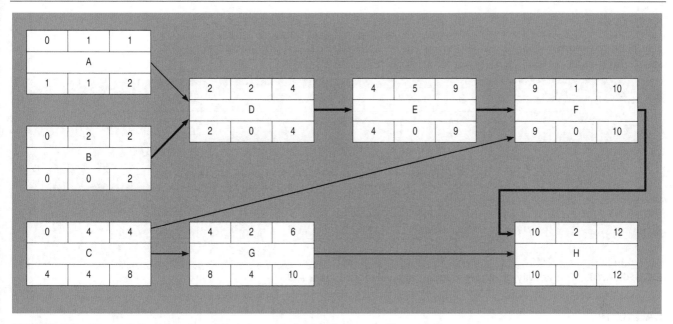

**FIGURE A.8** The activity-on-node network for well-digging (compare Figure A.4)

## SAQ 3.19

The completed precedence diagram is shown in Figure A.9. The layout of the activities on the page does not matter. If you had difficulty calculating the total float, remember that where there are multiple constraints you should use the formula:

total float = LFT − EST − duration.

Note in particular that EFT for activity F is 6, not 5, because it is constrained by the finish of Activity D.

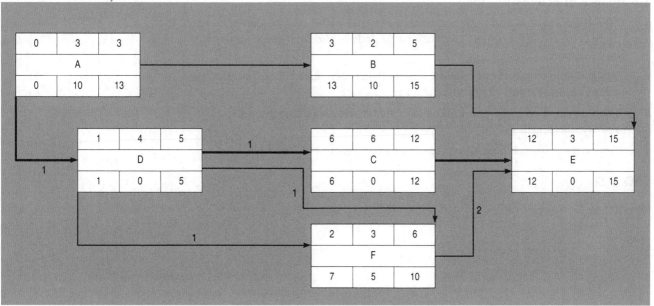

**FIGURE A.9** Answer to SAQ 3.19

## SAQ 3.20

The activity-on-arrow diagram is shown in Figure A.10. The earliest and latest starts and finishes of each activity agree, as expected, with Figure A.9.

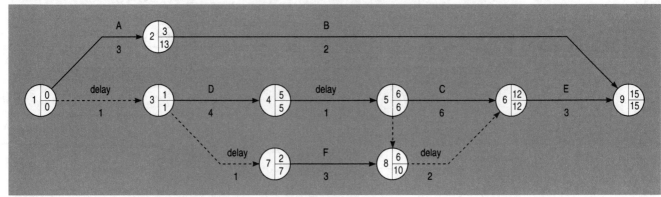

**FIGURE A.10**   The activity-on-arrow diagram equivalent to Figure A.9

## SAQ 3.21

You should have found most of the following features:

### Advantages of activity-on-arrow

- Diagrams are more compact with smaller, simpler, nodes.

- The timing of key events representing the completion of several parallel activities is displayed more clearly. In an activity-on-node diagram a dummy node could be needed to represent a milestone.

- Manual calculations may be slightly quicker because there is no redundant information on the diagram.

### Advantages of activity-on-node

- All the information about an individual activity is gathered into one node, so there is no need for further calculations to deduce the float on an activity for example.

- It is possible to represent relationships between activities other than the normal finish-to-start relationship.

- There is no need to invent dummy activities merely to achieve unique activity identification.

- Time delays *between* activities are easy to represent.

## SAQ 3.22

Figure A.11 shows the Gantt chart for this project.

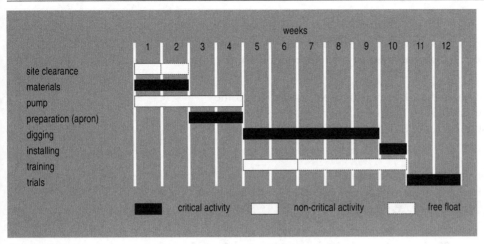

**FIGURE A.11** Gantt chart for well-digging showing free float

## SAQ 3.23

The time-scaled version of the network is shown in Figure A.12. You may have found that it was rather tedious to draw and hence conclude that you would not wish to repeat the exercise when it required updating.

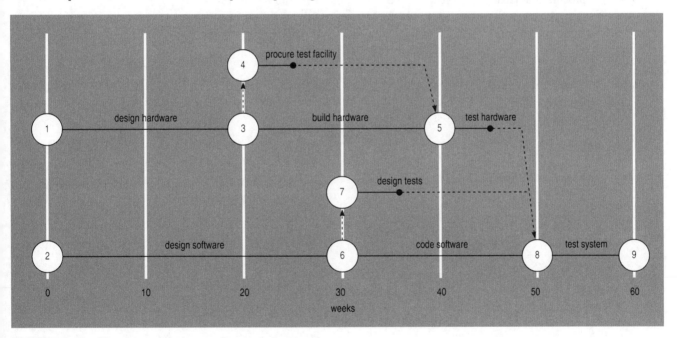

**FIGURE A.12** The time-scaled computer project network

## SAQ 3.24

One of the benefits of using a network is that it is amenable to change without redrawing. This benefit is lost as soon as a time-scaled version is employed because the position of an activity on the page depends on the time for which it is scheduled.

## SAQ 3.25

(a)  The total work required is 365 person-weeks. As the time limit is 60 weeks the minimum is 6.08 people working continuously, which rounds up to seven people.

(b)  A list of activities is required in order of increasing float. In Table A.6 they are already listed in order of increasing float and where activities have the same float in order of latest finish time. EST means earliest start time and LFT means latest finishing time.

**TABLE A.6**  Activities in order of increasing float (and then LFT)

| Reference | Description | Duration | Staff | EST | LFT | Float |
|-----------|-------------|----------|-------|-----|-----|-------|
| 2–6 | design software | 30 | 2 | 0 | 30 | 0 |
| 6–8 | code software | 20 | 4 | 30 | 50 | 0 |
| 8–9 | test system | 10 | 3 | 50 | 60 | 0 |
| 1–3 | design hardware | 20 | 3 | 0 | 25 | 5 |
| 3–5 | build hardware | 20 | 4 | 20 | 45 | 5 |
| 5–8 | test hardware | 5 | 3 | 40 | 50 | 5 |
| 4–5 | procure test facility | 10 | 3 | 20 | 45 | 15 |
| 7–8 | design tests | 5 | 2 | 30 | 50 | 15 |

(c) The initial resource loading built up by serial scheduling of the activities above at their earliest start time is as shown in Figure A.13. Notice that building the hardware is shown as a dislocated block because the load of critical activities underneath it forms an irregular base. The peak staff requirement (over weeks 31 to 35) is 10 people.

You might have noticed that the resource loading we have found in this example has the characteristic shape of many projects: it rises to a peak during the execution and tails off at the end of the project.

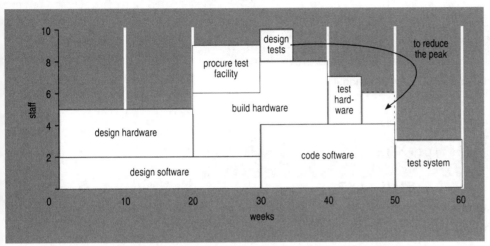

**FIGURE A.13** The initial resource loading for the time-limited schedule

(d) The optimum within the given constraints is obtained by deferring the design of the tests until after the hardware has been built. (The order of activities 5–8 and 7–8 is immaterial.)

(e) Since there is little scope for delaying any activities into the system testing period it seems best to think about ways in which some of the activity in weeks 20 to 30 might be brought forward into weeks 10 to 20. It may be possible to start building the hardware and/or procuring the test facility without waiting for all the hardware design to be completed. If it is possible to procure the test facility, using two people for 15 weeks starting after 15 weeks instead of three people for 10 weeks starting after 20 weeks, then the resource loading could be reduced to a peak of eight people.

## SAQ 3.26

Parallel scheduling considers all the activities eligible at any time in parallel, and uses some decision rule or rules to choose as many of them at that time as can be active within the resource constraint. This procedure is applied first at the start of the project and then repeated at all the points of time when resource is released by the completion of an activity.

## SAQ 3.27

(a) The seven staff resource-limited schedule for the computer project is shown in Figure A.14. The working is as shown in Table A.7.

396

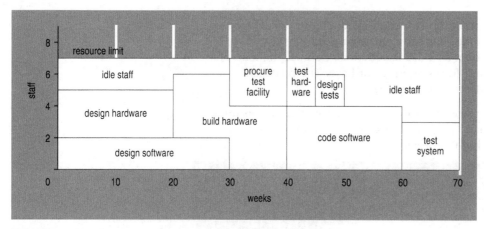

**FIGURE A.14**   The resource-limited computer project schedule

**TABLE A.7**   Producing the resource-limited schedule

| Time | Free staff | Eligible activities in LST order | | | Comment |
|------|-----------|----------|-------|-----|---------|
| | | **Activity** | **Staff** | **LST** | |
| 0 | 7 | design software | 2 | 0 | accept |
| | | design hardware | 3 | 5 | accept |
| 20 | 5 | build hardware | 4 | 25 | accept |
| | | procure test facility | 3 | 35 | insufficient staff |
| 30 | 3 | code software | 4 | 30 | insufficient staff |
| | | procure test facility | 3 | 35 | accept |
| | | design tests | 2 | 45 | insufficient staff |
| 40 | 7 | code software | 4 | 30 | accept |
| | | test hardware | 3 | 45 | accept |
| | | design tests | 2 | 45 | insufficient staff |
| 45 | 3 | design tests | 2 | 45 | accept |
| 60 | 7 | test system | 3 | 50 | accept |

Note: at time = 40, there are two activities equally eligible on the criterion of LST and both have the same duration. A further criterion may be used to choose between them: the criterion of accepting the activity with the higher staff requirement. In fact this has no effect on the overall project time.

(b)   The project is completed in 70 weeks.

(c)   This is the optimum given the constraint of seven staff. At the beginning the only eligible activities have both been scheduled, so nothing further could be scheduled until 20 weeks. As building hardware and coding software each use four staff, they must be sequential activities, taking a further 40 weeks. Since system testing requires coded software it cannot start until after 60 weeks, thus producing a project time which could not be reduced below 70 weeks unless there were more staff.

## SAQ 3.28

The technique described for the resource-limited approach, parallel scheduling, would be easier to implement. This is because selecting which activities to perform at a given time can be computed from the given set of rules without iteration or optimization.

## SAQ 3.29

(a) The project plan should be prepared by the project manager (with whatever assistance is required from the team).

(b) It is prepared, usually in outline form, before the project is sanctioned (contract signed) and elaborated in greater detail after the project is sanctioned. It continues to be updated throughout the project.

(c) There are three potential groups of readers: the contractor's management, the client, and members of the project team. Each may see a slightly different version, with sections omitted for confidentiality or summarized for brevity.

## SAQ 4.1

1 Setting or accepting overall goals and direction, interpreting these, reacting to changes in these, clarifying the problem and setting boundaries to it.

2 Identifying and obtaining resources by negotiating for them, keeping them for the project and managing their effective use.

3 Building a team structure and defining the roles within it.

4 Establishing good communications with various groups or individuals contributing to the project in such a way as to get their support and commitment.

5 Taking an overview of the project so as to be able to manage time and other resources, anticipate reactions from project stakeholders, spot links where they occur and anticipate the unexpected.

6 Taking action and accepting risk to keep the project going, especially when there are difficulties.

## SAQ 4.2

- Delegate not only the task but also the authority over resources for that task.

- Sell the task, discuss approaches, reassure, and then be willing to accept mistakes.

- Delegate to the lowest level possible, bearing in mind the delegatee's potential.

- Allow people to learn from their mistakes, but watch out for and prevent serious ones.

- Ensure that two-way feedback takes place: reports of progress on the one hand and guidance and acknowledgement on the other.

## SAQ 4.3

(a) Consider:

- who to negotiate with (i.e. who has the authority to loan the portables)

- if any members of the team currently have a portable that could be used

- your goal, and maximum and minimum positions

- what are the issues; why it is important to your project

- when you need the portables and in what numbers (when do you need the maximum number, and when can you manage with fewer)?

- constructing a 'no lose' negotiation 'script'.

(b) Main points in support of your case:

- the importance to the whole organization of this project

- that company time and money will be saved

- that you can be flexible and have different loan times for different machines

- that (say) two of the portable PCs could be on a 24-hour call-back arrangement, should the need arise

- that you know there are normally at least five in stock.

(c) The hoped-for outcome is (probably) six or perhaps seven portables, and the minimum (fall-back) position is three.

These are the main points, but you may have thought of other points that are equally valid.

## SAQ 4.4

(a) You should have listed three of the following and their drawbacks as shown in Table A.8.

**TABLE A.8** 'Negative' leadership skills and drawbacks

| | |
|---|---|
| Threatening | Cooperation is grudging; resistence to leadership is increased |
| Witholding information | Nasty surprises can result; others may not share important information with you |
| Blaming | Organizational paralysis can result; a blamer may lose respect |
| Delaying | If things go wrong it may be difficult to avoid blame for failure |
| Sacrificing the future to the present | Consequences will still remain to be dealt with later; it could have a very adverse effect on quality |

(b) You should have listed three of the following and listed at least one way each can help, as shown in Table A.9.

**TABLE A.9** 'Positive' leadership skills and ways they help

| Giving feedback | Encourages and motivates (if positive), can correct problems (if negative); can improve interpersonal relations |
| --- | --- |
| Recognizing progress and success | It can be perceived as compensation for a job and is free or very cheap; if documented it can aid future performance appraisals |
| Reward good performance | It can be free or cheap; shows that the 'boss' knows how hard or how well one has worked; it may result in improved conditions; it means that the person receiving the reward 'owes one' to the manager; the person is motivated to continue to perform well |
| Coaching and encouraging | It demonstrates the concern and interest of the manager for the subordinate; can result in improved performance or extra effort; may gain the manager respect and loyalty |
| Walking around | Enables 'intelligence' gathering at a level and in a way not possible from reading reports; subordinates get to know the manager; it encourages a supportive and open climate |

(c)     Good communication skills (listening, talking and writing).

## SAQ 4.5

(a)     Functionally arranged organizational hierarchy: clearly this is a set of routine functions with no project characteristics.

(b)     Project (single) team structure. Inputs to formulating the strategy would be needed from various user areas, plus professional and technical inputs. (For a relatively small organization a matrix structure might be used.)

(c)     Functional. While change-over work might well be done in teams the operation is routine. Elements which could be passed from one functional area to another are:

Production planning $\rightarrow$ engineering (fitters) $\rightarrow$ engineering (electrical) $\rightarrow$ manufacturing/production.

(d)     Matrix project (possibly project (single) team). Clearly this is a project because it is unique, but similar production lines will have been developed in the past. Significant inputs from various different specialists at different stages would be needed, suggesting a matrix project structure is most likely.

(e)     Functional, probably with a project manager or co-ordinator. Installing production lines will happen quite often in this industry, but the work will be the responsibility (almost entirely) of one department: engineering. This suggests using the existing functional organization, but the work will need some co-ordination. If a new process as well as new equipment were involved a project organization would be more likely.

(f)     This could be either a functional or a matrix project. Making incremental improvements would be the responsibility of the various line managers for the different functions involved; however, if new systems or radical change (e.g. process improvements or changes or business process re-engineering) were involved a project structure would be needed – probably of a matrix type because of the various different professional interests (academics, editors, TV producers, etc.).

(g) Functional. Formulating the cream would, most likely, take place exclusively in the research and development department (with some marketing department input).

(h) Functional, possibly with baton-pass, or with a project manager or co-ordinator if this is part of a wider project. The question did not mention a new system, so the straightforward computerization of an existing system with known requirements is implied – hence the choice of a functional approach.

(i) Project (single) team or matrix. A new system is being devised requiring various user and professional inputs (suggesting full project structure) but perhaps at different stages or to different degrees (suggesting matrix).

## SAQ 4.6

(a) Matrix structures for projects do seem to be used more frequently.

- The pace of scientific and technological advance is constantly accelerating, leading to changes in almost everyone's working life: this leads to many more 'change management' projects using all the different types of project organization, including matrix structures.

- Management and staff in many organizations are becoming more comfortable with matrix structures.

- The economic and competitive environments of the late 1980s and early 1990s have led to less job security and staff are more willing to participate in projects but prefer not to lose the security of a home base where their career interests are protected to some extent.

- Changes in social attitude have led to staff generally wanting a variety of job experiences, but also with an element of stability.

(b) Matrix structures are likely to be found in organizations going through:

- significant changes because of new technology

- a major change of strategic direction

- a reorganization.

Full project structures are likely to be found in organizations that:

- handle many projects as part of their core business (e.g. construction, software companies, media production businesses, consultancies)

- regularly need to change their product range (e.g. automobiles, electrical goods)

- use technical innovation as their competitive advantage.

(c) Problems with functional project co-ordination:

- difficulties in obtaining true project costs (costs are lumped together with operating costs)

- problems from having no clear owner or sponsor of the project

- information flow and communication difficulties when these are outside the 'normal' hierarchy

- no team synergy

- unclear objectives if these cannot be clearly differentiated from 'normal' operations.

## SAQ 4.7

(a) Major influences:

- executive and regional management

- customers.

(b) All staff are likely to be stakeholders in existing practices, but the stock clerk/book-keeper, the deputy manager and manager are likely to be most affected.

(c) The stakeholder map is shown in Figure A.15.

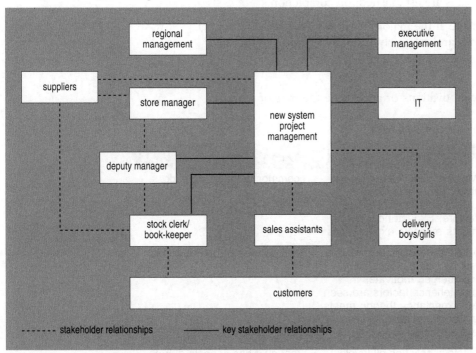

**FIGURE A.15** Stakeholder map for the newsagent's shop

## SAQ 4.8

(a) There should be regular contact; how regular depends on the style and culture of the business (and perhaps on the experience and status of the project manager). The contact would probably be informal face-to-face meetings (about every two weeks perhaps), with occasional formal reports discussed by the two people at the draft stage.

(b) All the executive board are stakeholders, but apart from the sponsor other key stakeholders are:

- the managing director

- the finance director

- the IS manager.

Contact probably would be informal and occasional (two to three times during the project perhaps) prior to the major (milestone) reports.

(c)  Other special 'managing-up' considerations:

- Ensure the managing director is kept well informed so that her support continues.

- Ensure that the sponsor is kept fully informed of major steps and is consulted about major problems (but not bothered with minor ones).

- Ensure that the sponsor is aware of other contacts with key stakeholders, and that the sponsor never receives news about the project from any source other than the project team.

- Milestone reports for the board should appear at key stages, e.g. at project initiation stage; when premises are found and full costs are known; when moving plans are established; on completion.

(d)  Formal reports should be made at the major milestones (see last point in (c) above); three or four at most, and relatively brief for a project of this size.

## SAQ 4.9

The following table shows likely motivations or applicable theories of work.

**TABLE A.10**  jobs and motivation or theories of work

| Job | Motivation | Theory of work |
|-----|-----------|----------------|
| (a) | Maslow: satisfies the lowest three levels; Herzberger: satisfies the maintenance factors; Expectancy theory: meets extrinsic expectations | commodity theory of work |
| (b) | Maslow: satisfies most of the levels, may satisfy all; Herzberger: motivates if maintenance factors are seen to; Expectancy theory: meets both extrinsic and intrinsic expectations | has aspects of both theories |
| (c) | Maslow: satisfies all levels; Herzberger: as with (b), though the individual may ignore maintenance factors unless they become untenable; Expectancy theory: intrinsic expectations are likely to predominate | though it has aspects of both theories, the humanistic theory is likely to predominate |

## SAQ 4.10

In terms of Maslow's hierarchy of needs, Alan will have safety needs satisfied by the permanence of his employment by the bank; Sally will only have a temporary fulfilment, limited by the terms of her contract, of those needs. Alan will probably have established relationships with his colleagues at the bank and so will have needs for relationships also satisfied. His regular hours of employment will allow him to plan for and fulfil his physiological needs for fresh air, exercise and regular meals easily, whereas Sally will be in the situation of having to establish relationships from scratch, and the hours demanded of her as a contractor may mean that she will not be able easily to plan to satisfy basic physiological needs. Alan may find his need for esteem amongst his colleagues met if the project is successful and he is seen to have had a successful role in the team. For Sally, esteem may be more difficult to obtain, since we assume she will move on to another job when this one is completed. However, a favourable report from the project manager about her contribution to the project may enhance her esteem in the eyes of future employers. Both may find their needs for self-fulfilment met by the project if it is successful and if they feel they've been challenged and risen to meet that challenge.

In terms of Herzberg's theory, both may have similar responses to the hygiene factors and motivators present, though (since contract personnel are frequently paid more) Sally's rate of pay may upset people like Alan, while Alan is more likely, since he is staying with the same firm, to gain advancement and recognition than Sally is, since she will be leaving at the end of the project.

## SAQ 5.1

The advantages of restricted communications include:

- more focusing by staff on their assigned tasks
- better control of the confidentiality of information
- less time wasted on reading papers and attending meetings
- reduced costs of paper and reproduction.

The disadvantages include:

- poorer understanding of global objectives
- weaker co-operation between staff in separate sections
- lack of mobility between job functions
- discouragement of team spirit.

The method seems appropriate only where confidentiality is paramount, because the disadvantages are likely to outweigh the time and cost savings. Top secret projects are an exception because the team is likely to understand the need for restricted communication in these circumstances and so will not be as demoralized by it.

## SAQ 5.2

Your answer should include six of the items listed below. Periodic reports could be used to:

- detect technical problems early
- detect cost overrun
- detect schedule slippage
- identify staff resource shortages
- reveal unforeseen events
- identify bottlenecks arising from limited facilities
- detect unplanned work being performed
- reveal the need to change priorities
- indicate that a contingency plan may need activating

- detect staff conflict
- monitor staff performance.

## SAQ 5.3

(a) Taking the value of partially completed elements as zero yields a lower bound for BCWP of £100 000. Taking the fraction complete of partially completed elements as 100% gives an upper bound for BCWP as £130 000.

(b) It is a very crude assumption to take the average of the upper and lower bounds for the actual value of BCWP. It is equivalent to assuming that all partially completed work is 50% complete.

(c) If the range of BCWP is to be reduced at this stage to 10% of the total budget, i.e. £15 000, it will be necessary to include extra milestones within activity F. As activity D accounts for only £4000 it will not refine the value of BCWP very much to insert extra milestones within it. So allowing for £4000 uncertainty in the BCWP of activity D means that BCWP of activity F must be assessed to within £11 000. This can be done by inserting two extra milestones reasonably spaced within it. (This assumes that suitable milestones representing significant events can be identified, which is not always possible.)

Note that at other stages in the project there are yet more elements that need to be broken down because they contribute large amounts to the budgeted cost.

(d) The value of BCWP at the end of the project will be £150 000. (This figure remains fixed unless the project budget, the total budgeted cost, is changed.)

## SAQ 5.4

The only term which remains constant is the project budget, PB. All the others will vary throughout the project.

## SAQ 5.5

(a) The cost performance index

$$\text{CPI} = \text{BCWP/ACWP} = 100/110.$$

The estimated cost at completion

$$\text{ECAC} = \text{PB/CPI} = £200\ 000 \times 110/100 = £220\ 000.$$

(b) The cost variance CV after 6 months is –£10 000.

If the remainder of the work is performed to budget the further costs to complete are £100 000.

The estimated cost at completion is

$$\text{ECAC} = \text{PB} - \text{CV} = £200\ 000 - (-£10\ 000) = £210\ 000.$$

## SAQ 5.6

The revised network is shown in Figure A.16. The revised estimated completion time is 25 weeks.

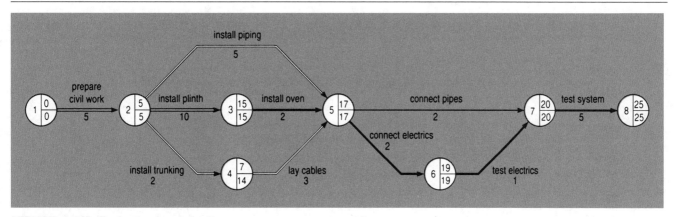

**FIGURE A.16** Revised network for the new oven

## SAQ 5.7

(a) On 1 May Milestone D is predicted to be passed at 19 June. It is confirmed as passed in the report on 10 July (but may have been passed on 3 July as last predicted – as the reports are fortnightly).

(b) It is not necessary for reports to be at *regular* intervals. The chart is neater if the report date rows are spaced regularly, but for example if one of the rows in the chart were missing then each milestone prediction date would remain at the previously reported date until a report was given to show differently.

(c) On 12 June Milestone D has been reported to have slipped by another week, yet Milestone E is still predicted to be unchanged from its last prediction. This would need to be justified since normally the slipping of one milestone will be expected to cause subsequent dates to slip similarly.

## SAQ 5.8

The main advantage of the milestone tracking chart is that it shows the *evolution* of key dates in an easily understood form (which could be included in a report to senior management). The absence of detail is an advantage for anyone who wants a quick overview of the *status* now and the *history* of progress, although this lack of detail would be a disadvantage to someone looking for the *reasons* for slippage.

## SAQ 5.9

(a) Table A.11 shows the expenditure on each activity in each 5-week period in thousands of pounds. For example the expenditure on activity A, designing the hardware, is £5000 in each of the first four periods. The value of £5000 is calculated from the given budgeted cost of £20 000 together with the known duration of 20 weeks, i.e. four periods. The values for the total expenditure in the period are calculated by adding up the entries in each row. Thus in the row for weeks 1–5 the total is 5 + 5 = 10. The cumulative BCWS is the accumulation of the total expenditure so far. Notice that the final value of BCWS is £150 000, the project budget, as you should expect.

**TABLE A.11** Calculations of BCWS for computer project

| Weeks | Expenditure on each activity | Total expenditure | Cumulative |
|---|---|---|---|

| | A | B | C | D | E | F | G | H | in period (£000) | BCWS (£000) |
|---|---|---|---|---|---|---|---|---|---|---|
| 1–5 | 5 | | | | 5 | | | | 10 | 10 |
| 6–10 | 5 | | | | 5 | | | | 10 | 20 |
| 11–15 | 5 | | | | 5 | | | | 10 | 30 |
| 16–20 | 5 | | | | 5 | | | | 10 | 40 |
| 21–25 | | 10 | 5 | | 5 | | | | 20 | 60 |
| 26–30 | | 10 | 5 | | 5 | | | | 20 | 80 |
| 31–35 | | 10 | | | | 6.5 | 5 | | 21.5 | 101.5 |
| 36–40 | | 10 | | | | 6.5 | | | 16.5 | 118 |
| 41–45 | | | | 4 | | 6.5 | | | 10.5 | 128.5 |
| 46–50 | | | | | | 6.5 | | | 6.5 | 135 |
| 51–55 | | | | | | | | 7.5 | 7.5 | 142.5 |
| 56–60 | | | | | | | | 7.5 | 7.5 | 150 |

(b) The graph of BCWS against time is shown in Figure A.17 Note that the curve is not very smooth; the changes in slope occur where there is a start or finish of an expensive activity. (If there were a larger number of activities starting at more random times the curve would be smoother.)

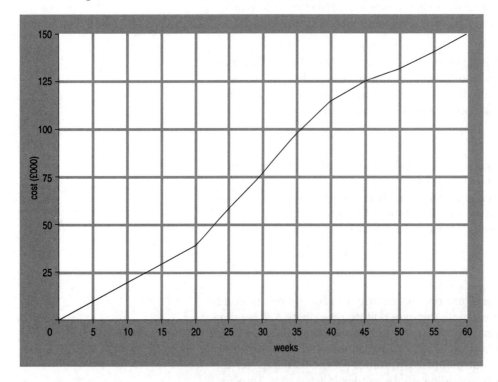

**FIGURE A.17**
BCWS for computer project

(c) The slope can never be negative because the curve is an accumulation of all the work planned. The slope is the rate of achievement so a negative slope would represent a negative rate of progress. This is certainly not something you plan for!

## SAQ 5.10

One possible assumption is that the remaining work is performed to schedule. An alternative is to assume that timescales are inflated by the same factor that has applied to work performance so far.

## SAQ 5.11

The answers to this question must be to some extent subjective, depending on how far you believe that the cause was an isolated historic event and to what extent you believe that there will be other similar events. A personal view from a member of the course team is as follows:

(a)   Assume a time inflation factor. The estimates for future work are likely to be equally optimistic.

(b)   Assume scheduled performance for the remainder of the work (provided the staff recruitment is now complete).

(c)   Assume a time inflation factor. These changes are likely to be followed by more changes unless you can convince the client that it will be more expensive at later stages in the project. If the changes persist you will need to be even more pessimistic because late changes have much greater impact!

(d)   Uncertain. If the design took longer than planned then possibly the job is bigger than expected and this will affect the coding and testing. If the job is the same size as expected and the design is good and complete then pessimism may be unjustified.

## SAQ 5.12

(a)   At the end of May the value of BCWP is virtually equal to the value of ACWP and hence the cost variance is zero. Financially the project is correctly to budget.

The value of BCWP is higher than the value of BCWS by about 5% of project budget and thus the work is ahead of schedule. The achievement at the end of May is roughly the same as planned for the end of June so the project is about a month ahead of schedule.

The slopes of the graphs might lead you to predict that the situation on both cost and schedule was likely to deteriorate. (In real life you would make such a prediction after taking into account information from progress meetings, etc.)

(b)   At the end of September the situation is quite different. ACWP is above BCWP by about 12% of project budget and so the value of CV is −12% of project budget, a significant overspend. You might predict from the slopes of the curves that this looks likely to get considerably worse.

The value of BCWP is below BCWS and the schedule variance SV is now about −10% of project budget. The achievement at the end of September is roughly what it should have been at the end of August. The achievement is therefore currently about one month behind schedule. From the slopes of the curves this looks likely to get considerably worse.

## SAQ 5.13

The graphs of the ideal project would look like Figure A.18. Successive revised estimates of cost ($E_1, E_2, E_3$, etc.) run horizontally across the top, and estimated completion dates ($S_1, S_2, S_3$ etc.) run vertically up the side. The graphs of ACWP and BCWP would coincide with BCWS as planned.

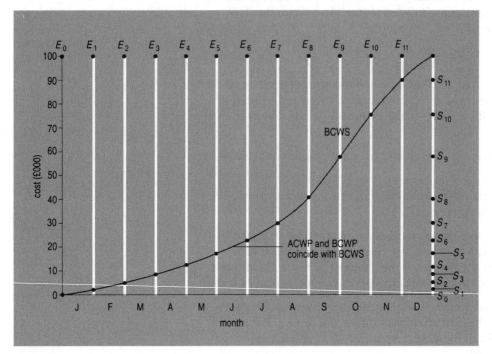

**FIGURE A.18**   The ideal project

## SAQ 6.1

The main differences are shown in Table A.12.

**TABLE A.12**   Differences between progress and quality reviews

| Progress review | Quality review |
| --- | --- |
| Usually held periodically – monthly or weekly | Held at fixed point in project, usually at the end of a major design phase |
| Attendees represent all functions within the project | Attendees are those able to comment on design and often concentrate on a single function |
| External contributors are not usually present | Attendees usually include non-project staff for their independent view |
| Scheduling issues often predominate over technical issues | Technical issues are the predominant subject |

## SAQ 6.2

A preliminary design review is likely to look at questions such as:

● Do we (the attendees) understand the requirements we are attempting to meet?

● Is this design following a proper path to reach our objectives?

● Is this design feasible?

● Have alternatives been considered? Have the advantages and disadvantages of the alternatives been fairly assessed?

You may have thought of other points.

## SAQ 6.3

When a unit is tested in isolation it is usually necessary to provide a test harness to simulate the environment in which the unit will work and additional code may be needed to enable the tester to see how the unit operates. After integration some of this will no longer be required and the unit can be tested in an environment closer to its final configuration. This may reveal faults that were not apparent before. At however late a stage a change is made to a module, it can have unforeseen side-effects, and regression testing is necessary to ensure that no such effects exist.

## SAQ 6.4

(a)    The answer appears in Table A.13.

**TABLE A.13**   Test type and quality aspect

| Quality | Unit test | Integration test | Subsystem test | Alpha test | Beta test |
|---|---|---|---|---|---|
| function | ✓✓ | ✓✓ | ✓✓ | ✓ | ✗ |
| correctness | ✓✓ | ✓ | ✓ | ✓ | ✗ |
| performance | ✗ | ✗ | ✓ | ✓✓ | ✓✓ |
| usability | ✗ | ✗ | ✓ | ✓✓ | ✓✓ |

(b)    Regression testing *repeats* other tests such as unit, integration and subsystem tests. At each stage the quality aspect tested for is the same as for the original tests.

## SAQ 6.5

(a)    Senior management visits are not formal enquiries. They usually rely on presentations by the project manager and team, without undertaking systematic enquiry.

(b)    Major design reviews may be very like project audits but they are not usually independent. They are usually conducted by members of the project team. Even quality assurance staff associated with the ongoing project should not be regarded as independent.

(c)    Progress reports are regular updates of status which are not external to the project.

(d)    Evaluation after termination will not assist the future conduct of a current problem.

## SAQ 6.6

A change control board set up to control changes across the client–contractor boundary of the project is unlikely to be appropriate for monitoring internal change because it likely has the wrong membership. Not all clients wish to be concerned with matters which are internal to the conduct of the contracting organization (although some clients may).

## SAQ 6.7

(a)    A design object may be freely changed by its designer, but a configuration item may be changed only under control and the change must be recorded.

(b)    While an item is being actively developed on a work bench or drawing board it would hamper progress if every change had to be approved.

(c)    An interface specification may be quite small compared with the components being interfaced. It is therefore easier for designers to concentrate just on the interface when reaching an agreement rather than being concerned with the design of the whole of the adjacent components.

(d)    Assuming that the configuration management system has been set up, the requirement specifications should become a configuration item (at the latest) when the contract is agreed. Any subsequent changes require approval and recording. (The requirements could become a single item but a grouping of items could be useful to allow more flexibility.)

## SAQ 6.8

Clearly an item cannot be dependent upon a design object which has not yet become a configuration item, because that object may be changed at any time without reference to anyone. So the direction of a dependency implies that the item being pointed to has to become a configuration item first. If the link is in both directions then both may be developed as design objects in parallel but they become configuration items at the same time.

## SAQ 6.9

(a)    The scope of configuration management is usually applicable to all documents or other items in a project which are products of the project in the widest sense, including items that are used for subsequent development. A configuration does not encompass the whole of the system under development: only those items that have matured sufficiently for change control to be applied. Items that are still being changed frequently are not put under change control and are called design objects.

(b)    The four principal elements of a configuration management system are identification, control, status accounting and auditing.

## SAQ 6.10

The answers must depend on the context of the configuration, but here is one judgement:

(a)    Quite good (slightly long?).

(b)    OK in the context of one bearing in one motor but not if there is more than one of either motors or bearings.

(c)    Not descriptive and therefore not memorable.

(d)    Likely not to be unique.

(e)    Poor. It is not very descriptive and fixes the position of this module in relation to others, so it may be difficult to move later if required.

## SAQ 6.11

The problem will be to identify precisely what this machine code software is. It may not be identifiable from an examination of the software itself unless some system of identifying the code has been employed. It may be necessary to rely on the label on the outside of the disk itself, but the contents may not match this label. Assuming that the label is correct, it may still not be possible to identify the particular version of the source code from which it came unless great care had been taken to keep machine code identification in step with changes of source code.

## SAQ 6.12

(a)   A baseline is a set of known and agreed items under change control.

(b)   Baselines render the development process more visible by providing the status at fixed points (usually major milestones) from which progress may be measured.

## SAQ 6.13

(a)   A variant could arise if a similar course were required for a different student population. For example, there could have been variants for those studying mainly CCI courses as opposed to those studying manufacturing, or if the course were translated into another language for use abroad.

(b)   After a course has been studied for a while experience shows that it could be improved. The original version has errors and omissions. A new version may be produced, superseding the old, perhaps with two or three of the units rewritten.

## SAQ 6.14

Once an item has been registered it may be in use by other team members and they will need to be aware of the original mistake and of the proposal to correct it. Even if the item is not being used it will subvert the status accounting system if changes are made without any record. Traceability will be compromised.

## SAQ 6.15

Last week the component was a design object. Nobody else placed reliance on it. This week other team members may already be using it and relying on the fact that any impending change, even a correction, will be notified to them, asking approval. If small improvements are allowed through without approval it will be impossible to draw a firm line.

## SAQ 6.16

The advantages of appointing a single authoritative person to control all items would be that everyone would know immediately who was responsible for approving all changes and that person would be aware of all the current change proposals. This could be satisfactory in a small project.

The disadvantages are that in a large project it would be difficult for one person to be sufficiently conversant with every aspect to make good decisions on change requests. Furthermore, it would involve a senior engineer unnecessarily in many trivial matters. This would slow down development enormously and the senior engineer would become a bottleneck. The system would also appear less democratic and would tend to arouse resentment.

## SAQ 6.17

Although this could often work satisfactorily in a small, informally organized project, several important stages are being by-passed. First, by omitting the formal change request there is no record of the reason for change. Secondly, the assessment of impact may not be adequate. Thirdly, no one else knows of the impending change until after the work has been done and it may then be too late to point out some defect in the proposal. The use of a custodian or a formal tool to take the role of the custodian should prevent this happening (as well as enforcing a disciplined approach by designers who see the benefit of configuration management).

## SAQ 6.18

(a) The configuration diagram shows what other items potentially depend on the item under consideration. If a change is made to the item then further changes may be needed to dependent items and to items dependent on these in turn.

(b) One advantage would be a reduction in the number of requests because this extra work would deter a requester; so the total throughput of work would be reduced. Another advantage would be an improvement in the quality of the request, since the act of making the assessment would enable the requester to improve the proposal or abandon an ill-advised request.

The disadvantages are that valuable requests may be left aside because of the additional burden and the requester may not have the skills required to make the assessment.

## SAQ 6.19

There may be more than one component placed under change control at contract but one essential item is the contract itself, or at least the part of the contract that specifies the work to be done. (Some parts of the contract, such as the commercial terms, may be someone else's province and subject to separate change control procedures.)

## SAQ 6.20

1   Too much time will be spent on the change control procedures.

2   Having to change his work to fit in with other people's changes too frequently will be unnecessarily disruptive to a designer. It may well be more efficient to accommodate the latest changes in a composite round-up after a suitable interval.

## SAQ 6.21

(a) The main purposes are: to report the current state of the system, or any items in it, and the history of events leading to this state; and to provide traceability.

(b) It is necessary to capture all significant events as they occur and store the data in some organized way so that reports can be produced quickly. A computer-based system is appropriate for this task.

## SAQ 6.22

(a) Configuration items such as the top-level design are identified unambiguously.

(b) The way that a change to the refrigeration unit has to be requested, approved by controllers and recorded.

(c) Recording all change by the administrator and answering questions about status and history.

(d) The questions asked by the quality manager.

## SAQ 7.1

| Tasks | Completed | By whom |
|---|---|---|
| Close internal work orders | | |
| Close external contracts | | |
| Check completion of all tasks | | |
| Summarize any outstanding commitments | | |
| Prune and complete the project file | | |
| Index the project file and store it | | |
| Ensure drawings are complete and indexed | | |
| Ensure maintenance procedures are documented | | |
| Dispose of unused equipment and materials | | |
| Hold a review meeting with users | | |
| Prepare final report on project | | |
| Present final report to management | | |

## SAQ 7.2

The purpose of the Project Manager's Final Report is primarily to review the conduct of the project for the benefit of future projects. The purpose of the Post-completion Review is to assess the extent to which the planned benefits are being reaped and the actions necessary to maximize those benefits.

# GLOSSARY

**activity breakdown structure**
See *work breakdown structure*.

**activity-on-arrow network**
'A network in which the arrows symbolize the activities' (BS 4335).

**activity-on-node network**
'A network in which the nodes symbolize the activities' (BS 4335).

**actual cost of work performed (ACWP)**
The costs actually incurred in carrying out work; not the same as budgeted cost of work performed.

**aim**
What one intends to do.

**archive**
See *configuration store*.

**asset**
Any property that can be sold to meet debts if necessary. *Tangible* assets are land, buildings, furniture, plant. *Intangible* assets include such things as mailing lists of customers, organizational goodwill, software.

**audit**
An official examination.

**backward pass**
The calculation of the latest time of each event in a network, so called because it starts at the time required for the finish node and works backwards through the network.

**base date**
The date on which an estimate is made; this becomes important for factoring in *cost escalation* through inflation.

**baseline**
In the context of planning it represents the completion of a major element of the work – often used to denote the specification of contractual requirements. In the context of *configuration management* it is a snapshot of the state of a *configuration item* and its component configuration items at a point in time. Baselines, plus approved changes from those baselines, constitute the current *configuration identification*.

**benefit**
Something gained such as income and cost savings.

**bid**
An *offer* made for a stated price or rate.

**bidder**
See *tenderer*.

### 'blue-book' estimating
See *standardized estimating*.

### budgeted cost of work performed (BCWP)
See *earned value*.

### budgeted cost of work scheduled (BCWS)
A method of comparing achievement with plan which is closely allied to *earned value*.

### budgeting
The preparation of financial plans, based on a project's objectives, for a future period. A budget relates to costs, revenues, working capital movements, capital expenditure and cash flow.

### capital
*Cash*, or anything readily convertible into cash, such as stock.

### capital cost
Costs incurred in the acquisition or enhancement of assets.

### cash
Money, money's worth, any form of funds or finance.

### cash flow
The movement of money into and out of a pre-defined area such as a *project*, department or company.

### cash flow statement
A document showing each *cash inflow* or *cash outflow* of a *project* or proposal.

### cash inflow
The benefits which a *project* is expected to provide. Any savings or reductions in costs are treated as cash inflows.

### cash outflow
The costs and expenses (whether capital or revenue in nature) needed to implement and run a *project*.

### cause and effect diagram
Graphical tool for establishing the relationship between an effect and the possible or actual causes of that effect; useful for exploring problems. Also known as *Ishikawa* or *fishbone diagrams*.

### champion
Someone who acts as an advocate for a proposal or *project*.

### change control
A means of organizing people in order to cope with change.

### change control board
A group which reviews proposed changes and approves (or disapproves) them. Also known as configuration control board.

### checkpoint
Points at which all people co-ordinate their work to the current *configuration*.

**client**

The *party* to a *contract* who commissions the work and pays for it upon satisfactory completion.

**closure phase**

Final phase of a *project*, when client acceptance is obtained and the project is 'signed off'.

**concurrency**

When activities from different phases in a project life-cycle overlap in time significantly.

**configuration**

The complete technical description required to build, test, install, operate and maintain and support a system. It includes all documentation pertaining to the system as well as the system itself.

**configuration administrator**

The central person to whom all change requests are sent.

**configuration auditing**

The process of verifying that all the required *configuration items* have been produced, that the current *version* agrees with the specified requirements, that the technical documentation completely and accurately describes the configuration items and that all change requests have been resolved.

**configuration control**

The process of evaluating, approving or disapproving, and co-ordinating changes to *configuration items* after formal establishment of their *configuration identification*.

**configuration control board**

See *change control board*.

**configuration identification**

The process of identifying uniquely all the items within the *configuration* and their relationship to each other.

**configuration item**

An entity within a *configuration* that can be uniquely identified at a given reference point. All configuration items are subject to *change control*.

**configuration management**

The discipline of identifying the components of a continuously evolving system (the *configuration*) at discrete points in time for the purposes of controlling changes to the configuration and maintaining integrity and *traceability* throughout the system life.

**configuration status accounting**

The recording of all *configuration item* descriptions together with the status of the proposed changes to the system and the implementation state of proposed changes

**configuration store**

A secure storage area for any component under change control. Also known as an archive.

**consortium**
An association of several companies or organizations.

**contingency allowance**
A percentage of a total or a particular amount of money allowed for an item line in an *estimate* or budget to allow the project manager to deal with uncertainty, e.g. changes in price of necessary components.

**contingency plan**
A plan stating steps to be taken if a risk arises.

**contingency reserves**
Reserves of money set aside to allow the project manager to cope with contingencies such as delay, hazard, etc. (also called *management reserves*). These may be in addition to any specific *contingency allowances*.

**contract**
A legally binding agreement between two *parties*.

**contract team**
A project team brought in from outside an organisation to do project work.

**contractor**
The *party* to a *contract* who agrees to do the specified tasks in return for the specified payment.

**cost**
Something lost, such as payments for labour, materials, rent etc.

**cost account level**
The level at which cost control is delegated to an individual. See *work package level*.

**cost–benefit analysis**
Identifying, specifying and evaluating a proposal's *costs* and *benefits*.

**cost breakdown structure**
A hierarchical structure setting out the cost categories and items for a project.

**cost escalation**
The increase in actual costs over *estimates* caused by inflation, delay or problems such as failure of suppliers to deliver or industrial disputes.

**cost–performance index**
The ratio of *budgeted cost of work performed* to *actual cost of work performed*.

**cost–plus contract**
The price of the *contract* is the *contractor's* costs plus an agreed percentage to be paid to the contractor by the client upon completion of the contract.

**cost reimbursement**
A type of contract in which the sum paid is based on actual costs incurred (see *cost–plus* and *time and materials contracts*).

**cost to complete**
Estimated cost at completion minus the *actual cost of work performed*.

### cost variance (CV)

The difference between *budgeted cost of work performed* and *actual cost of work performed*.

### counter-offer

A response to an *offer* that proposes changes to items discussed in the offer.

### critical path

Formally defined as 'a path with least float' (BS 4335), it is a path of sequential activities such that an increase in the duration of any one of them will increase the time required to complete the project.

### critical path scheduling

A term for variants of the network technique. Also used are critical path analysis and PERT (Project Evaluation and Review Technique).

### critical schedule

A schedule having at least one path with no *float*.

### custodian

Archivist or librarian empowered to ensure items in *configuration control* are changed only after authority has been granted.

### customer

Similar to *client*, its most common meaning is one who buys or a person with whom one is concerned, particularly in terms of quality.

### damages

Money owed by a *contractor* to a client equal to the client's financial loss if the contractor fails to complete the contract in a satisfactory way.

### dangling event

An event (other than the project start or project finish) which has either no prior activity or no succeeding activity. Also known as 'dangle'.

### decision tree

A graphical tool for representing decision possibilities and their various possible outcomes to decision-makers.

### definition phase

The initial stage in the life of a *project* where *objectives* are set, *scenarios* defined and *feasibility studies* are undertaken. The stage ends with a decision whether to proceed, or, where work is contracted, with the signing of the contract.

### delegation

Assigning a task or set of tasks, and some authority over the resources necessary, to someone else.

### deliverable

A product, which may be intangible (such as test results) to be delivered at a specified time during a project or at its end. (A project may have many deliverables.)

### depreciation

The loss of original value of an asset as it ages and wears out.

### design object
An area of project work which is allowed to be changed freely by its designer.

### design review
A formal documented examination intended to evaluate requirements and a design capability to meet them.

### discounted cash flow
The discounting at an appropriate rate of interest of future cash flows to ascertain their present value. Two commonly used methods are 'internal rate of return' and 'net present value'.

### dummy activity
An activity representing no actual work to be done but required for reasons of logic or nomenclature.

### earliest event time
The earliest time at which a node can be reached.

### earned value
A system of monitoring project costs against the value earned by the work done.

### escalation clause
A clause in a *contract* to protect the *contractor* against rising prices or wage settlements (usually tied to some agreed index such as the Retail Price Index).

### estimate
A prepared document setting out a proposed budget; also a *bidder's* document setting out the proposed cost to the *client* of work to be done.

### estimated completion date (ECD)
The date at which the project is estimated to be completed.

### estimated cost at completion (ECAC)
The difference between the project budget (PB) and *cost variance*.

### event
A point in time when all the activities have been completed which lead into the node under consideration.

### evolutionary development
A form of software development in which a system design is 'decomposed' into smaller units and developed and installed in a planned but piecemeal fashion over a longer period of time. The purpose is to reduce risk from novel developments, contain costs and speed the accrual of financial or operational benefits. It is also thought to reduce the risk of rejection by users.

### execution phase
The phase of a *project* in which work towards direct achievement of the project's objectives and the production of the project's deliverables occurs. This is sometimes called the implementation phase.

### feasibility phase
See *definition phase*.

### feasibility study

A study undertaken to assess whether something is achievable: this includes assessing economic, financial, human resource and technological factors (and may include ecological and social factors as well) that will influence whether something can be achieved and at what *cost* and to what *benefit*.

### feature

That aspect of an item considered to be important enough to evaluate on grounds other than cost.

### features analysis

A technique for enumerating, rating and ranking *features*.

### figure of merit

A number derived as a result of a *features analysis*, which can be used to compare similar products in order to choose which most closely meets *requirements*.

### financing cost

The *cost* of borrowing *capital* (e.g. the interest and any fees levied on a loan).

### fishbone diagram

See *cause and effect diagram*.

### fixed-price quotation

A *tender* for a *contract* in which the price stated is to be binding on the *contractor*. Also called a *lump sum quotation*.

### float

'The time available for an activity or path in addition to its duration' (BS 4335). Also known as *total float* or *path float*. (See also *free float*.)

### forward pass

The calculation of the earliest time of each event in a network.

### free float

'The time by which an activity may be delayed or extended without delaying the start of any succeeding activity.' (BS 4335)

### function point model

A method of estimating the cost of software production by using the number and complexity of the functions to be delivered.

### functional specification

A document specifying in some detail the functions that are required in the proposed system and the constraints that will apply.

### functional team

A team organized around a function such as design, research, marketing.

### Gantt chart

A chart with a timescale in which a bar represents the period over which each activity is scheduled to be performed.

### goal

A final point marking the desired end (e.g. of a race or game) or the object of desire, ambition or effort.

**historical method**
A method that uses historical information to estimate the costs of future activity.

**implementation phase**
See *execution phase*.

**inflation**
A general increase of prices and fall in the purchasing value of money.

**influencing**
A means of indirectly exercising power over another's action, usually by persuasion, *negotiation* or *leadership*.

**in-house project**
A project commissioned and carried out entirely within a single organization.

**injured party**
Any *party* to a *contract* who suffers a loss as a result of problems in the contract or the execution of work specified in the contract.

**inspection**
A group inspect a product such as a design document in detail and comment to the originator.

**intangible**
Of *costs*, *benefits* and *assets*, those items which have no physical existence (literally, cannot be touched).

**interpersonal skill**
A skill such as communicating, listening, conflict resolving that helps people to relate well to each other.

**Ishikawa diagram**
See *cause and effect diagram*.

**item controller**
The recognised authority for approving change to a *configuration item*.

**latest event time**
The latest time by which a node must be reached if the project is to finish by its required completion date.

**lead**
To direct, conduct, guide or use example to get others to do something. Usually implies that the leader 'goes first'.

**lead contractor**
The contractor who has overall project management and quality assurance responsibilities.

**leadership**
The ability to *lead*.

**letter of intent**
A letter indicating an intent to sign a *contract*, usually issued so that work can commence before the actual signing of that contract.

**linear responsibility chart**
See *responsibility matrix*.

**lump sum quotation**
See *fixed-price quotation*.

**management reserves**
See *contingency reserves*.

**matrix team**
A team structure where members report to different managers for different aspects of their work.

**method of potentials**
A type of *activity-on-node network* that allows only finish-to-start dependencies.

**milestone**
'An event selected for its importance in the project' (BS 4335).

**mission statement**
A brief description of what an organization believes to be the reason for its existence.

**negotiation**
Satisfying needs by reaching agreement or compromise with other parties.

**net cash flow**
The difference between the *cash outflows* and the *cash inflows*. Where the net cash flow is into a *project*, this is termed net *cash inflow*. Where the net cash flow is out of a project this is called net *cash outflow*.

**objective**
A means towards obtaining an *aim* or *goal*.

**offer**
A statement of the type, standard and cost of work that a *contractor* or *supplier* is willing to undertake if the *client* accepts.

**option**
A clause in a *tender* stating how long the tender *offer* remains valid, commonly 30 or 60 days.

**organization phase**
The *project* phase during which a project team, tools, methods and communications channels are put into place. This phase produces the infrastructure for project execution.

**outsourced supply team**
A form of *project team* which is situated remotely from the project manager.

**overheads**
The day-to-day *revenue* expenses (the running costs) charged against income which apply to the organization generally and are not directly attributable to any specific area within the organization (which is why they are sometimes called *indirect costs*).

## owner
See *client*.

## parallel scheduling
A method of scheduling in which all eligible activities are considered in parallel.

## Pareto analysis
A method of quantifying the importance in terms of value of the component parts of any problem. It consists of drawing columns proportional to the magnitude of a problem, or of aspects of a large problem. These columns are arranged in order of magnitude, starting with the largest.

## parties (to a contract)
The persons or companies who sign a *contract* with each other.

## path float
See *float*.

## payback period
Commonly used simple (but not especially reliable) method of justifying *projects* based on how long will it take to repay an initial investment.

## penalty
A sum payable to a *client* in addition to any *damages* owing if a contract cannot be completed satisfactorily.

## pilot
A method of software development in which the software implements basic functions and is installed, to be followed by *evolutionary development* of the remainder of the software. This is thought to reduce risk and contain cost but speed the accrual of any financial or operational benefits.

## planning
The process of formulating an organized method of achieving something which is to be done (e.g. a project) or of proceeding.

## precedence diagram
A type of *activity-on-node network* in which dependencies other than the normal finish-to-start link are allowed. Also known as *precedence network*.

## precedence network
See *precedence diagram*.

## product breakdown structure
A hierarchically arranged list of components that allows the project manager eventually to estimate the cost of the 'product'.

## programme
An organized and planned sequence of related projects aimed at achieving a long-term objective.

## project
Organized work towards a pre-defined *goal* or *objective* that has clear boundaries, requires resources and effort, is unique and therefore has an element of risk, and is assigned its own budget and schedule.

### project audit
An official appraisal of the technical status of a project or part of a project.

### project controller
The individual who undertakes the administrative work in larger projects. Also called the project control officer.

### project file custodian
A person charged with looking after project files and documentation.

### project mobilization
Getting all the activities of a project up and running.

### project plan
A collection of documents such as the budget, schedules, risk management plans, etc., that constitute the description of the project at the outset and during its execution.

### project support office
In very large projects a team of *project controllers* and perhaps also one or more *project file custodians*.

### project team
An organization structure in which all people work only on the project and report only to a project manager. Also called *single team*.

### prototyping
A method of development in which a prototype of the final design is built and tested, then either the prototype is refined, or the feedback from the prototype is used to develop the 'real' system. It is thought to help reduce risk in development and contain costs.

### quality
In the context of *projects* the totality of the features and characteristics of a project's deliverables that bear on their ability to satisfy given needs.

### quality audit
An official examination to determine whether practices conform to specified standards on a critical analysis of whether a deliverable meets quality criteria.

### quality plan
A document, sometimes contained within and sometimes separate from the *project plan* which sets out all those activities deemed to relate specifically to project quality.

### quality review
A review of the quality aspects of some part of the project work.

### rate
The cost of something per unit of time. For example, salary rates in estimating are generally stated in pounds per hour or pounds per day.

### rate of return
The profit from a *project* expressed in terms of the equivalence to a rate of interest on the capital invested.

### requirement
A statement of what is expected of a product or *project*, what role it is expected to fill or what it is expected to do.

### resource levelling
Rearranging activities to achieve resource usage which is as level as possible. (Sometimes used to mean scheduling so that resources are kept below a given level.)

### resource-limited scheduling
Scheduling within a fixed resource constraint (time variable).

### resource smoothing
Rearranging activities to achieve a smooth profile of resource usage, not necessarily constant.

### responsibility matrix
A tool for showing the involvement of individuals with the work elements of a project. Also called a *linear responsibility chart*.

### revenue
Earnings (income) and payments (disbursements).

### revenue cost
Any *cost* incurred other than for the acquisition or enhancement of *assets* (sometimes referred to as 'revenue expenditure' or *running costs*). For example, a motor car is a *capital* asset, and the costs of servicing it, filling it with fuel, etc., and purchasing consumable items like oil and tyres are revenue costs.

### risk
The probability of an undesired outcome.

### risk acceptance
Deciding not to do anything about a risk other than be watchful.

### risk assessment
An assessment of what can go wrong with a project that aims to identify risks, quantify their likelihood of occurring and assess their likely impact on the project; it is intended to allow *risk management* to take place.

### risk management
Strategies for dealing with risks, including avoidance, acceptance and reduction.

### risk reduction
Working to reduce the likelihood that a risk will occur or to reduce its impact if it does.

### risk transfer
Transferring the impact of having a risk occur to another party (e.g. by subcontracting, taking out insurance, etc.)

### running cost
See *revenue cost*.

### scenario

A brief description of a system, process or set of procedures that addresses previously identified inadequacies or meets previously identified objectives. It is used as a basis for a *feasibility study*.

### schedule–performance index

The ratio of the *budgeted cost of work performed* to the *budgeted cost of work scheduled*.

### schedule variance

A measure of how far work has progressed compared with the plan and expressed in cash terms.

### scheduling

Establishing the order of tasks, the timing of deliveries, etc.

### serial scheduling

A method of scheduling which considers each activity in some predefined order (e.g. in order of increasing *float*).

### single team

See *project team*.

### slack

'The calculated time span within which an event must occur' (BS 4335). In American literature it often means the same as *float*.

### software metrics

A numerical measure of some quality of software, e.g. the complexity.

### span of control

The number of people over whom one has direct or indirect authority.

### specification

A statement of the characteristics of something to be designed or done: dimensions, performance, etc., commonly in a quantifiable form (for example adherence to a standard, or to a common measure such as Ohms, millimetres, etc.).

### sponsor

The person providing the resources for the *project* who is responsible for ensuring that the project is successful at the highest organizational level.

### stage payments

Payments made during the life of a *contract*, either at set intervals or when some key milestone is achieved or deliverable accepted by the client.

### stakeholder

Someone for whom the success of the *project* is important.

### standardized estimating

An estimating method used when there is a sufficient body of detailed estimated and actual cost data allow statistically valid standards to be set for estimating (also called *'blue-book' estimating*).

### statement of work (SOW)

A document describing the work assigned to an individual defined either in the *work breakdown structure* if it is decomposed to the level of the individual, or drawn up using the *work package definition* by the person responsible for the package.

## strategic planning
Planning at a high organizational level that sets the direction and route for that organization.

## stress testing
Subjecting an object to tests which exceed its performance requirements.

## subcontractor
A *contractor* who undertakes part of some project work under the supervision of someone who is himself a contractor to a *client*.

## sunk costs
Money or time already spent; these cannot be recovered if a project is cancelled.

## supplier
Anyone who agrees to sell goods or products to a *client*.

## SWOT analysis
An acronym for Strengths, Weaknesses, Opportunities, Threats. A form of analysis that depends upon gathering information about the organization's environment and classifying each point as being an organizational strength, weakness, opportunity or threat.

## tangible
Anything (particularly used of *assets, capital, benefits* and *costs*) which has a physical existence, such as plant, buildings, cash.

## task list
A list of tasks that results from the first phase of developing a *work breakdown structure*.

## tender
A document proposing to meet a specification in a certain way and at a stated price (or on a particular financial basis), an offer of price and conditions under which the tenderer is willing to undertake work for the client.

## tenderer
The party proposing to do work for a potential *client*.

## terms of reference
A specification of a team member's responsibilities within the project.

## time and materials contract
A *contract* in which the *client* pays the *contractor* for the time spent, at an agreed rate, and for any materials.

## time-limited scheduling
Scheduling within a fixed project time constraint (resources variable).

## total float
See *float*.

## traceability

Recording information that will allow any investigation to reconstruct events, changes and reasons for change.

## turnkey project

A project where the contractor is expected to provide a finished product without a great deal of effort required on the part of the client.

## uncertainty

Doubt about the validity of either qualitative or quantitative data.

## value engineering

A technique for analysing qualitative and quantitative *costs* and *benefits* of component parts of a proposed system.

## value planning

A technique for assessing, before significant investment is made, the desirability of a proposal based on the value that will accrue to the organization from that proposal.

## value process

A process consisting of *value planning, value engineering* and value assessment.

## variant

A version of a component that co-exists with another (usually because it is used in a different application).

## version

A copy of a component which is uniquely identified by a reference number and is related to other versions with the same component name.

## walk-through

An informal method for reviewing a design document or program code in which the originator takes colleagues through step by step.

## work breakdown structure (WBS)

A hierarchical way of organizing work to be done into packages.

## work package definition

A document describing the work package defined in the *work breakdown structure*, setting out start and completion dates, responsibility, *deliverables* and milestones.

## work package level

A work package grouping tasks or sets of tasks together for the purposes of having an individual, such as a team leader, *contractor, subcontractor* or project manager in control of it. See *cost account level*.

# REFERENCES AND FURTHER READING

Archibald, R. D. (1992) *Managing High-Technology Programs and Projects* (2nd edn) John Wiley and Sons, Chichester.

A concise description of many project management techniques. It is a very good source of examples of charts and forms used in project management.

APM (1993) *Body of Knowledge* (revised), Association of Project Managers.

Babich, W. A. (1986) *Software Configuration Management: Coordination for Team Productivity*, Addison–Wesley, Reading, MA.

Mainly about software configuration management as a technique to co-ordinate programmers. Some of the nomenclature differs from that used in this book.

Beckhard, R. (1969) *Organizational Development: Strategies and Models,* Addison-Wesley, Reading MA.

Belbin, M. (1981) *Management Teams*, Heinemann, London.

Bennatan, E. M. (1992) *Software Project Management: a Practitioner's Approach,* (2nd edn) McGraw–Hill, London.

Bersoff, E. H., Henderson, V. D. and Siegel S. G. (1980) *Software Configuration Management: an Investment in Product Integrity*, Prentice Hall, Englewood Cliffs, NJ.

This book is primarily about software projects but the techniques described are applicable elsewhere. It contains numerous references.

Boddy, D. and Buchanan, D. A. (1992) *Take the Lead*, Prentice Hall, London.

Boehm, B. W. (1981) *Software Engineering Economics*, Prentice Hall, Englewood Cliffs, NJ.

Brooks, F. P. (1975) *The Mythical Man-Month*, Addison–Wesley, Reading, MA.

A classic and enjoyable read although now a bit dated technically.

Bryan, W., Chadbourne, C. and Siegel, S. (1980) *Tutorial: Software Configuration Management*, IEEE.

This tutorial brings together a number of articles on software configuration management. There is extensive coverage of management failures in the American defence contracting industry and the reasons for government agencies insisting on configuration management.

BS 4335 (1987) *Glossary of Terms used in Project Network Techniques*, British Standards Institution.

BS 6046 (1984, 1992) *Use of Network Techniques in Project Management*, Parts 1–4, British Standards Institution.

Buchanan, D. A. and Boddy, D. (1992) *The Expertise of the Change Agent: Public Performance and Backstage Activity*, Prentice Hall, London.

Buckle, I. K. (1982) *Software Configuration Management*, Macmillan, London.

Similar scope to Bersoff *et al.*, but British rather than American.

CCTA, (1993), *PRINCE User's guide to CRAMM (the CCTA Risk Analysis and Management Method)*, HMSO, London.

Checkland, P. (1981) *Systems Thinking, Systems Practice*, John Wiley & Sons, Chichester.

    An authoritative introduction to the foundations and philosophy of soft systems analysis.

Checkland, P. and Scholes, J. (1990) *Soft Systems Methodology in Action*, John Wiley & Sons, Chichester.

    A good introduction to the methods of soft systems analysis.

Chicken, J. C. (1994) *Managing Risks and Decisions in Major Projects*, Chapman & Hall, London.

    This book is a comprehensive survey of the methods of identifying risks and particularly of the statistical methods of undertaking risk assessment in respect of decision making in large projects and financial institutions. It is *not* a 'how-to' book.

Chilstrom, K. O. (1983) 'Project management audits' in Cleland and King *op. cit.* pp. 465–481.

Chomsky, N. (1991) 'Toward a Humanistic Conception of Education and Work', in Corson, D. (ed.) *Education for Work*, Multilingual Matters Ltd, Clevedon.

Cleland D. I. and King W. R. (eds) *Project Management Handbook*, Van Nostrand Reinhold, NY.

Crockford, N. (1980) *An Introduction to Risk Management*, Woodhead-Faulkner, Hemel Hempstead.

Czewinski, F. L., and Samaras T. T. (1971) *Fundamentals of Configuration Management*, John Wiley & Sons Inc., NY.

    A classic introduction to the subject: not software. You may have difficulty obtaining a copy as it is unfortunately out of print. It is included here for historical reasons.

de la Mare, R. F. (1982) *Manufacturing Systems Economics*, Holt, Rinehart & Winston, London.

DeMarco, T. (1982) *Controlling Software Projects*, Yourdon Press, New York.

Georgopoulos, B. S., Mahoney, G. M. and Jones, N. W. (1957) 'A path–goal approach to productivity', *Journal of Applied Psychology*, Vol. 41.

Gilb, T. (1988) *Principles of Software Engineering Management*, Addison–Wesley, Wokingham.

Gray, S. (1994) Private communication to the author.

Gunton, T. (1990) *A Dictionary of Information Technology and Computer Science*, NCC Blackwell, Oxford.

Hackman, J. G., Porter L. W. and Lawler, E. E. (1977) *Perspectives on Behaviour in Organizations*, McGraw-Hill, New York.

Handy, C. (1990) *Inside Organizations*, BBC Publications, London.

Hannaway, C. and Hunt, G. (1992) *The Management Skills Book*, Gower, Aldershot.

Harrison, F. L. (1992) *Advanced Project Management: a Structured Approach* (3rd edn) Gower, Aldershot.

This book provides a presentation of project management techniques which, in spite of its title, is quite down to earth.

Herzberg, F., Mausner, B. and Snyderman, B. B. (1986) *The Motivation to Work* (2nd edn), John Wiley and Sons, New York.

HMSO (1993) *Report of the Investigation of the London Ambulance Service* HMSO, London.

Ince, D., Sharp, H. and Woodman, M. (1993) *Introduction to Software Project Management and Quality Assurance*, McGraw-Hill, London.

Jordan, E. W. and Machesky, J. J. (1990) *Systems Development: Requirements, Evaluation, Design and Implementation*, PWS-Kent Publishing, Boston, MA.

Kerzner, H. (1984) *Project Management: a Systems Approach to Planning, Scheduling and Controlling*, Van Nostrand Reinhold, New York.

This is a very comprehensive book on project management. It sometimes seems rather verbose (937 pages) but it contains many case studies to illustrate the topics and plenty of problems to discuss. American context.

Kleim, R. L. and Ludin, I. S. (1992) *The People Side of Project Management*, Gower, Aldershot.

Lindley, D. V. (1985) *Making Decisions* (2nd edn), John Wiley & Sons, Chichester.

This is a widely used book concentrating on quantifying probabilities and treating decision-making in a disciplined, statistical way.

Lock, D. (1992) *Project Management* (5th edn) Gower, Aldershot.

This is a down-to-earth book describing many of the day-to-day activities required in the management of a project.

Lockyer, K. G. (1984) *Critical Path Analysis* (4th edn) Pitman, London.

A concise treatment of critical path analysis which is particularly valuable for project planning.

Machiavelli, N. (1513) *The Prince* (trans. Bull, G. 1970) Penguin, Harmondsworth.

He would have made a good project manager.

Markus, M.L. (1983) 'Power, politics and MIS implementation', *Communications of the ACM*, Vol. 26, No. 6, pp. 430–44.

Marsh, P. (1994a) 'Contract law' in Lock, D. (ed.) *Handbook of Project Management* (2nd edn), Gower, Aldershot, pp. 73–92.

_ (1994b) 'Contracts and payment structure' in Lock, D. (ed.), pp. 93–113.

_ (1994c) 'Contract administration' in Lock, D. (ed.), pp. 114–22.

Maslow, A. (1943) *Motivation and Personality,* revised by R. Frazer *et al.* (3rd edn 1970) Harper & Row, London.

Meredith, J. R. and Mantel, S. J. (1989) *Project Management: a Managerial Approach* (2nd edn) John Wiley and Sons, Chichester.

This well-presented book has many case studies and reproduces a number of published articles. It includes a discussion of probabilistic networks (Graphical Evaluation and Review Techniques, GERT). Contains substantial

432

chapters on monitoring, control, evaluation and termination and includes many case studies.

Moder, J. J., Phillips, C. R. and Davis, E. W. (1983) *Project Management with CPM, PERT and Precedence Diagramming*, Van Nostrand Reinhold, New York.

A very thorough treatment of planning and scheduling techniques.

Morris, P. W. G. (1994) *The Management of Projects*, Thomas Telford Services Ltd, London.

Mumford, E. (1983) *Designing Participatively*, Manchester Business School Publications, Manchester.

Norris, M., Rigby, P. and Payne, M. (1993) *The Healthy Software Project: a Guide to Successful Development and Management*, John Wiley & Sons, Chichester.

This book draws on the experiences of three senior software project managers at British Telecom.

Pearce, F. (1995) 'How to build greener bridges', *New Scientist*, 21 January, pp. 25–9.

Porter, L. W. and Lawler, E. E. (1968) *Managerial Attitudes and Performance*, R. D. Irwin, Homewood IL.

Pressman, R. S. (1988) *Making Software Engineering Happen*, Prentice Hall, London.

Rook, P. (1991) 'Project planning and control' in McDermid, J. A. (ed.) *Software Engineer's Reference Book*, Butterworth Heinemann, Oxford.

Russell, B. (1919) *Proposed Roads to Freedom: Anarchy, Socialism, and Syndicalism*, Holt and Company, New York.

Spirer, H. F. (1983) 'Phasing out the project' in Cleland and King *op. cit.*

Staw, B. M. and Ross, J. (1987) 'Knowing when to pull the plug', *Harvard Business Review*, March/April.

Stewart, R. W. and Fortune, J. (1994) 'The application of systems thinking to the identification, avoidance and prevention of risk', unpublished paper.

Thamhain, H. J. (1984) *Engineering Program Management*, John Wiley and Sons, Chichester.

This book contains a useful chapter on the preparation of a project plan.

This, L. E. (1974) *A Guide to Effective Management: Applications from Behavioral Science*, Addison-Wesley, Reading MA.

Townsend, R. (1971) *Up the Organization*, Coronet, London.

Turner, J. R. (1992) *The Handbook of Project-based Management*, McGraw-Hill, London.

Weiss, J. W. and Wysocki, R. (1994) *5-Phase Project Management: A Practical Planning and Implementation Guide,* Addison-Wesley, Reading, Mass.

Wellman, F. (1992) *Software Costing*, Prentice Hall, London.

Wesselius, J. and Ververs, F. (1990) 'Some elementary questions on software quality control', *Software Engineering Journal*, November.

# INDEX

Key terms are printed in **bold** both in the text and in the index; where there are several page references against a heading, important ones are printed in **bold**. Relevant SAQs and answers are indexed. *Italic* page references refer to information carried wholly or mainly in figures, tables, illustrations and captions.

# *ACKNOWLEDGEMENTS*

Grateful acknowledgement is made to the following sources for permission to reproduce material in this book:

## Chapter 1

*Text*

*Report of the Inquiry into the London Ambulance Service*, adapted by permission of South Thames Regional Health Authority.

*Figures*

*Figure 3.3:* de la Mare, R. F. (1982) *Manufacturing Systems Economics*, Holt, Rinehart & Winston; *Figure 4.3:* reproduced from Jordan, E. W. and Machesky, J. J. (1990) *Systems Development: Requirements, Evaluation and Implementation* with the permission of Boyd & Fraser Publishing Company Copyright © 1990 by Boyd & Fraser Publishing Company.

*Tables*

*Tables 3.2, 3.3:* de la Mare, R. F. (1982) *Manufacturing Systems Economics*, Holt, Rinehart & Winston; *Table 4.2:* Norris, M., Rigby, P. and Payne, M. (1993) *The Healthy Software Project: A Guide to Successful Development and Management*, Copyright © 1993 by John Wiley and Sons Ltd. Reprinted by permission of John Wiley and Sons Ltd.

## Chapter 2

*Text*

Harrison, F. L. (1992) *Advanced Project Management* (3rd edn), Gower

*Figure*

*Figure 1.6:* Courtesy of British Telecommunications plc; *Figure 3.1* adapted from Harrison, F. L. (1992) *Advanced Project Management* (3rd edn), Gower

*Table*

*Table 3.3:* Wellman, F. (1992) *Software Costing*, Prentice-Hall International (UK) Ltd; *Table 3.4:* adapted from Drummond, S. (1985) 'Measuring applications development performance', *Datamation*, 31 (4), 15th February 1985, p 104; *Table 5.1:* Marsh, P. (1994) 'Contracts and payment structure', in Lock, D. (ed.) *Handbook of Project Management* (2nd edn), Gower

## Chapter 3

*Figures*

*Figure 3.7:* Archibald, R. D. (1992) *Managing High Technology Programs and Projects*, 2nd edn, John Wiley and Sons Inc. Reprinted by permission of John Wiley and Sons Inc.; *Figure 3.32:* Courtesy of Roy Shepherd.

## Chapter 4

*Figure*

*Figure 4.1:* adapted from Norris, M., Rigby, P. and Payne, M. (1993) *The Healthy Software Project: a guide to successful development and management*, Copyright © 1993 by John Wiley and Sons Ltd, reprinted by permission of John Wiley and Sons Ltd.

## Chapter 5

*Figures*

*Figure 1.1:* Harrison, F. L. (1992) *Advanced Project Management, a Structured Approach,* 3rd edn, Gower; *Figures 4.2, 4.11:* adapted from Archibald, R. D. (1992) *Managing High-Technology Programs and Projects*, 2nd edn, John Wiley and Sons Inc. Reprinted by permission of John Wiley and Sons Inc.

## Chapter 6

*Figures*

*Figure 3.1:* Harrison, F. L. (1992) *Advanced Project Management, a Structured Approach*, Gower; *Figure 4.4:* Bersoff, E. H., Henderson, V. D. and Siegel, S. G. *Software Configuration Management, an Investment in Product Integrity*, © 1980 by Prentice-Hall, Inc., Englewood Cliffs, NJ; *Figure 5.1:* Spirer, H. F. (1983) 'Phasing out the project', in Cleland, D. and King, W. R. (eds) *Project Management Handbook*, Van Nostrand Reinhold Company Inc.

The authors would also like to acknowledge the contribution made by Mike Iles to the preparation of Chapter 4. Thanks also to John O'Dwyer (editing); Siân Lewis (design); Roy Lawrance, Steve Jones and Tony Seldon (artwork).